Regulating Migrant Integration in Europe

Immigration and Asylum Law and Policy in Europe

Edited by

Elspeth Guild
Valsamis Mitsilegas

VOLUME 54

The titles published in this series are listed at *brill.com/ialp*

Regulating Migrant Integration in Europe

The Case of Skills

By

Dáire McCormack-George

BRILL | NIJHOFF

LEIDEN | BOSTON

Library of Congress Cataloging-in-Publication Data

Names: McCormack-Georg, Dáire, author.
Title: Regulating migrant integration in Europe : the case of skills / Dáire McCormack-Georg.
Description: Leiden ; Boston : Brill/Nijhoff, 2025. | Series: Immigration and asylum law and policy in europe | Includes bibliographical references and index. | Summary: "In the European Union, migration is one of the foundations of shared prosperity, unity and diversity. Perhaps unsurprisingly, then, the phenomenon of migration to and within Europe calls for regulation. This book is about the role the law plays in facilitating migrants' integration and effective participation in the EU, whether coming to the EU for the first time or moving within the Single Market. Specifically, this book addresses the experience of one category of migrants accessing work in the Single Market, namely, third-country nationals. While third-country nationals play an important role in the EU by and through their work, they habitually experience inadequate skills' or qualification recognition and wrongful discrimination in accessing work, thereby inhibiting their well-being.
Identifiers: LCCN 2024061889 | ISBN 9789004719774 (hardback) | ISBN 9789004724068 (ebook)
Subjects: LCSH: Emigration and immigration law–European Union countries. | Immigrants–Cultural assimilation–European Union countries. | Immigrants–European Union countries. | Social integration–European Union countries.
Classification: LCC KJE6044 .M39 2025 | DDC 342.2408/2–dc23/eng/20250113
LC record available at https://lccn.loc.gov/2024061889

Typeface for the Latin, Greek, and Cyrillic scripts: "Brill". See and download: brill.com/brill-typeface.

ISSN 1568-2749
ISBN 978-90-04-71977-4 (hardback)
ISBN 978-90-04-72406-8 (e-book)
DOI 10.1163/9789004724068

Contents

Acknowledgements

This book is largely based on a doctoral thesis completed between 2017–2020 at Trinity College Dublin which I substantially revised and updated several years later. The thesis, awkwardly entitled *Well-Being, Skills and Work in a Neorepublican EU: The Case of Third-Country Nationals*, was awarded 'as it stands' and without corrections. Almost four years after I was awarded my doctorate, Akiko Hakuno of Brill informally approached me with information about the *Immigration and Asylum Law and Policy in Europe* series. I am grateful to Akiko for approaching me, her encouragement and kind stewardship throughout the publishing process, without which I would not have engaged in or continued with this endeavour.

As this book is based on a doctoral thesis, it would be 'remiss' of me to overlook the significant contribution made to its completion by those around me. My greatest debt of thanks is to my *doktorvater*, Prof Mark Bell. Mark provided excellent supervision – academic and personal – throughout my period of doctoral research. I am forever grateful for his kindness and generosity of spirit and his keen eye for minor but vital details. A special thank you to him for his long-standing friendship and continued support over the years. I also owe a significant intellectual debt to all the employment and labour law and legal and political theory teachers I had at Trinity College Dublin and the University of Oxford. In particular, I am grateful for the advice, guidance and commentary of Dr David Prendergast BL over many years. Dr Sonja Heppner read most of the doctoral thesis upon which this book is based. Other friends read and commented on parts of the doctoral thesis which are included in this text: Drs Alan Eustace, Isabel M Perera, and Sophie Van der Valk. Still others provided helpful feedback, guidance and direction at times during the doctoral process. They include Prof Dr Elise Muir, Dr Katharina Eisele and Judge Anthony M Collins SC (as he then was). Thanks are also due to my interim examiner, Dr Caoimhín Mac Maoláin, and the final examiners of the thesis, Prof Neville Cox BL and Dr Tom Hickey, for their comments and suggestions. Years later, Mark reviewed the book proposal for Brill and Naoise Duffy reviewed the book proposal and parts of the final manuscript.

Doctoral funding tends to be limited. I therefore wish to acknowledge the substantial funding I secured from Trinity College Dublin – a Non-Foundation Scholarship in 2014, a Postgraduate Research Studentship in 2017 and an Erasmus+ Traineeship Grant in 2019 – which enabled me to pursue a course of study that would not have been possible otherwise. The people I met, lived and dined with regularly during my period as a Scholar of the College significantly improved my life. I am grateful, in particular, for the friendship of Drs Conor Casey BL and James Rooney BL during our time as undergraduates and doctoral students. In addition, my friends, family and girlfriend supported me during the doctoral process and the subsequent preparation of this monograph, for which I am eternally grateful. Without them, I would not have made it this far.

This book and the thesis from which it is derived is literature-based. It largely draws on materials available at the Library of Trinity College Dublin. Thanks are due to Terry McDonald, Law Librarian, for her assistance in locating and obtaining many key texts. Occasional visits to the Bodleian Law Library, University of Oxford and the Institute of Advanced Legal Studies, University of London as well as numerous loans from various university libraries across the UK made my research much easier. During my doctoral studies, I also benefited greatly from periods as a Visiting Researcher at the Labour Rights Institute, Faculty of Laws, University College London and as a Visiting Scholar at the Institute for Labour Law, Katholieke Universiteit Leuven. Profs Nicola Countouris, Virginia Mantouvalou and Colm Ó Cinnéide provided helpful guidance and support at UCL; Profs Drs Frank Hendrickx and Valerio de Stefano were the perfect hosts at KU Leuven. Many years later, parts of this book were reorganised and restructured during a brief period of contemplation over a St Patrick's Day weekend at St Mary's Abbey, Glencairn. Much of the substantial revision and updating of the materials which now constitute this book was conducted in Dublin.

I was lucky to present some early versions of this work elsewhere prior to its collation and substantial revision here. Accordingly, I am grateful to audiences, anonymous referees and publishers for commenting on and permitting me to include elements of same. The idea for Chapter 1 originated in a structurally similar analysis of Irish law in 'The Right to Work in Irish Law' (2019) 42(1) DULJ 119. Chapter 2 is based on an updated version of 'Equal Treatment of Third-Country Nationals in the European Union: *Why Not?*' (2019) 21(1) EJML 53. Parts of Chapters 3 include materials which first appeared in 'Trade in Services, Migration and Recognition of Professional Qualifications post-Brexit' in Simon Tans and Marc Veenbrink (eds), *Upgrading Trade in Services in EU and International Trade Law* (Wolf 2019). Chapter 4 substantially reproduces, with some amendments and omissions, 'Recognition of Professional Qualifications in the Single Market: A Recap' (2019) 30(5) EBLR 785. Chapter 5 includes recent developments first noted in 'Recognition of Professional Qualifications of Third-Country Nationals in the European Union: A Comment' (2024) 15 ELLJ (forthcoming).

While my doctoral thesis and this book are, in a sense, not merely the fruits of my own labour but also of the community that shaped me, the views stated here are and remain mine alone, do not represent those of my employer and do not constitute or purport to be legal advice. Nonetheless, I have endeavoured to state the law accurately as at 29 August 2024.

Memorial of the Passion of St John the Baptist
Phibsborough
Dublin 7

Introduction

Introduction

In the European Union, migration is one of the foundations of shared prosperity, unity and diversity. Perhaps unsurprisingly, then, the phenomenon of migration to and within Europe calls for regulation. This book is about the role the law plays in facilitating migrants' integration and effective participation in the EU, whether coming to the EU for the first time or moving within the Single Market. Specifically, this book addresses the experience of one category of migrants accessing work in the Single Market, namely, third-country nationals. While third-country nationals play an important role in the EU by and through their work, they habitually experience inadequate skills' or qualification recognition and wrongful discrimination in accessing work, thereby inhibiting their well-being. This book proposes to describe and critically analyse the legal and policy architecture governing such migrants' access to work, equal treatment and non-discrimination and the recognition of their professional qualifications – in other words, some of the most important aspects of the regulation of migrants' integration in Europe. This book, in essence, is a study of the role that the regulation of skills' or qualification recognition plays in facilitating migrants' integration in Europe.

This introductory chapter is structured as follows. Section 1 outlines the problem this book addresses in greater detail. It does so by providing a high-level background to and partial overview of certain relevant statements of EU economic and social policy which identify the relevance of skilled migrants to the future of the European project. Section 1 also identifies and describes some empirical data which emphasises the need for third-country nationals to come to work in the EU, as well as some of the problems they actually face. Building on the policy documents and data outlined in Section 1, Section 2 identifies the central research question and contribution to scholarship which this book will make. Section 3 outlines the sources of law, policy and philosophy which this book draws on. Section 4 identifies a central theme which runs throughout this book, namely, that of governance or regulation. Before concluding, Section 5 provides an outline of the structure of the book, describing the contribution each chapter makes to the overall argument of the book.

 | DOI:10.1163/9789004724068_002

1 Setting the Scene

1.1 *A Vision for Europe?*

1.1.1 The Lisbon Strategy

On 23–24 March 2000, the European Council met in Lisbon, Portugal to agree on a new 'strategic goal' for the Union to 'strengthen employment, economic reform and social cohesion as part of a knowledge-based economy'.[1] The object of the so-called *Lisbon Strategy* was to transform Europe, with the aim of becoming 'the most competitive and dynamic knowledge-based economy in the world, capable of sustainable economic growth with more and better jobs and greater social cohesion'. The role which skills play in this process is emphasised throughout the strategy document: as '[p]eople are Europe's main asset (...) [i]nvesting in people (...) will be crucial (...) to Europe's place in the knowledge economy'.

But how does investment in people result in tangible economic benefits? The primary way is by regulating economic relations for competitiveness.[2] According to the *Lisbon Strategy,* harnessing people's innate capacities and developing those through continuous training and re-training provide the grounds for greater innovation, entrepreneurship and competitive performance in business. Not only are education and basic skills key to this, but greater flexibility on behalf of workers, through increased and improved training, recognition of qualifications and employability skills, also provides for a competitive edge in the labour market. The combination of these measures should result in the creation of conditions of full employment, avoiding social exclusion and poverty.

The central place occupied by skills in the agenda of the European Union was further consolidated in the mid-term review of the *Lisbon Strategy* in 2005.[3] In its relaunch of the Strategy in 2005, the Commission emphasised knowledge as a key factor in continued growth of the European economy. And knowledge is best developed through investment in education and skills. The use of skills is therefore viewed as central to harnessing economic growth and development in the European Union.

1 European Council, *Lisbon Conclusions* (23 and 24 March 2000).

2 See generally Hugh Collins, 'Regulating the Employment Relation for Competitiveness' (2001) 30 ILJ 17.

3 Commission, 'Working together for jobs and growth: A new start for the Lisbon Strategy' (Communication) COM(2005) 24 final.

1.1.2 Europe 2020

The *Europe 2020* strategy is the successor to the *Lisbon Strategy*, and the role which skills play in it is even more evident.[4] Launched in 2010, the *Europe 2020* strategy was centred around three pillars or priorities, namely, 'smart growth, sustainable growth and inclusive growth'. It is the last of these which is most relevant for present purposes. 'Inclusive growth' entails a high-employment economy delivering economic, social and territorial cohesion. In expanding on the 'inclusive growth' dimension, the Commission begins by acknowledging that Europe's working population is shrinking and that people's skills are increasingly being made redundant due to ill educational attainment and technological change.[5]

Two aspects of the *Europe 2020* strategy stood for present purposes. First, the Commission envisaged an 'Agenda for new skills and jobs', which entailed 'empowering people through the acquisition of new skills to enable our current and future workforce to adapt to new conditions and potential career shifts, reduce unemployment and raise labour productivity'. Second, the Commission aimed to launch a 'European Platform against Poverty', part of which will 'design and implement programmes to promote social innovation for the most vulnerable, in particular by providing innovative education, training, and employment opportunities for deprived communities'.[6] It is the former of these which is most prominent in the *Europe 2020* strategy, as evidenced in particular from the headline targets presented towards the end of the strategy document.[7] Two features of this envisaged initiative stand out. First, an object of the initiative is to facilitate greater intra-EU mobility, in particular through better matching of supply and demand. And second, member states will be required to implement the European Qualifications Framework (EQF) through the establishment of national qualification frameworks which facilitate comparison across and between qualifications. The EQF will be discussed in full insofar as it is relevant to this book in Chapter 5.

1.1.3 The European Pillar of Social Rights

The European Pillar of Social Rights was declared by the European Parliament, Council of the European Union and the European Commission at the Gothenburg Summit in 2017. A set of 20 rights and principles designed to put

4 Commission, 'Europe 2020: A strategy for smart, sustainable and inclusive growth' (Communication) COM(2010) 2020.

5 See also Commission, 'Migration' (Communication) COM(2011) 248 final, 4.

6 ibid 18.

7 ibid 30.

the 'social' back in 'social Europe',[8] some relevant rights and principles include the following:

> 1. Everyone has the right to quality and inclusive education, training and life-long learning in order to maintain and acquire skills that enable them to participate fully in society and manage successfully transitions in the labour market.
> 2. …
> 3. Regardless of gender, racial or ethnic origin, religion or belief, disability, age or sexual orientation, everyone has the right to equal treatment and opportunities regarding employment, social protection, education, and access to goods and services available to the public. Equal opportunities of under-represented groups shall be fostered.[9]

On foot of the declaration of the Pillar, the Commission adopted an action plan to implement the rights and principles contained therein. It included the three ambitious targets – 78% employment, 60% in training and 15 million fewer people at risk of poverty – to be achieved across the EU before 2030. This entails the creation of more and better jobs, improved skills and equality and greater social protection and inclusion. Examples of initiatives adopted by the EU to achieve these goals to date and which are of relevance to this book and the rights and principles outlined above are the *European Skills Agenda for Sustainable Competitiveness, Social Fairness and Resilience*, *Anti-Racism Action Plan*, *Action Plan on Integration and Inclusion* and the *Skills and Talent* package, some of which are discussed later in this chapter and in Chapter 5.

1.1.4 The European Green Deal

While not a successor to the *Europe 2020* strategy as such, the *European Green Deal*, approved in 2020, is the EU's latest and most significant statement of its strategic priorities. It is ambitiously described as,

> a new growth strategy that aims to transform the EU into a fair and prosperous society, with a modern, resource-efficient and competitive economy where there are no net emissions of greenhouse gases in 2050 and where economic growth is decoupled from resource use.[10]

---

8 Sacha Garben, 'The European Pillar of Social Rights: An Assessment of its Meaning and Significance' (2019) 21 CYELS 101.

9 Commission, 'Establishing a European Pillar of Social Rights' (Staff Working Document) SWD/2017/0201 final.

10 Commission, 'The European Green Deal' (Communication) COM(2018) 640 final.

This 'deeply transformative' agenda requires the design of a set of reform policies for increasing the EU's climate ambition for 2030 and 2050; supplying clean, affordable and secure energy; mobilising industry for a clean and circular economy; building and renovating in an energy and resource efficient way; accelerating the shift to sustainable and smart mobility; designing a fair, healthy and environmentally-friendly food system; preserving and restoring ecosystems and biodiversity; and creating a zero pollution ambition for a toxic-free environment.

Naturally, the 'mainstreaming' of sustainability across all of the EU's laws and policies required to achieve these ambitious goals envisages some stark 'reality checks' for the labour market and the expectation that workers' skills will drive the research and innovation required to meet these targets. Accordingly, while educational institutions are required to prepare students for a successful transition, 'pro-active re-skilling and upskilling are necessary to reap the benefits of the ecological transition'.[11] The Commission notes that the proposed European Social Fund+ will provide some of the necessary funding to facilitate the acquisition of new skills required to adapt to new processes, thereby enhancing employability and boosting productivity. This fund will be discussed at 5.

1.2 *The EU in the Global Market*

Global Europe, launched in 2006, is the EU's external trade strategy. Launched shortly after the renewed *Lisbon Strategy*, the Commission noted that the Single Market could not be completed successfully without complementary internal and external agendas. Accordingly, while the *Lisbon Strategy* directly states goals and objectives to be achieved within the EU, *Global Europe* relies on external relations and resources to ensure the achievement of these internal goals.[12] It is vital that the external dimension to the Union's action is viewed as a necessary corollary of the Union's internal action. As the Commission aptly notes, '[a]s globalisation collapses distinctions between domestic and international policies, our domestic policies will often have a determining influence on our external competitiveness and vice versa'.[13] According to the Commission, there are two areas which are vital to the success of the EU's economy: having the right internal policies in the Single Market and ensuring greater openness to and with other markets. And the primary way to achieve greater openness

11 ibid 19.

12 Commission, 'Global Europe: Competing in the World – A Contribution to the EU's Growth and Jobs Strategy' (Communication) COM(2006) 567 final, 2.

13 ibid.

to and with other markets is through the negotiation of trade agreements to advance trade and progressive market access, non-discrimination and liberalisation.[14] Progressive trade liberalisation should increase competition in markets by facilitating greater openness, bringing benefits to consumers and businesses. But barriers to trade liberalisation, in the form of tariff and non-tariff barriers, remain. For my purposes, it is the latter of these which are most significant.[15] As the Commission notes,

> [i]nstruments such as mutual recognition agreements, international standardisation and regulatory dialogues, as well as technical assistance to third countries, will play an increasingly important role in promoting trade and preventing distorting rules and standards.[16]

Such obstacles apply not only to goods in the form of product, technical and phytosanitary standards, but also to services in the form of qualification requirements and other technical standards. And, crucially, as services 'are the cornerstone of the EU economy', it is these with which this study should be most concerned.[17] Indeed, in *Trade for All: Towards a more responsible trade and investment policy*, the Commission noted that 'trade increasingly involves moving people and information, not just goods, across borders. This intensifies the ways in which trade boosts the exchange of ideas, skills and innovation'.[18] The Commission also noted the growing need to improve the recognition of professional qualifications in its external trade relations with third-countries. Specifically, the Commission concluded that it would promote the recognition of qualifications in its trade agreements negotiated with third-countries so as to facilitate exports and bridge skills gaps,[19] an issue which shall be addressed in full in Chapter 3.

---

14 ibid 5.

15 This position has been empirically verified: see, eg, Commission, 'European Competitiveness Report 2008' (Communication) COM(2008) 774 final; Commission, 'On the External Dimension of the Lisbon Strategy for Growth and Jobs: Reporting on market access and setting the regulatory framework for more effective international regulatory cooperation' (Communication) COM(2008) 874 final, 3.

16 'Global Europe: Competing in the World – A Contribution to the EU's Growth and Jobs Strategy' (n 10) 5–6.

17 ibid 6; Commission, 'Trade for All: Towards a more responsible trade and investment policy' (Communication) COM(2015) 497 final, 6.

18 'Trade for All: Towards a more responsible trade and investment policy' (n 17) 3.

19 ibid 7, 8.

Recent empirical data has confirmed the significance of qualification recognition in intra-EU professional services trade. In general, this research concludes that there is a positive correlation between trade in professional services and the recognition of qualifications. Furthermore, the more that one member state recognises the qualifications of those in another member state, the greater the chance of increased labour migration and service provision to that same member state.[20] The same should apply, mutatis mutandis, to external trade in services.

1.3 *The EU and Migration*

1.3.1 The Global Approach to Migration and Mobility

The *Global Approach to Migration and Mobility* (GAMM)[21] constitutes the EU's external policy on migration and is the culmination of years of work under the auspices of the Global Approach to Migration.[22] Originally designed as a 'balanced, global and coherent approach, covering policies to combat illegal migration and, in cooperation with third countries, harnessing the benefits of legal migration', the *Global Approach to Migration* has since become the EU's major policy in the context of external migration. Initially reviewed annually by the Commission, it was acknowledged in 2008, some three years after its launch, that '[a] more highly developed common European immigration policy will need to give more thought to ways of matching jobseekers to vacancies and to allowing for more flexible access for labour migrants'.[23] It is also important to recall the need to better match supply and demand, noted above. This echoes earlier observations of the Commission in several communications, where it noted that, in respect of third-country nationals, 'labour-matching'[24] tools should be developed, and, furthermore 'identifying [labour market] needs is not enough. Supply and demand have to match (…) [m]utual

20 Hildegunn Kyvik Nordås, 'Does Mutual Recognition of Professional Qualifications Stimulate Service Trade? The Case of the European Union' (2016) 48 Applied Economics 1852; and Stella Capuano and Silvia Migali, 'The Migration of Professionals within the EU: Any Barriers Left?' (2017) 25 Review of International Economics 760.

21 Commission, 'The Global Approach to Migration and Mobility' (Communication) COM(2011) 743 final. The *GAMM* was endorsed by the Council of the European Union on 29 May 2012.

22 European Council Conclusions (19 December 2005).

23 Commission, 'Strengthening the Global Approach to Migration: Increasing Coordination, Coherence and Synergies' (Communication) COM(2008) 611 final, 4.

24 ibid.

recognition of qualifications and skills by the EU and non-member countries will also be important for this.'[25]

In order to benefit from such measures, the Commission reissued and renewed the *Global Approach to Migration* as the *GAMM* in 2011, after consultation and recommendations from the European Council. Defined as the 'overarching framework of EU external migration policy', the Commission acknowledges that 'migration and mobility in the context of the Europe 2020 strategy aim to contribute to the vitality and competitiveness of the EU'.[26] It is thus vital to understand migration from this economic perspective. In the policies of the European Union, third-country nationals are considered economic actors contributing directly to EU integration through their participation in and contribution to its labour and service markets.[27] The *GAMM* has four 'pillars' around which policy actions should operate, namely,

(a) Organising and facilitating legal migration and mobility;
(b) Preventing and reducing irregular migration and trafficking in human beings;
(c) Promoting international protection and enhancing the external dimension of asylum policy; and
(d) Maximising the development impact of migration and mobility.[28]

It is the first of these – organising and facilitating legal migration and mobility – which is most relevant for the purposes of this book. Once again, there is a particularly strong focus on competitiveness, skills and labour market integration. Integration in and through the labour market is viewed as the primary vector of integration because it is 'key to ensuring that both migrants and receiving societies can benefit from the potential of migration';[29] and a 'particular emphasis is placed on strengthening the Union's capacity to anticipate

25 Commission, 'An Area of Freedom, Security and Justice serving the Citizen' (Communication) COM (2009) 262 final, 25.

26 'The Global Approach to Migration and Mobility' (n 19) 4. This theme is later echoed in a follow-up report, Commission, 'Report on the implementation of the Global Approach to Migration and Mobility' COM(2014) 96 final, 15 wherein it is observed that "[f]urther efforts should be made to better organise labour migration to the EU and to coordinate [member state] actions, ie, to progressively find a better balance between national competences (…) and the necessity of building an increasingly integrated EU labour market, which corresponds to the increasingly integrated Single Market."

27 Cf later comments at 6: 'The GAMM should also be migrant-centred. In essence, migration governance is not about 'flows', 'stocks' and 'routes', it is about people'.

28 ibid 7.

29 ibid 13.

labour market and skills needs'.[30] This latter aspect is considered a priority under the first pillar, as is broader cooperation between EU and third-country education and training institutions to ensure aligned curricula and qualifications, an issue which shall be addressed in Chapters 3 and 5.[31]

One might wonder whether the focus in the *GAMM* is exclusively on regular migration and partnership agreements with third-countries. The answer is no. The Commission does envisage the possibility of mobilising existing talent and skills of those third-country nationals already resident in the European Union, particularly those who are overqualified.[32] However, it must be admitted that the primary focus in the *GAMM* and other policy documents here reviewed is on regular migrants to the EU, not on third-country nationals currently resident therein nor on those who are likely most vulnerable and in need of migration, namely forced migrants. As the reader shall see in Chapter 5, however, at least some policies are directed towards these categories of migrant.

1.3.2 A European Agenda on Migration

Recent statistics confirm the view that external trade in services continues to provide reciprocal economic benefits to the EU and its international trading partners and that trade in services constitutes an increasingly larger proportion of total EU external trade in goods and services.[33] These statistics differentiate reasonably clearly between trade in different types of services which is helpful for the purposes of assessing the link between service trade and migration. While the statistics do not give details of the numbers of service providers involved, in practice these areas generally involve the (temporary) migration of persons for the supply of services. As the Eurostat report notes,

> The provision of services contributes a substantial share of the EU's economic wealth and accounts for more than 50% of GDP in each of the EU Member States. Nevertheless, the value of exports and imports of goods is generally two to three times higher than that of services. Part of this imbalance may be due to the nature of some services, for example, professional services that are bound by distinct national legislation. Another difference between goods and services concerns the immediacy

30 ibid.

31 ibid 15.

32 ibid 13.

33 Eurostat, 'Statistics Explained: International Trade in Services' <https://ec.europa.eu/eurostat/statistics-explained/index.php/International_trade_in_services> (accessed 21 December 2018).

> of the relationship between supplier and consumer: many services are non-transportable, in other words they require the physical proximity of the service provider and consumer, which implies that many services transactions involve factor mobility. For international trade in non-transportable services to take place, either the consumer must go to the service provider or the service provider must go to the consumer.[34]

The failure to further liberalise service regulation is therefore acknowledged as an obstacle to an increase in trade in services. The impact that this has on migration, temporary or otherwise, is also acknowledged. The link between service provision and migration has also been recognised and emphasised in a recent communication of the European Commission, *A European Agenda on Migration*.[35] According to the Commission, not only does the EU need to devise an attractive legal migration scheme for highly-skilled workers, '[t]he services sector includes well-trained, highly-skilled foreign professionals who need to travel to the EU for short periods in order to provide services'.[36] Evidence of the need to better achieve the goals of improved trade in services and satisfy European labour market demands is not only to be found in this and other communications of the European Commission.[37] The conclusions of the European Council in 2010,[38] 2011,[39] 2014,[40] 2015[41] 2016,[42] and 2018[43] also evince a concern for the need to improve migration management in the EU's external relations and thereby contribute to meeting European labour and service market demands. Furthermore, the long-running saga over the attempt to

34 ibid.

35 European Commission, 'A European Agenda on Migration' (Communication) COM(2015) 240 final. See Simon Tans, *Service Provision and Migration: EU and WTO Service Trade Liberalisation and Their Impact on Dutch and UK Immigration Rules* (Brill/Nijhoff 2017) and my review thereof in (2018) 9 ELLJ 218.

36 'A European Agenda on Migration' (n 33) 15.

37 Other relevant communications are European Commission, 'Europe 2020: A Strategy for Smart, Sustainable and Inclusive Growth' (Communication) COM(2010) 2020; and European Commission, 'The Global Approach to Migration and Mobility' (Communication) COM(2011) 743 final, 4.

38 European Council Conclusions (16 September 2010) 9.

39 European Council Conclusions (11 March 2011) 4; and European Council Conclusions (23–24 June 2011) 10–11.

40 European Council Conclusions (26–27 June 2014) 19.

41 European Council Conclusions (25–26 June 2015) 1.

42 European Council Conclusions (20–21 October 2016) 5.

43 European Council Conclusions (28 June 2018) 1.

reform the Blue Card Directive to better attract global talent to the EU provides further consistency with this view.[44]

1.3.3 A New Pact on Migration and Asylum

Announced in August 2020, the Commission's *New Pact on Migration and Asylum* aimed to provide a 'fresh start' at addressing the promises and pitfalls of migration. It captures the essence of the apparent problems both addressed and caused by migration, namely that:

> With a well-managed system, migration can contribute to growth, innovation and social dynamism. Key societal challenges faced by the world today – demography, climate change, security, the global race for talent, and inequality – all have an impact on migration. Policy imperatives such as free movement in the Schengen area, safeguarding fundamental rights, ensuring security, and filling skills gaps, all call for an effective migration policy. The task facing the EU and its Member States, while continuing to address urgent needs, is to build a system that manages and normalises migration for the long term and which is fully grounded in European values and international law.[45]

The Commission notes that, at the time of publication of the *New Pact on Migration and Asylum*, some 20.9 million third-country nationals were legally resident in the EU, amounting to approximately 5% of the total population of the Single Market. The *New Pact on Migration and Asylum* aimed to largely 'reset' the EU's approach to the regulation of migration. It is not necessary to address each element of this revised approach in this book. For the purposes of this study, however, it merits noting a number of important and relevant features thereof. First, the Commission proposed to launch Talent Partnerships between the EU and its key partner third-countries to provide a comprehensive EU policy framework and targeted funding support for cooperation with third-countries to better match labour and skills needs in the EU. Second, in addition to encouraging the European Parliament and the Council to adopt the revised EU Blue Card Directive, the Commission proposed to revise the Long-Term Residents Directive, the Single Permit Directive and to explore an EU Talent Pool for migrants which could 'operate as an EU-wide platform

44 See, eg, the articles in Kaleidoscope 2: Assessing the Blue Card reform: a matter of narrative in (2020) 26(3/4) ELJ 245–282.

45 Commission, 'A New Pact on Migration and Asylum' (Communication) COM(2020) 609 final.

for international recruitment, through which skilled third-country nationals could express their interest in migrating to the EU, and could be identified by EU migration authorities and employers based on their needs'.[46] These issues will be more fully explored at Chapter 5.

1.4 *Securing Europe's Future: Skills*[47]

> Skills are a pathway to employability and prosperity. With the right skills, people are equipped for good-quality jobs and can fulfil their potential as confident, active citizens. In a fast-changing global economy, skills will to a great extent determine competitiveness and the capacity to drive innovation. They are a pull factor for investment and a catalyst in the virtuous circle of job creation and growth. They are key to social cohesion.[48]

Thus begins the Commission's communication on *A New Skills Agenda for Europe*. This introductory paragraph highlights two important dimensions of skills. First, skills are linked to economic and social goals. The economic goals include employability and economic development, while the social goals extend to social inclusion and cohesion. Second, skills are seen as the aspect of people's abilities which can be mobilised for the purposes of value creation in a market society. This places skills at the heart of economic development in the EU.

The *New Skills Agenda* has three facets or 'strands': improving the quality and relevance of skills formation; making skills and qualifications more visible and comparable; and improving skills intelligence and information for better career choices.[49] For present purposes, the second of these is most relevant. Accordingly, the Commission notes the need to 'improve transparency and comparability of qualifications', particularly through the EQF.[50] The Commission further acknowledges that several third-countries 'have expressed interest in the EQF to enable their qualifications to be compared with European ones'.[51]

46 ibid 26.

47 Commission, 'New Skills for New Jobs' (Communication) COM(2008) 868 final and Commission, 'An Agenda for new skills and jobs: A European contribution towards full employment' (Communication) COM(2010) 682 final; and Commission, 'Rethinking Education: Investing in skills for better socio-economic outcomes' (Communication) COM(2012) 669 final.

48 Commission, 'A New Skills Agenda for Europe: Working together to strengthen human capital, employability and competitiveness' (Communication) COM(2016) 381 final, 1.

49 ibid 3.

50 ibid 9.

51 ibid.

It recognises that such an approach would help attract highly-skilled researchers and professionals from outside the EU, and would be consistent with the ambition to improve the Union's migration policy.[52] These were reiterated and expanded upon in the *European Skills Agenda for Sustainable Competitiveness, Social Fairness and Resilience* in 2020 which identified twelve actions to deliver upon the European Pillar of Social Rights. These included supporting strategic national upskilling actions and the development of a new Europass platform to support a fast track to recognition of academic and professional qualifications, reducing the administrative burden and decreasing fraud and supporting legally-resident migrants to showcase their skills and qualifications and facilitate their recognition through better information.

Fostering links between skills and migration, the Commission's 2022 communication on *Attracting Skills and Talent to the EU* placed great emphasis on the job shortages arising from the green transition and digital transition, estimated at 11 million. While the primary or overarching approach of the EU's strategic vision is to generate these jobs within the EU – through upskilling and reskilling – these actions alone are not enough. The future of the EU depends, at least in part, on its ability to attract global talent and provide a supportive environment to skilled migrants across Europe. Importantly, the communication on *Skills and Talent Mobility* notes that as many as 13% of key workers performing essential functions in the EU are third-country nationals and, in 2022, the member states issued more resident permits for employment purposes than ever before. Furthermore, occupations with shortages tend to have a higher share of workers born outside the EU. *Attracting Skills and Talent to the EU* set out three pillars of an ambitious and sustainable EU legal migration policy, involving legislative, operational and future-oriented policy measures. The legislative pillar focussed on recasting the Long-Term Residents Directive and the Single Permit Directive and intra-EU mobility of third-country nationals already resident in the EU. The operational pillar involves the development of Talent Partnerships and the key features of an EU Talent Pool, while the forward-looking policy pillar involves three specific priorities for action that should further guide the EU's policy on legal migration: care, youth and innovation.

The Commission subsequently built on the *European Skills Agenda* in its 2023 communication on *Skills and Talent Mobility*,[53] in which it was acknowledged that 'challenges linked to the recognition of qualifications of third-country

52 ibid.

53 Commission, 'Skills and Talent Mobility' (Communication) COM(2023) 715 final.

nationals are often [a] practical obstacle dissuading workers from coming to the EU.' In a lengthy but insightful passage, the Commission noted:

> The recognition of qualifications is essential to ensure that incoming workers in certain professions have sufficient education, training or experience. However, processes for the recognition of third country qualifications are often overly expensive, complex and time-consuming. They also represent a significant administrative burden for Member States, due to lack of information on third country qualifications systems, limited pooling of expertise and resources at EU level, and difficulties verifying the authenticity of documents.
>
> Many occupations facing shortages are not regulated. In these cases, employers have the discretion to decide whether third country nationals have the right profile based on their qualifications, experience and skills and a formal recognition process is not needed. However, employers' lack of understanding and trust in skills and qualifications gained in third countries necessary for recruitment to non-regulated professions is another significant barrier to talent and skills mobility.
>
> The result not only affects the EU's attractiveness but leads to 'brain waste' – third country nationals working below their qualification level. According to Eurostat, in 2022 over a quarter of third country nationals are highly qualified but 39.4% are overqualified for the job they do, with women more likely to be overqualified than men. The equivalent figure for EU citizens working in another Member State is 31.8% and for those residing in their own country just 21.1%. Facilitating the recognition of qualifications and validation of skills can therefore also help harness the untapped potential of third country nationals already in the EU.[54]

The specific measures envisaged by *Skills and Talent Mobility*, such as the Recommendation on the recognition of qualifications of all legally resident third-country nationals, will be addressed in full in Chapter 5.

1.5 *The Experience of Migrants to Date*

It is, or ought to be, now clear that, as a matter of policy, migrants are envisaged as playing at least some part in the widening and deepening of the project of EU integration by participating in the Single Market: third-country nationals

54 ibid 4.

may be relied upon to fill gaps in the EU's labour market. But what has their experience of doing so been to date?

Several sources help to explain and expand upon third-country nationals' experience to date. A first is the European Migration Network's (EMN) study on *Intra-EU Mobility of Third-Country Nationals* where it is observed that third-country nationals are even more likely to be mobile in the Single Market than member state nationals. However, the report also notes that the recognition of qualifications of third-country nationals is a significant obstacle to their mobility, particularly its cost, duration and documentation requirements.[55] This point is supported in subsequent research. The ECORYS/European Commission *Study on Obstacles to Recognition of Skills and Qualifications* notes that third-country nationals habitually experience inadequate qualification recognition which leads to inefficiencies between the level of qualifications obtained and labour market participation. In other words, third-country nationals often take up jobs they are overqualified to do. In most EU member states, the majority of resident non-citizens are third-country nationals and of those third-country nationals who come to the EU to work, 95% have a third-level qualification.[56] In 2023, the over-qualification rate was 39.4% for non-EU citizens and 31.3% for citizens of other EU countries compared with 20.8% for nationals.[57] A joint OECD/EU report also discloses similar data. According to that report, almost every EU labour market does not value third-country qualifications as highly as native ones. As a result, the employment rate of third-country nationals is significantly lower than that of member state nationals.[58] As the Eurostat figures for Europe 2020 made clear,

> Migrant workers from countries outside the EU tend to occupy low-skilled and insecure jobs with temporary contracts and poorer working conditions. Migrants are also among the first to lose their jobs during economic setbacks. Much lower employment rates are consequently reported for this group than for EU-born workers. In 2018, the employment rate of

55 European Migration Network Synthesis Report, *Intra-EU Mobility of Third-Country Nationals* (European Commission 2013) 5.

56 Vicky Donlevy, Mauriz Curtarelli, Andrew McCoshan and Anja Meierkord, *Study on Obstacles to Recognition of Skills and Qualifications: Final Report* (ECORYS/European Commission 2016).

57 Eurostat, 'Migrant integration statistics – over-qualification' (4 July 2024) <https://ec.europa.eu/eurostat/statistics-explained/index.php?title=Migrant_integration_statistics_-_over-qualification> (accessed 29 August 2024).

58 OECD/European Union, *Settling In 2018: Indicators of Immigrant Integration* (OECD Publishing 2018).

> people born outside the EU aged 20 to 64 was 8.7 percentage points below the total employment rate. Additionally, their employment rate has so far not recovered from the setback caused by the economic crisis, with the 2018 rate being still lower than the levels recorded in 2008.[59]

One of the main reasons third-country nationals occupy such low-skilled and insecure jobs is that their qualifications are undervalued. Third-country nationals are consequently forced to take up employment in jobs for which they are over-qualified. It should come as no wonder, then, that the rate of over-qualification is higher amongst third-country nationals in all EU member states. The same is not the case for those third-country nationals who come to the EU for education, however. For those third-country nationals, it is much easier to get a job commensurate with their qualifications.

Obstacles to integration and labour market participation do not solely arise from inadequate qualification recognition, however. Almost 20% of third-country nationals in the EU feel that they belong to a group which is discriminated against on the grounds of ethnicity, nationality or race. Perceived discrimination is most common amongst African nationals resident in the EU. Furthermore, a recent EMN study of the labour market integration and participation of third-country nationals provides further information which may help to explain these statistics. According to that study, the main reasons that first-generation third-country nationals come to the EU are for family reasons (44%), followed by work (33%), education (8%), asylum (6%) and other reasons (5%). The main challenges for third-country nationals participating in the labour market involved, inter alia, a lack of adequate language skills; the recognition and validation of qualifications and the consequent skills mismatch which comes therewith; and discrimination in recruitment processes or in the working environment, problems which are more pronounced when dealing with women or vulnerable groups. As to the recognition of qualifications, problems arose in certain member states such as the lack of any mechanism to evaluate the skills of third-country nationals, the length of accreditation procedures in Belgium and Spain, or the general incompatibility of qualifications in Finland. As to the discrimination experienced by third-country nationals, data from Ireland suggested that Sub-Saharan Africans were more likely to experience discrimination when looking for work. Third-country nationals were also discriminated against on account of their lack of knowledge of their

---

59 Eurostat, 'Europe 2020 indicators – employment' (August 2019) <https://ec.europa.eu/eurostat/statistics-explained/index.php?title=Archive:Europe_2020_indicators_-_employment> (accessed 12 May 2025).

labour rights, with some, especially in Greece and Lithuania, being exploited as a result.[60]

Of further assistance and guidance in this respect is the recent 'EU-MIDIS II' Survey conducted by the EU's Fundamental Rights Agency.[61] EU-MIDIS II is based on a sample of over 25,000 randomly selected respondents with different ethnic minority and immigrant backgrounds across all EU member states. In each member state, certain immigrant and ethnic minority groups were chosen for the purposes of the survey. In the main, immigrants and the descendants of immigrants from Turkey and Sub-Saharan Africa were chosen across the member states. That survey confirms the persistency of discrimination against immigrants, descendants of immigrants and minority ethnic groups across the EU, observing that 'a failure to deliver effective protection from discrimination and hate crime can undermine integration and social inclusion policies, affecting the social cohesion of our societies'.[62] For example, nearly a quarter of respondents felt discriminated against because of their ethnic or immigrant background in the last twelve months, with that figure rising to nearly 40% of respondents when expanded to take into account the past five years. Of particular relevance to this project is the affirmation that most discrimination is experienced in employment and when accessing public and private services. And while a majority of respondents know that such discrimination is prohibited, many are reluctant to report it because they do not feel anything will change.

It therefore seems that inadequate qualification recognition and wrongful discrimination – issues which migrants well-being – are the key problems to focus on in securing the role of third-country nationals in the process of EU integration.

1.6 *Synthesis and Summary*

The following picture emerges from this brief overview of EU economic and social policy and empirical data concerning the experiences of third-country nationals accessing work in the EU. First, skills are the ground upon which further development and growth shall emerge in the EU in the future; and the skills necessary to provide such growth are often in short supply. Second, this leads us to consider where to find new sources of skills. The answer lies, at least

60 European Migration Network, *Labour Market Integration of Third-Country Nationals in EU Member States: Synthesis Report for the EMN Study* (2019).

61 Fundamental Rights Agency, *Second European Union Minorities and Discrimination Survey: Main Results* (Publications Office of the European Union 2017).

62 ibid 13.

in part, in third-country nationals. But while third-country nationals provide new sources of human capital, empirical research suggests that such third-country nationals habitually experience discrimination in recruitment processes and inadequate qualification recognition. Moreover, it is an overarching goal of the EU to improve the matching of supply with demand and enabling the recognition of qualifications will be particularly important for this.

1.7 *Limitations and Criticisms*

It is important to reflect on what might be described as the 'technocratic' nature of the approach evinced by the European Commission in the above-discussed economic and social policy documents. While the Commission's case for the use of and reliance on the skills of migrants may be economically compelling,[63] it is nonetheless difficult to reconcile its approach with the significant backlash in recent years against migration generally in the EU, and especially against the immigration of third-country nationals in particular. In sum, the obvious economic case for migration needs to be accompanied by a compelling social case which renders migration satisfactory and acceptable to all. In the view of the Commission, the social case is to be provided primarily through economic reform: as noted in above, integration is to occur in and through the labour market. By joining and participating in the labour market, migrants should not be viewed as a drain on society and are instead understood as contributors in and to their community by and through their work.

It is clear, however, that there is not a consensus on such a position at EU level. The European migration crisis triggered the suspension of the Schengen area, resulting in country after country shutting its borders as each found its migration systems overwhelmed by refugees flooding in from the Middle East.[64] One of the key arguments in the Brexit campaign involved the claim that migration was undermining the well-being of the peoples of the United

63 I do not nor do I purport to have sufficient knowledge or expertise of the complex, dynamic and interactive relationship between migration, employment and economic development. For a review of some the theoretical basis and empirical evidence in respect of such relationship, see, *inter alia*, Tanja Bastia and Ronald Skeldon (eds), *Routledge Handbook of Migration and Development* (Routledge 2020); Cynthia Bansak, Nicole Simpson and Madeline Zavodny, *The Economics of Immigration* (2nd ed, Routledge 2021); Guglielmo Meardi (ed), *Research Handbook on Migration and Employment* (Edward Elgar 2024); and Hein de Haas, *How Migration Really Works: 22 Things You Need to Know about the Most Divisive Issue in Politics* (Penguin 2024).

64 Michela Ceccorulli, 'Back to Schengen: the collective securitisation of the EU free-border area' (2019) 42 West European Politics 302.

Kingdom.[65] Meanwhile, resistance to migration in eastern Europe, in particular, remains high.[66] At the time of writing, the EU has absorbed over 4 million persons fleeing Russia's invasion of Ukraine benefitting from temporary protection, a figure which many Europeans find unsustainable. Given that there is a lack of consensus on the viability of the Commission's plans in this respect, it merits noting, both here and throughout this book, that the proposed reforms made herein may be controversial and require a significant change in culture. They may require that the EU and its member states take more seriously not only the well-being of third-country nationals but of their own citizens too. A second concern arises from a challenge to the economic case advanced by the Commission itself. While labour migration may benefit the EU economically, a question arises as to whether and to what extent such labour migration may benefit the countries of origin of migrants. While, as noted above, the Commission suggests that external trade in services serves the interests of both the EU and its trading partners, this argument needs to be tested. Could such migration have a detrimental impact on the economies and societies of the countries of origin? While the issue will not be explored in this book, it merits noting that it is possible non-circular migration could result in a so-called 'brain drain', permanently draining developing countries of their most valued human resources.[67]

65 Jonathan Portes and Giuseppe Forte, 'The economic impact of Brexit-induced reductions in migration' (2017) 33 Oxford Review of Economic Policy S31; James Dennison and Andrew Geddes, 'Brexit and the perils of 'Europeanised' migration' (2018) 25 JEPP 1137; Catherine Barnard and Sarah Fraser Butlin, 'Free Movement v Fair Movement: Brexit and Managed Migration' (2018) 25 CML Rev 203.

66 Ivan Krastev, 'Eastern Europe's Illiberal Revolution' (2018) 97 Foreign Affairs 49.

67 See, inter alia, Fernando Tesón, 'Brain Drain' (2008) 45 San Diego L Rev 899; Tito Boeri, Herbert Brücker, Frédéric Docquier and Hillel Rapport, *Brain Drain and Brain Gain: The Global Competition to Attract High-Skilled Migrants* (OUP 2012) part 2; Kieran Oberman, 'Can Brain Drain Justify Immigration Restrictions?' (2013) 123 Ethics 427; Alex Sager, 'Reframing the brain drain' (2014) 17 Critical Review of International Social and Political Philosophy 560; Luara Ferracioli, 'Immigration, self-determination and the brain drain' (2015) 41 Review of International Studies 99; Gillian Brock and Michael Blake, *Debating Brain Drain: May Governments Restrict Emigration?* (OUP 2015); the articles the special issue of (2016) 9 Ethics and Global Politics 1; and the articles in the special issue of (2017) 36 South African Journal of Philosophy 1–176.

2 Central Research Questions

2.1 *Questions and Sub-questions*

In the light of the policy background provided thus far and the empirical data available concerning the experiences of third-country nationals participating in the Single Market to date, the central research question which this book investigates is the extent to which the EU guarantees the well-being of migrants in accessing work through its laws and policies, with a particular focus on skills' recognition and freedom from discrimination as aspects of their well-being, as a means to facilitate and enable their integration into European societies and economies. This question, while somewhat vague and high-level, is made clearer through exploring two overarching sub-questions which are addressed by Parts 1 and 2 of the book.

The first sub-question asks, what are the legal doctrinal foundations for migrants' entitlement to qualification recognition and non-discrimination in the EU? The purpose of asking this question is to identify the fundamental legal doctrinal foundations, in those parts of international and European law which are binding in the EU, of the rights of migrants to the recognition of their qualifications and to equality and non-discrimination. Part 1 accordingly sets out these foundations as based on two core rights of relevance to the lived experience of migrants in Europe, namely, the rights to work and to equality and non-discrimination. These rights, as they exist and are binding in international and European law, are described in detail. This description demonstrates the significance of these rights in facilitating effective access to and participation in the labour market. The application of these rights to migrants in Europe is considered. It is noted that the right to work is not generally guaranteed for migrants but only when they are granted equal treatment with member state nationals. Part 1 of the book concludes by arguing that migrants should generally be entitled to equal treatment with member state nationals.

The second sub-question asks, what are the specific contours of the right to the recognition of professional qualifications in Europe, both in general and in respect of migrants in particular? Part 2 of the book accordingly applies the doctrinal conclusions reached in Part 1 to migrants' right to have their skills or qualifications recognised when moving to and within the EU. This derivative right of the core right to work is currently afforded to third-country nationals through treating them more or less equally with EU nationals in circumstances when they are moving to the EU or within the Single Market itself. In Part 2, EU law and policy is described and analysed. Three areas of EU law and policy are considered: (a) the rules governing migration to Europe, (b) the rules governing migration within Europe and finally (c) soft laws, policies and legislative proposals governing both of those scenarios and, in particular, recent measures adopted in this space on foot of the Russo-Ukrainian War. It is suggested that certain parts of EU law as it stands are deficient in numerous respects insofar as they fail to treat migrants equally with EU nationals in respect of their right to have their skills or qualifications recognised and related legal and policy entitlements, such as labour market integration measures and access to education and training. Some possible and practical legal and policy reforms are suggested which would improve migrants' situation.

2.2 *Contribution to Scholarship and Originality*

This book responds to and attempts to fill several gaps in the literature at the intersection of EU migration (i.e., free movement[68] and migration and asylum),[69] equality and anti-discrimination[70] and external relations law.[71] The first contribution this book makes to these areas is the development of a nuanced focus and understanding of the role which equal treatment guarantees play in enabling migrants to bear rights and access opportunities when entering and moving within the EU. Two existing texts are helpful in this respect. The first is Katharina Eisele's doctoral dissertation on the external dimension of the EU's migration policy.[72] Her text examines the historical development of the EU's policies in this area, as well as the legal bases on which third-country nationals enter the EU. Important in this respect are entry schemes for regular migrants, as well as their entitlements to participate in the labour markets, social security systems and other entitlements of member state nationals. The second is Bjarney Friðriksdóttir's text concerning the construction of the equal treatment guarantee in the EU's migration acquis.[73] What emerges from Friðriksdóttir's text is that a close analysis of the equal treatment guarantees found in the EU's external labour migration acquis plays a vital part in analysing the place and treatment of third-country nationals

68 Catherine Barnard, *The Substantive Law of the EU: The Four Freedoms* (7th ed, OUP 2022).

69 Daniel Thym, *EU Migration Law* (OUP 2023) and Steve Peers, *EU Justice and Home Affairs Law Volume 1: EU Immigration and Asylum Law* (5th ed, OUP 2023).

70 Evelyn Ellis and Philippa Watson, *EU Equality and Anti-Discrimination Law* (2nd ed, OUP 2012).

71 Piet Eeckhout, *EU External Relations Law* (2nd ed, OUP 2011).

72 Katharina Eisele, *The External Dimension of the EU's Migration Policy: Different Legal Positions of Third-Country Nationals in the EU: A Comparative Perspective* (Brill/Nijhoff 2014).

73 Bjarney Friðriksdóttir, *What Happened to Equality? The Construction of the Right to Equal Treatment of Third-Country Nationals in European Union Law on Labour Migration* (Brill/Nijhoff 2017).

in and under EU law. The scope of the equal treatment guarantee is often a threshold issue for the recognition of third-country nationals' skills in the EU. Moreover, as it stands, nationality discrimination is not prohibited as a matter of EU anti-discrimination law. Accordingly, Chapter 2 argues that nationality should become a prohibited ground of discrimination to better tackle the discrimination which third-country nationals habitually face.

The second contribution which this book makes to these intersecting areas of scholarship, which results from this book's distinctive focus on skills, concerns the recognition of professional qualifications in the Single Market. Most existing legal scholarship at the intersection of these areas has focused either solely or mainly on the experiences of third-country nationals who are generally low-skilled, particularly those who undertake seasonal work,[74] enter the EU on so-called 'guestworker' schemes,[75] undertake 'precarious work'[76] or are irregular migrants undertaking work.[77] There is also an emerging body of work on highly qualified migrants, particularly as found in the scholarship of Lucie Cerna, who, alone[78] and in partnership with other academics,[79] has conducted

74 Judy Fudge and Petra Herzfeld Olsson, 'The EU Seasonal Workers Directive: When Immigration Control Meets Labour Rights' (2014) 16 EJML 439.

75 Stephen Castles, 'Guestworkers in Europe: A Resurrection?' (2007) 40 IMR 741; and Martin Ruhs and Philip Martin, 'Numbers vs Rights: Trade-Offs and Guest Worker Programs' (2008) 41 IMR 249.

76 Bridget Anderson, 'Migration, immigration controls and the fashioning of precarious workers' (2010) 24 WES 300.

77 Georg Menz, 'Employers and Migrant Legality: Liberalisation of Service Provision, Transnational Posting, and the Bifurcation of the European Labour Market' in Mark Freedland and Cathryn Costello (eds), *Migrants at Work: Immigration and Vulnerability in Labour Law* (OUP 2014).

78 Lucie Cerna, 'Understanding the diversity of EU migration policy in practice: the implementation of the Blue Card Directive' (2013) 34 Policy Studies 180; Lucie Cerna, 'The EU Blue Card: Preferences, Policies and Negotiations between Member States' (2014) 2 Migration Studies 73; Lucie Cerna, 'Attracting High-Skilled Immigrants: Policies in Comparative Perspective' (2014) 52 IM 69; Lucie Cerna, *Immigration Policies and the Global Competition for Talent* (Palgrave Macmillan 2016); Lucie Cerna, 'The crisis as an opportunity for change? High-skilled immigration policies across Europe' (2016) 42 Journal of Ethnic and Migration Studies 1610; and Lucie Cerna, 'European High-Skilled Migration Policy: Trends and Challenges' in Mathias Czaika (ed), *High-Skilled Migration: Drivers and Policies* (OUP 2018).

79 Alexander Betts and Lucie Cerna, 'High-Skilled Labour Migration' in Alexander Betts (ed), *Global Migration Governance* (OUP 2011); Lucie Cerna and Meng-Hsuan Chou, 'The regional dimension in the global competition for talent: Lessons from framing the European Scientific Visa and Blue Card' (2013) 21 JEPP 76; Lucie Cerna, James Hollifield and William Hynes, 'Trade, Migration and the Crisis of Globalisation' in Marion Panizzon, Gottfried Zürcher and Elisa Fornalé (eds), *The Palgrave Handbook of International Labour Migration* (Palgrave 2015); Lucia Cerna and Mathias Czaika, 'European Policies to Attract

extensive research into the EU and member states' high-skilled labour migration regimes. But Cerna and others' research does not generally consider the experiences of highly qualified third-country nationals in the EU; rather, her and others' work largely concerns the design of immigration norms and policies to best attract highly skilled third-country nationals to the EU. The contribution which this book makes, by contrast, is to address the real problems which third-country nationals, be they low-, middle- or highly-skilled, coming to or arriving in the EU habitually experience, namely inadequate skills' recognition and wrongful discrimination.

One important study in relation to the recognition of qualifications in the Single Market is Micheline van Riemsdijk's analysis of the experiences of certain accession state nationals.[80] While not dealing with third-country nationals,

Talent: The Crisis and Highly Skilled Migration Policies' in Anna Triandafyllidou and Irina Isaakyan (eds), *High Skill Migration and Recession: Gendered Perspectives* (Palgrave Macmillan 2015); and Lucie Cerna and Meng-Hsuan Chou, 'Defining 'Talent': Insights from Management and Migration Literatures for Policy Design' (2019) 47 PSJ 819.

80 Micheline van Riemsdijk, 'Obstacles to the Free Movement of Professionals: Mutual Recognition of Professional Qualifications in the European Union' (2013) 15 EJML 47; and Micheline van Riemsdijk, 'Politics of Free Movement in the European Union: Recognition and Transfer of Professional Qualifications' in Willem Maas (ed), *Democratic Citizenship and the Free Movement of People* (Brill 2013). On the recognition of qualifications in the EU generally, see Rolf Waegenbaur, 'Free Movement in the Professions: The New EEC Proposal on Professional Qualifications' (1986) 23 CML Rev 91; Julian Lonbay, 'Free Movement of Persons, Recognition of Qualifications and Working Conditions' (1989) 38(1) ICLQ 211; Malcom Ross, 'Freedom of Establishment and Freedom to Provide Services' (1989) 14 EL Rev 162; Julia Laslett, 'The Mutual Recognition of Diplomas, Certificates and other Evidence of Formal Qualifications in the European Community' (1990) 17 LIEI 1; Julian Lonbay, 'Free Movement of Persons, Recognition of Qualifications and Working Conditions' (1994) 43 ICLQ 217; Miek Peeters, 'Free Movement of Medical Doctors: The New Directive 2005/36/EC on Recognition of Professional Qualifications' (2005) 12(4) EJHL 373; Sacha Garben, 'On Recognition of Qualifications for Academic and Professional Purposes' (2011) 16 TLR 127; Micheline van Riemsdijk, 'Obstacles to the Free Movement of Professionals: Mutual Recognition of Professional Qualifications in the European Union' (2013) 15(1) EJML 47; Micheline van Riemsdijk, 'Politics of Free Movement in the European Union: Recognition and Transfer of Professional Qualifications' in Willem Maas (ed), *Democratic Citizenship and the Free Movement of People* (Brill 2013); Lavinia Kortese, 'Exploring Professional Recognition in the EU: A Legal Perspective' (2016) 4(1) Journal of International Mobility 43; Silvia Adamo and Tom Binder, 'Union Citizens and the Recognition of Professional Qualifications: Where Do We Go from Here?' in Sybe de Vries, Elena Ioriatti, Paulo Guarda and Elisabetta Pulice (eds), *EU Citizens Economic Rights in Action: Re-Thinking Legal and Factual Barriers in the Internal Market* (Edward Elgar 2018); and Barend van Leeuwen, 'The Doctor in Free Movement Law: Expertise, Duty and Accountability' (2023) CYELS 1. On the recognition of qualifications of third-country nationals specifically, see Katherina Eisele, 'Falling Through the Cracks: Third-Country Nationals and the Recognition of Qualifications in the EU' in Sergio Carrera, Elspeth

her study is nonetheless a helpful starting point in recognising the significance of existing skills in providing access to and participation in the labour market. Moreover, while the studies noted thus far have focused on different categories of skilled workers – i.e., low skilled, middle skilled and highly-skilled (or perhaps 'differently skilled') – they have not always done so in a skills-conscious manner. That is, these studies have not always located such workers within a broader paradigm or model of work as skilled activity which contributes to people's well-being, nor have they noted the stratified and discriminatory nature of the EU's labour migration acquis on the ground of skills.[81]

As is by now clear from the analysis of the EU's economic and social policies in Section 1, the recognition of qualifications plays an important role in facilitating labour mobility and boosting trade in services both within the EU and between the EU and third-countries. Further evidence of this is provided by Simon Tans' text linking service provision and migration.[82] For while migrants contribute to the satisfaction of demand in labour markets by and through their work, they can also contribute to service markets insofar as they provide, by means of their skills, valuable services which are in demand. The contribution to the study of qualification recognition this book makes has two dimensions,

---

Guild and Katherina Eisele (eds), *Rethinking the Attractiveness of EU Labour Immigration Policies: Comparative Perspectives on the EU, the US, Canada and Beyond* (CEPS 2014); Roos Pijpers, Pascal Beckers, Niels Grootjans, Ton van Naerssen, Lars Paardekooper and Lothar Smith, *Skills Recognition, Diversity Management and Voluntary Work with regard to Third Country Nationals in the Netherlands: A Case Study on the Healthcare Sector in the Arnhem-Nijmegen Region* (Radboud University 2015); Dáire McCormack-George, 'Trade in Services, Migration and Recognition of Professional Qualifications post-Brexit' in Simon Tans and Marc Veenbrink (eds), *Upgrading Trade and Services in EU and International Trade Law* (Wolf Publishing 2019); Dáire McCormack-George, 'Recognition of Professional Qualifications in the Single Market: A Recap' (2019) 30(5) EBLR 785; Ton Van den Brink and Sybie de Vries, 'A Silk Road for Professional Qualifications? EU Models of Integration and their Potential in Sino-EU Relations' in Marijk Van Der Wende, William C Kirby, Nian Cai Liu and Simon Marginson (eds), *China and Europe on the New Silk Road: Connecting Universities across Eurasia* (OUP 2020); Dáire McCormack-George, *Well-Being, Skills and Work in a Neorepublican EU: The Case of Third-Country Nationals* (Trinity College Dublin PhD Thesis 2020) chs 5 and 6; Natalie Camila Wiesner, *Recognition of Third-Country Professional Qualifications: An Evaluation of the Current Framework in the European Union. The Case of Healthcare Workers* (Utrect University LLM Thesis 2023); and Živa Šuta and Karmen Pišek Šuta, 'Professional Qualifications Recognition of Doctors in the EU: A Perspective on EU Citizens and Third-Country Nationals' (2023) 16(1) Medicine, Law and Society 149.

81 See my review of *What Happened to Equality?* (n 73) in (2018) 55 CML Rev 1647 and Chapter 2 of this book.

82 *Service Provision and Migration* (n 35).

external and internal. The external dimension concerns the circumstances in which third-country nationals can have their qualifications recognised when coming to the EU for the first time. Again: in what circumstances, if any, can third-country nationals have their qualifications recognised when moving to the EU? The response to this question is provided in Chapter 3. By contrast, the internal dimension concerns the recognition of professional qualifications within the Single Market. In what circumstances, if any, can third-country nationals have their qualifications recognised when moving within the Single Market? The response to this question is provided in Chapter 4. Both of these dimensions are imbued with and logically follow from the analysis of equal treatment in Chapter 2.

There is a final element of this book's contribution to research on qualification recognition. That is an attempt to understand what makes qualification recognition work well. There is some evidence to suggest that prior coordination of education and training facilitates qualification recognition. If this is the case, then, for the sake of completeness, it is worth considering the extent to which the EU already does this with third-countries, something I investigate in part in Chapters 3 and 5.

3 Sources

3.1 *Sources of Law*

While this book concerns certain aspects of the well-being of third-country nationals in accessing work in the EU, it is not concerned solely with the manner in which EU law secures their well-being. There are at least two other sources of transnational legal regulation which bind and influence the EU and its member states, namely, various forms of international law (international human rights, labour and economic law), on the one hand, and European human rights and labour law as found in the measures of the Council of Europe, on the other hand.[83] Why take these into account? For one, some of these sources of law are binding either on the EU, its member states or both. The EU and its member states also participate, to various degrees, in the workings of the various international and European institutions associated with

83 A helpful overview is provided by Bernard Ryan and Virginia Mantouvalou, 'The Labour and Social Rights of Migrants in International Law' in Ruth Rubio Martin (ed), *Human Rights and Immigration* (OUP 2014). See further Edoardo Ales, Mark Bell, Olaf Deinert and Sophie Robin-Olivier (eds), *International and European Labour Law: A Commentary* (Nomos/Hart 2018).

these sources of law. Finally, and crucially, EU and member states' courts occasionally take these sources of law into account in deciding cases in a manner which has been described by Virginia Mantouvalou in her pioneering work as an 'integrated approach' to legal interpretation: that is, an approach to interpreting a provision of law which takes into account international and European human rights law obligations relevant to the provision in question.[84] The EU and its member states, therefore, not only have an interest in securing the well-being of third-country nationals for purely self-interested reasons (as suggested in Section 1 above) but also because and insofar they do or should adopt an integrated approach to interpreting and applying EU law and policy.

3.2 *Sources of Normativity*

This book is a contribution to the academic study of the regulation of migrant integration in Europe, taking as a case study the recognition of professional qualifications or skills of migrants. While, as noted below, this book addresses both 'hard' and 'soft' forms of regulation, other sources of 'normativity' are occasionally drawn upon to critically analyse and reflect upon the legal and policy materials. This book does not expressly rely on any single overarching theory or philosophy of law or politics, although the doctoral thesis upon which it is based did so. Rather, it draws on discrete aspects of contemporary legal and political theory which make contributions to the often-controversial issues raised in this text, such as the proper approach to the integration of migrants, the right of migrants to equal treatment with citizens in numerous respects, the appropriateness of skills-selective immigration laws and policies and the potential for a 'brain drain' of third-countries.[85] It is not a goal of this book to provide a single or harmonious interpretation of the legal and policy governance of migrants' integration in Europe in the light of a particular legal or political theory, although it might at times seem that it is. At best, it is hoped to identify, present and briefly reflect upon some of the relevant theoretical issues or debates which bear upon the regulation of migrant integration, such

84 Virginia Mantouvalou, 'Labour Rights in the European Convention on Human Rights: An Intellectual Justification for an Integrated Approach to Interpretation' (2013) 13 HRLR 529.

85 The principal theoretical sources relied upon in this respect are Joseph Carens, *The Ethics of Immigration* (OUP 2013); Iseult Honohan and Marit Hovdal-Moan (eds), *Domination, Migration and Non-Citizens* (Routledge 2015); Sarah Fine and Lea Ypi (eds), *Migration in Political Theory: The Ethics of Movement and Membership* (OUP 2016); David Miller, *Strangers in Our Midst: The Political Philosophy of Immigration* (HUP 2016); Sarah Song, *Immigration and Democracy* (OUP 2019); and Désirée Lim, *Immigration and Social Equality: The Ethics of Skill-Selective Immigration Policy* (OUP 2023).

as those noted above, and to attempt to articulate the link, if any, between such theoretical debates and the need for concrete legal and policy reforms.

4 The Theme of Governance

There is an important theme underlying the competing modes and levels of governance just noted. That is the theme of governance itself. Governance is the setting of standards – the establishment of norms which guide people's behaviour and enable them to live their lives. A leading scholar on regulation is Gunther Teubner[86] and his work has spawned much further work.[87] Teubner distinguishes between formal legal rules and substantive legal rules. Formal legal rules are designed to protect a sphere of private or personal autonomy. By contrast, substantive legal rules require that specific action be taken to achieve a goal; they are goal-oriented. Substantive legal rules are, however, weak because law operates in one of numerous discrete heterarchical social systems. To put it another way, goal-oriented legal regulation cannot successfully govern society in a 'top-down' fashion. Because society is not hierarchically ordered, law cannot impose on and achieve goals in society in a 'command-and-control' fashion. Rather, often, each social system or 'sub-system' – e.g., law, politics, religion, etc – speaks past each other, using and adopting its own language and internal logic. Acts of communication between sub-systems are then translated and re-translated in and according to each sub-system's own internal logic and language.[88]

How, then, can law come to govern other sub-systems? How can we ensure that the goals we pursue through legal regulation are achieved? Ultimately, what is required is change from within: law must adjust itself in a manner which has come to be described as 'reflexive law'. 'Reflexive law' suggests a need for a multiplicity of modes of governance, not simply adopting a single, traditional model of governance but rather accepting the different languages and internal logics of separate social systems, synthesising them and

86 Gunther Teubner, 'Substantive and Reflexive Elements in Modern Law' (1983) 17 Law and Society Review 239.

87 Julia Black, 'Constitutionalising Self-Regulation' (1996) 59 MLR 24; Hugh Collins, *Regulating Contracts* (OUP 1999); Julia Black, 'Proceduralising Regulation, Part 2' (2001) 21 OJLS 33; and Sandra Fredman, *Human Rights Transformed: Positive Rights and Positive Duties* (OUP 2008) ch 6. I draw heavily on Fredman in this section.

88 Juergen Habermas, *Between Facts and Norms: Contributions to a Discourse Theory of Law and Democracy* (Polity Press 1997) section 2.1.

responding to them in their own language. Only in this way can law come to govern other social systems – often by assimilating and, to some extent, ameliorating its goals and ambitions to suit those of other social systems. And the primary way of doing this is through adopting diverse modes and means of governance, ranging from adopting modes of governance which have varying legal force or weight to those which facilitate decentralised deliberation and decision-making through local organisations and committees.

In EU law specifically, the theme of governance has attracted a great deal of critical attention.[89] In a well-known paper, Joanne Scott and David Trubek provide a helpful overview of different modes of governance operating in the EU. According to Scott and Trubek, the starting point for any analysis of regulation in the EU should be the 'classic Community Method', namely, the (almost) exclusive right of legislative initiative of the European Commission, as well as the legislative powers of the European Parliament and the Council. Such a traditional approach to regulation as top-down or 'command-and-control' is consonant with conventional views of legal regulation more generally. However, it is by now clear that the EU adopts many and varied modes of governance to achieve its various legal and policy goals. Examples of such varied models of governance include the social dialogue, the Open Method of Coordination and what is now the cornerstone of new governance in the EU, the European Semester, and the coordination of economic and employment policies on the basis of arts 121, 136 and 146 of the Treaty on the Functioning of the European Union.[90]

According to Scott and Trubek, these and other forms of governance share a number of important features. They include participation and power-sharing; multi-level integration of modes of governance; accepting diversity and decentralisation in modes of governance; facilitating deliberation; permitting flexibility and revisability of measures; and permitting experimentation

89 A good starting point is Joanne Scott and David Trubek, 'Mind the Gap: Law and New Approaches to Governance in the European Union' (2002) 8 ELJ 1 and the other articles in that special issue. See also Olivier de Schutter and Simon Deakin, 'Reflexive Governance and the Dilemmas of Social Regulation' in Olivier de Schutter and Simon Deakin (eds), *Social Rights and Market Forces: Is the Open Coordination of Employment and Social Policies the Future of Europe?* (Bruylant 2005); Gráinne de Búrca and Joanne Scott (eds), *Law and New Governance in the EU and the US* (Hart 2006); Mark Dawson, *New Governance and the Transformation of European Law: Coordinating EU Social Law and Policy* (CUP 2011); and Mark Dawson, 'New governance and the displacement of Social Europe: the case of the European Semester' (2018) 14 EUConst 191.

90 'New governance and the displacement of Social Europe: the case of the European Semester' (n 89).

and knowledge creation.[91] Soft law can be given effect in a number of ways. Trubek, Patrick Cottrell and Mark Nance identify several: shaming; diffusion through mimesis; diffusion through discourse; networking; deliberation; and peer learning.[92]

The European Semester itself is a good example of this. The successor to the Open Method of Coordination, the European Semester requires that country-specific recommendations are made, while national performance is benchmarked and compared across a number of indicators.[93] And given the flexibility of such modes of governance, the goals of legal regulation can adapt over time, constantly readjusting in the light of the capacity of the particular mode of governance to achieve new goals and ensure compliance. Such modes of governance can even consist of multiple levels of compliance, mandating strict compliance with those goals most imminently necessary and lower levels of compliance for less important goals. Once again, the European Semester serves as a good example of this: with the possibility of imposing financial sanctions on member states for consistent failure to adhere to recommendations, states are incentivised to comply early in the process.[94]

This book is primarily concerned with the 'hard' law regulation of certain aspects of third-country nationals' well-being at work, viz wrongful discrimination and inadequate skills' recognition. However, that is not to say that it is solely concerned with traditional 'command-and-control' methods of regulation. Several other forms of regulation are considered. Much international legal regulation which is discussed and relied upon in this book is – in substance, if not in principle – a form of soft law. Furthermore, when it comes to the measures which the EU adopts in areas which it shares competence with the member states, these generally constitute more timid forms of regulation but are, in practice, often very effective. One prominent example of this has already been mentioned and shall be addressed in full detail in Chapter 5, namely, the EQF. Other regulatory approaches, such as the adoption and provision of supportive, non-binding tools by the European Commission will also be addressed in Chapter 5.

---

91 'Mind the Gap: Law and New Approaches to Governance in the European Union' (2002) 8 ELJ 1 (n 89) 5–6.

92 David Trubek, Patrick Cottrell and Mark Nance, ''Soft Law', 'Hard Law' and EU Integration' in *Law and New Governance in the EU and the US* (n 89) 79.

93 'New governance and the displacement of Social Europe: the case of the European Semester' (n 89) 197.

94 Parliament and Council Regulation 1303/2013/EU on Structural Funding [2013] OJ L 347/320, Annex 1.

5 Structure of the Book

Part 1 constitutes the doctrinal foundations of this book. It is prefaced by a brief summary of the background to or theoretical basis for the doctrinal foundations of the book. This background can be summarily stated as lying in a concern for migrant's quality of life, their freedom of choice and the effective use and development of their skills as core constituents thereof. The rights to work and to equal treatment and non-discrimination are necessary to instantiate people's welfare generally and migrants' well-being in particular. Chapter 1 begins the doctrinal foundations for the book. It does so by describing, in detail, the right to work as a fundamental legal right in international and European law. The importance of this right cannot be understated. It is one of the foundations of EU employment and labour law, from which many other rights derive. It must be understood as facilitating access and integration into the labour market of migrants, in particular, as well as playing a crucial corrective and constitutive role in the construction of a Single Market in labour. Some general remarks and reflections on the nature of the Single Market in labour are made in the light of the legal construction of the right to work. It is noted, however, that at least as a matter of EU law, migrants are only granted the right to work when and insofar as they are granted equal treatment with member state nationals in respect of that right. It therefore becomes necessary to explore this latter right before determining when, and to what extent, migrants enjoy the right to work in Europe.

Chapter 2 concludes the doctrinal foundations of the book. It does so by describing and analysing the right to equal treatment and non-discrimination as it applies to third-country nationals. Migrants are granted this right in a variety of ways (e.g., the prohibition of discrimination on the grounds of gender or religion). However, for the purposes of this book, the most important context in which migrants are granted this right is in respect of their labour rights. This amounts to non-discrimination on the basis of nationality. Indeed, for migrants, the right to equality and non-discrimination on the on the ground of nationality functions as the 'right to have rights'. This chapter commences by providing a high-level overview of the link between the right to equality and non-discrimination, migration and skills. It is suggested that it is a fundamental function of the labour market to facilitate and enable discrimination on the ground of skills. However, other grounds of discrimination, such as nationality, should generally be prohibited. The chapter then outlines relevant measures of international and European law in respect of this issue. It argues that migrants should generally be granted equal treatment with EU nationals by way of generally prohibiting discrimination on the ground of nationality. The right of migrants to equal treatment with EU nationals is the trigger or gateway to being afforded other rights, such as the right to work. It may also serve to reduce the discrimination which third-country nationals habitually face. The question then arises as to whether migrants should be afforded equal treatment with citizens in particular circumstances. There are a wide range of such particular circumstances which could be investigated, such as socio-economic rights. However, the particular situation investigated in the remainder of this book is in respect is migrants' equal treatment in respect of the right to have their qualifications recognised and related rights.

Part 2 describes and analyses in detail the recognition of qualifications of migrants in Europe. It is prefaced by a brief note describing, in outline, what the right to qualification is and entails. It is simply described as a derivative right of the core right to work, enabling persons to access and participate in the labour market generally or certain regulated professions specifically. Practical examples are provided as to when the right to have one's qualifications recognised is engaged and to illustrate the important but under-explored role qualification recognition plays in facilitating labour market integration. Chapter 3 commences the analysis of the right to the recognition of a person's skills or professional qualifications in EU law. It describes the application of that right in the context of external migration, i.e., as it applies to and is implemented in the context of migrants coming to the EU. This requires a description and analysis of certain parts of EU migration and asylum law, as well as EU external relations law, such as the EU's trade and association agreements with third-countries. This chapter identifies the circumstances in which that right may be engaged and argues that these areas of EU law are somewhat deficient in a number of respects. Chapter 4 turns to the application of the recognition of qualifications when migrants move within the Single Market. This chapter largely deals with Directive 2005/36/EC on the recognition of professional qualifications. It outlines what this legislative instrument does, the case law interpreting it and the extent to which third-country nationals may benefit from it. The chapter concludes that third-country nationals should, in principle, benefit from this measure in certain narrowly defined circumstances and that there may be reason to explore expanding those circumstances in future. In so concluding, this chapter draws on and contributes to the ongoing debate over the scope of the free movement rights which migrants enjoy when living in the EU. Chapter 5 explores the EU's soft law and policy measures, as well as emerging legislative developments, in the context of both internal and external migration. These include integration measures specifically targeted at third-country nationals, the EU's Neighbourhood and Enlargement policies, mobility partnerships, international development and cooperation policy, the European Commission's recent recommendations on the recognition of professional qualifications of third-country nationals generally and migrants fleeing the Russo-Ukrainian War in particular, as well as the proposal for a Regulation establishing an EU Talent Pool. These and other measures, as well as relevant EU funds, are described and analysed in detail.

The concluding chapter summarises the entire book and makes a series of practical suggestions as to how EU law could better cohere with the theoretical and doctrinal foundations laid out earlier in the text. In the light of critical reflections made throughout this book, it is suggested that the EU should consider adopting a specific legislative instrument, such as a Directive, governing the recognition of qualifications of third-country nationals. Some of the core elements of such an instrument are identified in outline. Other and further issues for future research are also identified in outline.

Conclusion

This chapter has highlighted the increasingly prominent role which skills play in the policies of the European Union, particularly as they relate to third-country nationals, and some empirical evidence identifying some of the problems third-country nationals habitually experience in accessing the EU's labour market. On the basis of this background, the central research question which this book investigates has been outlined. That question, as stated in earlier, is the extent to which the EU guarantees the well-being of migrants in accessing work through its laws and policies, with a particular focus on skills' recognition and freedom from discrimination as aspects of their well-being, as a means to facilitate and enable their integration into European societies and economies. In the light of this question, this chapter outlined the various contributions to scholarship which this book shall make. The remainder of this book constitutes these contributions. This chapter has also highlighted the diverse sources of regulation which shall be drawn on in this book. It has discussed the importance of governance as a theme concerning the recognition of the skills of third-country nationals in the EU. It outlined the structure of the book to guide the reader in what is to come. Accordingly, it is now time to commence the response to the questions which this book seeks to answer.

PART 1

The Legal Foundations of Migrant Integration

Introduction to Part 1

This book, being focussed on migrants' integration in Europe, is, ultimately, concerned with their well-being. At a high level of abstraction, the theoretical or philosophical perspective this book implicitly relies upon is that the hallmark of personal well-being lies in a rich conception of human freedom, such that people's freedom of choice informs their past, present and future welfare. People use their skills to freely make choices which affect their well-being. One such choice is to work. Work therefore contributes to the quality of peoples' lives and naturally, a person's choice to undertake any particular job, career or employment represents one of the most important aspects of their welfare. The use and development of a person's skills at, in and through work is therefore crucial to their quality of life. This book focuses on migrants' opportunities to use their skills at, in and through their work to effectively and meaningfully participate in European societies and economies as the primary (but not only) means of their integration in the EU.

This part of the book seeks to identify and exposit some (not all) of the legal preconditions to or foundations necessary for the exercise and implementation of such a conception of personal well-being and human freedom. That is, it is the aim of this part of the book to identify and explain certain of the doctrinal foundations of a legal system which facilitates the free choice of work and the use and development of a person's skills at, in and through their work. In Europe, there are two correlative rights which form the foundations of such a system for migrants: the right to work and the right to equal treatment and non-discrimination. The right to work is recognised as a fundamental right in international, European and EU law. It is amongst the legal doctrinal foundations of employment and labour law in Europe. It is, in other words, a core right from which many other rights derive, such as the right to the recognition of professional qualifications, the subject of Part 2 of this book. One of the most important dimensions of the right to work is its facilitation of access to and participation in the workforce. It should therefore be understood as being of central significance for migrants seeking to access work in the EU because and insofar as it facilitates their access to the labour market when they are granted that right. However, crucially, their right to work is generally contingent on their right to equal treatment or non-discrimination with member state nationals on the ground of nationality. In other words, migrants, generally speaking, are not entitled to access the labour market without first being granted equal treatment with EU member state nationals in respect of the right to work.

 | DOI:10.1163/9789004724068_003

In the European Union, the right to equal treatment and non-discrimination on the basis of nationality constitutes the 'right to have rights'[1] for migrants: it determines many of migrants' rights in Europe, such as the right to work and the right to the recognition of their professional qualifications. Given the discrimination that migrants habitually experience in Europe, they should generally be entitled to equal treatment with member state nationals on the ground of nationality. This view generally finds support in international and European law. However, EU law does not currently cohere with the requirements of international and European law in this respect. There are some good reasons – legal doctrinal, political, conceptual and sociological – which suggest a change is necessary. In other words, migrants should generally be entitled to equal treatment with member state nationals as a matter of EU law. If this conclusion is correct, then we have reason to reassess the balance of reasons as it currently stands in respect of migrants' right to the recognition of their professional qualifications. In other words, it gives us reason to pause and reconsider whether the law as it stands is up to scratch from a normative perspective.

1 Hannah Arendt, 'The Rights of Man: What are They?' (1949) 3(1) Modern Review 467.

CHAPTER 1

The Right to Work

Introduction

This chapter commences the outline of some of the legal doctrinal foundations of the recognition of skills or qualifications of migrants in the EU. It seeks to start to answer the first sub-question which this book investigates, namely, what are the legal doctrinal foundations for migrants' entitlement to qualification recognition and non-discrimination in the EU? It does so by outlining the right to work in the European Union, a right which should be understood as fundamental for the purposes of facilitating people's access to and participation in the workforce. This chapter does not purport to provide a comprehensive description and analysis of all aspects of the right to work in the EU, for there have been many other such contributions made elsewhere which are cited here extensively for reference. Rather, this chapter aims to provide a concise, accessible and contextual description and analysis of the right to work in Europe which is relevant to and for the purposes of this book.

It is important to note that the right to work has a controversial history.[1] It is often read as entailing or implying a 'right to a job'. No such assumption is made in this book. But the right to work is nonetheless widely considered to be amongst the theoretical and doctrinal foundations of employment and labour law, a 'core' right from which many other labour rights derive.[2] On this point, the author agrees. For this reason, the right to work might also be described as a 'structural right'[3] because and insofar as it plays a central and organisational role in the design of the law governing work in general. Accordingly, when considering any part of employment and labour law, it is important to bear in mind the relevant dimension of the right to work which is applicable. The purpose of this chapter is primarily to emphasise the right to work's role in facilitating access to the labour market: it is the first right which a person must have to be able to contract for work. It is the foundation stone upon which every relation of production is built. The broader implications of the right to

1 See the essays in Virginia Mantouvalou (ed), *The Right to Work: Legal and Philosophical Perspectives* (Hart 2014).

2 Joseph Raz, *The Morality of Freedom* (OUP 1986) 168–170.

3 Cf Hiba Hafiz, 'Structural Labour Rights' (2021) 119(4) MichLRev 651.

 | DOI:10.1163/9789004724068_004

work for the nature of employment and labour law in the European Union will also be touched on briefly.

This chapter is structured as follows. It first considers the right to work in international and European law (Section 1). What emerges from this analysis is, first, that the right to work is universally considered to be a fundamental human right; second, it is a multidimensional right; third, that the most important dimension for the purposes of this book is the access dimension; and fourth, the multiple and overlapping modes of governance in operation to guarantee that right effectively. The chapter then considers the right to work in EU law, tracing its origins and genesis (Section 2). Particular attention is paid to the beneficiaries of the right to work, especially migrants, which are the focus of this book (Section 2.4.2). A short conclusion follows which summarises the key points of this chapter and indicates the link between this chapter and the remainder of this Part of the book.

1 The Right to Work in International and European Law

1.1 *International Law*

1.1.1 International Human Rights Law

Article 23(1) of the Universal Declaration of Human Rights (UDHR) recognises the right to work as a fundamental right of everyone: '[e]veryone has the right to work, to free choice of employment, to just and favourable conditions of work and to protection against unemployment'.[4] The right to work is also guaranteed in several other international human rights treaties, namely, in and through art 8(3)(a) International Covenant on Civil and Political Rights (ICCPR),[5] art 6 of the International Covenant on Economic, Social and Cultural Rights (ICESCR),[6] art 11(1)(a) of the Convention on the Elimination of All Forms of Discrimination Against Women (CEDAW),[7] art 5(e)(i) of the International

4 Colm Ó Cinnéide, 'The Right to Work in International Human Rights Law' in Virginia Mantouvalou (ed), *The Right to Work: Legal and Philosophical Perspectives* (Hart 2014).

5 Sarah Joseph and Melissa Castan, *The International Covenant on Civil and Political Rights: Cases, Materials and Commentary* (3rd edn, OUP 2013) ch 10.

6 Ben Saul, David Kinley and Jacqueline Mowbray, *The International Covenant on Economic, Social and Cultural Rights: Commentary, Cases and Materials* (OUP 2014) ch 8.

7 Frances Raday, 'Article 11' in Marsha Freeman, Christine Chinkin and Beate Rudolf (eds), *The UN Convention on the Elimination of All Forms of Discrimination Against Women: A Commentary* (OUP 2012).

Convention on the Elimination of All Forms of Racial Discrimination (CERD),[8] art 27(1) of the Convention on the Rights of Persons with Disabilities (CRPD),[9] art 32 of the Convention on the Rights of the Child (CRC)[10] and in arts 11, 25, 26, 40, 52 and 54 of the International Convention on the Protection of the Rights of All Migrant Workers and Members of Their Families (ICRMW). All member states of the European Union are parties to these respective human rights treaties (except the ICRMW, to which only a minority of member states are party)[11] and, according to art 3 TEU, the EU is committed to respecting, protecting and promoting human rights. It is thus essential that the EU, in its laws and policies, respects, protects and promotes the right to work to ensure its compliance with international human rights law. Of the guarantees of the right to work here mentioned, only the ICESCR and the ICRMW shall be considered in full below because the ICESCR 'deals more comprehensively than any other instrument with this right'[12] and the ICRMW is directly related to the place of migrant workers.

Article 6(1) ICESCR proclaims 'the right to work, which includes the right of everyone to the opportunity to gain his living by work which he freely chooses or accepts'. This text is significant in its implications for third-country nationals. It seems to suggest that everyone in the jurisdiction and subject to the powers of the state has the right to work. The Committee on Economic, Social and Cultural Rights also emphasises the need to allocate adequate resources to those who are disadvantaged, such as migrant groups.[13] There are also a number of 'core obligations' under the ICESCR; namely, to ensure the right of access to employment; to avoid any measures that result in discrimination and unequal treatment; and to adopt a national employment strategy and plan of action to implement the right to work.[14] Clearly, then, access to employment

8 Patrick Thornberry, *The International Convention on the Elimination of All Forms of Racial Discrimination: A Commentary* (OUP 2016) ch 12.

9 Ilias Bantekas, Facundo Pennilas and Stefan Trömel, 'Article 27' in Ilias Bantekas, Michael Ashley Stein and Dimitris Anastasiou (eds), *The UN Convention on the Rights of Persons with Disabilities: A Commentary* (OUP 2018).

10 Philip Alston, 'Article 32' in John Tobin (ed), *The UN Convention on the Rights of the Child: A Commentary* (OUP 2019).

11 Euan MacDonald and Ryszard Cholewinski, 'The ICRMW and the European Union' in Paul de Guchteneire, Antoine Pecoud and Ryszard Cholewinski (eds), *Migrants and Human Rights: The United Nations Convention on Migrant Workers' Rights* (CUP 2009).

12 CESCR, 'The Right to Work: General Comment No 18' (24 November 2005) 2; *The International Covenant on Economic, Social and Cultural Rights: Commentary, Cases and Materials* (n 3) ch 8.

13 ibid 8.

14 ibid 9.

is key in the overall schema of the right to work as laid out in the ICESCR. The right to work should therefore be understood as vital in enabling people to participate in the labour market.

In its Comment, the Committee on Economic, Social and Cultural Rights also observes that the following are required to guarantee the right to work, namely, the availability of work, accessibility to work and acceptability of work – hence the multidimensionality of the right to work. It is the accessibility to work which is most relevant to this book's aims and purposes. According to the CESCR, 'the labour market must be open to everyone under the jurisdiction of the State parties'.[15] This means that any discrimination on the grounds of, inter alia, national or social origin, is prohibited. However, discrimination on the ground of immigration status is not expressly prohibited. This point is raised in the ICRMW, art 7 of which provides that states are obliged to afford migrant workers the rights guaranteed therein without discrimination based on, inter alia, nationality. For the purposes of the ICRMW, a 'migrant worker' is simply any worker who has, is or will be engaged in work in a state of which s/he is not a national. While this seems broad, similar to the ICESCR, art 35 ICRMW expressly provides that

> [n]othing in the present part of the Convention shall be interpreted as implying the regularization of the situation of migrant workers or members of their families who are non-documented or in an irregular situation or any right to such regularization of their situation, nor shall it prejudice the measures intended to ensure sound and equitable-conditions for international migration.

It is, therefore, important to distinguish quite sharply between prohibited discrimination on the ground of nationality, on the one hand and permitted discrimination on the grounds of immigration status, on the other hand. While the ICESCR guarantees the rights therein to all persons in the state without discrimination, the ICRMW guarantees those rights only insofar as migrant workers are in a regular situation. Indeed, Part VI of the ICRMW contains provisions concerning the return of irregular migrants to their state of origin. Article 67 provides for the cooperation of states in ensuring the return of migrants when their authorisation to work has expired or their status in the jurisdiction has become irregular and art 68 requires states to bring the employment of irregular migrants to an end, including adopting sanctions on employers

15 ibid 4.

for employing irregular migrants. Accordingly, international human rights law prohibits any discrimination on the ground of, inter alia, nationality in respect of the right to work. But it does not prohibit discrimination on the ground of immigration status. The EU and its member states should also do so to comply with their international legal obligations, an issue which shall be addressed in full in the next chapter.

1.1.2 International Labour Law

Perhaps surprisingly, the right to work is not expressly guaranteed as a right in international labour law. However, it is noted as being given effect to in a number of conventions. The Preamble to the Employment Policy Convention 1964 (No 122) notes the guarantee in the UDHR of the right to work and states that the Convention, alongside other conventions, should be seen as a programme for 'economic expansion on the basis of full, productive and freely chosen employment'. Article 1 of the Convention requires that each member shall declare and pursue the goal of full, productive and freely chosen employment and adopt a policy in pursuit of that goal. According to art 1(2), that policy shall aim at ensuring, inter alia, work is as productive as possible. Article 1(3) of the Convention states that the policy shall take into account the relationship between employment objectives and other economic and social objectives. In its reports, the International Labour Organisation's Committee of Experts on the Application of Conventions and Recommendations regularly considers the link between such policies and education and training laws and policies, suggesting a need for coherence between both.[16] However, no account is taken, either in the Preamble or the text of the Convention of the role which non-nationals might play in the labour market and what rights they may have or deserve. But to be clear, migrant workers are afforded a wide range of rights under international labour law, in particular under the Conventions on Freedom of Association and Protection of the Right to Organise 1948 (No 87), Migration for Employment (Revised) 1949 (No 97), Discrimination (Employment and Occupation) 1958 (No 111), Equality of Treatment (Social Security) 1962 (No 118) and Migrant Workers (Supplemental Provisions) 1975 (No 143). The relevance and applicability of these measures shall be discussed in Chapter 2.

16 See, eg, ILO, *Application of International Labour Standards 2018: Report of the Committee of Experts on the Application of Conventions and Recommendations* (*Report III Part A*), Part 2.

1.1.3 International Economic Law

Article I of the General Agreement on Trade in Services provides that the agreement applies to measures by member states affecting trade in services, defined as the supply of a service

- From the territory of one member into the territory of another;
- In the territory of one member into the territory of any other another;
- By a service supplier of one member, through commercial presence in the territory of any other member; or
- By a service supplier of one member, through presence of natural persons of a member in the territory of any other member.

The last of these, so-called 'Mode 4' GATS, provides for the temporary presence of a service supplier from one member state in the territory of another member state. Access by service providers of one member state to the market of another member state is a fundamental part of the GATS but is not granted automatically. To put it another way, as a matter of international economic law, service providers are only permitted access to the market of a given state if a specific commitment in a relevant sector of the economy has been made by the host state. Under the GATS, member states must undertake commitments in respect of each sector of the economy which are contained in a series of schedules to the GATS. A series of minimum, harmonised preferences apply to the EU. Thus, for example, market access is generally unrestricted for Mode 4 service suppliers entering the EU except for certain categories of natural persons, namely self-employed persons; business visitors; highly-skilled workers; intra-corporate transferees; and posted workers.[17] These persons must obtain a visa from national authorities. In the case of self-employed service providers availing of visas under default GATS rules in the Annex on Movement of Natural Persons supplying Services under the Agreement, those rules are often practically unenforceable due both to the nature of the rules as deriving from an international economic order, which are difficult to enforce in practice, and the failure of WTO member states to properly implement these rules in domestic law.

For example, Simon Tans has demonstrated that the Netherlands and the UK failed to implement their obligations under the GATS appropriately because (i) their implementation lacked sufficient clarity due to the mode of governance adopted (often, executive policy documents rather than legislation) and

17 Simon Tans, *Service Provision and Migration: EU and WTO Service Trade Liberalisation and Their Impact on Dutch and UK Immigration Rules* (Brill Nijhoff 2017) chs 5–6 and see my review in (2018) 9 ELLJ 218.

the language used; (ii) the restrictions imposed on service providers domestically went beyond what was required under the GATS; and (iii) GATS rules generally lack enforceability at a domestic level. Thus, in terms of facilitating the market access of self-employed persons, much will rest on the good faith of the domestic authorities in designing and implementing these rules.[18] Market access is not, therefore, the default position as a matter of international economic law. If a member state specifically (as opposed to generally) permits market access in a given sector, then it is prohibited from, inter alia, imposing any limitations on the number of service suppliers which may enter the jurisdiction.[19]

1.2 *European Law*

1.2.1 The European Convention on Human Rights

The text of the ECHR does not expressly recognise or protect the right to work and the European Court of Human Rights has held that there is 'no general right to employment'.[20, 21] However, in protecting certain express rights in the ECHR, the ECtHR has effectively protected the right to work to some extent. Rory O'Connell, in his analysis of the case law of the ECtHR, outlines a number of areas in which the Court has effectively protected the right to work: under arts 6 (fair procedures), 8 (respect for private and family life), 9 (freedom of thought, conscience and religion) and 14 (non-discrimination). Only the Court's case law based on art 8 ECHR will be discussed here as it is most relevant.

In *Sidabras v Lithuania*, two former KGB agents were dismissed from public employment in Lithuania due to their involvement in the KGB.[22] By virtue of a provision of national law, the applicants were also prohibited from applying for various jobs in the private sector. They argued that their dismissal violated art 8 on its own and in conjunction with art 14 ECHR. The Court first assessed whether there was a difference in treatment of the applicants and then considered whether the facts of the case fell within the ambit of art 8 ECHR. The Court first concluded that there was a difference of treatment between the applicants and persons who had not worked for the KGB. In turning to the

18 ibid ch 7.

19 GATS, art XVI(2)(a).

20 Rory O'Connell, 'The Right to work in the ECHR' [2012] EHRLR 176; Filip Dorssemont, Klaus Lörcher and Isabelle Schömann (eds), *The European Convention on Human Rights and the Employment Relation* (Hart 2014); and Virginia Mantouvalou, 'The Protection of the Right to Work through the European Convention on Human Rights' (2014) 16 CYELS 313.

21 *Ţîmpău v Romania* [2023] ECHR 982 [148].

22 (2006) 42 EHRR 6.

second question, the ECtHR had regard to art 1 of the European Social Charter and the ILO's Convention on Discrimination (Employment and Occupation) 1958 (No 111) and concluded that 'a far-reaching ban on taking up private-sector employment does affect "private life"'.[23] While the ECtHR accepted that the ECHR does not guarantee a right of access to a particular profession,[24] nevertheless 'state imposed restrictions on the possibility for a person to find employment with a private company for reasons of lack of loyalty to the state cannot be justified (…) in the same manner as restrictions governing access to their employment in the public service'.[25] Accordingly, the restrictions in place were disproportionate and violated art 8 in conjunction with art 14 ECHR. *Sidabras* thus identifies access to work as a vital constituent element of a person's life and their well-being.

Campagnano v Italy concerned a bankruptcy case.[26] The applicant's name was entered in the bankruptcy register and as a result, she argued, was unable to engage in any business activity and several other activities, thereby violating her right to private and family life under art 8 ECHR. The scope of application of the restrictions included a prohibition on being appointed a guardian, a prohibition on being appointed as the director or trustee in bankruptcy of a commercial or cooperative company and the inability to carry on the occupations of trustee in bankruptcy, stockbroker, auditor or arbitrator. The applicant was also prohibited from participating in certain professions, such as the legal profession. Because these restrictions on a bankrupt affected 'the applicant's ability to develop relationships with the outside world',[27] the ECtHR found that they fell within the ambit of art 8 ECHR. According to the Court, being listed on the bankruptcy register clearly amounted to an interference with the applicant's right to respect for her private life.[28] Given the wide-ranging nature of these restrictions and the length of time before rehabilitation could be obtained (a period of five years), the Court considered that infringement of the applicant's art 8 rights were not 'necessary in a democratic society'.[29] *Campagnano* therefore locates work as a central source of meaning and identity in people's lives and emphasises the contribution of participation in the labour market to a person's well-being.

23 (2006) 42 EHRR 6 [47].
24 (2006) 42 EHRR 6 [52].
25 (2006) 42 EHRR 6 [58].
26 (2009) 48 EHRR 43.
27 (2009) 48 EHRR 43 [54].
28 (2009) 48 EHRR 43 [58].
29 (2009) 48 EHRR 43 [66].

These cases can, however, be distinguished from two more recent cases of the ECtHR concerning the right to work or, more specifically, the right of access to a profession. In *Jankauskas v Lithuania (No 2)*, the applicant, who had committed several crimes while working as a law enforcement officer, sought to be enrolled as a trainee advocate in Lithuania.[30] The applicant did not disclose the fact of his previous convictions in his application and the Bar Association accordingly rejected his application. The applicant appealed this decision throughout Lithuania before it was eventually affirmed by the Supreme Court. Similarly, in *Lekavičienė v Lithuania*, the applicant had been admitted to the Bar and subsequently committed several criminal offences involving fraud.[31] She was then removed from the list of practising advocates and subsequently sought readmission but was refused. While the applicant's conviction had expired, she nonetheless lacked the necessary high moral character required to be a practising advocate.

In both cases, while the ECtHR found that there had been an infringement of the applicants' right to respect for private and family life, the restrictions were nonetheless justified. They were prescribed by law, pursued the legitimate aim of underlining 'the advocates' obligations towards clients, courts and society and the need to safeguard the functioning of the justice system overall'[32] and did not permanently prohibit the applicants from later applying to be admitted to the Bar when their moral standing in the community had recovered.[33] Both *Jankauskas* and *Lekavičienė* stand out from *Sidabras and Dziautus* and *Campagnano* because of the obvious criminal wrongdoing and previous criminal behaviour of the applicants. But it is possible to reach a stronger conclusion in relation to these cases. In all the above discussed cases, there was some fault on behalf of the applicants – in the latter two, merely civil in nature; in the former two, criminal. Such fault triggered the restrictions imposed. Nonetheless, the restrictions prima facie infringed their right to respect for private and family life and were found to actually infringe that same right in *Sidabras and Dziautus* and *Campagnano*. In the context of migrant workers, however, there is no such fault justifying restrictions on their right to work.

Finally and conversely, Hugh Collins has argued that recent case law of the ECtHR under art 8 effectively guarantees a right to protection against unjustified dismissal.[34] The landmark case establishing this point for Collins is *Denisov*

30 (2018) 66 EHRR 16.

31 (2018) 67 EHRR 5.

32 (2018) 66 EHRR 16 [73]; (2018) 67 EHRR 5 [50].

33 (2018) 66 EHRR 16 [79]; (2018) 67 EHRR 5 [55].

34 Hugh Collins, 'An Emerging Human Right to Protection against Unjustified Dismissal' (2020) 50(1) ILJ 36.

v Ukraine[35] in which the applicant, a judge, was removed from office on the ground of 'significant shortcomings, omissions and errors and grave violation of the foundation of the organisation and administration of justice'. While the applicant's case was unsuccessful under art 8, the ECtHR nonetheless made a number of important remarks relating to the emerging right to protection against unjustified dismissal. The purpose of describing the Court's observations is as follows: if exclusion from employment by way of dismissal may constitute a breach of art 8 ECHR, then the converse must also be true: namely, that exclusion from the good of work in general may, if sufficiently serious, violate art 8.

The Court in *Denisov* began by affirming that, while there is no right to employment or to take up any particular profession under the ECHR, nonetheless, '[p]rofessional life is (…) part of the zone of interaction between a person and others which, even in a public context, may, under certain circumstances, fall within the scope of "private life"'.[36] The Court then distinguished between two different approaches it takes to employment-related cases. The first it called a 'reason-based approach', viz, where 'factors relating to private life were regarded as qualifying criteria for the function in question and when the impugned measure was based on reasons encroaching upon the individual's freedom of choice'.[37] The second the ECtHR described as the 'consequence-based approach', viz, where the 'impugned measure has or may have serious negative effects on the individual's private life'.[38] In relation to this approach, the Court has considered negative consequences on a person's 'inner circle', their opportunity to 'develop connections with the outside world' and their social and professional reputation. Moreover, any impugned measures or restrictions on any of these areas of a person's life must meet a threshold level of severity: in the case of the 'consequence-based approach', '[t]he applicant has to present evidence substantiating consequences of the impugned measure' and '[t]he Court will only accept that article 8 is applicable where these consequences are very serious and affect his or her private life to a very significant degree'.[39]

The ECtHR has since expanded the scope of application of this reasoning to include not only dismissal but also measures falling somewhat short of dismissal, such as suspension, as well as measures equivalent to dismissal in

35 [2018] ECHR 1061.
36 [2018] ECHR 1061 [100].
37 [2018] ECHR 1061 [103].
38 [2018] ECHR 1061 [107].
39 [2018] ECHR 1061 [116].

certain professions, such as the disbarment of a lawyer or removal from the register of medical practitioners. For example, in *Bagirov v Azerbaijan*, the ECtHR considered the case of a lawyer who was suspended for public criticism of police brutality and later disbarred for disrespectful remarks about a judge made in a courtroom while representing a client. In that case, it was not disputed that the lawyer's suspension from practising law for a period of one year and his subsequent disbarment for professional misconduct prevented him from exercising his profession and therefore 'affected a wide range of his professional and other relationships and encouraged upon his professional and social reputation'.[40] This, coupled with the significant loss of earnings, was sufficient to engage art 8 ECHR.

These relatively recent developments in the case law of the ECtHR provoke a question of relevance to the present work. If exclusion from the domain of work by way of unjustified dismissal is a violation of a person's human rights, then is the unjustified exclusion from work or the labour market in general for other reasons also a violation of a person's human rights? The question is important because it suggests that, on the assumption that there is or ought to be a parallel sort of reasoning in both cases, the reasons excluding a person from accessing the labour market, whether in whole or in part, need to be scrutinised. The total or even partial exclusion from access to the labour market seems, as a matter of principle, very likely to, at least, diminish, if not completely destroy, a person's autonomy and dignity. The case law outlined above seems to at least establish that exclusion from access to certain professions can violate a person's human rights if it is unjustified. Therefore, a conscientious and sustained focus on the reasons justifying exclusion from a particular domain of the labour market or the entirety thereof needs to be maintained.

No case law of the ECtHR to date has discussed the protection of the right to work in respect of migrants. Nonetheless, it might be possible to foster a connection between the right to work and the right to non-discrimination under art 14 ECHR. It may be the case that treating migrants differently from host state nationals in some respect, such as in respect of their labour rights, could amount to unlawful discrimination. The possibility of making this connection shall be investigated in full in Chapter 2.

40 *Bagirov v Azerbaijan* [2020] ECHR 488.

1.2.2 The European Social Charter and Revised European Social Charter

Article 1 ESC guarantees the right to work and provides as follows:[41]

> With a view to ensuring the effective exercise of the right to work, the Parties undertake:
> 1. to accept as one of their primary aims and responsibilities the achievement and maintenance of as high and stable a level of employment as possible, with a view to the attainment of full employment;
> 2. to protect effectively the right of the worker to earn his living in an occupation freely entered upon;
> 3. to establish or maintain free employment services for all workers;
> 4. to provide or promote appropriate vocational guidance, training and rehabilitation.

As Simon Deakin has observed, '[l]ooking at these provisions as a whole (…) it can be argued that the unifying idea in Article 1 is that of a *right to access the labour market*'.[42] According to Deakin, there are three senses in which it guarantees a right to access the labour market. A first is the way it protects the property right – the right to sell one's labour – in the market. It accurately acknowledges that labour is indeed a commodity in a social market economy. Second, the conception of the labour market developed therein is a social one: art 1 ESC protects a social market economy. And third, art 1 ESC 'assumes that the state and the legal system constitute the labour market not in an abstract sense, but with a particular instrumental goal in mind: this is the goal of protecting and enhancing the capabilities of market actors'.[43] And, according to Edoardo Ales,

> the right to work as affirmed by Article 1 RESC can be qualified as a social right to work (…) In order to realise a social right to work, a strong institutional (public or public authorised and supervised) intervention on the labour market is needed. However, it does not oblige (sic) to look at the

41 Diamond Ashiagbor, 'The Right to Work' in Gráinne de Búrca and Brunno de Witte (eds), *Social Rights in Europe* (OUP 2005); Simon Deakin, 'Article 1: The Right to Work' in Nikklas Bruun, Klaus Lörcher, Isabelle Schömann and Stefan Clauwaert (eds), *The European Social Charter and the Employment Relation* (Hart 2017); and Edoardo Ales, 'Article 1 RESC' in Edoardo Ales, Mark Bell, Olaf Deinert and Sophie Robin-Olivier (eds), *International and European Labour Law: A Commentary* (Nomos/Hart 2018).

42 Deakin, 'Article 1: The Right to Work' (n 41) 148 (emphasis original).

43 ibid 149.

> labour market as an institution itself. On the contrary, the institutionalised intervention is meaningful only if one looks at the labour market as a free place of encounter between labour demand and supply, encouraged, facilitated and assisted in its transitions by the institutionalised intervention.[44]

Colm Ó Cinnéide notes, art 1(2) ESC is 'in many ways the 'core' of the right to work'.[45] The European Committee of Social Rights has identified three different types of protection which states may adopt in respect of art 1(2) ESC: the prohibition of all forms of discrimination in employment; the prohibition of forced or compulsory labour; and the prohibition of any practice that might interfere with workers' right to earn their living in an occupation freely entered upon.[46] While the ESC does prohibit discrimination generally, in respect of nationality discrimination, the ECSR has stated that no nationality discrimination is permitted in respect of persons who are legally in the jurisdiction of the state, except on certain limited grounds of, e.g., national security or the exercise of public authority.[47]

2 The Right to Work in EU Law

2.1 *Origins*

The most obvious manifestation of the right to work in EU law first emerged in *Nold*,[48] wherein the applicant, a wholesaler in the coal industry, challenged a decision of the Commission concerning the establishment of conditions required for the acquisition of the status of 'direct wholesaler' in the industry. Those rules required, amongst other things, the acceptance of minimum purchase arrangements from a consolidated coal consortium in the Ruhr area of Germany. The applicant, however, was unable to meet these minimum requirements. In essence, the applicant's business was too small to survive in heightened conditions of competition. As the applicant argued, 'the effect of the new terms of business [was] to favour the concentration of this distribution into the hands of a small number of major dealers'.[49]

44 Ales, 'Article 1 RESC' (n 41) 253.
45 'The Right to Work in International Human Rights Law' (n 1) 115.
46 ECSR, 'Conclusions II, Statement of Interpretation on Article 1(2)' 4.
47 'The Right to Work in International Human Rights Law' (n 1) 117.
48 Case 4/73 *Nold* [1974] ECR 491. See also Case 44/79 *Hauer* [1979] ECR 3727.
49 [1974] ECR 491, 499.

The European Court of Justice rejected the applicant's challenge to the decision of the Commission on the grounds of discrimination and breach of fundamental rights. For the purposes of this chapter, the most relevant aspect of the Court's judgment is that part concerning fundamental rights. According to the Court, the right to free pursuit of a business activity, as protected by the German Basic Law and in the constitutions of the other member states, must be considered as a fundamental right which forms an integral part of the general principles of EU law.[50] The ECJ then went on to note the social nature of the right to choose and practice a trade or profession, in holding that such a right and analogue rights must be considered in the light of their social function: such rights 'are protected by law subject always to limitations laid down in accordance with the public interest'.[51] In the instant case, while the applicant's right to practice its profession was engaged, it was not infringed: 'the disadvantages claimed by the applicant are in fact the result of economic change'.[52]

Nold is important for a number of reasons. First, the Court grounded the right to work in the constitutional traditions of the member states. According to Michele Everson and Rui Correia Goncalves, such constitutional traditions share, at least, an elementary or basic republican heritage, emerging in particular out of the Weimar Constitution. Specifically, the constitutions of Ireland,[53] Luxembourg, Spain and Portugal, which draw on the Weimar Constitution to some extent, all guarantee the right to work in some shape or form. In addition, the right to work can also be traced, albeit more obliquely, in the constitutional traditions and jurisprudence of the UK, France, Austria, Germany, Greece, Sweden and Finland.[54] A second and vital point emerges from *Nold* concerning the nature of our culture. The right to work as explicated therein can be understood as functioning in at least three dimensions or vectors. It is, therefore, a multidimensional right. First, and most fundamentally, the right to work logically entails a right of access to the market. This is a de minimis condition with regards to the exercise of one's freedom to work. If anyone is prohibited from working tout court, then, given the centrality of work in European culture, there ought to be very weighty reasons justifying such a prohibition. Second, the right to work is also constitutive of the labour market because it,

---

50 [1974] ECR 491 [12]-[13].

51 [1974] ECR 491 [14].

52 [1974] ECR 491 [15].

53 See my 'The Right to Work in Irish Law' (2020) 42 DULJ 119.

54 Michele Everson and Rui Correia Goncalves, 'Article 16' in Steve Peers, Tamara Hervey, Jeff Kenner and Angela Ward (eds), *The EU Charter of Fundamental Rights: A Commentary* (2nd ed, Hart 2021).

amongst other norms, delineates the contours of the labour market.[55] While the right to work guarantees people's freedom of choice insofar as people are, at a minimum, enabled to contractually sell their labour, restrictions on the exercise of that right in the public interest (eg, not permitting children under a certain age to work, working time regulations, etc) ensure that people's well-being is secured. This point is, in effect, noted by the Court in *Nold*, when it is observed that the right to work may be 'subject to certain limits justified by the overall objectives pursued by the Community'.[56] Further evidence of this point is found in numerous later cases which acknowledge that the fundamental freedoms and right to work,

> may be restricted, particularly in the context of a common organization of a market, provided that those restrictions in fact correspond to objectives of general interest pursued by the Community and do not constitute a disproportionate and intolerable interference, impairing the very substance of the rights guaranteed.[57]

The right to work is thus a vital tool for the construction of a common competitive culture of work in the European Union. A final dimension to the right to work is its corrective nature. In contrast to its constitutive dimension, the corrective dimension of the right to work provides people with the ability to challenge existing limitations, by way of judicial review, on the exercise of the right to work (as opposed to access to work itself). This dimension of the right to work is made quite clear in *Nold* itself where the applicant attempted to challenge the apparently unfair regulations in place. Although the applicant's claim failed on the facts, what is important is that the applicant was enabled to review the seemingly oppressive regulation on the ground of its infringing the right to work.

Third, it is significant that the Court did not consider that the applicant's right to work was infringed. In particular, the fact that the Court did not intervene in the economic changes evident in the coal industry suggests that the

55 I borrow this reasoning from Wolfgang Streeck, 'From Market Making to State Building? Reflections on the Political Economy of European Social Policy' in Stephan Liebfried and Paul Pierson (eds), *European Social Policy: Between Fragmentation and Integration* (Brookings Institute 1995).

56 [1947] ECR 491 [14] (emphasis added).

57 Case C-177/90 *Kühn* [1992] ECR I-35 [16] (emphasis added); Case C-280/93 *Germany v Council* [1994] ECR I-4973 [78]; Case C-44/94 *Fishermen's Organisations and Others* [1995] ECR I-3115 [55]; Case C-200/96 *Metronome Musik* [1998] ECR I-1953 [21]; and Joined Cases C-20/00 and C-64/00 *Booker Aquacultur and Hydro Seafood* [2003] ECR I-7411 [68].

Court was reluctant to give legal – as opposed to moral – effect, in a strident manner, to the corrective dimension of the right to work in this context. While, in principle, the applicant's right to access the market was guaranteed, little more than access was ensured. This conclusion raises interesting questions concerning the potential imbalance between the three dimensions of the right to work. For, in *Nold*, the constitutive dimension trumped the corrective dimension to the right to work insofar as the right to work was not used to amend the regulations in question but to affirm them. However, the Court's reasoning for this is unclear and somewhat limited. It would have been preferable for the Court to identify an internal hierarchy amongst these possible dimensions, deploying them in a reasoned manner. One plausible reason for this outcome is that the Court adopted a moral approach to the corrective dimension; that is, the Court did enforce the corrective approach morally rather than legally. This leaves it up to the applicant to bring the challenge elsewhere, through perhaps appropriate executive or legislative lobbying. Another and probably the most plausible reason may be the evolution of the Court's role in developing EU law. In the early case law on the general principles of EU law, the reasoning provided was often very brief.[58] Certainly, going forward, it would be helpful if such a hierarchy amongst the different dimensions or vectors of the right to work was identified by the CJEU or the EU's legislative bodies, so as to serve as guidance to law and policy makers when implementing the constitutional vision of work regulation in the EU. From the perspective of this book, the access dimension would likely merit positioning at the top of the hierarchy given the overarching interest of every person in the EU in being able to participate in the good of work. Its constitutive and corrective dimensions may then follow suit in that order. The corrective dimension should be understood as a catch-all mechanism facilitating the review of the legality of restrictions on the right to work in the light of some sort of balancing or proportionality test between the different rights at play, a possibility to be considered presently.

2.2 *Genesis*

It is worth considering, albeit briefly, some of the key cases touching on the structural dimension of the right to work in recent years: namely, *Schmidberger*,[59] *Omega Spielhallen*,[60]

58 See Ulf Bernitz, Xavier Groussot and Felix Schulyok (eds), *General Principles of EU Law and European Private Law* (Wolters Kluwer 2013); Chiara Amalfitano, *General Principles of EU Law and the Protection of Fundamental Rights* (Edward Elgar 2018); and Takis Tridimas, *The General Principles of EU Law* (3rd edn, OUP 2019).

59 Case C-112/00 *Schmidberger* [2003] ECR I-5659.

60 Case C-36/02 *Omega Spielhalen* [2004] ECR I-9609.

Viking[61] and *Laval*.[62] While not expressly dealing with the right to work, these cases are nonetheless very important in developing our understanding of the structure or organisation of the law governing work in general by virtue of the architectonic role they play in structuring the regulation of work in the EU.

In *Schmidberger*, an association to protect the biosphere in the Alpine region held a demonstration, resulting in the closure of a motorway. The demonstration was not banned. HGVs consequently were unable to use this motorway. The applicant in this case was an international transport undertaking which generally used that motorway between Germany and Austria, hence bringing a cross-border element to the case and triggering EU law. It was argued that the failure to prohibit the demonstration constituted an infringement of the free movement of goods. The European Court of Justice held that where two or more fundamental rights are in conflict, a double proportionality[63] analysis must be deployed. That is, in the context of the right to work and other rights, 'in addition to assessing the proportionality of restrictions that labour rights impose on the exercise of economic freedoms, courts should examine whether the exercise of economic freedoms is justified and proportionate given their capacity to restrict the exercise of collective labour rights'.[64] The ECJ emphasised that national courts are afforded a wide margin of discretion in developing such an analysis and, on the facts of this case, were entitled to conclude that the restriction on the free movement of goods was proportionate. This case therefore implies that the right to work, amongst other rights related to work, must be balanced against seemingly conflicting rights, such as the fundamental economic freedoms, when there is an alleged conflict between the interests of workers and the interests of others, such as other actors in the market generally. The question in each case will likely be a highly complex one, involving legal doctrinal, economic and other theoretical perspectives explaining and justifying the introduction or removal of laws and norms governing work.

Omega Spielhallen provides a good example of such double proportionality analysis at work. In that case, the applicant was a German company which produced a 'laserdrome' game. The police authority issued an order against the applicant forbidding it from 'facilitating or allowing in its (…) establishment games with the object of firing on human targets using a laser beam or other

61 Case C-438/05 *Viking* [2007] ECR I-10779.

62 Case C-341/05 *Laval* [2007] ECR I-11767.

63 Hugh Collins, 'On the (In)compatability of Human Rights Discourse and Private Law' in Hans-W Micklitz (ed), *Constitutionalisation of European Private Law* (OUP 2014) 49–51.

64 Vilija Velyvyte, 'The Right to Strike in the European Union after Accession to the European Convention on Human Rights' (2015) 15 HRLR 73, 97.

technical devices (such as infrared, for example), thereby, by recording shots hitting their targets, 'playing at killing' people', on pain of a DEM 10,000 fine for each game played in breach of the order. The national court was concerned that the order constituted an infringement of the free provision of services. The ECJ upheld the restriction on the freedom to provide services in the public interest, where the public conception of a fundamental right (in this case, the right to human dignity) in the national constitution supported such a restriction.[65] In essence, the domestic court was given a significant margin of discretion, against a background where the prevailing public policy of the state ostensibly supported such a restriction, to determine the legitimacy of that restriction. The Court also noted that it is not necessary 'for the restrictive measure issued by the authorities of a member state to correspond to a conception shared by all member states as regards the precise way in which the fundamental right or legitimate interest in question is to be protected'; however, such a convergence of values across member states may offer stronger support than a single member state's values alone.[66]

In *Viking*, the applicant ferry, running between Finland and Estonia, was flagged in Finland and the wages of the crew were regulated by a collective agreement in Finland. As the ferry was running at a loss, the applicant sought to reduce its costs by reflagging the ferry in Estonia where wages were lower, with a view to reaching a collective agreement with an Estonian trade union. The respondent, an international association of trade unions, called on its affiliated trade unions in Estonia not to enter into negotiations with the applicant, while its affiliated trade union in Finland threatened strike action. In other words, the respondent threatened transnational strike action against the applicant. The applicant accordingly issued proceedings seeking to have the threatened strike action rendered as an unlawful infringement of EU free movement law. The ECJ reasoned as follows. It began by acknowledging that the right to strike was a fundamental right which was guaranteed by EU law, notwithstanding that such a right was expressly excluded from the scope of the EU's constitutional texts. It then held that such collective action constituted a restriction on the freedom of establishment. While the Court accepted that national competent authorities would have a significant discretion to assess the extent to which such a restriction was justified, it nonetheless held that such national authorities could not conclude that the restriction was justified if it could be established that the jobs or conditions of employment were not jeopardised or

65 [2004] ECR I-9609 [32].
66 [2004] ECR I-9609 [37].

under serious threat. Moreover, even if workers' jobs or conditions of employment were jeopardised or under serious threat, it would need to be further demonstrated whether the collective action taken was proportionate.

Laval concerned posted workers. The applicant posted construction workers from Latvia to Sweden to work on sites operated by a company which was wholly owned by the applicant. While the workers were bound by and benefited from collective agreements made in Latvia, they were not bound by nor did they benefit from similar collective agreements in Sweden. A branch of the respondent trade union in Sweden entered into negotiations with a view to reaching a collective agreement with the applicant on the conditions of employment of its posted workers in Sweden. Elements of this collective agreement provided for further negotiations in respect of, inter alia, pay. The applicant refused to sign the collective agreement and the respondent initiated collective action in the form of blockading sites on which the applicant's posted workers worked. Sympathy action followed from other trade unions in Sweden until the applicant's wholly owned company in Sweden went bankrupt. The question for the ECJ was whether such collective action violated the freedom to provide services. As in *Viking*, the Court began by acknowledging that the right to take collective action was indeed a fundamental right guaranteed by EU law. However, the Court then held that the collective action in question constituted a restriction on the freedom to provide services since it was likely to make it less attractive for market actors to exercise that same freedom. While the Court accepted that collective action was in principle a justifiable restriction on that freedom, nonetheless, in this case, where the negotiations on pay formed 'part of a national context characterised by a lack of provisions, of any kind, which are sufficiently precise and accessible',[67] such a restriction was not justifiable.

What is the relevant point which emerges from this brief overview of *Viking* and *Laval*? Criticisms of these cases abound and this is not the place to consider many or all of them.[68] Furthermore, as the CJEU has subsequently confirmed, these cases no longer apply as broadly as was once thought.[69] Two brief points do, however, merit noting. A first is the failure to apply the double proportionality test envisaged in *Schmidberger*. Instead of first considering the right to strike as a restriction on the freedom to provide services and the

67 [2007] ECR I-11767 [110].

68 See, inter alia, Mark Freedland and Jeremias Prassl (eds), *Viking, Laval and Beyond* (Hart 2014).

69 See Case C-413/3 *FNV Kunstetn Informatie en Media v The Netherlands* ECLI:EU:C:2014:2411; and Case C-437/09 *AG2R Prévoynce v Beaudout Père et Fils SARL* ECLI:EU:C:2011:112.

freedom of establishment and then considering the converse, the Court simply considered the right to take collective action as a restriction on EU free movement law which required justification. No assessment was undertaken of the extent to which EU free movement law restricted the right to strike. This is deeply lamentable. A second and related point emerges from the first, namely, that the Court thereby established an internal hierarchy amongst rights to free movement and certain collective aspects of EU labour law. It unduly privileged parts of EU free movement law over elements of EU labour law without any real justification, beyond citing the fundamental need to establish an internal market in the EU. This hierarchy entrenches a certain economic vision of the Union within at least part of the EU's legal system, namely, one which emphasises commercial freedom and certainty.[70] While this occurred solely in relation to the possibility of transnational collective action, given that these cases are so significant for the nature of work and community in the EU, then the possibility of a similarly unsympathetic hierarchy between rights or within the internal dimensions of multidimensional rights becoming entrenched in other areas of EU law must be kept in mind with due caution. As suggested in relation to the right to work in the previous section, while some sort of hierarchy between the different dimensions of that right should be established, overemphasising any one of them may have detrimental effects. For example, one could envisage the right to work in its access dimension being used to challenge ostensibly protective regulation restricting access to certain professions, thereby making it easier for more and more people to participate in the labour market but with less effective consumer and labour protective regulation. This possibility is explored, derivatively, in Chapter 4.

In relation to the right to work more generally, it is trite to say that access to and participation in the labour market will be either enabled or hindered by rules governing work and the right to work can be used to challenge and liberalise such measures in its access, constitutive and corrective dimensions. The question in each case will thus be whether the relevant laws and norms are more or less likely, empirically speaking, to facilitate people's access to and participation in the market, sufficiently broadly construed to include the self-employed. This is an extremely difficult question to answer. It will be necessary to consider the extent to which existing laws and norms governing access to and participation in the relevant part of the labour market are justified by empirical considerations relating to people's well-being. The regulation of

70 Hilary Hogan, 'The Origins and Development of Article 16 of the Charter of Fundamental Rights' (2023) 2 European Law Open 753.

business reorganisation[71] provides an example of laws and norms designed, within certain limits, to double or even triple balance the rights of businesses, workers and consumers, a balance which must be rigorously adhered to and developed.

2.3 *The Charter of Fundamental Rights of the European Union*

The culmination of the analysis thus far is the rights now expressly stated in arts 15 and 16 CFREU.[72] Article 15, the explanatory notes to which refer to art 1 ESC already discussed, extends to 'everyone' the right to work and pursue a freely chosen occupation. This general expression of the right to work is then applied, more particularly, to certain categories of person in the sub-clauses of art 15. Thus, art 15(2) provides that Union citizens have the freedom to seek employment, to work and to exercise the right of establishment and to provide services in the territory of the member states. By contrast, according to art 15(3) CFREU, third-country nationals who are duly authorised to work are merely afforded working conditions 'equivalent' to those of member state nationals. In other words, lawfully-resident migrants with permission to work are entitled to equivalent, but not equal, treatment in respect of their working conditions under EU law.

Article 16 CFREU provides for the freedom to conduct a business 'in accordance with Union law and national laws and practices'. While arts 15 and 16 thus

---

71 Council Directive 2001/23/EC on the transfer of undertakings [2001] OJ L 82/16.

72 See further Valeria Bonavita, 'The EU Charter of Fundamental Rights and the Social Dimension of International Trade' in Giacomo Di Federico (ed), *The EU Charter of Fundamental Rights: From Declaration to Binding Instrument* (Springer 2011) 259–260; Jeremias Prassl, 'Freedom of Contract as a General Principle of EU Law? Transfers of Undertakings and the Protection of Employer Rights in EU Labour Law' (2013) 42 ILJ 434; Stephen Weatherill, 'Use and Abuse of the EU's Charter of Fundamental Rights: On the Improper Veneration of 'Freedom of Contract'' (2014) 10 ERCL 167; Stefan Giubboni, 'Freedom to Conduct a Business and EU Labour Law' (2018) 14 EUConst 172; Simon Deakin, 'Article 15' and Bruno Veneziani, 'Article 16' in Filip Dorssemont, Klaus Lörcher, Stefan Clauwaert and Mélanie Schmitt (eds), *The Charter of Fundamental Rights of the European Union and the Employment Relation* (Hart 2019); Nils Wahl, 'The Freedom to Conduct a Business' in Fabian Amtenbrink, Gareth Davies, Dimitry Kochenov and Justin Lindeboom (eds), *The Internal Market and the Future of European Integration: Essays in Honour of Lawrence Gormley* (CUP 2019); Niall O'Connor, 'Whose Autonomy is it Anyway? Freedom of Contract, the Right to Work and the General Principles of EU Law' (2020) 49(3) ILJ 285; Eleni Frantziou and Virginia Mantouvalou, 'Article 15' and Everson and Correia Goncalves, 'Article 16' in *The EU Charter of Fundamental Rights: A Commentary* (n 54); and Hilary Hogan, *The Freedom to Conduct a Business: The Origins and Development of Article 16 of the Charter of Fundamental Rights of the European Union* (European University Institute PhD Thesis 2024).

express different rights, they must emanate from the same central freedom, namely, to work, be it as an employed person, or a self-employed person or service provider. In his Opinion in *Alemo-Herron*, AG Cruz Villalón made a number of helpful comments in relation to art 16 CFREU.[73] The AG first noted that art 16 is based not only on case law concerning the freedom to pursue an economic activity but also contractual freedom and the principle of free competition.[74] Second and relatedly, the AG made several comments on the nature of art 16 CFREU as a market norm, similar to those made earlier in respect of the right to work evidenced in *Nold*. The AG first observed that the freedom to conduct a business 'acts as a limit on the actions of the Union in its legislative and executive role as well as on the actions of the Member States in their application of European Union law'.[75] Second and relatedly, the AG emphasised that the freedom to conduct a business 'protects economic initiative and the ability to participate in a market'.[76] Once again, the significance of the right to work in facilitating access to the labour market can be seen. Finally, AG Cruz Villalón emphasised the possibility of using art 16 CFREU as a 'counterweight' to other fundamental rights.[77] This suggests a need to balance competing concerns through the sort of double proportionality analysis as envisaged in *Schmidberger*.

2.4 *Beneficiaries*

2.4.1 Citizens

According to art 15(1) CFREU, the right to work is enjoyed by 'everyone'. But art 15(2) CFREU acknowledges that only 'citizens' have the 'freedom to seek employment' and exercise their freedom of movement for the purposes of work, service provision or establishment anywhere in the Union. Intuitively, then, 'workers'[78] and so-called 'work-seekers'[79] can avail of the right to work;[80] but what of employers, the self-employed and the unemployed? And what of

---

73 Case C-426/11 *Alemo-Herron* [2014] 1 CMLR 21.

74 [2014] 1 CMLR 21 [AG48].

75 [2014] 1 CMLR 21 [AG50].

76 [2014] 1 CMLR 21 [AG51].

77 [2014] 1 CMLR 21 [AG52].

78 Nicola Countouris, 'The Concept of 'Worker' in European Labour Law: Fragmentation, Autonomy and Scope' (2018) 47 ILJ 192.

79 Catherine Barnard, 'Free movement of natural persons and citizenship of the Union' in Catherine Barnard and Steve Peers (eds), *European Union Law* (2nd edn, OUP 2017) 377.

80 Case C-179/90 *Merci Convenzionali Porto di Genova SpA v Siderurgica Gabrielli SpA* [1991] ECR I-5923 (dock workers); Case C-355/93 *Eroglu v Land Baden-Wurttemberg* [1994] ECR I-5116 (Turkish workers).

those undertaking unpaid personal work? The case law to date makes it clear that self-employed persons,[81] co-operatives,[82] SMEs[83] and other substantially-sized economic operators and employers on the market can and do avail of the right to work and the freedom to conduct a business.[84] By virtue of the duality of the right to work and the freedom to conduct a business, arts 15 and 16 CFREU can be relied on not only by natural persons, who are the traditional concern of human rights law, but also by non-natural legal persons.

2.4.2 Non-citizens

What, then, of non-citizens? The answer to this question is surely crucial in the context of this book. To be clear, third-country nationals are only entitled to the right to work when and to the extent that they are entitled to equal treatment with member state nationals, are lawfully resident in the EU and have permission to work in a member state, in particular on the basis of some visa scheme, circumstances which I explore in more detail in the next chapter.[85] Article 15 CFREU does not itself regulate the parameters of granting authorisation to work in the EU.[86] However, as Eleni Frantziou and Virginia Mantouvalou have noted, in one case, the CJEU appear to have suggested that, taken in conjunction with art 7 CFREU, the right to work 'may be found to amount to a right not to be excluded from the labour market in certain circumstances'.[87] Nonetheless, they conclude that art 15(3) CFREU,

> does not change the legal position of third-country nationals in terms of rights of access to national labour markets or free movement within the EU. To do so would have had the effect of extending EU

81 Joined Cases C-184/02 and C-223/02 *Spain v Council* [2004] ECR I-7829.

82 Case C-44/94 *Fishermen's Organisations and Others* [1995] ECR I-3115.

83 Case 4/73 *Nold* [1974] ECR 491.

84 Case 44/79 *Hauer* [1979] ECR 3727; Case C-134/15 *Lidl* ECLI:EU:C:2016:498; Case C-534/16 *Finančné riaditeľstvo Slovenskej republiky v BB construct s. r. o.*, ECLI:EU:C:2017:820; Case T-732/14 *Sberbank of Russia OAO v Council* ECLI:EU:T:2018:541; Case T-734/14 *VTB Bank OAO v Council* ECLI:EU:T:2018:542; Cases T-735/14 and T-799/14 *Gazprom Neft PAO v Council* ECLI:EU:T:2018:548; Case T-798/14 *DenizBank AS v Council* ECLI:EU:T:2018:546; and Case T-207/15 *National Iranian Tanker Company v Council* ECLI:EU:T:2016:471.

85 Catherine Barnard, *EU Employment Law* (4th edn, OUP 2012) 182–188.

86 Eleni Frantziou and Virginia Mantouvalou, 'Article 15' in *The EU Charter of Fundamental Rights: A Commentary* (n 54) 452.

87 ibid, citing Joined Cases C-391/16 *M v Ministerstvo vnitra* and Cases C-77-78/17 *X v Commissaire général aux réfugiés et aux apatrides* [2019] EU:C:2018:486 [109].

> competence – modifying the powers of the Union, contrary to the restriction in Article 51(2) of the EU Charter.[88]

But given that third-country nationals habitually experience wrongful discrimination and inadequate skills recognition in access to employment, is the right to work a sufficient protection of the well-being of third-country nationals currently in or coming to the EU? To answer this question, it is necessary to make two points. The first point concerns the circumstances in and extent to which third-country nationals are entitled to equal treatment with member state nationals. If and when third-country nationals are entitled to equal treatment with member state nationals, then it may be possible to challenge the wrongful discrimination they regularly face through anti-discrimination law. To put the point another way, third-country nationals' equal treatment with member state nationals enables us to apply anti-discrimination norms to their circumstances. The possibility of so doing is the subject of the next chapter. The second point is the relationship between core and derivative rights.[89] While the right to work is the core right based upon the basic liberty to work and therefore of significant importance in and of itself, there is a vital derivative right which merits special consideration in response to the inadequate skills recognition which third-country nationals habitually face. The derivative right in question, namely, the right to have one's qualifications recognised for the purposes of access to and participation in the labour market, is the major subject of Part 2 of this book. The nature, scope of application, limitations of and relationship between this right and other legal rights shall be described there in full detail.

2.5 *Scope*

The scope of the right to work is broad. While the CJEU has not stated any single overarching objective for or scope of the right to work, it has nonetheless deployed it in a wide variety of circumstances. In addition to those cases discussed earlier in this section, the right to work has been deployed in the context of the rights of migrant family members,[90] numerous commercial activities,[91] intellectual property rights,[92] product labelling,[93] the regulation

88 ibid 457.

89 Joseph Raz, *The Morality of Freedom* (OUP 1986) 168–170.

90 Case 267/83 *Diatta v Land Berlin* [1985] ECR 574.

91 Joined Cases 63 and 147/84 *Finsider v Commission* [1985] ECR 2857; Case C-112/00 *Schmidberger* [2003] ECR I-5659; Case C-36/02 *Omega Spielhalen* [2004] ECR I-9609.

92 Case C-200/96 *Metronome Musik* [1998] ECR I-1953.

93 Case 234/85 *Keller* [1986] ECR 2897; Case C-134/15 *Lidl* ECLI:EU:C:2016:498.

of professional bodies[94] and working time.[95] In so deploying the right to work, the Court often uses what may be described as 'labour market reasoning', namely, an approach characterised by its addressing the structural conditions in the labour market.

This point is perhaps made most clear in the CJEU's age discrimination case law. For example, in *Fuchs*, the Court considered the legitimacy of a mandatory retirement law for state prosecutors in Germany.[96] In addressing the question of whether such a law pursued a legitimate aim, the Court noted that a mandatory retirement law can have the effect of facilitating intergenerational fairness in the labour market, enabling young people to access jobs which would otherwise be unavailable. The Court then noted that, while the member states enjoyed a broad margin of discretion in defining measures capable of achieving the aim of intergenerational fairness, the member states may not frustrate the prohibition on age discrimination set down in the Framework Directive.[97] Moreover, the Court noted, the prohibition on age discrimination must be read in the light of the right to work in art 15 CFREU. According to the Court, it followed that 'particular attention must be paid to the participation of older workers in the labour force and thus in economic, cultural and social life'.[98] The right to work has therefore not only been deployed in diverse areas of law but has also played an important role in designing or structuring the labour market, as previously suggested in respect of *Nold*.

These are the recorded instances of the right to work being invoked before the CJEU. Naturally, the right to work in EU law can only be invoked against those who are also subject to and fall within the ambit of a particular provision of EU law and it has accordingly been relied upon most often to challenge provisions of EU law or the conduct of EU institutions. But by virtue of the doctrines of (vertical and horizontal) direct effect and supremacy, it can also be deployed against member states, as well as emanations of the state, and even natural persons in certain circumstances. In addition, it may also be used to interpret provisions of secondary EU legislation and member state law which implements EU law, by virtue of the obligation to give indirect effect to EU law. The application of these traditional or fundamental doctrines of EU law to the right to work suggest that its scope is therefore very wide-ranging,

94 Case C-237/18 *Stiernon* ECLI:EU:C:2018:630.

95 Joined Cases C-184/02 and C-223/02 *Spain v Council* [2004] ECR I-7829.

96 Case C-159/10 *Fuchs* ECLI:EU:C:2011:508.

97 Council Directive 2000/78/EC establishing a general framework for equal treatment in employment and occupation [2000] OJ L 303/16.

98 ECLI:EU:C:2011:508 [63].

entailing deep impacts in the governance of the labour market of each member state. As noted earlier in this chapter, the right to work is a structural and multidimensional right in that it plays both a constitutive and corrective role in regulating the labour market. This applies not only to the labour and service markets of EU as a whole but to each labour and service market of the member states. Individuals in the EU may therefore challenge any domestic regulations which could (≠ necessarily does) infringe their right to work under EU law, particularly where those regulations restrict, set limits or regulate access to, participation in and exit from domestic labour or service markets or ancillary benefits associated therewith, such as social advantages and social assistance. It follows therefore, as Frantziou and Mantouvalou note, that the right to work 'entails a duty to respect the right of individuals to freely enter a chosen profession by the EU and the member states and allows its enforcement against EU and member state authorities before national and EU courts.'[99]

2.6 *Restrictions and Limitations*

Restrictions on the right to work may be made through statute, administrative practice or contract. The standard of review of restrictions has varied slightly, from assessing whether the restriction in question are proportionate or violate the very substance of the right.[100] Restrictions of various kinds have been considered by the Court of Justice. Prominent among them are those regulatory restrictions on the exercise of the right to work of the self-employed,[101] restrictions on collective action taken by workers[102] and restrictions on the operations of certain financial service providers[103] while fewer restrictions on the right to work of workers and non-nationals have been considered. This is probably because it is more difficult for such individuals to access the CJEU but also because the right to work can more effectively be applied and deliberated upon by member state courts in respect of such persons. While this author is not familiar with nor does this book purport to take into account comprehensively the case law of the member states, it would be interesting to develop

99 Eleni Frantziou and Virginia Mantouvalou, 'Article 15' in *The EU Charter of Fundamental Rights: A Commentary* (n 54) 459.

100 Case 4/73 *Nold* [1974] ECR 491; Case C-280/93 *Germany v Council* [1994] ECR I-4973.

101 Case C-177/90 *Kühn* [1992] ECR I-35 (milk quotas); Joined Cases C-184/02 and C-223/02 *Spain v Council* [2004] ECR I-7829 (working time of self-employed lorry drivers).

102 Case C-341/05 *Laval* [2007] ECR I-11767; Case C-438/05 *Viking* [2007] ECR I-10779.

103 Case C-304/16 *American Express* ECLI:EU:C:2017:524; Case C-534/16 *Finančné riaditeľstvo Slovenskej republiky v BB construct s. r. o.*, ECLI:EU:C:2017:820; Case T-732/14 *Sberbank of Russia OAO v Council* ECLI:EU:T:2018:541; Case T-734/14 *VTB Bank OAO v Council* ECLI:EU:T:2018:542; Case T-798/14 *DenizBank AS v Council* ECLI:EU:T:2018:546.

knowledge and understanding of the extent to which natural and legal persons do rely on the right to work to challenge domestic legislation and policy. Indeed, given that 'everyone' in the EU has the right to work, one might expect that anyone in the EU could rely on it, at least in correspondence with member state authorities or departments, to challenge restrictions thereon. In assessing whether such restrictions are permissible, the CJEU may seek specific evidence of detriment suffered[104] and the negation of other options which might reasonably be open to an applicant.[105] However, as indicated in the analysis of *Nold* in Section 2.1 above, the CJEU has not always strictly or rigidly adhered to its own principles in this respect and it is thus probable that when member state courts are considering restrictions or limitations on the right to work, they are not necessarily following those principles either.

Conclusion

This short chapter commenced the response to the first sub-question this book investigates, namely, what are the legal doctrinal foundations for migrants' entitlement to qualification recognition and non-discrimination in the EU? Specifically, it began the consideration of the first of two core rights necessary to secure the well-being of migrants accessing work in the EU, namely, the right to work. This chapter has established a number of important and relevant conclusions concerning the right to work, particularly as it relates to third-country nationals.

First, as can be seen from the high-level description and analysis of certain relevant provisions of international and European law, the overarching significance of the right to work lies in its facilitating access to and participation in the labour market, which is possibly the primary way in which people can both contribute to society and receive the necessary means of subsistence and development. It is recognised as a fundamental right in international human rights, labour and economic law and in European human rights and labour law, a basic or core right from which many other legal rights, entitlements and permissions derive in the context of work. Furthermore, the case law of the ECtHR suggests that any restriction on access to or exclusion from the labour market must be very carefully scrutinised lest they infringe a person's human rights.

104 Case C-177/90 *Kühn* [1992] ECR I-35.
105 Case C-36/02 *Omega Spielhalen* [2004] ECR I-9609 [36].

Second and relatedly, the right to work in EU law can and should be understood as a vital ingredient in the ongoing construction and deepening of the Single Market. From workers to businesses, the right to work provides part of the fundamental normative basis for structuring a social market economy in the EU. It is a multidimensional right, which both constitutes the labour market and enables its beneficiaries to seek to correct it in numerous ways and contexts. It accordingly provides people with opportunities for deregulation and reregulation; that is, to challenge over-regulation and under-regulation of productive activity which contributes to people's well-being. This means that the right to work can be relied upon to challenge restrictions on access to the workforce, on the basis that such restrictions or exclusions constitute a disproportionate infringement of the right to work or violate the very substance of that right. However, evidence of detriment suffered and the negation of other options reasonably open to the beneficiary of the right to work will need to be considered in determining whether that right has been violated by such restrictions. This could, in principle, be relevant to migrants at work in Europe who are seeking access to certain professions, are finding it difficult to have their qualifications recognised or are indeed being discriminated against in some other respect.

Third and finally, the right to work enables migrants to participate in the workforce. Although the art 15(1) CFREU declares that 'everyone' in the EU has the right to work, the conventional reading of EU law is that migrants are only entitled to work when and to the extent that they are entitled to equal treatment with member state nationals in respect of the right to access the labour market. In other words, migrants must at least have what we might describe as a 'bare' right to work if they are to be permitted to access and participate in the labour market, however narrow or broad in scope that right or permission might be, whatever other rights they may have and however or on whatever conditions they may have them. Such right or permission usually has a clear, specific and narrow basis in EU and member state law. The precise circumstances in and extent to which third-country nationals are so entitled to equal treatment with EU nationals in respect of the right to work and other derivative rights will, therefore, be vital. The nature and legitimacy of such circumstances are the subject of the next chapter, where consideration is given to the possibility of expanding the circumstances in which migrants are entitled to equal treatment with member state nationals, so that they may effectively rely on the right to work and its derivative rights in a wider range of circumstances.

CHAPTER 2

The Right to Equal Treatment and Non-discrimination

Introduction

The previous chapter concluded by noting the important role which a guarantee of equal treatment or non-discrimination plays in enabling migrants to rely on the right to work. This chapter, therefore, is concerned with the extent to which such migrants benefit from a right to equal treatment or non-discrimination with member state nationals. For the right to work of third-country nationals is contingent on their status in EU law and permission to work in a member state and the primary way the right to work is guaranteed for third-country nationals is through guaranteeing them equal treatment, to varying degrees, with member state nationals under EU migration and asylum law in respect of their access to and participation in the labour market. Strictly speaking, it will not always be the case that the right to work forms part of an express equal treatment guarantee as such; but where it does not, it will nonetheless be an implicit precondition which migrants must satisfy before accessing the labour market of the member state in question. Migrants will therefore need to rely on comparative reasoning to challenge their difference in treatment from member state nationals.

Migrants are entitled to differing degrees of equal treatment with member state nationals in respect of certain rights and entitlements, such as the right to work, depending both on the nature and purpose of their migrating and residence – labour,[1]

1 Parliament and Council Directive 2011/98/EU on a single application procedure for a single permit for third-country nationals to reside and work in the territory of a Member State and on a common set of rights for third-country workers legally residing in a Member State [2011] OJ L343/1 (Single Permit Directive), art 12; Parliament and Council Directive (EU) 2021/1883 on the conditions of entry and residence of third-country nationals for the purposes of highly qualified employment [2021] OJ L382/1 (Blue Card Directive), art 15; Parliament and Council Directive 2014/36/EU on the conditions of entry and stay of third-country nationals for the purpose of employment as seasonal workers [2014] OJ L94/375 (Seasonal Workers' Directive), art 23; Parliament and Council Directive 2014/66/EU on the conditions of entry and residence of third-country nationals in the framework of an intra-corporate transfer [2014] OJ L157/1 (ICT Directive), art 15; posted workers under art 56 TFEU (see Case

 | DOI:10.1163/9789004724068_005

voluntary,[2] or forced[3] – and the length of time spent in the EU.[4] The same sort of reasoning also applies, mutatis mutandis, to EU nationals – such as workers and their family members – exercising free movement rights in the EU.[5] Unsurprisingly, these guarantees are often heavily circumscribed in their scope. In particular, the scope of such equal treatment guarantee constructs the extent to which migrants can participate in the host member state. Thus, for example, it can be said that more rights facilitating migrants' integration or participation in a member state's economy and society are given to those who are considered to be more valuable to the EU, whereas less rights are afforded to migrants who are considered less valuable.[6]

The guarantees of equal treatment found in EU migration law (i.e., EU migration and asylum law and EU free movement law) concern persons who

C-43/93 *Van der Elst* [1994] ECR I-3803; Case C-299/02 *Commission v Netherlands* [2004] ECR I-9761); persons entering the EU on the basis of association and trade agreements; and Parliament and Council Directive (EU) 2016/801 on the conditions of entry and residence of third-country nationals for the purposes of research, studies, training, voluntary service, pupil exchange schemes or educational projects and au pairing (recast) [2016] OJ L132/21 (Researchers', Students', Volunteers' and Au Pairs' Directive), art 22.

2 Council Directive 2003/86/EC on the right to family reunification [2003] OJ L251/12 (Family Reunification Directive), art 14. However, Council Directive 2004/38/EC on the right of citizens of the Union and their family members to move and reside freely within the territory of the Member States [2004] OJ L158/77 (Free Movement Directive), art 24 is an essential companion to the Family Reunification Directive. In addition, some association agreements, such as the EEA Agreement, may provide for family reunification schemes. See also Council Directive 2003/109/EC concerning the status of third-country nationals who are long-term residents [2004] OJ L16/44 (Long Term Residents Directive), art 11.

3 Council Directive 2001/55/EC on minimum standards for giving temporary protection in the event of a mass influx of displaced persons and on measures promoting a balance of efforts between Member States in receiving such persons and bearing the consequences thereof [2001] OJ L212/12 (Temporary Protection Directive); Parliament and Council Directive 2013/33/EU laying down standards for the reception of applicants for international protection (recast) [2013] OJ L180/96 (Reception Directive); and Parliament and Council Directive 2011/95/EU on standards for the qualification of third-country nationals or stateless persons as beneficiaries of international protection, for a uniform status for refugees or for persons eligible for subsidiary protection, and for the content of the protection granted (recast) [2011] OJ L337/9 (Uniform Status Directive).

4 See in particular, the Long-Term Residents' Directive.

5 See, eg, the Free Movement Directive; Parliament and Council Regulation 492/2011/EU on freedom of movement for workers within the Union [2011] OJ L 141/1 (Free Movement Regulation), art 7; Parliament and Council Regulation 883/2004/EC on the coordination of social security systems [2004] OJ L 166/1 (Social Security Systems Regulation), art 4; and Anne Pieter van der Mei, 'The Outer Limits of the Prohibition of Discrimination on Grounds of Nationality: A Look through the Lens of the European Union' (2011) 18 MJ 62.

6 Cf the Blue Card Directive and the Seasonal Workers' Directive.

are moving or migrating across borders. The scope of these equal treatment guarantees – which may be broader than the explicit guarantee of equal treatment in the relevant legal measure – condition or permit migrants' integration, particularly their participation in the labour market. They do so by treating them equally, to differing degrees and in different respects, with member state nationals, be they home state nationals (in the case of third-country nationals moving to the EU) or host state nationals (in the case of member state nationals or third-country nationals moving within the EU). In other words, these various guarantees of equality and non-discrimination prohibit discrimination on the ground of nationality in respect of some fundamental freedom. It should therefore come as no surprise that the CJEU has repeatedly confirmed that these guarantees of equal treatment contribute to the integration of migrants in their host state.[7]

By contrast with these guarantees of equal treatment and non-discrimination found in EU migration law, EU equality and anti-discrimination law itself does not prohibit discrimination on the ground of nationality. Rather, it prohibits discrimination on the grounds of sex, race or ethnicity, sexual orientation, religion or belief, age and disability.[8] It is only once a person enters a member state that EU equality and anti-discrimination law is triggered and works to reduce the discrimination people experience in, inter alia, access to employment. For third-country nationals, this means that once labour market access has been granted,[9] EU equality and anti-discrimination law reduces obstacles to their actual participation in the labour market. But it does not prohibit discrimination on the ground of their nationality.

These prohibitions on discrimination on different grounds in different contexts prompt a number of questions. A first question concerns the conceptual link between discrimination and migration. When should migrants be entitled to equal treatment with member state nationals as a matter of principle?

7 See the discussion in Herwig Verschueren, 'Equal Treatment as an Instrument of Integration: The CJEU's Case Law on Social Rights for Third-Country Nationals under the EU Migration Directives' (2023) 25(3) ELLJ 243.

8 See, eg, Council Directive 2000/43/EC implementing the principle of equal treatment between persons irrespective of racial or ethnic origin [2000] OJ L 180/22 (Racial Equality Directive); Council Directive 2000/78/EC establishing a general framework for equal treatment in employment and occupation [2000] OJ L303/16 (Framework Equality Directive); and Parliament and Council Directive 2006/54/EC on the implementation of the principle of equal opportunities and equal treatment of men and women in matters of employment and occupation (recast) [2006] OJ L204/23 (Recast Sex Directive).

9 It will only be necessary to grant labour market access to those who do not already have it; in general, non-nationals.

Section 1 of this chapter considers whether and to what extent third-country nationals should be entitled to equal treatment with member state nationals – the threshold condition for being entitled to the right to work and all other derivative rights at work in the EU. The answer is that, given certain empirical facts about the discrimination which third-country nationals habitually face, third-country nationals should generally benefit from equality and anti-discrimination norms in the EU. More specifically, they should generally benefit from a prohibition of discrimination on the ground of nationality.

A second question is whether, as a matter of legal doctrine, third-country nationals can ever benefit from EU equality and anti-discrimination law. The response to this question is provided in Sections 2 and 3. Section 2 concludes that much of international and European law requires that nationality discrimination be abolished in general. Section 3 notes that third-country nationals can benefit from EU equality and anti-discrimination law when they are entitled to be treated equally with member state nationals on the ground of nationality. But, as has already been noted, EU equality and anti-discrimination law does not prohibit discrimination on the ground of nationality. Where EU law does specifically do so, such as in EU migration law, third-country nationals can then benefit from EU equality and anti-discrimination law. Section 3 explores the doctrinal reasons for the status quo and finds them somewhat unconvincing, suggesting that EU law should generally prohibit discrimination on the ground of nationality in accordance with binding international and European law.

A third question, which follows from the second, is whether and to what extent the prohibitions of discrimination found in EU migration law, on the one hand, and EU equality and anti-discrimination law are truly different. While the second question has been addressed on numerous occasions by scholars, this third question is often overlooked. The response to this issue is provided by Section 4. Specifically, this section considers the extent to which the reasons which explain and justify the differences between these prohibitions are compelling. The answer is that there are reasons – which I shall categorise and describe roughly as political, conceptual and sociological – to believe that these prohibitions are not that different. As such, we have reason to unify them, in whole or in part. Reflecting on the theme of governance running throughout this book, Section 4 suggests that we should assimilate these conceptions in part to avoid the further fragmentation or proliferation of different conceptions of equal treatment in the EU. In other words, it calls for the further entrenchment or constitutionalisation of a general norm of equal treatment and non-discrimination in the EU. A short conclusion follows.

1 Discrimination, Migration and Nationality

1.1 *Overview*

This section attempts to provide a concise but nonetheless accurate description and analysis of certain dimensions of the conceptual or theoretical link between freedom, discrimination and migration. It does so by defining aspects of these concepts and certain of their implications. Like many such abstract theoretical inquiries, this one starts somewhere in the middle. It will abound with many undefended and unarticulated assumptions about the nature of the concepts of freedom, discrimination and migration. These assumptions will be used to defend a particular view of the nature of discrimination, the relationship between human freedom and discrimination, the role discrimination does and ought to play in the regulation of the labour market and immigration as well as the role that discrimination should not play in regulating relations of production and borders. Many of the claims made here are not necessarily a priori or conceptual truths. Rather, they draw on and attempt to describe, if true, certain general features of human experience of freedom, discrimination and migration. While I do not attempt to justify them, I aim to validate them by effectively using and relying upon them later in this chapter and in subsequent chapters. The proof will be in their usefulness.

1.2 *Discrimination, Skills and Migration*

1.2.1 Discrimination, Freedom and Domination

Discrimination as an activity can be a good or a bad thing. It is good to be a discerning individual, making good friends and turning a cold shoulder to those one cannot rely on. Discrimination of this kind is a virtuous character trait. But this sort of discrimination is not what attracts most attention. Rather, the kind of discrimination we are most concerned with occurs when people use certain actual or imputed characteristics to treat people differently and, in particular, detrimentally so. For example, some people do not employ women because they think women are inferior or because women are statistically more likely to take time of work to have a family. The former reason is invalid while the latter ought to be excluded as a reason justifying differential treatment because of the intrinsic wrongfulness and consequential effects, in our culture, of such treatment on people's ability to flourish.[10] This last sentence should suggest to the reader that there is an important link between discrimination and

10 This paragraph effectively summarises the understanding of discrimination articulated by John Gardner, 'Discrimination: The Good, the Bad and the Wrongful' (2018) 118(1) Proceedings of the Aristotelian Society 55.

human freedom. My freedom to choose who to employ is significantly limited by equality and anti-discrimination norms; and contrastively my freedom to seek and change employment is significantly hindered by discrimination. Discrimination of the kind we are most often concerned with – on the grounds of sex, religion, race or sexual orientation and so forth – is a paradigm form of domination in our culture. If I am seeking work and at each turn being rejected because of my sexual orientation, whether directly or indirectly, then I am being subjected to the direct or indirect will of another in a way which undermines my ability to look others in the eye with a sense of self-respect, restricts my ability to access and participate in some of the essential elements of society and on the whole frustrates my ability to exercise my will.[11]

1.2.2 Discrimination, Skills and Migration

That is not to say that no discrimination between people and peoples at all is permitted. Rather, whether a certain kind of discrimination is permitted or not will largely depend on the particular political community in question. What is clear from EU migration law, for example, is that discrimination on the ground of skills is not only considered unproblematic but is actually necessary. That is, it is legitimate to distinguish between people and peoples on the basis of their skills. Such discrimination is necessary for the proper functioning of the Single Market. Being able to discriminate on the ground of skills enables improved matching of supply and demand in the market because those demanding skilled workers (ie, member states, employers, consumers, etc) can filter the supply of workers, assessing and distinguishing workers for certain qualities such as certain levels of experience, qualifications and so forth. Those workers who are in high demand are able to attract higher prices – often in the form of increased rights – while workers in low demand generally attract a lower price – generally, fewer rights.[12] Discriminating on the ground of people's skills

11 Tarunabh Khaitan, *A Theory of Discrimination Law* (OUP 2015) ch 5 provides a similar set of reasons explaining the link between freedom and discrimination. See similarly Sophia Moreau, 'What is Discrimination?' (2010) 38 Phil and Pub Aff 143; Sophia Moreau, 'In Defence of a Liberty-based Account of Discrimination' in Deborah Hellman and Sophia Moreau (eds), *Philosophical Foundations of Discrimination Law* (OUP 2013); Kasper Lippert-Rasmussen, *Born Free and Equal? A Philosophical Inquiry into the Nature of Discrimination* (OUP 2014) ch 6; and Sophia Moreau, 'Discrimination and Freedom' in Kasper Lippert-Rasmussen (ed), *The Routledge Handbook of the Ethics of Discrimination* (Routledge 2018).

12 Harald Bauder, *Labour Movement: How Migration Regulates Labour Markets* (OUP 2006); Martin Ruhs and Philip Martin, 'Numbers vs Rights: Trade-Offs and Guest Worker Programs' (2008) 42 IMR 249; Martin Ruhs, 'Migrant Rights, Immigration Policy and Human Development' (2010) 11 Journal of Human Development and Capabilities 259; and

is nothing more than a basic and fundamental function of a modern and efficient labour market.

However, that is not to say that there is necessarily a morally-neutral link between skills-based discrimination and migration, but it is a position with which at least some scholars of the ethics of migration agree. For example, David Miller notes that

> the admission of economic migrants should be understood in terms of mutual advantage – both parties must expect to gain from the decision to admit. The receiving state has certain policy goals – for example, it is aiming for economic growth or to provide its citizens with generous welfare services – and it is entitled to use immigration policy as one of the means to achieve such goals. This explains why selecting immigrants according to the particular skills that they can deploy is a justifiable criterion. Moreover, it is also a criterion that prospective immigrants ought to accept, given the relationship that they wish to establish with the state they are trying to enter, which depends upon mutual advantage.[13]

Naturally, not all theorists are in agreement with Miller's views. For example, Ayelet Shachar, while welcoming the 'paradigm shift' in immigration policies away from nationality and race towards skill-selective immigration policies, identifies at least three problems with skills-selective immigration policies: potential unfairness to other migrants, unfairness to immigrants' country of origin and unfairness to other people in immigrants' country of origin (the so-called 'brain drain').[14] Similarly, Desireé Lim argues that 'we have strong reasons to rethink skill-selective immigration policies that advantage highly skilled migrants and disadvantage low-skilled migrants ... social equality requires states to regulate their exclusionary practices so that they do not demean or subordinate low-skilled migrants'.[15] Lim's interesting and challenging argument is grounded in the fundamental principle of equal respect for all persons, from which she derives certain novel obligations of justice that states

---

Martin Ruhs, *The Price of Rights: Regulating International Labour Migration* (Princeton University Press 2013).

13 David Miller, *Strangers in Our Midst: The Political Philosophy of Immigration* (HUP 2016) 105–106.

14 Aylet Shachar, 'The Brave New World of Stratified Mobility' in Sarah Fine and Lea Ypi (eds), *Migration in Political Theory: The Ethics of Movement and Membership* (OUP 2016).

15 Désireé Lim, *Immigration and Social Equality: The Ethics of Skill-Selective Immigration Policy* (OUP 2023) 22.

owe immigrants. For example, she argues that the principle of equal respect for persons implies that skill-selective immigration policies have 'the expressive effect of reproducing and legitimising demeaning social beliefs about low-skilled non-citizens',[16] while also indirectly discriminating against migrants on other grounds of discrimination, such as sex or race. In addition, Lim argues that skill-selective immigration policies risk perpetuating historical patterns of racial exploitation.

Lim's views are valuable and certainly merit noting when considering any potential wholescale reform of EU migration law. However, in the present context, they are subject to at least two important caveats. First, Lim's analysis only applies to the regulation of certain types of regular migration. Naturally, different considerations apply to the regulation of irregular or forced migration, which largely occurs for different reasons. Second, this book does not challenge the legitimate authority of nation states to control their borders. While it does apply a critical lens to the EU's regulation of migration with a view to making its regulatory system more coherent, rational and fair, in doing so, it does not challenge the skills' selective nature of much of EU migration law per se but rather points to incoherencies, irrationalities and unfairness in same.

1.3 *Discrimination, Migration and Nationality*

Discrimination on the grounds of nationality is fundamental to the process of EU integration. Reducing discrimination on the ground of nationality enables EU integration because it facilitates greater and more open competition on relevant grounds, such as skills, between peoples through a reduction of barriers to information, movement and so forth. But widespread discrimination on the ground of residence and, therefore, indirect nationality discrimination, remains permissible across the EU. As noted in the introduction to this chapter, while nationality is a prohibited ground of discrimination *to some extent* as a matter of EU migration law, EU anti-discrimination and equality law does not prohibit discrimination on the ground of nationality. Abolishing discrimination on the ground of nationality altogether would mean that EU nationals could migrate freely across the EU as they can in their own country. Such a development may even require widespread harmonisation of social security, tax and other entitlements, essentially entailing a single EU state or, at the very least, a much greater degree of free movement on behalf of EU nationals. There is, naturally, a degree of speculation involved in considering what exactly abolishing nationality discrimination would entail in practice.

16 ibid 25.

Nonetheless, abolishing nationality discrimination in general would be a very significant step towards further and deeper EU integration.[17]

So much for the role of nationality discrimination in the process of EU integration generally. But what of third-country nationals' ability to participate in the project of EU integration? While migrants are considered to be essential to the future of the EU, we know that third-country nationals in the EU habitually experience discrimination in recruitment processes. Furthermore, third-country nationals are regularly at risk of domination insofar as they are subject to the arbitrary will of the state through member states' sovereign power to regulate immigration, depending on the intensity and extent of the domination such immigration controls exercise over migrants. As Iseult Honohan puts it in a lengthy but important passage,

> The intensity of domination (…) will depend on the degree of arbitrariness; the ease of exclusion; and the severity of the measures excluding foreigners. (…) The arbitrariness of migration controls appears in the way in which the exact requirements for migration are liable to change according to the will of the admitting state (…) The intensity is increased by the arbitrariness that arises from the greater prevalence of discretionary powers in the area of migration than in most areas of domestic policy: here agencies and officials are given wide powers, often laid down without legislative provision or oversight; their decisions are often not subject to review, judicial or otherwise; the framework within which they make decisions is often neither clearly laid out nor well known to citizens as well as non-citizens. As to the ease of exclusion, while states have difficulty in excluding migrants entirely, they can readily restrict legal access, and impose illegal status on those who breach entry controls; and they can shift the burden of controlling borders to others (other states, carriers, etc.). Finally, the severity of the procedures, which (even when not discretionary in practice) range from exclusion by walls and barbed-wire fences, through deportation to detention or incarceration of illegal migrants.
>
> …
>
> The extent of domination will depend, first, on the range of areas of their lives affected, and the degree to which their options are limited for those who are excluded. On this basis, evidence suggests that the extent

17 Joseph Carens, *The Ethics of Immigration* (OUP 2013) ch 11. On the link between equal treatment and the process of EU integration, see Elise Muir, *EU Equality Law: The First Fundamental Rights Policy of the EU* (OUP 2018) 3–5.

> of domination by migration controls is significant. The whole lives of potential migrants who lack the basics of a reasonable level of subsistence may be determined by the difficulty of migration, which leaves them unable to access the preconditions for a flourishing life – even if they are not continuously subject to interference in each aspect of their lives.[18]

The question which must be asked is, how can we avoid or minimise such forms of domination? One way to address this problem is to make nationality a protected ground of discrimination. Doing this will reduce the arbitrary power to which third-country nationals are regularly subjected[19] and better ensure their freedom by targeting obstacles, such as discrimination in recruitment processes, which they regularly face. By being required to provide good reasons for discrimination on the ground of nationality, member states and market actors would reduce the discrimination third-country nationals habitually experience and the consequent risk of domination third-country nationals face. It would expose the EU's institutions, member states and market actors' intentions to contestation and deliberation, allowing us to more clearly consider and contest the reasons in favour of or against the status quo. In addition, it would also constitute a significant step in the project of EU integration.

To be clear, however, (i) nothing so far implies that abolishing discrimination on the ground of nationality would be some sort of panacea (ii) nor is it strictly a logical necessity to so abolish nationality discrimination in seeking to address the discrimination which third-country nationals habitually face. First, as third-country nationals regularly experience discrimination, I am implicitly assuming that EU equality and anti-discrimination law as it stands must be deficient in some way; and one way of remedying such deficiency is through making nationality a prohibited ground of discrimination. It is, of course, plausible that the real problem is not that EU equality and anti-discrimination law as it is currently constituted is inadequate to address the discrimination which third-country nationals face but rather that its enforcement in practice has not addressed the problems third-country nationals experience. It is possible, for example, that third-country nationals are not fully aware of their rights under EU anti-discrimination and equality law. I do not explore this possibility here. A full analysis of the remedies necessary to address the discrimination

18 Iseult Honohan, 'Domination and migration: an alternative approach to the legitimacy of migration controls' in Iseult Honohan and Marit Hovdal-Moan (eds), *Domination, Migration and Non-Citizens* (Routledge 2015) 40.

19 Sarah Fine, 'Non-domination and the ethics of migration' in *Domination, Migration and Non-Citizens* (n 18) 19–24.

third-country nationals face would need to take into account such theoretical and practical obstacles. Second, it could be objected that discrimination on other grounds, such as third-country nationals' migration status, socio-economic standing[20] or cultural background could also result in, at least, the risk of domination. Why not abolish discrimination on one of these grounds instead? On the one hand, doing so would make it necessary for states and others to proffer good reasons every time they establish norms which distinguish between people on one of those grounds. This may be beneficial insofar as it further reduces the domination to which third-country nationals are habitually subject. On the other hand, nationality is the relevant and fundamental ground according to which third-country nationals are to be distinguished from member state nationals, as the language of the relevant provisions of the TFEU suggests.[21] Moreover, abolishing nationality discrimination in general should, in many cases, entail the functional reduction of discrimination on some of the other aforementioned grounds.

However, to make nationality a protected ground of discrimination requires further clarification of the prevalent conceptions of equal treatment in EU migration law, on the one hand, and EU equality and anti-discrimination law, on the other hand, referred to in the introduction to this chapter. Accordingly, it is to an analysis of these concepts in international, European and EU law which I now turn.

2 The Right to Equal Treatment and Non-discrimination in International and European Law

2.1 *International Law*

2.1.1 International Human Rights Law

Article 2 UDHR guarantees the rights contained therein without discrimination on the basis of, inter alia, national or social origin. Thus, the right to work guaranteed in art 23(1) UDHR benefits all persons regardless of national or social origin. The right to equality and non-discrimination on the ground of nationality is also guaranteed in arts 2(1) and 26 ICCPR,[22] arts 2 and 7 ICESCR,[23] art 2

20 Shreya Atrey, 'The Intersectional Case of Poverty in Discrimination Law' (2018) 18 HRLR 411.

21 Part Three, Title V, Chapter 2 TFEU refers to third-country nationals.

22 Sarah Joseph and Melissa Castan, *The International Covenant on Civil and Political Rights: Cases, Materials and Commentary* (3rd edn, OUP 2013) ch 23.

23 Ben Saul, David Kinley and Jacqueline Mowbray, *The International Covenant on Economic, Social and Cultural Rights: Commentary, Cases and Materials* (OUP 2014) ch 4.

CRC[24] and arts 1 and 7 ICRMW.[25] All member states of the European Union are parties to these respective human rights treaties (except the ICRMW, to which only a minority of member states are party) and, according to art 3 TEU, the EU is committed to the respect, protection and promotion of human and fundamental rights. It is thus essential that the EU, in its laws and policies, respect, protect and promote the right to non-discrimination to ensure its compliance with international human rights law. Furthermore, it is important to note here that art 21 TEU obliges the EU to respect the principles of international law. Accordingly, EU law should follow the approach under international law of generally affording third-country nationals' equal treatment and providing reasons for discriminating against them. Of the guarantees stated here, only the ICCPR, ICESCR and ICRMW will be considered in further detail.

In respect of the ICCPR, the Human Rights Committee in its General Comment No 18 has observed that prohibited discrimination involves

> any distinction, exclusion, restriction or preference which is based on any ground such as (…) national or social origin (…) and which has the purpose or effect of nullifying or impairing the recognition, enjoyment or exercise by all persons, on an equal footing, of all rights and freedoms.[26]

According to the Human Rights Committee, non-discrimination 'constitute[s] a basic and general principle relating to the protection of human rights'.[27] The Committee also acknowledges that not all discrimination is prohibited discrimination; some distinctions and differentiations are legitimate. This is consistent with the view that discrimination on the grounds of, inter alia, skills is permissible. The Human Rights Committee has considered the possibility of nationality discrimination in a number of cases.[28] In *Gueye v France*, retired Senegalese members of the French army complained of discrimination on the ground of race in relation to their pension entitlements. While not finding discrimination on the ground of race, the Human Rights Committee did conclude that there had been discrimination on the ground of nationality. According to

24 Samantha Besson and Eleonor Kleber, 'Article 2' in John Tobin (ed), *The UN Convention on the Rights of the Child: A Commentary* (OUP 2019).

25 Joo-Cheong Tham, 'Equality and Community for Migrant Workers' in Alan Bogg, James Rowbottom and Alison Young (eds), *The Constitution of Social Democracy: Essays in Honour of Keith Ewing* (Hart 2020).

26 CCPR, 'General Comment No 18: Non-discrimination' (10 November 1989) para 7.

27 ibid para 1.

28 *Gueye v France* (196/85); *Adam v Czech Republic* (589/94); and *Karakurt v Austria* (965/00). Cf *Van Oord v The Netherlands* (658/1995).

the Human Rights Committee, 'mere administrative inconvenience or the possibility of some abuse of pension rights cannot be invoked to justify unequal treatment'.[29] *Karakurt v Austria* concerned the right of a Turkish national, in possession of an open-ended residence permit to live in Austria, to be elected to a work-council. The applicant's election as a member of the work-council was challenged on the ground that the relevant provision of Austrian labour law limited the entitlement of non-nationals to stand for election to such work-councils. In the domestic courts, this challenge was successful. However, the Human Rights Committee found that, although an international agreement which grants preferential treatment to certain nationals of a state party to that agreement might constitute an objective and reasonable ground for differentiation,[30] no general rule of discrimination could be drawn therefrom. Accordingly, the Human Rights Committee found that the applicant had been subjected to prohibited discrimination on the ground of nationality. This case is particularly interesting because it acknowledges that an international agreement between states may justify discrimination on the ground of nationality.

In Chapter 1, I noted that, according to art 6 ICESCR, 'everyone' is entitled to the right to work. Accordingly, discrimination on the ground of, inter alia, nationality is prohibited. Unlike art 26 ICCPR, however, art 2 ICESCR is not a free-standing guarantee of equality; rather, it is a parasitic guarantee of equality, requiring violation of some other right in the ICESCR to be triggered. This may be because equality has been considered 'the dominant single theme of the Covenant'.[31] But, like the ICCPR, the guarantee of equality in art 2 ICESCR is non-exhaustive; it extends to grounds other than those listed therein. According to art 2(2) ICESCR, states party to the ICESCR undertake to guarantee the rights stated therein 'without discrimination of any kind as to (…) national or social origin, property, birth or other status'. It is important to point out that while this guarantee seems very broad, it does not apply to all possible distinctions.[32]

In interpreting the ICESCR, the CESCR adopts the same approach as the HRC and the ECtHR. Accordingly, decisions of these other bodies are likely to

29 *Gueye v France* (196/85) para 9.5.

30 *Van Oord v The Netherlands* (658/1995).

31 Matthew Craven, *The International Covenant on Economic, Social and Cultural Rights: A Perspective on its Development* (OUP 1998) 153–154, quoting Bertrand Ramcharan, 'Equality and Non-discrimination' in Louise Henkin (ed), *The International Bill of Rights: The Covenant on Civil and Political Rights* (Columbia University Press 1981) 246.

32 *The International Covenant on Economic, Social and Cultural Rights: Commentary, Cases and Materials* (n 23) 177.

inform the approach of the CESCR.[33] They should therefore be read together. In respect of the ground of discrimination – 'national or social origin' – the CESCR has interpreted this as including 'a person's State, nation or place of origin'.[34] In addition, and contrary to the expressed intentions of many states parties,

> [t]he ground of nationality should not bar access to Covenant rights (…) The Covenant rights apply to everyone including non-nationals, such as refugees, asylum-seekers, stateless persons, migrant workers, and victims of international trafficking, regardless of legal status and documentation.[35]

At least one group of leading commentators, in an attempt to reconcile the views of the CESCR with those of states party to the ICESCR, have argued that 'what is prohibited is *arbitrary* distinctions in treatment based on nationality, that is, distinctions for which there is no 'objective and reasonable justification'.'[36] In the light of the discussion in Chapter 1 and in Section 1 of this chapter, reducing arbitrary power and the risk of domination inherent therein is a valuable goal of the law in this area. However, as noted in Chapter 1, art 7 ICRMW prohibits discrimination on the ground of nationality but is without prejudice to distinctions drawn on the basis of immigration status. Accordingly, discrimination on the ground of immigration status is permitted under art 7 ICRMW.[37]

2.1.2 International Labour Law[38]

In relation to international labour law, the relevant measures are the Conventions on Freedom of Association and Protection of the Right to Organise 1948 (No 87), Migration for Employment (Revised) 1949 (No 97),

33 ibid 179.

34 CESCR, 'General Comment No 20: Non-discrimination in economic, social and cultural rights' (2 July 2009) para 24.

35 ibid para 30.

36 *The International Covenant on Economic, Social and Cultural Rights: Commentary, Cases and Materials* (n 23) 198.

37 Bernard Ryan, 'In Defence of the Migrant Workers Convention: Standard Setting for Contemporary Migration' in Satvinder Juss (ed), *The Ashgate Research Companion to Migration Theory and Policy* (Ashgate 2013) 494–495.

38 See Shauna Olney and Ryszard Cholewinski, 'Migrant Workers and the Right to Non-discrimination and Equality' in Cathryn Costello and Mark Freedland (ed), *Migrants at Work: Immigration and Vulnerability in Labour Law* (OUP 2014) and Joo-Cheong Tham, 'Equality and Community for Migrant Workers' (n 25).

Discrimination (Employment and Occupation) 1958 (No 111), Equality of Treatment (Social Security) 1962 (No 118) and Migrant Workers (Supplemental Provisions) 1975 (No 143).[39] While all EU member states have ratified Conventions No 87 and 111, only a minority of member states have ratified the remaining three conventions. Indeed, Convention No 143 has only been ratified by five EU member states. These latter conventions are therefore not binding on the member states. Nonetheless, the ILO states that all conventions apply to migrant workers unless otherwise stated. In general, all conventions noted require non-discrimination in respect of migrant workers, although Convention No 97 states that its terms do not apply to irregular migrants.

Convention No 111 on Discrimination, one of the core conventions of the ILO, defines, in art 1(a), discrimination as 'any distinction, exclusion or preference made on the basis of race, colour, sex, religion, political opinion, national extraction or social origin, which has the effect of nullifying or impairing equality of opportunity or treatment in employment or occupation'. By contrast, and consistently with the approach adopted in this book, discrimination on the grounds of job requirements – ie, skills – is expressly permitted. As art 1(2) of the Convention states, 'any distinction, exclusion or preference' in respect of a particular job 'based on the inherent requirements thereof' shall not be considered prohibited discrimination. In other words, where a job requires certain skills, employers are entitled to discriminate between people on the basis of their skills. Accordingly, given that, under international labour law, discrimination on the grounds of nationality – 'national extraction or social origin' – is generally prohibited, it is submitted that the EU should amend its position by prohibiting nationality discrimination in general to ensure compliance with international labour law. While, as noted in the introductory chapter, the EU is not a subject of international law and is not, therefore, strictly bound by international labour law, the EU does participate in the work of the ILO and the Court of Justice has cited certain provisions of international labour law in its judgments.[40]

2.1.3 International Economic Law

In the previous chapter, I highlighted the relevance of granting market access in international economic law. Equality and non-discrimination come in two forms in international economic law. The first is the so-called

39 See generally ILO, *Migrant Workers* (Geneva 1980), ILO, *Migrant Workers* (Geneva 1999) and ILO, *Promoting fair migration* (Geneva 2016).

40 Tzehainesh Teklè, 'Labour Rights and the Case Law of the European Court of Justice: What Role for International Labour Standards?' (2018) 9 ELLJ 236.

'most-favoured-nation' obligation. Article II(1) GATS provides that each member state of the WTO shall 'accord immediately and unconditionally to services and service suppliers' of any other member state 'treatment no less favourable than that it accords to like services and service suppliers of any other country'. This is most pertinent to the possibility of third-country nationals accessing and participating in the Single Market on equal terms with one another. However, art II(2) GATS goes on to provide that any member state may maintain a discriminatory measure provided that it is listed in the Annex on art II exemptions. Under international economic law, therefore, states are given a wide-ranging power of exemption from the obligation to treat other states equally. But the thrust of the position under international economic law is similar to that which is advocated for in this chapter; namely, that discrimination on the ground of nationality should be generally prohibited subject to specific exceptions. A general principle can be maintained subject to many specific and reasoned exceptions. And exceptions based on valid, valuable reasons are perfectly justifiable.

By contrast, the second obligation of equality and non-discrimination in international economic law is, as we shall see shortly, very like EU law at present. Like the market access obligation considered in the previous chapter, art XVII GATS provides for 'national treatment' in specific as opposed to general circumstances, where listed in the schedules of WTO member states. According to art XVII(1) GATS, each member state of the WTO shall give services and service suppliers of other member states 'treatment no less favourable than it accords its own services and service suppliers'. In other words, the default position in international economic law generally permits discrimination on the ground of nationality. Only in specific circumstances will third-countries be afforded equal treatment with home state nationals.

2.2 *European Law*

2.2.1 European Convention on Human Rights

Although nationality discrimination is not expressly prohibited by art 14 ECHR,[41] it does fall within the scope of that article and requires

41 Generally, see Rory O'Connell, 'Cinderella comes to the ball: Article 14 and the right to non-discrimination in the ECHR' (2009) 29 LS 211; Oddny Mjöll Arnardóttir, 'The Differences that Make a Difference: Recent Developments on the Discrimination Grounds and the Margin of Appreciation under Article 14 of the European Convention on Human Rights' (2014) 14 HRL Rev 647; and Sandra Fredman, 'Emerging from the Shadows: Substantive Equality and Article 14 of the European Convention on Human Rights' (2016) 16 HRL Rev 273; and specifically Sonia Morano-Foadi and Stelios Andreadakis, 'The Convergence of

justification.[42] As the ECtHR noted in *Gaygusuz v Austria*, 'very weighty reasons would have to be put forward before the Court could regard a difference of treatment based exclusively on the ground of nationality as compatible with the Convention'.[43] However, as Claire Kilpatrick has noted, the ECtHR has long acknowledged the legitimacy of differences between EU nationals and third-country nationals.[44] Moreover, the weight to be attached to differences of treatment based on nationality is very different from that to be attached to differences based on immigration status. Because immigration status as a characteristic is not immutable and involves an element of choice, distinctions made on the grounds of immigration status are less weighty, or less morally significant, than those based on nationality.[45] Of relevance in this context is the wide discretion granted to contracting parties 'when it comes to general measures of economic or social strategy'.[46] Indeed, the Court has confirmed that for any welfare or resource-redistribution system to operate effectively, the state may need to make distinctions and broad categorisations between different groups.[47]

Three cases of the ECtHR stand out in their treatment of third-country nationals. The first is *Ponomaryovi v Bulgaria*. In that case, the applicants, two brothers, were Russian nationals who had been taken to live in Bulgaria by their mother, a Russian national, in virtue of her marriage to a Bulgarian national. The applicants' mother obtained a permanent residence permit, on the basis of which the applicants resided and remained in the jurisdiction lawfully until their eighteenth birthday. At this point, the applicants' immigration status in Bulgaria became irregular. The applicants were then required to pay fees to complete their secondary school education which were only levied on foreign nationals. The applicants challenged the decision to levy fees on them

the European Legal System in the Treatment of Third-Country Nationals: The ECJ and ECtHR Jurisprudence' (2011) 22 EJIL 1071.

42 See *Gaygusuz v Austria* (1996) 23 EHRR 364; *Zeibek v Greece* App no 46368/06 (ECtHR, 9 July 2009); and *Poirrez v France* App no 40892/98 (ECtHR, 30 September 2003).

43 (1996) 23 EHRR 364 [42].

44 Claire Kilpatrick and Hanna Eklund, 'Article 21' in Steve Peers, Tamara Hervey, Jeff Kenner and Angela Ward (eds), *The EU Charter of Fundamental Rights: A Commentary* (2nd ed, Hart 2021) 624 citing *Moustaquim v Belgium* (1991) 13 EHRR 802 and *Ponomaryovi v Bulgaria* (2014) 59 EHRR 20.

45 *Bah v United Kingdom* (2012) 54 EHRR 21 [46]-[48].

46 *James v United Kingdom* (1986) 8 EHRR 123 [46]; *National and Provincial Building Society v United Kingdom* (1998) 25 EHRR 27 [80]; and *Bah v United Kingdom* (2012) 54 EHRR 21 [37].

47 *Runkee v United Kingdom* App 42949/98 (ECtHR, 10 May 2007) [39]; and *Ponomaryovi v Bulgaria* (2014) 59 EHRR 20 [54].

arguing that it violated their rights under the Convention, in particular art 2 of Protocol 1 to the Convention (the right to education) in conjunction with art 14 (the right to non-discrimination).

The ECtHR first noted that education fell within the scope of art 14. The Court then held that the applicants were being discriminated against solely on the basis of their nationality and immigration status: 'the applicants were thus clearly treated less favourably than others in a relevantly similar situation, on account of a personal characteristic'.[48] The Court finally turned to the question of justification. Although contracting parties are entitled to a wide margin of appreciation in respect of expensive and resource-intensive public services, given that the right to education forms an important part of the Convention's framework, this margin must be narrowed in respect thereof. Moreover, the Court observed, in the present case, the applicants were highly integrated in Bulgarian society, having lived in Bulgaria for more than 10 years and being fluent in Bulgarian; the applicants had taken steps to regularise their immigration status; and the applicants' conduct could in no way be described as abusive of Bulgaria's public services. In the light of these considerations, the ECtHR concluded that the discrimination against the applicants on the basis of their nationality and immigration status was unjustifiable and in contravention of art 2 of Protocol 1 in conjunction with art 14 ECHR.

Ponomaryovi is important for a number of reasons. First, the Court placed great emphasis on nationality and immigration status as constituting a 'personal characteristic' of the applicants. This contrasts strongly with EU law in a number of ways. For although nationality is a ground of prohibited discrimination as a matter of EU free movement law, the same is not the case as a matter of EU equality and anti-discrimination law and nowhere in EU law is immigration status considered as a ground of discrimination. A second point is the fact that the applicants' immigration status was irregular. The fact that (i) the applicants had been in the jurisdiction for so long and that, (ii) by the time the case reached the Court, they had obtained permanent resident status, may have given the Court reason to be sympathetic. But the result is nonetheless significant; that irregular migrants might ground a successful claim for discrimination is an outlier. Indeed, in other cases concerning irregular migration, the Court has not been so sympathetic.[49]

48 (2014) 59 EHRR 20 [50].

49 *Osungu and Lokongo v France* App nos 78860/11 and 51354/13 (ECtHR, 8 September 2015).

The second case of relevance is *Dhahbi v Italy*.[50] In that case, the applicant, a Tunisian national legally resident and working in Italy, claimed certain social welfare entitlements on behalf of himself and his family. His application was rejected. The applicant challenged this outcome on the basis of, inter alia, an equal treatment guarantee in the Euro-Mediterranean Association Agreement.[51] The ECtHR initially accepted that there had been differential treatment on the basis of a personal characteristic between the applicant and member state nationals. The Court then turned to the question of justification: could restricting access to such benefits for third-country nationals be justified? According to the Court, the answer was 'no'. The applicant was lawfully resident, working and contributing to the funding of public services; and the sole reason for denying the applicant the allowance was his nationality. Although not expressly acknowledged in the Court's reasoning, the fact that the applicant had subsequently (and at the time of the hearing) become a naturalised Italian citizen, may also have been relevant.

Dhahbi is particularly relevant to my discussion here insofar as the applicant relied on the existence of an equal treatment guarantee in one of the EU's many international agreements. While a full exploration of these guarantees is undertaken in Chapter 3, it merits noting summarily that similar terms are found in the Ankara Agreement,[52] EU-Andean Trade Agreement,[53] Euro Mediterranean Agreement with Algeria,[54] EC-Azerbaijan Agreement,[55] Bosnia and Herzegovina Stabilisation and Association Agreement,[56] EC-Georgia

50 App no 17120/09 (ECtHR, 8 April 2014). See also *Fawsie v Greece* App no 40080/07 (ECtHR, 28 October 2010) and *Saidoun v Greece* App no 40083/07 (ECtHR, 28 October 2010).

51 Euro-Mediterranean Agreement establishing an association between the European Communities and their Member states, of the one part, and the Republic of Tunisia, of the other part [1998] OJ L97/2, art 64.

52 Agreement establishing an Association between the European Economic Community and Turkey [1977] OJ L361/1, art 9.

53 Trade Agreement between the European Union and its member states, of the one part, and Columbia and Peru, of the other part [2012] OJ L353/3, arts 269 and 276.

54 Euro-Mediterranean Agreement establishing an Association between the European Community and its Member states, of the one part, and the People's Democratic Republic of Algeria, of the other part [2005] OJ L265/2, art 67.

55 Partnership and Cooperation Agreement between the European Communities and their Member States, of the one part, and the Republic of Azerbaijan, of the other part [1999] OJ L246/3, art 20.

56 Stabilisation and Association Agreement between the European Communities and their Member states, of the one part, and Bosnia and Herzegovina, of the other part [2015] OJ L164/2, art 47.

Association Agreement,[57] EU-Kazakhstan Partnership and Cooperation Agreement,[58] Euro-Mediterranean Agreement with Morocco,[59] EC-Moldova Association Agreement,[60] EC-Russia Partnership and Cooperation Agreement,[61] EC-Serbia Stabilisation and Association Agreement,[62] and EU-Ukraine Association Agreement.[63] In principle, therefore, provided that nationals of those countries enter the EU lawfully, they should be entitled, under EU law, to equal treatment with member state nationals in respect of their working conditions. The extent of the measures which migrants might benefit from equal treatment with EU member state nationals by virtue of an express guarantee of equal treatment in the EU's partnership, trade and association agreements is considered in Chapter 3.

The final case of relevance is *Hode and Ali v United Kingdom*,[64] which concerned elements of the UK's asylum code. The first applicant had been granted asylum in 2006 and was given leave to remain in the UK until 2011. The first applicant subsequently married the second applicant in Djibouti in 2007. The second applicant applied for a visa to enter the UK, but this application was rejected on the ground that the applicants did not qualify for family reunion. At the time, the family reunification rules in the UK's immigration code applied only to the spouses of refugees who were part of the refugee's family before they had left the country of origin. The applicants challenged these rules as infringing art 8 (the right to family life) in conjunction with art 14. The

57 Association Agreement between the European Union and the European Atomic Energy Community and their Member states, of the one part, and Georgia, of the other part [2014] OJ L261/4, art 416.

58 Partnership and Cooperation Agreement establishing a partnership between the European Communities and their Member states, of the one part, and the Republic of Kazakhstan, of the other part [2016] OJ L29/3, art 19.

59 Euro-Mediterranean Agreement establishing an association between the European Communities and their Member states, of the one part, and the Kingdom of Morocco, of the other part [2000] OJ L70/2, art 64.

60 Association Agreement between the European Union and the European Atomic Energy Community and their Member states, of the one part, and the Republic of Moldova, of the other part [2014] OJ L260/4, art 447.

61 Agreement on partnership and cooperation establishing a partnership between the European Communities and their Member States, of one part, and the Russian Federation, of the other part [1997] OJ L327/3, art 23.

62 Stabilisation and Association Agreement between the European Communities and their Member states of the one part, and the Republic of Serbia, on the other part [2013] OJ L278/16, art 49.

63 Association Agreement between the European Union and its Member States, of the one part, and Ukraine, of the other part [2014] OJ L161/3, art 17.

64 (2013) 56 EHRR 27. See also *Biao v Denmark* (2017) 64 EHRR 1.

ECtHR agreed. First, the Court confirmed that there had been discrimination on the basis of immigration status: the ground for treating the applicants differently was the first applicant's status as a refugee. The Court then turned to the question of justification. It accepted that, in principle, 'offering incentives to certain groups of immigrants may amount to a legitimate aim'.[65] The UK Government argued that in providing preferential treatment to the spouses of students and workers coming to the UK, it was providing such incentives in a legitimate manner. However, the Court disagreed because the respondent government had never relied on such a justification domestically and, moreover,

> the Court sees no justification for treating refugees who married post-flight differently from those who married pre-flight. The Court accepts that in permitting refugees to be joined by pre-flight spouses, the United Kingdom was honouring its international obligations. However, where a measure results in the different treatment of persons in analogous positions, the fact that it fulfilled the state's international obligation will not in itself justify the difference in treatment.[66]

Hode and Ali is important for two reasons. First, it acknowledges the legitimacy of providing benefits and incentives to certain types of immigrants. This may appear to support the type of differentiation in rights provided to migrants which are evident in labour migration regimes generally, particularly as evident in the EU's labour migration acquis, consistently with my earlier comments in respect of the legitimacy of discrimination on the grounds of skills. Second, and most significantly, the decision challenges a rule which forms part of the immigration code as *itself* being discriminatory on the ground of immigration status. The significance of this element of the decision cannot be understated. The CJEU has not yet questioned whether EU migration law is in compliance with international or regional human rights norms but the ECtHR here concluded that part of the UK's immigration regime was inherently discriminatory on a ground closely associated with nationality, namely, immigration status. This entails at least two conclusions.

First, it is possible for the courts to review many areas of law, including immigration and asylum law, as to whether same is discriminatory on the basis of nationality and/or immigration status. Second and derivatively, recall my comment in the previous chapter to the effect that treating migrants

65 (2013) 56 EHRR 27 [53].
66 (2013) 56 EHRR 27 [55].

differently from EU member state nationals in some respect, such as in respect of their labour rights, could amount to unlawful discrimination which infringes migrants' human rights. In the light of the abovementioned case law, it appears that it could be argued, as a matter of principle, that such differential treatment between migrants and EU member state nationals in respect of at least certain of their labour rights could amount to unlawful discrimination on the basis of nationality. In addition, it could be further argued that differential treatment of different categories of migrants – i.e., by providing different categories of migrants with different labour rights – could amount to unlawful discrimination on the basis of immigration status. However, in both cases, such discrimination would not necessarily be unjustifiable, but it does seem that at least a prima facie case of unlawful discrimination could be made out. This argument is explored in further detail in the next chapter.

2.2.2 Revised European Social Charter[67]

Article E RESC commences Part V thereof concerning implementation and enforcement, 'thereby indicating its primary role in securing the effective and equal enjoyment of all rights under the Charter'.[68] Article E RESC is, like art 14 ECHR, a parasitic right. It is not a free-standing guarantee of equality; rather, it requires that some other right be infringed. And art E applies to all provisions in Part 2 RESC.

However, two points merit noting. First, while 'national extraction' is a prohibited ground of discrimination, nationality or citizenship is not: differential treatment on the ground of citizenship is permitted.[69] Second, third-country nationals are in general expressly excluded from the scope of application of the RESC: art 1 of the Annex to the RESC provides that the persons covered by the RESC 'includes foreigners only insofar as they are nationals of other parties lawfully resident or working regularly within the territory of the party concerned'. However, refugees and stateless persons lawfully present in the jurisdiction of the parties to the RESC are entitled to treatment not less favourable than that required under the parties' international obligations. Furthermore, in extreme cases, the ECSR has considered that the RESC can apply to third-country nationals 'on a right of fundamental importance to the individual'.[70]

67 Colm Ó Cinnéide, 'Migrant Rights under the European Social Charter' in *Migrants at Work: Immigration and Vulnerability in Labour Law* (n 38).

68 Csilla Kollonay-Lehoczy, 'Article E: Non-Discrimination' in Niklas Bruun, Klaus Lörcher, Isabelle Schömann and Stefan Clauwaert (eds), *The European Social Charter and the Employment Relation* (Hart 2017).

69 Explanatory Report to the European Social Charter (Revised) para 137.

70 *FIDH v France* (Collective Complaint No 14/2003) paras 30–32.

While the Committee has not yet applied art E RESC to irregular third-country nationals,[71] it is nonetheless possible that in future cases it may apply that article to third-country nationals. And given the centrality of work to people's well-being, it would seem that the right to work and equality of access to the labour market should be understood as being of 'fundamental importance' to the individual. In other words, third-country nationals should be guaranteed equal treatment with member state nationals when exercising their right to work.

3 The Right to Equal Treatment and Non-discrimination in EU Law

3.1 *Article 18 TFEU*

Article 18 TFEU is the fundamental textual expression of equality and non-discrimination in EU law. In general, art 18 TFEU applies as an independent guarantee of equality unless a specific guarantee of equality has been provided elsewhere in EU law.[72] Of course, that is not to say that art 18 TFEU cannot be used as a source of inspiration and interpretation for those other, more specific guarantees of equality; indeed, it has been so used on numerous occasions.[73] The text of art 18 provides that non-discrimination on the basis of nationality shall be guaranteed 'within the scope of application of the Treaties'. Who, then, falls within the scope of EU law? The answer is all those persons who are within the territory of the EU member states or overseas territories, are EU nationals or are entitled to equal treatment therewith.[74]

If third-country nationals are entitled to equal treatment with EU nationals on the ground of nationality, then they can rely on EU equality and anti-discrimination law because the former, logically, entails the latter. To put it

71 *DCI v The Netherlands* (Collective Complaint No 48/2008).

72 Case C-379/92 *Peralta* [1994] ECR I-3453 [18]; Case C-55/00 *Gottardo* [2002] ECR I-413 [21]; Case C-91/08 *Wall* [2010] ECR I-2815 [32]; Case C-195/16 *I* ECLI:EU:C:2017:815 [70]; and Case C-25/10 *Missionswerk Werner Heukelbach eV* [2011] 2 CMLR 35 [18].

73 Case C-73/08 *Bressol* [2010] ECR I-2735 [86]; Case C-391/09 *Runevič-Vardyn v Vilniaus miesto savivaldybės administracija* [2011] 3 CMLR 13 [43]; and Case C-42/11 *Lopes de Silva* ECLI:EU:C:2012:517 [59].

74 Elspeth Guild and Steve Peers, 'Out of the Ghetto? The Personal Scope of EU Law' in Steve Peers and Nicola Rogers (eds), *EU Immigration and Asylum Law: Text and Commentary* (Brill 2006); and Eleanor Spaventa, 'Seeing the Wood for the Trees? On the Scope of Union Citizenship and its Constitutional Effects' (2008) 45 CML Rev 13. The CJEU has, however, equivocated at times on this point: cf Case C-233/14 *Commission v The Netherlands* [2017] 1 CMLR 5 [76] and Case C-182/15 *Petruhhin* [2017] 1 CMLR 28 [30].

another way, once migrants are guaranteed equal treatment on the ground of nationality, they are then entitled to equal treatment on other grounds. Equal treatment on the ground of nationality is a threshold condition for equal treatment in many other respects. However, the Court of Justice has asserted that art 12 EC – now art 18 TFEU – does not apply to third-country nationals. As the Court of Justice noted in *Vatsouras and Koupatantze*, that article

> concerns situations coming within the scope of Community law in which a national of one Member State suffers discriminatory treatment in relation to nationals of another Member State solely on the basis of his nationality and is not intended to apply to cases of a possible difference in treatment between nationals of Member States and nationals of non-member countries.[75]

This position has been affirmed in several post-Lisbon cases.[76] In *Hadj Ahmed*, for example, the applicant was an Algerian national resident in Belgium holding a valid resident permit and had entered Belgium on the basis of the Family Reunification Directive to be united with her partner there, who was a French national. The couple had a child together of French nationality and the applicant had another child of Algerian nationality. The couple subsequently separated and the applicant, who was not dependent on her partner, was then reliant on social assistance in Belgium. Shortly thereafter, the applicant stopped receiving allowances for her child of Algerian nationality. The applicant applied for such benefits, but her application was rejected on the basis that she had not been resident in Belgium for five years or more. The applicant challenged this decision and the ground for it, namely the five-year residency requirement.

A number of questions relating to this challenge were referred to the Court of Justice, the most pertinent for my purposes being whether the applicant was entitled to equal treatment with member state nationals on the basis of the Family Reunification Directive, in particular arts 13(2) and 14 thereof. According to the Court, given that (i) the applicant's circumstances fell outside the scope of arts 13(2) and 14 of the Family Reunification Directive and (ii) the fact that the applicant had a resident permit did not, in and of itself, entitle her to equal treatment with member state nationals in accordance with

75 Case C-122/96 *Saldanha and MTS* [1997] ECR I-5325 [15]; and Cases C-22/08 and C-23/08 *Vatsouras and Koupatantze* [2009] ECR I-4585 [52].

76 Case C-291/09 *Francesco Guarnieri and Cie* ECLI:EU:C:2011:217 [20]; and Case C-42/11 *Lopes de Silva* ECLI:EU:C:2012:517; Case C-45/12 *Hadj Ahmed* ECLI:EU:C:2013:390.

art 18 TFEU, the applicant was accordingly not entitled to equal treatment with member state nationals. Specifically, the Court noted that as the background to art 18 TFEU was Union citizenship, art 18 TFEU could not apply 'as it stands' to third-country nationals holding a resident permit in a member state. Reflecting on the Court's approach, however, Evelien Brouwer and Karin de Vries observe, rightly in my view, that

> [u]sing the wording 'as it stands' (…) seems to indicate that Article 18 TFEU could apply to TCNs, but only if their situation is covered by EU law. In this case, the CJEU found that the person invoking Article 18 TFEU (and Articles 20 and 21 of the Charter) did not fall within the categories of persons protected by EU law: neither the mother nor her daughter, for whom she applied for family benefits, fell within the scope of Directive 2004/38 or Regulation 1612/68 or of Directive 2003/109.[77]

In the light of this case law, it is clear that in no case has the CJEU expressly held art 18 TFEU applicable to third-country nationals. But the case law is, at least, consistent with the following view: namely, that art 18 TFEU, as an expression of equal treatment in general, may apply to third-country nationals only when they fall within the scope of some other, more specific, expression of that conception. In other words, while third-country nationals are not generally entitled to equal treatment with member state nationals as a matter of EU law, they are so entitled in specifically enumerated circumstances, such as under the terms of the Family Reunification Directive. This is consistent with other case law concerning art 18 TFEU. In general, that article will not be invoked if an alternative and specific guarantee of equality exists. However, it has been acknowledged that, if such a specific guarantee does exist, then art 18 can be used to interpret that guarantee, giving it greater breadth.

Given this possibility, it is not entirely clear, as a matter of legal doctrine, why the CJEU has refused to recognise the general application of art 18 TFEU to third-country nationals. Indeed, a general principle may be subject to many exceptions and so such a position may be roughly the same, in practice, with

77 Evelyn Brouwer and Karin de Vries, 'Third-country nationals and discrimination on the ground of nationality: article 18 TFEU in the context of article 14 ECHR and EU migration law: time for a new approach' in Marjolein van de Brink, Susanne Burri and Jenny Goldschmidt (eds), *Equality and Human Rights: Nothing but Trouble? Liber amicorum Titia Loenen* (SIM 2015) 141. See further Karin de Vries, 'The Non-National as 'The Other': What Role for Non-Discrimination Law?' in Moritz Jesse (ed), *European Societies, Migration and the Law: The 'Others' amongst 'Us'* (CUP 2021).

the current legal protection of the rights of third-country nationals in EU law. One reason for this may be that the CJEU has left the definition of the specific guarantees of equality for third-country nationals to the EU's legislative institutions. That much is evident, at least in the case of third-country nationals, from the legislative history of the drafting of much of the EU's migration acquis. For, as Bjarney Friðriksdóttir has outlined, the extent of the equal treatment guaranteed to third-country nationals in many of the EU's migration measures was a matter of a great debate and lobbying on behalf of the member states.[78] While this legislative and political reality is certainly enlightening, it does not explain, as a matter of legal doctrine, why art 18 TFEU does not apply in principle to third-country nationals.[79]

3.2 *Article 21 CFREU*

It is also necessary to consider art 21(2) CFREU, which is textually similar to art 18 TFEU, and states that '[w]ithin the scope of application of the Treaties and without prejudice to any of their specific provisions, any discrimination on grounds of nationality shall be prohibited'. This appears to designate art 21(2) CFREU as something of an exception or derogation to art 21(1) CFREU,[80] a point which has been borne out in subsequent case law.[81] For example, *Kamberaj* concerned an application by an Albanian national, resident and working in Italy, for a housing allowance. The allocated funding for housing allowance was divided into two categories, for EU national residents and non-EU national

78 Bjarney Friðriksdóttir, *What Happened to Equality? The Construction of the Right to Equal Treatment of Third-Country Nationals in European Union Law on Labour Migration* (Brill Nijhoff 2017) ch 9. See also Sonia Morano-Foadi and Karin de Vries, 'The Equality Clauses in the EU Directives on Non-discrimination and Migration/Asylum' in Sonia Morano-Foadi and Micaela Malena (eds), *Integration for Third-Country Nationals in the European Union: The Equality Challenge* (Edward Elgar 2012).

79 It is plausible to think that the reason art 18 TFEU does not apply to third-country nationals is because it is designed to strengthen EU citizenship. But this does not explain why art 18 apparently ignores legal doctrine. There is an important difference between the actual or potential purpose of a law and its actual coherence within the legal system of which it is a part.

80 Mark Bell, 'Article 20' and Claire Kilpatrick and Hanna Eklund, 'Article 21' in *The EU Charter of Fundamental Rights: A Commentary* (n 44).

81 Case C-508/10 *Commission v The Netherlands* [2012] 2 CMLR 48; Case C-571/10 *Kamberaj* [2012] 2 CMLR 43; Cases C-443 and C-443/14 *Kreis Warendorf* [2016] 3 CMLR 11; Case C-579/13 *P and S* [2015] 3 CMLR 44; *Sannah v Work and Pensions Secretary* [2015] 2 CMLR 27; Karin de Vries, 'Towards Integration and Equality for Third-Country Nationals? Reflections on *Kamberaj*' (2013) 38 EL Rev 248; and Steve Peers, 'The Court of Justice lays the Foundations for the Long-Term Residents Directive: *Kamberaj, Commission v Netherlands, Mangat Singh*' (2013) 50 CML Rev 529.

residents respectively. The applicant challenged this distinction as being discriminatory on grounds of nationality but was unsuccessful. Ultimately, the Court of Justice avoided addressing the issue under art 21(2) CFREU, instead addressing the issue under art 34 CFREU concerning rights to social assistance and social security. The structure of the Court's reasoning is nonetheless interesting to consider.

The Court first noted that the referring court had failed to make a concrete link between, inter alia, arts 18 TFEU and 21 CFREU and the case before it. The CJEU then turned to a specific equal treatment guarantee for third-country nationals in the Long-Term Residents' Directive. Noting that, according to the terms thereof, the member states are entitled to restrict equal treatment in respect of social assistance and social protection to 'core benefits', the Court then considered the meaning of 'core benefits' in the light of art 34 of the Charter. The Court concluded that the allocative distinction made in national law fell within this concept and was therefore contrary to the terms of the Long-Term Residents' Directive. It thus appears that rather than addressing the scope of the equal treatment guarantee as defined in the Long-Term Residents' Directive, the Court instead began from the terms thereof, taking for granted a priori that the Directive granted third-country nationals' equal treatment with member state nationals. Rather than challenging this position, as made by the EU's legislative institutions in drafting the Directive, the Court accepted it and continued its reasoning therefrom. The Court's reasoning can be reconstructed, more simply, as follows:

(i) [Third-country nationals are entitled to equal treatment with member state nationals.][82]
(ii) The TFEU and CFREU do not specify the extent of third-country nationals' entitlement to equal treatment with member state nationals clearly.
(iii) The Long-Term Residents' Directive provides one clear specification of same.
Third-country nationals who fall within the scope of the Long-Term Residents' Directive are entitled to equal treatment with member state nationals as defined therein.

A similar phenomenon is also evident in subsequent case law. In *Kreis Warendorf*, the Court addressed certain restrictions on the free movement of beneficiaries of subsidiary protection in Germany under the Uniform Status

82 I state this as a necessary, but enthymematic, premise in the reasoning.

Directive. The Court referred neither to the TFEU nor the CFREU, but the language of equality imbues much of the judgment. Specifically, in assessing whether a residence condition, which had as its object the integration of third-country nationals, was permissible, the Court held that beneficiaries of subsidiary protection may not be in an 'objectively comparable situation' to other third-country nationals in this respect and so the question of equal treatment will not arise. However, the Advocate General, in his analysis, did refer expressly to art 21 CFREU. He noted that, notwithstanding that there was no reference to it in the Charter, immigration status must be a prohibited ground of discrimination, an interpretation which he suggested would bring art 21 CFREU into line with art 14 ECHR.[83]

At issue in *Commission v The Netherlands* were charges for resident permits for third-country nationals who had obtained long-term resident status elsewhere in the EU and wished to move to the Netherlands. No reference was made to the equality guarantees in the Union's constitutional documents in the judgment of the Court. However, the Advocate General did conclude that, on the basis of the equal treatment guarantee in the Long-Term Residents' Directive, 'the principle of non-discrimination seems to me to preclude the establishment of charges the amounts of which have a deterrent effect on third-country nationals who do not have sufficient financial resources'.[84] The Advocate General's comments are, unfortunately, ambiguous between discrimination on different grounds. On the one hand, the Advocate General could be here referring to indirect nationality discrimination. If, statistically, it could be established that nationals from certain third-countries are less able to afford the charges for the resident permits than others, then those third-country nationals are being discriminated against indirectly on the ground of nationality. On the other hand, the Advocate General could merely be referring to direct discrimination on the grounds of socio-economic standing. If this is the case, then the question of nationality discrimination does not necessarily arise. If we prefer the former interpretation, at least for the sake of argument, then it seems clear that the Advocate General is offering us a potentially robust conception of equal treatment in the context of the design of immigration regimes. Specifically, on this view, the EU's migration acquis would need to be (re)designed so as to avoid, at least, indirect nationality discrimination.

Finally, *Petrov*[85] and *Voigt*[86] concerned the withdrawal of security clearance for several Russian nationals to enter and use certain facilities at the European

83 [2016] 3 CMLR 11 [AG77].
84 [2012] 2 CMLR 48 [AG69].
85 Case T-452/15 *Petrov* ECLI:EU:T:2017:822.
86 Case T-618/15 *Voigt* ECLI:EU:T:2017:821.

Parliament. Mr Voigt, a member of the European Parliament, applied to use certain facilities at the Parliament to host a political forum and working meeting. Several Russian citizens were due to attend. Security clearance is required of all non-members of the Parliament and, although security clearance was initially granted to all attendees, it was subsequently withdrawn for all Russian guests. The applicants in both cases argued, inter alia, that this decision was discriminatory. The General Court's response, in both judgments, was as follows. First, the Court considered the interpretation of art 21(2) CFREU. It held that, on the basis of the explanations accompanying the Charter, art 21(2) is equivalent to art 18 TFEU and has the same scope. Accordingly, the Court returned to the meaning of art 18 TFEU, affirming the application of *Vatsouras and Koupatantze* to art 21(2) CFREU. In other words, the applicants could not rely on art 18 TFEU. In so doing, the Court did not refer to any of the more recent case law outlined above. With respect, this is a significant failing in an otherwise opportune case to address the issue this chapter raises. Instead, the General Court went on to observe that art 21 CFREU,

> is a particular expression of the principle of equal treatment (…) and both that principle and the prohibition of any discrimination are simply two labels for a single general principle of law, which prohibits both treating similar situations differently and treating different situations in the same way unless there are objective reasons for such treatment.[87]

3.3 *The Argument for Expanding the Scope of Application of the Right to Equal Treatment and Non-discrimination*

Numerous scholars have argued for a shift away from the status quo in EU law due to, inter alia, the post-Lisbon change in the structure and operation of the Union and move away from the so-called 'pillar' system. This view implies that the areas of migration and asylum, previously governed by quite distinct rules, now fall, at least to some extent, under general provisions of the treaties. As such, third-country nationals should in principle benefit from equal treatment with member state nationals as embodied in arts 18 TFEU and 21 CFREU.[88] In

87 ECLI:EU:T:2017:821 [98]; ECLI:EU:T:2017:822 [53]. See also Case C-897/19 PPU *I.N.* ECLI:EU:C:2020:262 [40]; Case C-930/19 *X* ECLI:EU:C:2021:657 [50].

88 See 'Out of the Ghetto? The Personal Scope of EU Law' (n 74); Kees Groenendijk, 'Citizens and third-country nationals: differential treatment or discrimination' in Jean-Yves Carlier and Elspeth Guild (eds), *The Future of Free Movement of Persons in the EU* (Bruylant 2006);

other words, third-country nationals should generally be afforded equal treatment with member state nationals. However, even at first grant, two problems arise with this argument.

First, even post-Lisbon, the CJEU has distinguished to some extent, in the scope and exercise of its jurisdiction, between the Union's external and internal dimensions. While, post-Lisbon, the Court has expressed a willingness to exercise jurisdiction in cases concerning the Union's common foreign and security policy, in general, this is a jurisdiction which it exercises lightly. In particular, the General Court has acknowledged that the Council has a broad discretion in this area.[89] This may suggest that the Court will not exercise jurisdiction to adjudicate on the rights of third-country nationals as such, thus maintaining the deference to the EU's legislative institutions and the member states which has been the conventional practice of the Court to date. However, the CJEU has also acknowledged the possibility of judicial review of activities in this area and academic commentary suggests that the Court's jurisdiction is only expanding, albeit slowly and incrementally.[90] Moreover, in some cases, the Court has interpreted the Council's discretionary powers in a manner

Moritz Jesse, 'Missing in Action: Effective Protection for Third-Country Nationals from Discrimination under Community Law' in Elspeth Guild, Kees Groenendijk and Sergio Carerra (eds), *Illiberal Liberal States: Immigration, Citizenship and Integration in the EU* (Ashgate 2009); Kees Groenendijk, 'Are third-country nationals protected by the Union law prohibition of discrimination on grounds of nationality?' in Klaus Barwig and Rainer Dobbelstein (eds), *Den Fremden akzeptieren – Festschrift fuer Gisbert Brinkmann* (Nomos 2012); Sara Iglesias Sánchez, 'Fundamental Rights Protection for Third-Country Nationals and Citizens of the Union: Principles for Enhancing Coherence' (2013) 15 EJML 137; Theodore Konstadinides and Noreen O'Meara, 'Fundamental Rights and Judicial Protection' in Diego Acosta Arcarazo and Cian Murphy (eds), *EU Security and Justice Law: After Lisbon and Stockholm* (Hart 2014); Katharina Eisele, *The External Dimension of the EU's Migration Policy: Different Legal Positions of Third-Country Nationals in the EU: A Comparative Perspective* (Brill Nijhoff 2014); Daniel Thym and Margarite Zoeteweij-Turhan (eds), *Rights of Third-Country Nationals under EU Association Agreements: Degrees of Free Movement and Citizenship* (Brill Nijhoff 2015); Steve Peers, *EU Justice and Home Affairs Law Volume 1: EU Immigration and Asylum Law* (OUP 2016) ch 6; and *What Happened to Equality?* (n 78) ch 2.

89 Case T-63/14 *Iran Insurance Company* ECLI:EU:T:2016:264 [90].

90 Case T-255/15 *'Almaz-Antey' Air and Space Defence* ECLI:EU:T:2017:25 [99]; Christina Eckes, 'Common Foreign and Security Policy: The Consequences of the Court's Extended Jurisdiction' (2016) 22 ELJ 492; Graham Butler, 'The Coming of Age of the Court's Jurisdiction in the Common Foreign and Security Policy' (2017) 13 EUConst 673; and Panos Koutrakos, 'Judicial Review in the EU's Common Foreign and Security Policy' (2018) 67 ICLQ 1.

consistent with the fundamental rights and values of the Union.[91] It is therefore arguable that, in principle, the CJEU does have jurisdiction over areas of the EU's external dimension which it heretofore did not have and can exercise it in a manner consistent with the rights of third-country nationals. As such, it is no longer necessary, as a matter of legal doctrine, for the Court to defer to the EU's legislative institutions in this area. Rather, the Court can pave its own way and provide its own interpretation and definition of the scope of the conception of equal treatment with member state nationals.

A second problem concerns a similar issue arising out of the wording of the Treaties. Articles 67(2) and 79 TFEU expressly refer to the need to treat third-country nationals 'fairly'. An ordinary reading of these articles may imply the non-application of the conception of equal treatment with member state nationals to third-country nationals. However, this guarantee needs to be read in the light of the EU's general objectives in the context of its external action, laid down in art 21 TEU, to recognise, advance and promote, inter alia, respect for human dignity, the principles of equality and solidarity, and the protection of human rights and fundamental freedoms. As such, the obligation to treat third-country nationals 'fairly' should not be implemented in a manner inconsistent with the fundamental values of the Union, such as equality, espoused in art 21 TEU. As a matter of interpretation, therefore, the possibility of affording third-country nationals equal treatment in accordance with EU law and, therefore, in principle the protection of arts 18 TFEU and 21 CFREU, is possible.

In relation to the scope of application of the equal treatment guarantee in arts 18 TFEU and 21 CFREU themselves, semantic differences in these and other articles provide grounds for the view that third-country nationals are generally entitled to equal treatment with member state nationals. One obvious example is the guarantee of equality before the law in art 20 CFREU, which simply states that 'everyone' shall benefit therefrom. This may be a simple guarantee of procedural fairness.[92] But it could also constitute a sign of the fundamental, unitary concept of equality underlying all equal treatment and non-discrimination norms, which the EU institutions shape and develop. Indeed, as art 20 prefaces the entirety of the 'equality' title of the Charter, it might indicate the generality of the guarantee of equality for all persons. Later instantiations

91 See Gráinne de Búrca, 'The European Court of Justice and the International Legal Order after *Kadi*' (2010) 51 Harv Int'l LJ 1; Case T-68/14 *Post Bank Iran* ECLI:EU:T:2016:263 [91]; 'The Coming of Age of the Court's Jurisdiction in the Common Foreign and Security Policy' (n 90) 680, 700; and Peter van Elsuwege, 'Upholding the rule of law in the Common Foreign and Security Policy: *H v Council*' (2017) 54 CML Rev 841.

92 Bell, 'Article 20' (n 80).

of the equality guarantee, particularly in arts 21 and 23–26 CFREU, delineate different conceptions.[93] If this is the case, then art 20 CFREU, like art 18 TFEU, could be used as a source of inspiration and expansion of those conceptions.[94]

For example, in *X*, the Court of Justice had to determine whether art 13(2) of the Free Movement Directive was valid in the light of arts 20 and 21 CFREU and, in particular, whether art 13(2) of the Free Movement Directive may lead to discrimination against third-country nationals who are victims of acts of domestic violence and whose spouses are EU citizens compared with those whose spouses are also third-country nationals. The Court reiterated its standard position in respect of the potential application of art 21 CFREU, viz., that it is not intended to apply to discrimination as against or between third-country nationals. However, the Court of Justice then deployed art 20 CFREU to analyse the position of third-country nationals who are victims of acts of domestic violence and whose spouses are EU citizens, under the Free Movement Directive, relative to those whose spouses are also third-country nationals, under the Family Reunification Directive. While the Court did not go so far as to compare the positions of third-country nationals and member state nationals, it did rely on art 20 CFREU to compare the relative positions of two categories of third-country nationals within EU migration law. At the very least, *X* provides direct evidence of the Court's reliance on and use of art 20 CFREU to assess the coherence of the relative treatment of different categories of third-country nationals within EU migration law.

Furthermore, while it is undoubtedly true that art 18 TFEU has its origins in the emergence and genesis of EU citizenship law,[95] that does not mean that art 18 cannot inspire and imbue other areas of EU law. For, first, art 18 has already been so used.[96] Second, the Court of Justice has also done so in respect of other articles of the Treaties, even broadening their scope of application to areas of law which were expressly excluded by the treaties.[97] And third, it is not inconsistent or incoherent to expand the scope of application of art 18 TFEU

93 In Case C-528/13 *Léger* ECLI:EU:C:2015:288 [48], the Court noted that art 21(1) CFREU is a 'particular expression of the principle of equal treatment, which is a general principle of EU law enshrined in Article 20 [CFREU]'.

94 Case C-333/13 *Dano* [2015] 1 CMLR 48 [61].

95 Daniel Thym, 'EU Migration Law and its Constitutional Rationale: A Cosmopolitan Outlook' (2013) 50 CML Rev 709; Daniel Thym, "Citizens' and 'Foreigners' in EU Law. Migration Law and its Cosmopolitan Outlook' (2016) 22 ELJ 296; and Case C-45/12 *Radia Hadj Hamed* ECLI:EU:C:2013:390.

96 See the cases cited at (n 73).

97 Most famously, Case C-438/05 *Viking* [2007] ECR I-10779 and Case C-341/05 *Laval* [2007] ECR I-11767.

to third-country nationals given that, as a matter of first principles, all persons must, in general, be entitled to equal treatment.[98] Indeed, it would be inconsistent, incoherent[99] and, in accordance with my analysis in Section 1 above, discriminatory and dominating for the EU to claim to be based on the values of freedom, human dignity, equality and solidarity while nonetheless refusing in general to recognise the right of third-country nationals to equal treatment. Another reason to be hesitant of the truth of the orthodox view is the existence of a general principle of equality and non-discrimination[100] and the fundamental right to non-discrimination in EU law.[101] The general principles of EU law and fundamental rights, as drawn from the constitutional traditions of the member states, are of equal importance to the texts of the constitutional documents but their scope of application is unclear. Moreover, while in principle they are of equal normative significance to the constitutional documents, and therefore normatively superior within the EU hierarchy of norms as a whole, they are not of decisive weight.[102] As with many provisions of the constitutional texts, the general principles and fundamental rights always lie in the background, forming a repository of norms which courts, in particular, draw on to explain and justify a particular interpretation or approach. The general principle of equality and the fundamental right to non-discrimination have not featured heavily in the context of nationality discrimination nor has their application to third-country nationals been denied or rejected as of yet. It is therefore certainly possible that third-country nationals do benefit from the application of the general principle of equality and the fundamental right to non-discrimination. A final reason, similar in form to the previous, is the

98 Cf Case C-52/81 *Faust v Commission* [1982] ECR 3745 [25]; Case C-122/95 *Germany v EU Council* [1998] 3 CMLR 570 [60]; and Case C-272/15 *Swiss International Air Lines* EU:C:2016:993 [14].

99 Armin von Bogdandy, Matthias Kottmann, Carlino Antpöhler, Johanna Dickschen, Simon Hentrei and Maja Smrkolj, '*Reverse Solange* – Protecting the Essence of Fundamental Rights against EU Member States' (2012) 49 CML Rev 489, 516–517.

100 Case 117/76 *Ruckdeschel* [1979] 2 CMLR 445 [7]; Case 106/83 *Sermide SpA v Cassa Conguaglio Zucchero* [1984] ECR 4209 [28]; Case C-189/01 *Jippes v Minister van Landbouw, Natuurbeheer en Visserij* [2001] ECR I-5689 [129]; Case C-149/96 *Portugal v Council* [1999] ECR I-8395 [91]; and Case C-411/98 *Angelo Ferlini v Centre Hospitalier de Luxembourg* [2000] ECR I-08081; and Evelyn Ellis and Philippa Watson, *EU Anti-Discrimination Law* (2nd edn, OUP 2012) ch 3.

101 Case C-442/00 *Caballero v Fondo de Garantia Salarial (Fogasa)* [2002] ECR I-11915 [32].

102 Deirdre Curtin and Tatevik Manucharyan, 'Legal Acts and Hierarchy of Norms in EU Law' in Damien Chalmers and Anthony Arnull (eds), *The Oxford Handbook of European Union Law* (OUP 2015); and Paul Craig and Gráinne de Búrca, *EU Law: Texts, Cases and Materials* (6th edn, OUP 2015) ch 4.

obligation in EU law to interpret derogations and exceptions narrowly.[103] This is particularly relevant for analysing art 21(2). However, as of yet, this obligation has not been applied stringently at the level of the Charter, although it is often applied in respect of EU legislation. Other norms and principles of EU law, therefore, provide grounds for an expanded interpretation of the equal treatment guarantee.

A general recognition of equal treatment with member state nationals for third-country nationals implies that EU law could be reviewed on the grounds of nationality discrimination by third-country nationals. This might seem like a bold claim but holding that the law is subject to a certain type of review is of course different from suggesting that the law must adopt a specific interpretation, conception or concept of equality. It merely suggests that EU law and decisions based thereon must be reviewed in the light of equality and anti-discrimination norms. This leaves member states with a(n unspecified) degree of discretion to justify their discriminatory decisions and laws. For example, one type of justifiable nationality discrimination may be that found in preferential trade and association agreements. Moreover, holding that third-country nationals are generally entitled to equal treatment may not be, in practice, that different from holding that third-country nationals are only entitled to equal treatment in certain, specifically defined circumstances. Under my suggested approach, the practical difference may be that third-country nationals will have a right to review certain decisions affecting them taken under EU law on the grounds of nationality discrimination. This, minimally, provides another ground for review of legality. The result, more often than not, will be an obligation to provide reasons for decisions heretofore immune from review on this ground. It requires that member states act on valid, valuable *reasons* in exercising their discretion. It requires that laws and policies be drafted taking into consideration the rights of nationals and the potential for (direct and indirect) discrimination.

3.4 *Some Objections*

A number of objections to the analysis thus far merit consideration. A first is the sample size: I have drawn on a very limited range of case law to justify my view of the trends and many of the comments identified as justifying my view are those of Advocates General. This is an objection I feel bound to accept. Hopefully, given time, the sample size will increase and the CJEU will adopt the

103 Case C-75/11 *Commission v Austria* [2013] 1 CMLR 17 [54]; Case C-46/12 *N* ECLI:EU:C:2013:97 [33]; Case C-233/14 *Commission v Netherlands* [2017] 1 CMLR 5 [86].

Advocate Generals' reasoning. A second objection concerns the role of conventional practices in the area of nationality discrimination. As Friðriksdóttir noted, the EU's legislative institutions played a predominant role in delineating the scope of third-country nationals' right to equal treatment. This may provide a reason for the Court of Justice *not* to adopt a new approach, given that by convention the EU's legislative institutions have definitional authority in this area. This objection, too, is powerful. For, given the increasing cultural and political significance of the securitisation of border controls in Europe and the Global North generally, it seems unlikely that courts are going to lead the way in this area in a manner which is politically palatable. Third, the suggestion that the general principles of EU law may provide an opportunity for expanded protection for third-country nationals seems misplaced, particularly when the CJEU has rejected an expansion of the obvious textual guarantees of equality. That is, if the CJEU has rejected the obvious textual guarantees of equality as opportunities for expanded protection for third-country nationals, then it seems highly unlikely that the Court would rely on unspecified guarantees of equality to do the same work, controversial as it is. At present, this objection is strong, but given the CJEU's reputation for expanding into new territory without obvious textual justification this possibility should not be disregarded lightly.

There is a final and significant recent objection from Elise Muir to the line of reasoning developed so far in this section. Muir's objection runs as follows. In some contexts, provisions of the constitutional treaties have been used to expand the rights located in more specific legislative instantiations of the right to equal treatment.[104] However, in the context of the EU's migration and asylum acquis, this has not been done. Rather, the case law to date suggests that the equal treatment guarantees in the relevant legislation are 'understood as directly and exclusively related to the dynamics of legislation-making on migration, thereby avoiding an organic connection with the constitutional version of the right to equal treatment.'[105] In making this point, Muir relies on *Kamberaj* (previously discussed), *P and S*[106] and *Martinez Silva*.[107] *P and S* case

104 In correspondence on this point, Muir referred the author, as illustrative, to the recent cases of Case C-193/17 *Achatzi* ECLI:EU:C:2019:43, Case C-684/16 *Shimizu* ECLI:EU:C:2018:874, Joined Cases C-569/16 and C-570/16 *Bauer and Broßonn* ECLI:EU:C:2018:871, Case C-68/17 *JQ* ECLI:EU:C:2018:696, Case C-414/16 *Egenberger* ECLI:EU:C:2018:257 and Case C-22/18 *Biffi* ECLI:EU:C:2019:497.

105 *EU Equality Law* (n 17) 135.

106 Case C-579/13 *P and S* [2015] 3 CMLR 44.

107 Case C-449/16 *Martinez Silva* ECLI:EU:C:2017:485.

concerned a civic integration course the applicant long-term residents were required to undertake after they had been granted long-term resident status; and given that such a course was not required of member state nationals, nor should it be required of long-term residents on the basis of the guarantee of equal treatment contained in the Long-Term Residents' Directive. However, the CJEU reasoned that third-country nationals are not in a comparable situation to member state nationals given that member state nationals are more likely to have a knowledge of the national language; and as the principal purpose of the Long-Term Residents' Directive is to facilitate the integration of third-country nationals, a civic integration course is consistent with its aims. For Muir, it is 'remarkable' that the CJEU in *P and S* 'only refers to the 'principle' of equal treatment and not to the 'general principle' of equal treatment which has the same content, thereby exclusively locating its analysis at a legislative level'.[108] While not a damning criticism, this does echo the criticism made earlier that the CJEU's approach to date must be considered to operate on the implicit assumption that third-country nationals are entitled to equal treatment with member state nationals but only in specific circumstances.

Martinez Silva concerned a cash benefit intended to meet family expenses claimed by the applicant third-country national who entered the EU on the basis of the Single Permit Directive. The member state in question refused to grant the applicant the benefit on the basis that she was not a long-term resident. The Court of Justice first held that the benefit in question was a social security benefit for the purposes of EU law and was therefore one which third-country nationals were, in principle, entitled to on the basis of an equal treatment guarantee in the Single Permit Directive. The Court then considered, in detail, whether denying certain third-country nationals the benefit was consistent with the Directive. The Court noted that member states are entitled to rely on certain derogations from the equal treatment guarantee provided in the Single Permit Directive so long as they state that they are relying on them in advance of adopting any measure restricting third-country nationals' equal treatment with member state nationals. However, that had not occurred in the case before the Court. Accordingly, the member state measure restricting the applicant's access to the cash benefit was contrary to EU law. Again, however, as Muir notes, 'the Court barely discussed the content of the prohibition of discrimination and drew no parallels with EU equality law'.[109]

108 *EU Equality Law* (n 17) 136.
109 ibid.

It therefore turns out that, on a close analysis of Muir's argument, rather than taking the current approach of the CJEU as justified, Muir would actually support the normative arguments made thus far in this section in favour of a more integrated approach – an approach according to which the CJEU could and should make connections and links between EU equality law, on the one hand, and EU migration law, on the other hand.

4 Converging Conceptions of Equal Treatment and Non-discrimination in EU Law

4.1 *Competing Conceptions of Equal Treatment and Non-discrimination*

4.1.1 Overview

As noted in the introduction to this chapter, EU migration law prohibits discrimination on the ground of nationally to different degrees, while EU equality and anti-discrimination law prohibits discrimination on many other grounds.[110] The Framework Equality Directive, for example, one of the foundational measures of EU equality and anti-discrimination law, does not 'cover differences of treatment based on nationality'.[111] The reasons for the exclusion of the ground of nationality from EU anti-discrimination law were, and no doubt remain, primarily political.[112] Such 'political' motivations are generally considered to point one way, targeting third-country nationals only and thereby protecting EU citizens. But it is undoubtedly the case that the exclusion of nationality discrimination from EU equality and anti-discrimination law impacts on member state nationals too. For if discrimination on the ground of nationality was prohibited by the Framework Directive, then the scope of application of EU law may expand very significantly into areas of domestic

110 Elise Muir, 'Enhancing the Protection of Third-Country Nationals against Discrimination: Putting EU Anti-Discrimination Law to the Test' (2011) 18 MJ 136, 141.

111 Framework Equality Directive, art 3(2). See Sonia Morano-Foadi, 'Third Country Nationals Versus EU Citizens: Discrimination Based on Nationality and the Equality Directives' (21 December 2010) available at <https://papers.ssrn.com/sol3/papers.cfm?abstract_id=1729141> (accessed 9 July 2019).

112 Mark Bell, *Racism and Equality in the European Union* (OUP 2008) ch 7; Sara Benedi Lahuerta, 'Race Equality and TCNs, or How to Fight Discrimination with a Discriminatory Law' (2009) 15 ELJ 738; Chloé Hublet, 'The Scope of Article 12 of the Treaty of the European Communities *vis-à-vis* Third-Country Nationals: Evolution at Last?' (2009) 15 ELJ 757; 'Enhancing the Protection of Third-Country Nationals against Discrimination: Putting EU Anti-Discrimination Law to the Test' (n 110); 'EU Migration Law and its Constitutional Rationale: A Cosmopolitan Outlook' (n 95); Citizens' and 'Foreigners' in EU Law. Migration Law and its Cosmopolitan Outlook' (n 95) and *What Happened to Equality?* (n 78).

law heretofore not addressed by EU free movement law. Indeed, it may entail the partial or total abolition or amendment of the 'purely internal situation' rule.[113] If this rule was abolished, for example, it may enable the CJEU to provide answers to preliminary questions, in a wider array of cases than is currently possible, where the facts of the case are confined within a single member state.[114] This is but one example among many; abolishing completely or restricting the application of the purely internal situation rule in part would nonetheless pave the way for a significant expansion of the scope of application of EU law. Abolishing discrimination on the ground of nationality, then, is a vital ingredient in the deepening of the project of EU integration. Moreover, it may have particularly beneficial effects for third-country nationals, enabling them to avail of anti-discrimination norms in a wider range of circumstances than is currently possible.

Having thus identified the relevant difference between these conceptions of equal treatment, the question which then arises is whether these differences are legitimate or necessary. To interrogate the legitimacy or necessity of these differences, it is helpful to analyse the reasons underlying the distinction drawn between discrimination on the grounds of nationality, on the one hand, and discrimination on other grounds, on the other hand. In addition to the legal doctrinal reasons previously discussed, there are at least three types of reasons which are relevant to the legitimacy and necessity of the distinction between these two conceptions of equal treatment: moral or political reasons; conceptual reasons; and sociological reasons.

4.1.2 Political Reasons

Recall that the CJEU has effectively adopted a position of total deference in the context of nationality discrimination in EU migration law, leaving the definition and scope of equal treatment a matter for the EU's legislative institutions to address. As suggested above, there are certainly some legal doctrinal reasons for disagreeing with this approach. There may also be moral or political reasons for doubting that justification. If, as Colm Ó Cinnéide notes, 'a consensus

113 Niamh Nic Shuibhne, 'Free Movement of Persons and the Wholly Internal Rule: Time to Move On?' (2002) 39 CML Rev 731; Alina Tryfonidou, 'The Outer Limits of Article 28 EC: Purely Internal Situations and the Development of the Court's Approach through the Years' in Catherine Barnard and Okeoghene Odudu (eds), *The Outer Limits of European Union Law* (Hart 2009); and Sara Iglesias Sánchez, 'Purely Internal Situations and the Limits of EU Law: A Consolidated Case Law or a Notion to be Abandoned?' (2018) 14 EUConst 7.

114 Case C-268/15 *Ullens de Schooten* ECLU:EU:C:2016:864.

emerged that EU law should reflect and give effect to a strongly substantive concept of equality', then perhaps the CJEU would change its approach.[115] In other words, if equality became a general norm of the EU, then the CJEU should change its approach. But such a change would require a significant change in culture and the practice of the CJEU and, more generally, the EU as a whole. The explanation and justification for such changes are intimately tied up with a distinctive moral or political theory.[116]

While this book does not adopt any single moral or political theory, as suggested in Section 1 of this chapter, one implication of the link fostered there between discrimination and migration was the adoption of a guarantee of non-discrimination not only in respect of citizens but also in respect of those other people who are at risk of domination, such as at least some non-citizens. The suggested way of implementing this requirement in practice was to make nationality a protected ground of discrimination as a matter of EU anti-discrimination and equality law. Accordingly, there are normative moral or political implications for the role of the CJEU in participating in social and legal change. Given that these factors suggest that change is necessary, they may legitimise the CJEU taking part in developing a general norm of equality in the EU. It is therefore argued that there are both legal doctrinal and moral or political reasons which weigh in favour of entrenching a general prohibition of discrimination on the ground of nationality in EU law, extended in particular to at least some third-country nationals.

Of course, whether it is legitimate all-things-considered[117] for the CJEU to spearhead such change by expanding the scope of application of EU law is a larger question about the role of the CJEU in the project of EU integration more generally.[118] The argument of this chapter thus far does not identify the

115 Colm Ó Cinnéide, 'The Constitutionalisation of Equality within the EU Legal Order: Sexual Orientation as a Testing Ground' (2015) 22 MJ 370, 383–384.

116 'EU Migration Law and its Constitutional Rationale: A Cosmopolitan Outlook' (n 95); and "Citizens' and 'Foreigners' in EU Law. Migration Law and its Cosmopolitan Outlook' (n 95).

117 On the distinction between pro tanto judgments and all-things-considered judgments, see David Ross, *The Right and the Good* (OUP 1930) 18–33 and Skelly Kagan's corrective thereof in *The Limits of Morality* (OUP 1989) 17.

118 See, inter alia, Gráinne de Búrca and JHH Weiler (eds), *The European Court of Justice* (OUP 2001); Anthony Arnull, *The European Union and its Court of Justice* (2nd edn, OUP 2006); Bruno de Witte, Elise Muir and Mark Dawson (eds), *Judicial Activism at the European Court of Justice: Causes, Responses and Solutions* (Edward Elgar 2013); Dorte Sindbjerg Martinsen, *An Ever More Powerful Court? The Political Constraints of Legal Integration in the European Union* (OUP 2015); Susanne K Schmidt, *The European Court of Justice and the Policy Process: The Shadow of Case Law* (OUP 2018); and Thomas Horsley, *The Court of*

precise role of the CJEU in such process of change but it does suggest that there are at least some reasons in favour of that change and that those reasons may be relevant to and feature in the CJEU's process of reasoned adjudication. It does not afford those reasons decisive weight in that process but merely suggests that they are relevant and worthy of articulation, consideration and critical reflection.

4.1.3 Conceptual Reasons

Conceptual reasons explain and justify, at least in part, the nature and structure of a given concept. In this context, the following is an example of reasoning about concepts:

(i) A is constituted by rules (1, 2, 3, … n).
(ii) B is constituted by rules (1x, 2x, 3x, … xn).
A and B are different.

What relevance is this to the conceptions of equal treatment under discussion in this chapter? Some egalitarian legal scholars claim, for example, that sex discrimination is of a different type or kind from nationality discrimination. They appeal to the rules applying to each to explain and justify this claim in a manner similar to the sample reasoning provided at the beginning of this subsection. For example, the fact that equality between the sexes attracts greater legal protection than other forms of discrimination may or may not suggest a difference in the kind or type of wrong being addressed.[119]

It is, however, far from clear that this is the case for at least two reasons. First, there is a difference, in principle, between disagreements over concepts and disagreements over competing conceptions of the same concept.[120] Some egalitarian legal scholars claim that what the law should aspire to protect is a certain conception of equality, such as 'equality of opportunity', 'substantive equality' or 'multi-dimensional equality'.[121] Such egalitarian legal scholars,

---

Justice of the European Union as an Institutional Actor: Judicial Lawmaking and its Limits (CUP 2018).

119 Cf Christopher McCrudden, 'Theorising European Equality Law', in Cathryn Costello and Barry (eds), *Equality in Diversity: The New Equality Directives* (Irish Centre for European Law 2003); Mark Bell and Lisa Waddington, 'Reflecting on Inequalities in European Equality Law' (2003) 28 EL Rev 349; Erica Howard, 'The Case for a Considered Hierarchy of Discrimination Grounds in EU Law' (2006) 13 MJ 445; and Sara Benedi Lahuerta, 'Taking EU Equality Law to the Next Level: In Search of Coherence' (2017) 7 ELLJ 348.

120 On the distinction between concepts and conceptions, see Ronald Dworkin, *Law's Empire* (HUP 1986) 90–96.

121 For a helpful overview of such competing conceptions, see Christopher McCrudden and Haris Kountouris, 'Human Rights and European Equality Law' in Helen Meenan

however, would be wrong in believing that those conceptions are different concepts; rather, they are merely a particular conception of the same concept – the concept of equality. Others, however, appeal to different concepts as explaining and justifying the existence of certain rules for different reasons. Some egalitarian legal scholars do advocate apparently egalitarian rules but for non-egalitarian purposes. Ó Cinnéide suggests, for example, that 'a strongly substantive concept of equality (…) [would] be informed by a strong commitment to human dignity'.[122] Here, two interpretations are possible: either Ó Cinnéide is advocating a dignitarian conception of the concept of equality or he is advocating for a concept of dignity which entails egalitarian principles.

What is the implication of this for the present discussion? It is to clarify that, in principle, it is certainly possible for a single concept of equality, along with competing conceptions of that same concept, to achieve egalitarian goals. The existence of competing conceptions of equality and possibly competing conceptions of some other concept, such as dignity mentioned by Ó Cinnéide, in EU law does, however, suggest a tension in the ultimacy and primacy of egalitarian goals within the EU's legal order.[123] Moreover, the greater the number of conceptions of the same concept there is, the more likely it is that the ability to achieve the goals and aims espoused by subscribers to that same concept will diverge to a greater degree.[124] What is therefore required is convergence and standardisation in respect of one or several, but in general fewer, conceptions of equality. Greater focus and attention to fewer conceptions of equality may better aim and achieve egalitarian goals. Hence the recent prominence in academic debates of the 'constitutionalisation' of certain issues, such as equality, in EU law. This imperative gives us at least one reason to assimilate the prohibitions on discrimination previously outlined.

From here, the second reason to doubt the claim that different types of discrimination involve different types of wrongs emerges more clearly. Discrimination always involves a certain type of conduct – the use a certain criteria, property or ground to distinguish and differentiate between people for some purpose – but what makes discrimination wrongful is the fact that the particular criteria, property or ground – be it sex, gender, race, ethnicity,

(ed), *Equality Law in an Enlarged European Union* (CUP 2007) and Sandra Fredman, *Discrimination Law* (2nd edn, OUP 2011) ch 1.

122 'The Constitutionalisation of Equality within the EU Legal Order: Sexual Orientation as a Testing Ground' (n 115) 383–384.

123 Colm Ó Cinnéide, 'The Uncertain Foundations of Contemporary Anti-Discrimination Law' (2011) 7 IJDL 7.

124 This is a probabilistic claim.

etc – tends to attract, in a given society, certain kinds of disadvantages, be it socially, economically, politically, etc, to different degrees.[125] Thus, the fact that discrimination on the ground of sex is viewed as being particularly wrongful is because our culture, now at least, recognises it as such. By contrast, our culture has not always, or even recently, viewed discrimination on the basis of other grounds as wrongful, sexual orientation being an obvious example. The goal of egalitarian legal scholars should be, it seems, to attempt to create a culture in which discrimination on each such ground is recognised as being equally wrongful in proportion to the detrimental effects which exist in respect of that discrimination on that ground – hence the desire and impetus to assimilate the currently many competing conceptions of equality to fewer conceptions thereof. To put it another way, the conceptual distinction between the different prohibitions of discrimination, the subject of this chapter, should not be treated as definitive. Rather, the aim should be to assimilate and consolidate both of these prohibitions as found in EU migration law and EU equality and anti-discrimination law.

4.1.4 Sociological Reasons

However, we may have reason to resist this move on the basis of other types of reasons. According to what I shall call 'sociological reasons', the immediate consolidation and expansion of EU equality and anti-discrimination law into a single body or category of law may actually weaken the law's ability to achieve its egalitarian goals. Suppose that both conceptions of equality here discussed were wholly assimilated tomorrow. In principle, vast swathes of immigration and asylum law across the EU would become vulnerable to comprehensive deconstruction by anti-discrimination norms.[126] Immigration and asylum laws would need to be immunised from challenge on the basis of nationality discrimination, direct and indirect. If that did happen, such laws may require significant redrafting because we know that many immigration and asylum regimes are riddled with either or both forms of discrimination. Some of the case law discussed in section II.B of this chapter illustrates that point and much the same can be said of the EU's labour migration regime itself. Beyond immigration law, norms prohibiting nationality discrimination could also be

125 This paragraph relies on the position articulated by John Gardner in 'Liberals and Unlawful Discrimination' (1989) 9 OJLS 1; 'Discrimination as Injustice' (1996) 16 OJLS 353; 'On the Ground of Her Sex(uality)' (1998) 18 OJLS 167; and 'Discrimination: the Good, the Bad and the Wrongful' (n 10).

126 I am of course assuming that immigration and asylum law can be subjected to the rigour of anti-discrimination and equality law, something which may not be possible at present.

used to challenge otherwise immune provisions of domestic laws. Logically, this would entail abandoning, in full or in part, the purely internal rule in EU law. The need to reconfigure many areas of the law is not, itself, an obstacle to the achievement of egalitarian goals; indeed, it may be a necessary step in the pursuit thereof. But unless legal change is preceded by a significant cultural and societal shift in the recognition and acknowledgement of the wrongfulness of nationality discrimination, then equality law may not operate effectively to challenge nationality discrimination. In other words, a comprehensive top-down approach to nationality discrimination may be useless in the absence of an appropriately similar comprehensive bottom-up societal response.[127]

That is not to say that equality and anti-discrimination law, for example, cannot and has not achieved at least some of its goals by relying on traditional modes of governance. Geoffrey Brennan, Lina Eriksson, Robert Goodin and Nicholas Southwood describe the different ways in which norms emerge. Sometimes, norms emerge on the basis of top-down processes; on other occasions, norms emerge due to their widespread adoption by more diffuse, decentralised sources. Neither mode of emergence is necessarily preferred here. Rather, it is suggested that a combination of modes of emergence of norms is most likely to serve egalitarian goals. Relying on both top-down and bottom-up approaches is more likely to result in the emergence and creation of a (more) egalitarian culture.[128] More detailed political science discussions may be led concerning the ability of interest groups to have their norms established for the general public but I do not explore those here.

Whether there is or is not a significant cultural acknowledgement of the wrong of nationality discrimination is essentially an empirical one. To come to a conclusive view on this question, one would need to ascertain the current levels of nationality discrimination in Europe generally, differentiating between discrimination against EU nationals (intra-EU discrimination) and third-country nationals (extra-EU discrimination). Such data is not generally collected across the Union and so one might quickly conclude that there is not a significant cultural recognition of the phenomenon. A helpful alternative starting point, however, is data concerning the prevalence of racial and ethnic discrimination in the Union. According to the most recent Eurobarometer on discrimination, Europeans are more comfortable than ever with having a

127 'Discrimination: the Good, the Bad and the Wrongful' (n 10) 76–78.

128 Geoffrey Brennan, Lina Eriksson, Robert Goodin and Nicholas Southwood, *Explaining Norms* (OUP 2013) ch 5. See further Edna Ullmann-Margalit, *The Emergence of Norms* (OUP 1977).

person of a different ethnicity elected to the highest political office.[129] This may suggest that rates of ethnic and racial discrimination are declining and that there is a significant cultural recognition of the wrongfulness of racial and ethnic discrimination in Europe; or it may not. The empirical data provided to date by the Eurobarometer is too indefinite to rely on to be sure.

Recall further the recent 'EU-MIDIS II' Survey conducted by the EU's Fundamental Rights Agency, outlined in section I.E of the introductory chapter.[130] That survey confirms the persistency of discrimination against immigrants, descendants of immigrants and minority ethnic groups across the EU, observing that 'a failure to deliver effective protection from discrimination and hate crime can undermine integration and social inclusion policies, affecting the social cohesion of our societies'.[131] This suggests that we should perhaps not be as hopeful of the reduction in discrimination as the Eurobarometer may imply. It reinvigorates the need for strong legal action coupled with educational and awareness-raising programmes to ensure real equality for all in the Union.

Of final relevance is the fact that nationality is expressly included as a ground of discrimination in the anti-discrimination guarantees of almost every EU member state in some form, being variously described as 'nationality', 'national origin', 'national or social origin', 'origin', 'place of birth', etc, except in Greece, Ireland and Sweden, where the definitions of 'race' and 'ethnic' discrimination include discrimination on the grounds of nationality. Of course, immigration law is generally excluded from the scope of these laws. Accordingly, in the light of the relatively limited EU-wide empirical evidence presently available, we do have *some* reason to believe that assimilating the norms of discrimination into a single (or fewer) principle(s) would not necessarily undermine egalitarian goals. Nonetheless, the risk remains that total consolidation of these areas may undermine egalitarian aspirations, something which we should be loathe to do.

4.2 *A Partial Unitary Conception of Equality and Non-discrimination?*

4.2.1 The Goal

If, as suggested, total assimilation of competing conceptions of equality may risk fracturing the concept of equality, then perhaps partial consolidation and

129 Special Eurobarometer 437, *Discrimination in the EU in 2015: Report* (European Commission 2015) para 2.2.1.

130 FRA, *Second European Union Minorities and Discrimination Survey: Main Results* (Publications Office of the European Union 2017).

131 ibid 13.

assimilation could nonetheless be effective. Recall the General Court's observation in *Petrov* and *Voigt* that art 21 CFREU,

> is a particular expression of the principle of equal treatment (…) and both that principle and the prohibition of any discrimination are simply two labels for a single general principle of law, which prohibits both treating similar situations differently and treating different situations in the same way unless there are objective reasons for such treatment[132]

This statement provides the grounds for recognising, albeit at a highly abstract, constitutional level, the assimilation and consolidation of the prohibitions of discrimination on the ground of nationality in EU migration and asylum and free movement law, on the one hand, and EU equality and anti-discrimination law, on the other hand, into a single prohibition of discrimination. This is, or should be, the fundamental implication of the analysis so far. What other evidence is there of this phenomenon and how might it support a partial unitary conception of equality? In addition to the empirical evidence provided at the end of the previous section, which suggested that nationality, immigration status and ethnicity tend to be considered together, the case law of the ECtHR discussed previously certainly points to increasing convergence on a single conception of equality. There are, however, other signals of this shift elsewhere in the respective courts' case law too.

4.2.2 Hopeful Beginnings …

At times, both the CJEU and ECtHR have been willing to blur the lines between the grounds of nationality, ethnicity, race and social origin.[133] In *CHEZ*, the Court of Justice observed that 'the concept of ethnicity (…) has its origin in the idea of societal groups marked in particular by common nationality, religious faith, language, cultural and traditional origins and backgrounds'.[134] In so observing, the Court referred to and endorsed several judgments of the ECtHR

132 ECLI:EU:T:2017:821 [98]; ECLI:EU:T:2017:822 [53].

133 Case C-54/07 *Centrum voor gelijkheid van kansen en voor racismebestrijding v Firma Feryn NV* [2008] ECR I-5187; Case C-83/14 *CHEZ Razpredelenie Bulgaria AD v Komisia za zashtita ot diskriminatsia* [2016] 1 CMLR 14; and Case C-668/15 *Jyske Finans A/S v Ligebehandlingsnaevnet* [2017] 3 CMLR 29. See further Shreya Atrey, 'Redefining Frontiers in EU Discrimination Law' [2017] PL 185; Shreya Atrey, 'Race discrimination in EU Law after *Jyske Finans*' (2018) 55 CML Rev 625; and generally Shreya Atrey, *Intersectional Discrimination* (OUP 2019).

134 [2016] 1 CMLR 14 [46].

on this issue, namely, *Nachova v Bulgaria*[135] and *Sejdić and Finci v Bosnia and Herzegovina*.[136] In *CHEZ*, the applicant, a Bulgarian national, claimed that she had been discriminated against on the basis of her nationality or Bulgarian ethnicity in an area where electricity metres were raised higher than in other areas due to concerns of criminal activity by members of the Roma community in the area. Even though the discriminatory conduct appears to have detrimentally effected Roma people more, the fact that the applicant was resident in an area mainly populated by Roma people implied that she too suffered. This was sufficient for the Court of Justice to consider the applicant a victim of discrimination.

Firma Feryn concerned an action by a Belgian public authority, empowered to promote equal treatment, against a private company which sought to recruit fitters. One of the directors of the latter publicly commented that it could not recruit 'immigrants' because its customers would not permit such person's access to their premises. While the Court of Justice did not directly address the question of whether the reference to 'immigrants' constituted a type or ground of discrimination, it can be inferred from the judgment that it assimilated such comments with ethnic discrimination. Specifically, the Court noted that

> public statements by which an employer lets it be known that under its recruitment policy it will not recruit any employees of a certain ethnic or racial origin are sufficient for a presumption of the existence of a recruitment policy which is directly discriminatory.[137]

This appears to suggest that discrimination on the grounds of immigration status can, at least in some cases, be assimilated to, or overlap with, ethnic discrimination.[138] Finally, in *Jyske Finans A/S*, a credit institution required further identification documents from an applicant for a loan who was born in Bosnia and Herzegovina, notwithstanding that the applicant had subsequently acquired Danish nationality. By contrast, it was not the practice of the credit institution to request such further identification documentation from persons born in the EU. The question for the Court of Justice was whether such

135 [2004] ECHR 90. See also *Timishev v Russia* App no 55974/00 (ECtHR, 13 December 2005) [55].

136 App nos 27996/06 and 34836/06 (ECtHR, 22 December 2009) [45]-[50].

137 [2008] ECR I-5187 [34].

138 Sandra Fredman 'Combating Racism with Human Rights: The Right to Equality' in Sandra Fredman (ed), *Discrimination and Human Rights: The Case of Racism* (OUP 2001); and *Racism and Equality in the European Union* (n 112) ch 1.

a practice constituted prohibited discrimination, direct or indirect, under the terms of the Racial Equality Directive. The comments of the Advocate General and the judgment of the Court itself offer some interesting points of reflection.

Beginning with the former's views, AG Wahl adopted a somewhat conservative interpretation of the CJEU's previous case law. Notwithstanding the position of the Court in *CHEZ* noted above, the AG held that discrimination on the grounds of nationality was not prohibited under the Racial Equality Directive and such discrimination, as well as discrimination on the grounds of ethnic origin or birth, should not be conflated.[139] But AG Wahl did see *some* connection between discrimination on the grounds of ethnic origin and discrimination on the grounds of nationality; as he observed, 'nationality in the 'ethnic' sense of the word (…) is merely one factor which distinguishes a given ethnicity'.[140] Similarly, he acknowledged that there was no automatic connection between a place of birth and ethnicity but nonetheless birth may be a factor going to ethnicity.[141] Turning thence to the views of the Court of Justice, the views of AG Wahl were bolstered. According to the Court, '[e]thnic origin cannot be determined on the basis of a single criterion but, on the contrary, is based on a whole number of factors'.[142]

4.2.3 … or Hope in Vain?

However, more recently, the Court of Justice has expressly resiled from recognising the implications of these conceptual connections. In *Land Oberösterreich v KV*,[143] the Court was asked to consider whether the Racial Equality Directive precluded member state legislation pursuant to which the grant of housing assistance to third-country nationals who are long-term residents was subject to the condition that they provide proof that they have a basic command of the language of that member state. The Court noted that the Racial Equality Directive only applies to direct or indirect discrimination based on racial or ethnic origin. The Court expressly noted that the Racial Equality Directive

> does not cover differences in treatment based on nationality and is without prejudice to provisions and conditions relating to the entry into and residence of third-country nationals and stateless persons on the territory

139 [2017] 3 CMLR 29 [AG39]-[AG40].
140 [2017] 3 CMLR 29 [AG40].
141 [2017] 3 CMLR 29 [AG43]-[AG44].
142 [2017] 3 CMLR 29 [19].
143 Case C-94/20 *Land Oberösterreich v KV* ECLI:EU:C:2021:477.

> of Member States, and to any treatment which arises from the legal status of the third-country nationals and stateless persons concerned.[144]

Because the difference in treatment of third-country nationals with long-term resident status vis-à-vis resident nationals was based on their status qua nationals, it was considered not to fall within the scope of the Racial Equality Directive. In addition, although the Court went on to consider whether the provision of national law in question indirectly discriminated against third-country nationals, citing *CHEZ* and *Jyske Finans* to that effect, it concluded that because the provision of national law applied to third-country nationals 'without distinction', it did not place persons of a particular ethnic origin at a disadvantage.[145] However, the Court did not cite any evidence, empirical or otherwise, to justify its view in this respect. In the light of the earlier case law described above, *Land Oberösterreich v KV* should be read as narrowing the potential for an integrated or unitary conception of equality to emerge and reasserting the orthodox position repeatedly articulated by the CJEU in respect of the Treaties as being applicable to secondary EU legislation.

Conclusion

This chapter concluded the response to the first sub-question this book investigates, namely, namely, what are the legal doctrinal foundations for migrants' entitlement to qualification recognition and non-discrimination in the EU? Specifically, it considered the second of two core rights necessary to secure the well-being of migrants accessing work in the EU, namely, the right to equal treatment and non-discrimination. The argument made in this chapter, which forms part of the response to that sub-question, can be summarised as follows.

First, it outlined and clarified the understanding of the relationship between discrimination and migration upon which this book proceeds. EU migration law generally discriminates on the ground of skills. It also discriminates on the ground of nationality. Not only is reducing nationality discrimination a fundamental part of the project of EU integration; it can also serve to better facilitate the integration of migrants in Europe. Accordingly, it was argued that making nationality a protected ground of discrimination as a matter of EU equality

144 ECLI:EU:C:2021:477 [51].

145 ECLI:EU:C:2021:477 [56].

and anti-discrimination law could both better enable migrants' integration in Europe and facilitate further and deeper EU integration.

Second, the actual entitlement of migrants at work in Europe to equal treatment and non-discrimination on the ground of nationality was described and analysed. Many forms of binding international and European law, including European human rights law, require the general abolition of discrimination on the basis of nationality – and, in some cases, immigration status – which may only be subject to specific and reasoned exceptions. However, as a matter of EU law, third-country nationals are not generally entitled to equal treatment with member state nationals in EU law. The default position in EU law is that migrants are only guaranteed equal treatment with member state nationals in specifically defined circumstances. This position is clearly inconsistent with important sources of international and European law which bind the EU and its member states. In addition, it was argued that third-country nationals should generally be entitled to equal treatment with member state nationals in EU law as a matter of EU legal doctrine. Some potential objections to this argument were considered. On balance, it is at least arguable that the current position in EU law as regards discrimination on the ground of nationality should be debated further.

Finally, several other types of reasons relevant to the claim that migrants should generally be afforded equal treatment with member state nationals were outlined. These reasons weighed in favour of consolidating existing egalitarian norms in the EU through further entrenchment, thus raising the theme of governance in this book quite directly. These reasons did not, however, conclusively suggest that courts should spearhead change but rather left open the role which courts may play. In the light of those reasons, Section 3 considered to what extent the process of assimilating both conceptions of equal treatment is already evident. While this process appeared to be underway, recent case law of the Court of Justice has resiled from this development and reasserted the orthodox position that migrants are not generally entitled to equal treatment with member state nationals. Given the theoretical position articulated in Section 1 of this chapter and the argument developed in Sections 2 and 3, this is a regrettable development.

PART 2

The Case of Skills

Introduction to Part 2

Part 1 of this book attempted to provide an outline description and critical analysis of part of the legal foundations of migrant integration in Europe. This outline essentially comprised two legal rights of relevance to migrants seeking access to work in the EU. Those were the rights to work and to equal treatment or non-discrimination. The right to work facilitates people's access to the labour market but is generally contingent on one's entitlement to equal treatment with member state nationals. There is, however, another right which is a practical necessity to the effective implementation of the right to work and only comes to light as a result of this book's focus on people's skills. It is a derivative right of the (core) right to work:[1] namely, that the qualifications – that is, the formal expression of the people's skills – be recognised so that, in practice, they are able to access their given profession or occupation. Indeed, without having one's qualifications recognised by appropriate authorities – those governing access to professions or employers within the labour market more generally – one would not be able to participate and move within the labour market effectively because one would not be valued as a person with certain skills. Nor would one be able to advertise and promote one's skills without effective recognition being given to them. To put it another way, the use of one's skills frequently requires recognition of them. A failure to have one's qualifications adequately recognised would result in an inability to take up work commensurate therewith, thereby inhibiting one's well-being. Part 2 of this book concerns the implementation of this right in EU law and policy.

There are at least two types or groups of authorities which may require that one's qualifications are recognised for the purposes of exercising one's right to work. The first are employers.[2] Employers are amongst the authorities acting in the labour market which seek to differentiate between people on the ground of their skills. If, for example, an employer refuses to hire me on the basis that I am inadequately qualified, the employer is restricting my right to work – my ability to access and participate in the labour market – in a manner which could be challenged on procedural grounds. Such procedural grounds are largely a matter of domestic employment and labour law. The more prominent authorities – and the ones this Part is primarily concerned with – are those

1 On the relationship between core and derivative rights, see Joseph Raz, *The Morality of Freedom* (OUP 1986) 168–170.

2 See, e.g., Chris Selby Smith and Lee Ridoutt, 'The importance employers attach to employee qualifications' (2007) 45 Asia Pacific Journal of Human Resources 180.

 | DOI:10.1163/9789004724068_006

governing access to and participation in professions, such as professional regulatory bodies. Suppose, for example, a person holding a medical qualification obtained outside the EU seeks to obtain employment as a doctor within the Single Market. It is almost invariably the case that doing so will require the recognition of their professional qualification as a doctor by a local, regional or national medical council as at least equivalent or similar to a qualification obtained in the EU. Only once this process has been completed will such a person be able to practise medicine in the EU and, in some circumstances, may only be permitted to do so subject to supervision or further education and training.

Accordingly, Chapter 3 is primarily concerned with the extent to which migrants can have their qualifications recognised by appropriate regulatory authorities of the EU's member states when first moving to the EU. It explores relevant parts of EU migration and asylum law and EU external relations law in this respect. Chapter 4 deals with the circumstances in which migrants may have their qualifications recognised when moving within the Single Market. It does so by describing and analysing the law concerning the mutual recognition of professional qualifications which constitutes part of the substantive law of the EU, i.e., EU free movement law. Finally, Chapter 5 considers soft law and policy measures as well as suggestions for reform to the law and practice of the recognition of professional qualifications in EU law. The totality of Part 2 will describe, critically analyse and make practical suggestions for reforming EU law to make it more coherent, effective and fair so as to better enable migrant integration in Europe. In sum, in describing and analysing the implementation of the right to have one's qualifications recognised in EU law, Part 2 of this book should provide at least a partial remedial response to the inadequate qualification recognition third-country nationals habitually experience in the EU.

CHAPTER 3

External Migration

Introduction

This chapter concerns the extent to which migrants are provided with the right to have their professional qualifications recognised before or on arrival in the EU. In other words, it is concerned with the provision of the right to the recognition of professional qualifications in the context of external migration to the EU. The next chapter deals with the manner in and extent to which migrants are provided with the right to have their professional qualifications recognised when moving within the EU. It addresses, in other words, internal migration. The present chapter is structured as follows. It first sets out the relatively bare position in international and European law governing the recognition of professional qualifications (Section 1). The chapter then commences the substantial description and critical analysis of the regulation of the recognition of professional qualifications in EU law which Part 2 of this book seeks to undertake. It first considers certain aspects of EU migration and asylum law (Section 2). It identifies, describes and critically reflects upon the relevant provisions of EU migration and asylum law which provide for the right to the recognition of professional qualifications to migrants of all categories when they arrive in the EU. This chapter then addresses certain aspects of EU external relations law – specifically some of the EU's partnership, association and trade agreements – which complements EU migration and asylum law insofar as it provides migrants with the right to the recognition of professional qualifications in EU law when entering the EU (Section 3). A short conclusion follows.

1 International and European Law

1.1 *International Law*[1]

1.1.1 International Human Rights Law

There are two sources of international human rights law of relevance to the right to the recognition of professional qualifications, both of which provide

1 See generally Christof Roos and Natascha Zaun, 'Norms Matter! The Role of International Norms in EU Policies on Asylum and Immigration' (2014) 16 EJML 45.

 | DOI:10.1163/9789004724068_007

relatively limited guidance. The first is the right to work as guaranteed by the ICESCR. As noted in the introduction to this chapter, the right to have one's qualifications recognised should be understood as a derivative right of the (core) right to work. Because the right to have one's qualifications recognised affects one's ability to participate in the labour market, that right can be understood as operating to facilitate people's access to and participation in the labour market. The right functions in a similar manner to the right to work when it is being used to challenge regulation (or a failure to regulate) to facilitate people's access to the labour market. The right to have one's qualifications recognised can therefore be understood as deriving from the access dimension of the right to work. But does the right to work, as provided for in the ICESCR, guarantee people's right to have their qualifications recognised? Expressly, there is no such guarantee. But it is plausible that the access dimension of the right to work in the ICESCR could be interpreted to include such a right. 'The labour market', for example, 'must be open to everyone under the jurisdiction of states parties'.[2] It is possible that such openness should require that states implement a recognition procedure, facilitating the effective participation of non-nationals in their labour market. The point is merely one of plausibility. But the very plausibility of the point may be bolstered by the views of the CESCR that the principle of non-discrimination guaranteed in the ICESCR and ICRMW should apply equally to migrant workers.[3] For example, given that (home) state nationals do often have to undergo recognition procedures to certify their qualification, even where these are simplified relative to those applied to non-nationals, it seems that non-nationals should have access to at least some qualification recognition procedure to facilitate their effective participation in the labour market. Only if this is the case could a state discharge its obligations of non-discrimination towards third-country nationals.

The second source of international human rights law worth considering is the ICRMW, art 52(2) of which states that the state of employment of a migrant worker may restrict the right to work in accordance with its legislation concerning the recognition of qualifications.[4] However, in doing so, states are nonetheless obliged to endeavour to provide for the recognition of qualifications which third-country nationals hold. In essence, then, migrants ought to

2 CESCR, 'The Right to Work: General Comment No 18' (24 November 2005) 4.

3 ibid 6.

4 The Committee on Migrant Workers has considered potential breaches of this article on two occasions only. See its Concluding observations on the initial report of Uruguay (2 May 2014) paras 37–38; and Concluding observations on the initial report of Turkey (31 May 2016) paras 11–12.

be able to have their qualifications considered through some sort of recognition procedure, even if they are not recognised as being substantively equivalent to qualifications of workers of the host state. In other words, states are not obligated to actually recognise migrants' professional qualifications; they must merely consider them in determining whether migrants should be entitled to access and participate in their particular profession. In addition, it is important to recall that, as noted in Chapter 2, under the ICRMW labour migrants are entitled to equal treatment with host state nationals. But how extensive is the guarantee of equal treatment in international human rights law? According to art 25 ICRMW, labour migrants are entitled to equal treatment with persons in their state of employment in respect of 'working conditions' and 'terms of employment'. While this may include equal treatment in respect of the right to have one's professional qualifications recognised, no integration measures specifically targeted at migrants are required as a matter of international human rights law. Moreover, it should be recalled that the EU and its member states are not bound by the ICRMW.

1.1.2 International Labour Law

Part VI of the ILO's Human Resources Development Recommendation 2004 (No 195), which replaced the Human Resources Development Recommendation 1975 (No 142), provides quite extensive guidance on the recognition of qualifications.[5] The guidance comes in three parts.

First, it recommends that states should adopt a transparent mechanism for the assessment, certification and recognition of skills regardless of where the qualifications have been obtained, whether formally or informally. The Recommendation thus covers the need to recognise formal qualifications, obtained after a period of training and/or education, and non-formal or informal qualifications. Second, according to the Recommendation, the actual assessment of qualifications should be based on objective, non-discriminatory and standardised criteria. In other words, the procedure for recognising qualifications should be a fair and impartial one based on skills rather than other, irrelevant considerations. This is consistent with, say, permitting discrimination on the ground of skills but not on the basis of other irrelevant grounds, such as nationality, considered in the previous chapter. Finally, the 2004

5 See generally ILO, *General Survey of Reports on the Paid Educational Leave Convention (No 140) and Recommendation (No 148) 1974, and the Human Resources Development Convention (No 142) and Recommendation (No 150) 1975* (ILO 1991); and Vania Brino, 'ILO Conventions 122 and 142' in Edoardo Ales, Mark Bell, Olaf Deinert and Sophie Robin-Olivier (eds), *International and European Labour Law: A Commentary* (Nomos /Hart 2018).

Recommendation sparsely suggests that 'special provisions' should be made to ensure the recognition of qualifications of migrant workers. Some guidance from what this provision may mean can be gleaned from a consideration of the equivalent provision in the 1975 Recommendation. The ILO, in its general survey of reports on, inter alia, the 1975 Recommendation, acknowledged that the reason the provisions of the Recommendation are so sparse in relation to migrant workers is that 'the question of migrant workers was a separate item on the agenda of the 59th and 60th Sessions of the Conference'. The ILO recognises that the most frequently used measure in respect of migrant workers are specialised language courses, although the recognition of qualifications is also facilitated by some states.[6]

There are a number of other measures of international labour law of relevance: the Migration for Employment Convention (Revised) 1949 (No 97); the Migration for Employment Recommendation (Revised) 1949 (No 86); the Migrant Workers (Supplementary Provisions) Convention 1975 (No 143); and the Migrant Workers Recommendation 1975 (No 151).[7] The rights guaranteed by these measures are very similar to those provided for under international human rights law. While not referring to qualification recognition specifically, they are of general relevance in considering the external dimension to qualification recognition, as will become clear throughout this chapter. First, according to these measures, labour migrants must have their human rights guaranteed.[8] Second, labour migrants are entitled to equal treatment in respect of working conditions and terms of employment.[9] Third, states are required to facilitate the 'departure, journey and reception' of labour migrants.[10] This may provide grounds for developing integration measures targeted at labour migrants.

A final element of international labour law of relevance is the availability of a model agreement for temporary or permanent labour migration in the Annex to the Migration for Employment Recommendation (Revised) 1949 (No 86). Of particular relevance to the present book is the possibility of identifying 'the number, the categories and the occupational qualifications of the migrants desired',[11] as well determining the conditions to be met for the purposes of

6 *General Survey of Reports* (n 6) paras 305–306.

7 Shauna Olney and Ryszard Cholewinski, 'Migrant Workers and the Right to Non-discrimination and Equality' in Cathryn Costello and Mark Freedland (ed), *Migrants at Work: Immigration and Vulnerability in Labour Law* (OUP 2014).

8 Migrant Workers (Supplementary Provisions) Convention 1975 (No 143), art 1.

9 Migration for Employment Convention (Revised) 1949 (No 97), art 6.

10 Migration for Employment Convention (Revised) 1949 (No 97), art 4.

11 Migration for Employment Recommendation (Revised) 1949 (No 86), Annex, art 1(1)(b).

recognition of any document issued by the state of emigration, such as occupational qualifications.[12] And relatedly, parties to such agreements shall also stipulate any qualification requirements necessary on behalf of migrant workers and their families.[13] Such agreements were quite popular in the second half of the twentieth century[14] and the EU's Mobility Partnerships, about which more shall be said in chapter 5, now serve a similar function. However, they are generally non-binding and therefore do not afford individuals rights which they can rely on. Moreover, as with the ICRMW, these measures of international labour law are not binding on the EU or its member states, the majority of which have not ratified them.

1.1.3 International Economic Law

International economic law does not regulate labour in general, only certain types of service provision. Yet varying kinds of labour regulation are often found in international trade agreements. One increasingly relevant but perhaps controversial example is where states parties agree to cooperate to some extent in respect of their labour standards to support sustainable development.[15] Another, less well-known source of labour regulation in international trade agreements is where states parties put in place measures to facilitate labour mobility, such as qualification recognition systems and guarantees of

12 Migration for Employment Recommendation (Revised) 1949 (No 86), Annex, art 4(1)(c).

13 Migration for Employment Recommendation (Revised) 1949 (No 86), Annex, art 5.

14 Aderanti Adepoju, Femke van Noorloos and Annelies Zoomers, 'Europe's Migration Agreements with Migrant-Sending Countries in the Global South: A Critical Review' (2010) 48 IM 42.

15 See, inter alia, Tonia Novitz, 'Legal Power and Normative Sources in the Field of Social Policy: Normative Power Europe at Work?' in Jan Orbie (ed), *Europe's Global Role: External Policies of the European Union* (Ashgate 2008); the articles on labour standards and sustainable development in (2015) 31 IJCLLIR 233–349; Axel Marx, Brecht Lein and Nicolás Brando, 'The Protection of Labour Rights in Trade Agreements: The Case of the EU-Columbia Agreement' (2016) 50 JWT 587; the articles on labour rights in international agreements in (2016) 155 Int'l Lab Rev 339–475; the articles on labour standards in a global environment in (2017) 5 Politics and Governance 1–105; Billy Melo Araujo, 'Labour Provisions in EU and US Mega-Regional Trade Agreements: Rhetoric and Reality' (2018) 67 ICLQ 233; Jonas Aissi, Rafael Peels and Daniel Samaan, 'Evaluating the effectiveness of labour provisions in trade agreements: An analytical and methodological framework' (2018) 157 Int'l Lab Rev 671; James Harrison, Mirela Barbu, Liam Campling, Ben Richardson and Adrian Smith, 'Governing Labour Standards through Free Trade Agreements: Limits of the European Union's Trade and Sustainable Development Chapters' (2019) 57 JCMS 260; and Clair Gammage, '(Re)Imagining the Trade-Labour Linkage: The Capabilities Approach' in Brian Langille (ed), *The Capability Approach to Labour Law* (OUP 2019).

equal treatment.[16] International trade law does provide default rules concerning qualification recognition in respect of service providers. According to art VII GATS, WTO members are entitled to recognise the licences or certifications of service providers of other members for the purposes of satisfying their own market standards. Recognition of foreign qualifications may be provided through agreement or independently of any prior agreement. Importantly, WTO members are not obliged to treat each other equally or on the basis of the most favoured nation principle in this area. Rather, WTO members may recognise foreign standards but must offer all WTO members the opportunity to negotiate an agreement, or accession to an existing agreement, covering the recognition of professional qualifications. However, this is subject to the general condition that members must not grant recognition in a discriminatory manner nor in a way which would constitute a disguised restriction on trade in services. According to art VI.6, if WTO members have made a commitment to service liberalisation in a given sector, then they must implement a procedure by which to review the professional qualifications of foreign service providers. Article VI.4 provides that all measures affecting service trade are applied in a 'reasonable, objective and impartial manner'. Specific disciplines have also been developed for the accountancy professions, but these do not expressly endorse the recognition of professional qualifications as such. Rather, they require member states to 'take account of' accountancy qualifications.[17]

1.2 *European Law*

1.2.1 The Convention on the Recognition of Qualifications Concerning Higher Education in the European Region 1997

The Lisbon Convention is the flagship measure of the Council of Europe on the recognition of qualifications and is binding on those states party to it. At present, the EU and all its member states, except Greece, have ratified the Lisbon Convention. In addition, the terms of the Convention are generally confined to

16 See, inter alia, Jacques Poot and Anna Strutt, 'International Trade Agreements and International Migration' (2010) 33 The World Economy 1923; the essays in Marion Panizzon, Gottfried Zürcher and Elisa Fornalé (eds), *The Palgrave Handbook of International Labour Migration: Law and Policy Perspectives* (Palgrave Macmillan 2015) part I; and Åsa Odin Ekman and Samuel Engblom, 'Expanding the Movement of Natural Persons Through Free Trade Agreements? A Review of CETA, TPP and ChAFTA' (2019) 35 IJCLLIR 163.

17 This paragraph draws on Julia Nielson, 'Trade Agreements and Recognition' in *Quality and Recognition in Higher Education* (OECD 2004); and Wolfgang Kerber and Roger Van den Bergh, 'Mutual Recognition in the Global Trade Regime: Lessons from the EU Experience' in Ioannis Lianos and Okeoghene Odudu (eds), *Regulating Trade in Services in the EU and the WTO: Trust, Distrust and Economic Integration* (CUP 2012).

holders of qualifications 'issued in one of the Parties' to the Convention.[18] In other words, the Lisbon Convention does not apply to holders of qualifications issued in a state which is not a party to it. However, that does not mean that third-country nationals are automatically excluded from the scope of application of the Lisbon Convention. Indeed, art III.1.2 thereof prohibits any discrimination on the grounds of, inter alia, nationality. Rather, recognition is to be based 'solely on the basis of the knowledge and skills achieved'.

So, what are the key requirements of the Lisbon Convention?[19] First, holders of a qualification issued in one of the parties to the Convention must have 'adequate access' to an assessment of their qualifications when in the territory of another state party. What 'adequate access' requires is, strictly speaking, undefined. However, it is possible to glean some understanding of the requirement of adequacy from other provisions of the Convention. For example, states party must instruct or encourage educational systems to comply with any reasonable request for information for the purpose of assessing qualifications earned at those same institutions.[20] Each state party must also ensure that adequate and clear information concerning its education system is provided.[21] Second, such assessment and recognition procedures must be transparent, coherent and reliable.[22] Third, assessment decisions must themselves be made within a reasonable time limit.[23]

What are the implications of recognition? What does recognition mean? As noted earlier in this chapter, the recognition of professional qualifications may facilitate access to the labour market. And given the increasing transnationalisation of the labour market – in other words, the creation of a single labour market across the European Union – '[e]mployers will increasingly need reliable information on foreign qualifications'.[24] This is surely the most pressing implication of the recognition of professional qualifications in the context of this book. But there are two other implications of recognition. First,

18 The Lisbon Convention, art III.1.1.

19 See also Committee of the Convention on the Recognition of Qualifications concerning Higher Education in the European Region, 'Revised Recommendation on Criteria for the Assessment of Foreign Qualifications' (Strasbourg, 23 June 2010).

20 The Lisbon Convention, art III.3.4.

21 The Lisbon Convention, art III.4.

22 The Lisbon Convention, art III.2.

23 The Lisbon Convention, art III.5.

24 Steering Committee for Higher Education and Research, 'Policies and Instruments for Recognition of Qualifications and Mobility: Reference Document' (Strasbourg, 21–22 September 2004) para 17.

recognition may facilitate access to further higher education studies. And second, recognition may permit the use of an academic title.

1.2.2 Recommendation on the Recognition of Refugees' Qualifications

The Committee of the Convention on the Recognition of Qualifications concerning Higher Education in the European Region – the Committee empowered to oversee, promote and facilitate the implementation of the Lisbon Convention – is empowered to issue recommendations concerning the application of the Lisbon Convention. One such recent recommendation is that concerning refugees' qualifications, issued sometime after the European Migrant Crisis.[25] Given that most refugees – indeed, most third-country nationals – hold qualifications from outside the European Union and Europe generally, this recommendation goes somewhat further than the Lisbon Convention, requiring states parties to recognise qualifications obtained in third-countries.

That is not to say that states parties are obliged to recognise them as equivalent, but '[s]uch qualifications should be recognised unless a substantial difference can be shown between the refugees' qualification for which recognition is sought and the comparable qualification in the Party in which recognition is sought'.[26] The primary emphasis, therefore, is on facilitating the recognition of refugees' skills to enable them to access further education and training or, in some cases, to participate in the labour market. The procedures applicable to refugees are much the same as those under the Lisbon Convention, except that the possibility of recognising refugees' qualifications even in the absence of documentation is envisaged. Paragraph 9 of the Recommendation provides that refugees, displaced persons and 'persons in a refugee-like situation', as the Recommendation defines it, are entitled to have their qualifications recognised even in the absence of any documentation providing proof of those qualifications. Such recognition mechanisms should also be affordable for refugees and refugees should not be prevented from seeking recognition because of the costs involved.[27]

25 Committee of the Convention on the Recognition of Qualifications concerning Higher Education in the European Region, 'Recommendation on the Recognition of Refugees' Qualifications under the Lisbon Recognition Convention and Explanatory Memorandum' (Strasbourg, 14 November 2017).

26 ibid 1.

27 ibid 6.

2 EU Migration and Asylum Law

2.1 *Overview*

The rights of migrants coming to the EU have largely been constructed under the terms of Part Three, Title V, Chapter 3 TFEU and particularly arts 78–79 thereof. Interestingly, no specific legislative form is envisaged by these provisions. It is therefore possible that regulations may be adopted. Furthermore, the reader should recall that art 79(1) TFEU obliges the Union to develop a common immigration policy which facilitates the 'fair treatment' of third-country nationals. Notwithstanding this language, in Chapter 2 it was argued that it would be inegalitarian for the EU not to generally guarantee third-country nationals' equal treatment with member state nationals. In other words, it was argued that migrants should generally be entitled to equal treatment with member state nationals on the ground of nationality. Accordingly, this section describes (Section 2.2) and critiques (Section 2.3) the circumstances in which three categories of third-country national can have their qualification recognised in the EU, namely, regular migrants, forced migrants and irregular migrants. Such migrants may wish to have their qualifications recognised in either and/or both of two scenarios: (a) before departing their country of origin; or (b) on arrival and during their stay in the EU. A table summarising what the law appears to be is provided at the end of Section 2.2.

2.2 *Categories of Migrant*

2.2.1 Regular Migrants

2.2.1.1 *Labour Migrants*[28]

Labour migrants enter the EU on the basis of one of the EU's labour migration schemes, namely: the Single Permit Directive;[29] the Blue Card Directive;[30] the

28 Elaine Dewhurst, 'Labour Rights of Third-Country National Workers in the European Union' in *International and European Labour Law: A Commentary* (n 6); and Herwig Verschueren, 'Employment and Social Security Rights of Third-Country Nationals under the EU Labour Migration Directives' (2018) 20 EJSS 100.

29 Parliament and Council Directive 2011/98/EU on a single application procedure for a single permit for third-country nationals to reside and work in the territory of a Member State and on a common set of rights for third-country workers legally residing in a Member State [2011] OJ L343/1 (Single Permit Directive).

30 Parliament and Council Directive (EU) 2021/1883 on the conditions of entry and residence of third-country nationals for the purposes of highly qualified employment [2021] OJ L382/1 (Blue Card Directive).

Seasonal Workers' Directive;[31] the ICT Directive;[32] as posted workers under art 56 TFEU;[33] association and/or trade agreements between the EU, the member states and third-countries;[34] or researchers, students, trainees, volunteers or au pairs.[35] In respect of scenario (a), no such procedure generally exists at present. In respect of scenario (b), by contrast, any recognition procedure that is applied to a member state's own nationals must also be applied to all labour migrants, except for some trainees, volunteers or au pairs who are not working or students without the right to work, by virtue of a guarantee of equal treatment.[36] Specifically, labour migrants are entitled to 'equal treatment with nationals of the member state (…) as regards (…) recognition of diplomas, certificates and other professional qualifications in accordance with relevant national procedures'.

2.2.1.2 *Voluntary Migrants*

Voluntary migrants enter the EU on the basis of one of the EU's family reunification schemes.[37] The same reasoning which applies to labour migrants in respect of scenarios (a) and (b) roughly applies to voluntary migrants. Strictly speaking, voluntary migrants are not afforded equal treatment with member state nationals in respect of their access to qualification recognition procedures, but it is likely implicit in the guarantee of their equal access to

---

31 Parliament and Council Directive 2014/36/EU on the conditions of entry and stay of third-country nationals for the purpose of employment as seasonal workers [2014] OJ L94/375 (Seasonal Workers' Directive).

32 Parliament and Council Directive 2014/66/EU on the conditions of entry and residence of third-country nationals in the framework of an intra-corporate transfer [2014] OJ L157/1 (ICT Directive).

33 Case C-43/93 *Van der Elst* [1994] ECR I-3803; Case C-299/02 *Commission v Netherlands* [2004] ECR I-9761.

34 TFEU, arts 207 and 217.

35 Parliament and Council Directive 2016/801/EU on the conditions of entry and residence of third-country nationals for the purposes of research, studies, training, voluntary service, pupil exchange schemes or educational projects and au pairing (recast) [2016] OJ L132/21 (Researchers', Students', Volunteers' and Au Pairs' Directive).

36 Single Permit Directive, art 12(1)(d); Blue Card Directive, art 16(1)(d); Seasonal Workers' Directive, art 23(1)(h); ICT Directive, art 18(1)(b); and Researchers', Students', Volunteers' and Au Pairs' Directive, art 22.

37 The primary scheme is embodied in Council Directive 2003/86/EC on the right to family reunification [2003] OJ L251/12 (Family Reunification Directive). However, Council Directive 2004/38/EC on the right of citizens of the Union and their family members to move and reside freely within the territory of the Member States [2004] OJ L158/77 is an essential companion to the Family Reunification Directive. In addition, some association agreements, such as the EEA Agreement, may provide for family reunification schemes.

employment and self-employment with their sponsor that they too shall have access to qualification recognition procedures.[38] Voluntary migrants are also entitled to access education on equal terms with their sponsor.[39] Furthermore, member states may require voluntary migrants to comply with 'integration measures'.[40] Such integration measures generally include language proficiency, as well as knowledge of the history, legal order and values of the host country. Of course, this is not to say that the application of all integration requirements by the member states to date has been appropriate. In *P and S*,[41] discussed briefly in Chapter 2, a Dutch requirement for long-term residents to partake in mandatory civic integration courses was challenged by two long-term residents on the basis that failure to pass the course resulted in the imposition of a fine. The Court of Justice held that while the obligation to take such a course was consistent with the spirit of the Long-Term Residents' Directive, the payment of a fine (€1,000), in addition to the costs incurred in relation to the course, was liable to jeopardise the achievement of the integration objectives of the Directive.

2.2.1.3 *Long-Term Residents*

For such migrants, only scenario (b) is relevant.[42] Long-term residents are entitled to equal treatment with member state nationals as regards 'recognition of professional diplomas, certificates and other qualifications, in accordance with the relevant national procedures',[43] education and training, including grants and loans,[44] and like the Family Reunification Directive, the Long-Term Residents' Directive provides that one of the conditions for acquiring long-term resident status which the member states may impose on migrants is that they 'comply with integration conditions'.[45]

---

38 Family Reunification Directive, art 14(1)(b).

39 Family Reunification Directive, art 14(1)(a).

40 Family Reunification Directive, art 7(2).

41 Case C-579/13 *P and S* [2015] 3 CMLR 44. See further Daniel Thym, 'Towards a contextual conception of social integration in EU immigration law. Comments on *P and S* and *K and A*' (2016) 18 EJML 89; and Moritz Jesse, 'Integration measures, integration exams and immigration control: *P and S* and *K and A*' (2016) 53 CML Rev 1065.

42 Council Directive 2003/109/EC concerning the status of third-country nationals who are long-term residents [2004] OJ L16/44 (Long-Term Residents' Directive).

43 Long-Term Residents' Directive, art 11(1)(c).

44 Long-Term Residents' Directive, art 11(1)(b).

45 Long-Term Residents' Directive, art 5(2).

2.2.2 Forced Migrants[46]

2.2.2.1 *Persons Seeking Temporary Protection*[47]

No question of scenario (a) arises for persons seeking temporary protection, since the terms of the Temporary Protection Directive do not apply until such persons are in the EU. The only scenario of relevance is scenario (b). According to art 12 of the Temporary Protection Directive, member states must permit beneficiaries of temporary protection to access employment or self-employment, 'subject to rules applicable to the profession' and educational opportunities linked to employment, such as vocational education for the duration of the temporary protection given. Article 12 is, however, ambiguous as to whether beneficiaries of temporary protection are entitled to such public goods on the basis of equal treatment. Member states are permitted to distinguish between member state nationals, certain other third-country nationals and beneficiaries of temporary protection in relation to their unemployment benefit policies 'for reasons of labour market policies'. Article 12 also states that the 'general law in force' concerning remuneration, access to social security systems and other employment conditions will apply. The only reference to non-discrimination in the Temporary Protection Directive is in recital 16, which provides that the member states are bound by obligations under international law which prohibit discrimination, but no reference is made to any specific measures of international law. And, according to art 14(2), member states 'may' allow adults enjoying temporary protection access to their general education system. This ambiguity may be a source of domination for such vulnerable third-country nationals insofar as it is unclear what their rights are and many enable member states to exercise arbitrary power over them.

2.2.2.2 *Asylum Seekers*

Like persons seeking temporary protection, the only situation of relevance to asylum seekers is scenario (b).[48] Asylum seekers must be given access to the labour market within nine months of the date of first application if a decision has not been made by the competent authority as to their asylum application.

---

46 See generally Franziska Weber, 'Labour Market Access for Asylum Seekers and Refugees under the Common European Asylum System' (2016) 18 EJML 34.

47 Council Directive 2001/55/EC on minimum standards for giving temporary protection in the event of a mass influx of displaced persons and on measures promoting a balance of efforts between Member States in receiving such persons and bearing the consequences thereof [2001] OJ L212/12 (Temporary Protection Directive); and see Meltem Ineli-Ciger, *Temporary Protection in Law and Practice* (Brill Nijhoff 2018).

48 Parliament and Council Directive 2013/33/EU laying down standards for the reception of applicants for international protection (recast) [2013] OJ L180/96 (Reception Directive).

However, member states are free to decide the conditions for effective access to the labour market of asylum seekers 'in accordance with national law'.[49] Member states are entitled to differentiate between asylum seekers, EU citizens, nationals of EEA states and other legal migrants in their labour market policies.[50] Member states may also permit asylum seekers to access vocational education and training[51] but no integration measures are envisaged. As with persons seeking temporary protection, this ambiguity as to the rights of asylum seekers may be a source of domination for them.

2.2.2.3 *Refugees and Persons Eligible for Subsidiary Protection Status*

As with persons seeking temporary protection and asylum seekers, only scenario (b) is of relevance for refugees and persons eligible for subsidiary protection.[52] According to the Uniform Status Directive, refugees and persons eligible for subsidiary protection are expressly entitled to labour market access immediately after their status has been confirmed, access to employment-related education and skills training and upgrading opportunities on terms equivalent to nationals of the member state,[53] and equal treatment with member state nationals in relation to procedures for the recognition of their professional qualifications.[54] Specifically, art 28(2) provides that member states 'shall endeavour' to facilitate the former two categories of forced migrant to access assessment schemes for their prior learning and skills, especially for those who cannot provide the documentary evidence of their skills which is generally necessary. Article 34 also guarantees such beneficiaries of international protection access to integration programmes in the member states.

2.2.3 Irregular Migrants

There are three categories of irregular migrant of relevance, namely, those who enter the EU unlawfully, certain victims of trafficking who enter the

49 Reception Directive, art 15(1). The reference to 'national law' must include provisions of EU law which are directly effective too, but given that the terms of the Reception Directive provides member states with a power to distinguish between asylum seekers and other nationals, any more general EU equality guarantee must be displaced by this measure.

50 Reception Directive, art 15(2).

51 Reception Directive, art 16.

52 Parliament and Council Directive 2011/95/EU on standards for the qualification of third-country nationals or stateless persons as beneficiaries of international protection, for a uniform status for refugees or for persons eligible for subsidiary protection, and for the content of the protection granted (recast) [2011] OJ L337/9 (Uniform Status Directive).

53 Uniform Status Directive, art 26.

54 Uniform Status Directive, art 28.

EU unlawfully[55] and those whose status as legal migrants becomes irregular whilst in the EU. Only scenario (b) is of relevance for irregular migrants. In respect of the first and third categories of irregular migrant, although the EU does not have the competence to regulate irregular employment, the EU has indirectly regulated irregular employment by prohibiting employers operating in the EU from employing irregular migrants.[56] Thus, under EU law it is not unlawful per se for an irregular migrant to work and potentially even benefit from the necessary guarantees surrounding work, such as the recognition of their professional qualifications. However, given that it is unlawful for employers to employ irregular migrants and the member states are under a duty to return irregular migrants to their country of origin, the chances of this happening are probably quite slim. This is the case regardless of the length of time spent in the jurisdiction prior to the migrant's status becoming irregular.

By contrast, victims of trafficking who have been granted a residence permit must be given access to the labour market,[57] and to professional skills enhancement courses.[58] However, as with certain categories of forced migrants, there is no general or specific equal treatment guarantee in respect of victims of trafficking, and so member states are entitled to define the conditions in which such irregular migrants may access the labour market and the recognition procedures and standards for their professional qualifications. In general, no equal treatment guarantee is provided for irregular migrants in respect of the recognition of their professional qualifications in scenario (b); they must rely on any available national procedure in those scenarios.

55 Council Directive 2004/81/EC on the residence permit issued to third-country nationals who are victims of trafficking in human beings or who have been the subject of an action to facilitate illegal immigration, who cooperate with the competent authorities [2004] OJ L261/19 (Victims of Trafficking Resident Permit Directive).

56 Parliament and Council Directive 2009/52/EC providing for minimum standards on sanctions and measures against employers of illegally staying third-country nationals [2009] OJ L168/24.

57 Victims of Trafficking Resident Permit Directive, art 11.

58 Victims of Trafficking Resident Permit Directive, art 12.

TABLE 3.1 Rights enjoyed by different types of migrant

Type of migrant/ rights	Recognition of qualifications	Integration measures	Education and training
Labour migrants	Yes, except trainees, volunteers and au pairs when not working	No	All except ICTs; access to loans and grants can be restricted
Voluntary migrants	Yes	Yes	Yes, depending on sponsor's rights
Long-term residents	Yes	Yes	Yes, including grants and loans
Persons seeking temporary protection	Unclear on the basis of the Directive	No	Limited access
Asylum seekers	Unclear on the basis of the Directive	No	Limited access
Refugees and persons eligible for subsidiary protection status	Yes, even if documentary evidence is unavailable	Yes	Yes, including grants and loans
Irregular migrants (generally)	No	No	No
Victims of human trafficking	Yes	Yes	Yes

2.3 *Analysis*

2.3.1 General Observations

In respect of scenario (a), as the Commission quite damningly admitted in its *Fitness Check on EU Legislation on legal migration*, '[d]epending on the laws of the country of destination, TCNs may (…) face more onerous requirements for recognition of their qualifications than EU citizens holding a similar EU or non-EU qualification'.[59] This seems like an obvious instance of unequal treatment. Further, in a lengthy but insightful passage, the Commission observed,

> Recognition of diplomas is a widely posed requirement, especially for work-related permits, but its existence and the related guidance are relatively difficult to find. This, together with the complex process of recognition itself and the multitude of requirements especially concerning regulated professions make recognition one of the more burdensome requirements for TCNs. It has been documented that when there are requirements in terms of qualification level in order to be eligible to a work-related residence permit, some potential highly skilled migrant workers are sometimes excluded because of the excessive requirements or procedures, the impossibility to have access to recognition procedures from outside the country or the lack of knowledge in the destination country (by the administration or by the employer) about the value of the non-EU qualification.[60]

Even in the absence of harmonisation in respect of scenario (a), simply setting up a common EU website or repository of member state practices would go a long way to overcoming this obvious uncertainty. Indeed, this absence was particularly relevant during the COVID-19 pandemic when migrants may not be able to travel to the EU to have their qualifications recognised. Putting in place measures to enable migrants to have their qualifications recognised before coming to the EU is therefore must pressing.

Turning thence to scenario (b), a number of questions arise. First, the guarantee of equal treatment 'in accordance with the relevant national procedures' is in relation to member state nationals. However, for the most part, particularly where member state nationals hold qualifications obtained in the relevant member state, no question of recognition arises. Rather, their qualifications are automatically recognised by the relevant authority. This does not mean, however, that third-country nationals are not entitled to equal treatment. Indeed, if they hold qualifications obtained within the member state, then they are equally entitled to such automatic recognition. In general, though, most third-country nationals do not hold qualifications obtained from within the EU. Accordingly, for those third-country nationals who hold qualifications

---

59 Commission, 'Fitness Check on EU Legislation on legal migration' (Staff Working Document) SWD(2019) 1055 final, 128.

60 ibid, citing European Commission, *Obstacles to Recognition of Qualifications* (2017); and OECD and EU, *Recruiting Immigrant Workers: Europe 2016* (2016).

obtained from outside the EU, they will be entitled to the same procedural treatment granted to member state nationals who obtain qualifications from outside the EU.

It is now that the amorphous phrase 'in accordance with the relevant national procedures' comes to the fore. This can only mean one thing: permitted discrimination. Allow me to explain. Suppose a member state national obtains a qualification outside the EU and seeks to have it recognised by an authority within the EU. That authority is obligated to compare it with equivalent qualifications obtained within the EU. If that authority concludes that the qualification obtained outside the EU is equivalent to that obtained within the EU, then it is obliged to recognise it. If, by contrast, the authority concludes that the non-EU qualification is not equivalent to the EU qualification, then it is not required to recognise it. Returning, then, to those third-country nationals who hold non-EU qualifications: like member state nationals holding non-EU qualifications they are simply entitled to have their qualifications compared with relevant member state qualifications. This is a limited guarantee of procedural equality in respect of the recognition test applicable to non-EU qualifications. But, crucially, it does not determine the grounds upon which comparison is to be made. Suppose, for example, that a member state authority is comparing a non-EU qualification with an EU qualification. There is nothing stopping that authority developing criteria which discriminate against non-EU qualifications provided that the recognition procedure is applied to EU and non-EU nationals alike. To put the point another way, while third-country nationals are entitled to procedural equality with member state nationals in respect of qualification recognition, that procedural equality may be substantively unequal.

All of this, of course, is only of relevance to third-country nationals who are clearly granted equal treatment in respect of qualification recognition procedures in accordance with member state procedures. But not all third-country nationals are so entitled. For voluntary migrants, for example, no such express guarantee of equal treatment is provided; and for persons seeking temporary protection and asylum seekers, there is no such guarantee of equal treatment. Even though asylum seekers are entitled to labour market access within nine months of the date of their application for asylum, it cannot be said that, on the basis of the text of the relevant directive, they are entitled to equal treatment with member state nationals in respect of access to qualification recognition procedures. Similarly, victims of human trafficking, who must be given access to the labour market, are not expressly entitled to equal treatment in respect of qualification recognition procedures. These differences in treatment are difficult to rationalise. They range from being entitled to equal treatment in respect of qualification recognition even in the absence of proof of qualifications in the case of refugees and persons seeking subsidiary protection – who might be considered to benefit from the 'gold standard' of protection – to no equal treatment whatsoever, as in the case of irregular migrants generally and victims of human trafficking in particular. Even in the recitals to the relevant directives, there is little reasoning provided as to why, if at all, such differences of treatment exist. For these reasons, it is possible that the status quo is in breach of the general principle of legal certainty in EU law, according to which '[i]ndividuals must be able to ascertain unequivocally what their rights and obligations are and take steps accordingly'.[61]

However, there is a particular moral ideal which can enlighten and respond to the uncertainty created for third-country nationals seeking to have their qualifications recognised, one which has attracted the attention of some migration theorists in recent years.[62] It is the ideal of freedom as non-domination. It transcends the conceptual point that people's well-being or welfare is partly determined through their free choice of options available and holds that freedom of choice in the absence of arbitrary, uncontrolled or discretionary power is a vital constituent element of people's well-being. In the context of migration specifically, the ideal of freedom as non-domination can be used to clearly identify and highlight the intensity and extent of domination in the lives of migrants. As Iseult Honohan puts it,

> The intensity of domination ... will depend on the degree of arbitrariness; the ease of exclusion; and the severity of the measures excluding foreigners ... The arbitrariness of migration controls appears in the way in which the exact requirements for migration are liable to change according to the will of the admitting state ...
>
> The extent of domination will depend, first, on the range of areas of their lives affected, and the degree to which their options are limited for those who are excluded. On this basis, evidence suggests that the extent of domination by migration controls is significant.[63]

I am here concerned with only one aspect of migrants' vulnerability to domination: namely, their entitlement to have their qualifications recognised. It is

61 Case C-158/06 *ROM-projecten* [2007] ECR I-5103 [25].

62 See, *e.g.*, Iseult Honohan and Marit Hovdal-Moan (eds), *Domination, Migration and Non-Citizens* (Routledge 2015).

63 Iseult Honohan, 'Domination and migration: an alternative approach to the legitimacy of migration controls' in Iseult Honohan and Marit Hovdal-Moan (eds), *Domination, Migration and Non-Citizens* (Routledge 2015) 40.

now clear that migrants have very different rights in respect thereof depending on their migration status. Yet, little to no reasoning is provided by the EU in its laws as to why this is the case. To drill down into the criteria identified by Honohan, then, let us dwell on the intensity and extent of domination caused by this uncertainty. As to the intensity of domination, this is clearly evident in the case of voluntary migrants, persons seeking temporary protection, asylum seekers and victims of human trafficking. Their right to have their qualifications recognised is not clearly guaranteed and, in the case of victims of human trafficking, is likely not guaranteed at all. This is a major source of anxiety for such migrants and leaves them particularly vulnerable to the exercise of arbitrary, uncontrolled or discretionary power by relevant member state actors. If their rights are not clearly identified, then they may not be fulfilled; and if they are not guaranteed at all, then their well-being will be negatively affected. As to the extent of domination, this is also significant given that what we are concerned with here is the ability to access the labour market. Failing to consider qualifications because of the uncertainty surrounding third-country nationals' actual entitlement thereto constitutes a significant obstacle to labour market access – something which we know, empirically-speaking, is the case. This is due to a lack of clear rules and procedures and, consequently, a form of arbitrary, uncontrolled or discretionary power – in other words, domination. But how can such domination be reduced or eliminated? The simple answer is to reduce arbitrariness, an absence of controls and discretionary powers. One way in which this can be achieved is simply by clearly stating the rights and entitlements of third-country nationals coming to the EU. Notice that the ideal of freedom as non-domination does not demand that all migrants be afforded the same rights. However, it does require, at a minimum, clarity and fairness in the rights and entitlements afforded to migrants. By clearly stating the reasons for differential treatment as well as the actual differences in treatment, the domination migrants habitually experience would be significantly reduced.

There is a further and separate point worth noting. As suggested in Chapters 1 and 2, in at least some circumstances, discriminating between migrants and EU member state nationals in respect of certain of their legal rights may constitute unlawful discrimination on the ground of nationality under European human rights law. It was also suggested that, in at least some circumstances, discriminating between different categories of migrant in respect certain of their legal rights may constitute unlawful discrimination on the ground of immigration status under European human rights law. By affording migrants different rights, there is at least a risk that such discriminatory treatment, which is inherent in EU migration and asylum law as it stands, is unlawful and cannot be justified. The viability of these arguments, as a matter of principle only, is now explored in respect of each category of migrant noted earlier.

2.3.2 Regular Migrants

It is arguable that regular migrants should be entitled to equal treatment with member state nationals in respect of at least some measures ensuring justice at work, such as the right to have their professional qualifications recognised, labour market integration measures, education and training and so forth. This argument could be developed by interpreting the express guarantees of equal treatment in the EU's regular migration acquis creatively or expansively. It could be suggested, for example, that although some parts of the EU's regular migration acquis are expressly silent on these issues, nonetheless they constitute implicit or implied requirements of the express guarantee of equal treatment, so as to give practical and meaningful effect thereto.

However, a number of potential objections to this position arise. First, while it may be conceded that migrants are generally entitled to equal treatment with member state nationals, that does not mean that no discrimination between third-country nationals and member state nationals and amongst the different categories of third-country nationals is permitted. Indeed, as noted in Chapter 2, discrimination on the ground of nationality and immigration is justifiable. One obvious source of permitted discrimination, it could be argued, is to ensure that migrants do not benefit from certain public goods, such as social welfare or assistance, on equal terms with member state nationals. It is one thing for some migrants to so benefit from welfare measures after they have lived and worked in the jurisdiction for some time; it is quite another for migrants to be immediately afforded access to such welfare schemes.[64] Moreover, as is well known, EU member state nationals migrating within the EU are themselves restricted in access to social welfare schemes, with such restrictions being reduced, until removed completely, over time. This is a powerful objection, but there are at least three ways of responding to this objection.

The first is to argue, like political philosophers Joseph Carens and David Miller, that migrants should, nevertheless, have their human rights guaranteed. Accordingly, given the fundamental nature of the rights to work and equal treatment and the right to have one's qualifications recognised as a derivative right of the right to work in international and European law, as outlined in the previous section, it may be arguable that effective protection of

64 See Joseph Carens, *The Ethics of Immigration* (OUP 2013) chs 5–7; and David Miller, *Strangers in Our Midst: The Political Philosophy of Immigration* (HUP 2016) chs 5–7.

those rights for third-country nationals requires additional measures to secure their human rights similar to those granted to EU citizens as a matter of justice. Recall, for example, that, as a matter of international labour law migrants should have opportunities to have their qualifications recognised on objective, non-discriminatory grounds and that 'special measures' should be taken to provide for the recognition of qualifications of migrant nationals. Such special measures may consist of novel recognition procedures, targeted integration measures or reducing or eliminating the costs associated with the recognition process. The provision of targeted education and training and upskilling or reskilling measures is also a possibility. The problem with this response, however, is that the EU and its member states are not bound by many of the instruments discussed in the previous section. Moreover, many of the instruments there discussed are sufficiently vague so as to provide the EU and its member states with a significant degree of discretion in their implementation to justify the status quo as satisfying the requirements thereof. The fact that the right to have one's qualifications recognised has not attracted a great degree of juridical attention in international and European law to date means that the law in this area is somewhat underdeveloped. Without wishing to set up a straw man, it is probably fair to say that a significant degree creative legal interpretation would be needed to justify the imposition of such measures on the basis of international and European law alone.

The second response to the objection is theoretical. Partially conceding the point, it accepts that some distinctions between migrants and EU citizens are necessary and appropriate. But the existence of unequal residence statuses and the correlate differences in rights highlights a tension between the need to treat migrants equally, on the one hand, and the need to establish exclusive, exclusionary categories of citizenship, on the other hand. And the way to resolve this tension at the level of principle is to appeal to some higher political theory. Many contemporary political theories do not logically entail a commitment to full equality of treatment between non-citizens and citizens in all respects. Specifically, most contemporary political theories only require partial or specific equality of treatment. In this context, partial equal treatment with member state nationals in access to labour rights and integration measures may require that migrants should be given access to some, but not all, measures which are provided to member state nationals. Such partial equality of treatment can be tiered so that migrants living and working temporarily in the EU have less rights than those permanently resident non-citizens. Overtime, migrants should then be able to acquire more rights, ultimately approximating with citizens, given the increasing contribution they make to shared social schemes, such as general taxation.[65] One problem with this approach, however, is that it is largely consistent with the status quo and is, once again, sufficiently vague to provide the EU and its member states with a significant degree of discretion in affording third-country nationals additional resources. Consistently with affording third-country nationals' equal treatment with member state nationals in general, it gives the EU great discretion to discriminate against third-country nationals in specific circumstances. So, is there any alternative response available to the objections made earlier?

The third response and approach here favoured recognises that one could consider the equal treatment of migrants with respect to such measures as a matter of policy.[66] Accordingly, if it could be empirically demonstrated that migrants were less likely to be affected by inadequate qualification recognition by immediately affording them equal treatment with member state nationals in access to qualification recognition procedures and other measures, then there would be a strong policy case in favour of affording third-country nationals equal treatment with member state nationals in respect of such measures immediately. To make the point more concrete, one can provide at least two relevant examples. If it could be demonstrated that, by affording migrants equal treatment with member state nationals in respect of qualification recognition procedures in scenarios (a) and (b), they were less likely to be affected by inadequate skills' recognition, then there would be a compelling policy case in favour of such a change. Similarly, if it could be demonstrated that by affording migrants equal treatment with member state nationals in respect of other measures, such as integration measures and opportunities for education and training, they were less likely to experience inadequate skills' recognition, then there would be a compelling policy case in favour of such a change.

However, even accepting this response to the objection, the question which naturally arises is, what precise measures are actually necessary? Based on the empirical evidence presented in the introduction to this book, it seems that migrants should generally be provided with equal treatment in access to qualification recognition measures either before entering or on arrival in the EU: this simply means that they should be entitled to have their qualifications assessed in the same manner as member state nationals. In other words, migrants should be entitled to strict procedural equality in respect of the recognition of their qualifications when moving to the EU. National procedures must not

65 Marit Hovdal-Moan, 'Unequal residence statuses and the ideal of non-domination' in Iseult Honohan and Marit Hovdal-Moan (eds), *Domination, Migration and Non-Citizens* (Routledge 2015).

66 *Strangers in Our Midst* (n 64) 124–125.

assume that the qualifications of third-country nationals are of a lesser quality than member state nationals' qualifications; rigorous procedural equality must be provided. That is not to say that member state authorities must recognise the qualifications of third-country nationals as at least equivalent to the qualifications of member state nationals, but it does suggest that non-recognition on arbitrary grounds should not be permitted. By contrast, as suggested in Chapter 2, while differentiating between people on the ground of their skills is not problematic, it may become so when it indirectly discriminates on some protected ground, such as nationality. It seems plausible to assume that third-country nationals are being indirectly discriminated against on the ground of their nationality insofar as they are not able to participate in the Single Market in a manner commensurate with their qualifications. To put the point another way, by systematically treating third-country nationals as inadequately skilled for the purposes of their participation in the labour market, the EU and/or its member states discriminates indirectly on the ground of nationality.

The matter thus becomes a policy question of what redistributive remedy is most likely to alleviate such indirect or structural domination which migrants habitually experience. Given that the question is essentially a policy one, only some highly general and somewhat speculative reflections can be provided here as to the nature and extent of such policies. First, the availability of targeted integration measures designed to ensure that migrants have an opportunity to participate in the labour market will be vital. These could include mandatory language training, which may be a condition to their entitlement to practise their profession. No such measures are made available in the EU's labour migration acquis, although the EU does have an independent competence to develop such measures. These measures are addressed in Chapter 5. Such integration measures may be similar to those currently required for voluntary migrants and long-term residents. Second, the availability of education and training to upskill and reskill is also likely to be vital for migrants whose qualifications are inadequate to meet market demands in the EU. At present, most labour migrants are entitled to equal treatment with member state nationals in respect of access to education and training,[67] but member states are nonetheless empowered to restrict third-country nationals' access to study and maintenance grants and loans.[68]

67 Single Permit Directive, art 12(1)(c); Blue Card Directive, art 16(1)(c); Seasonal Workers' Directive, art 23(1)(g); and Researchers', Students', Volunteers' and Au Pairs' Directive, art 22.

68 Single Permit Directive, art 12(2)(a); Blue Card Directive, art 14(2); Seasonal Workers' Directive, art 23(2)(ii); and Researchers', Students', Volunteers' and Au Pairs' Directive, art 22.

Such policy arguments for affording certain rights and entitlements to migrants could feed into and justify the argument that the specific discriminatory treatment (on the basis of either nationality or immigration status) of regular migrants relative to EU member state nationals in respect of these measures is unjustifiable. For example, such data could be used to indicate that the EU and its member states' discriminatory immigration regimes do not have a legitimate or accurate empirical foundation and that the discrimination therein is consequently arbitrary, irrational or unreasonable. However, the other arguments noted above that are derived from political theory – those based on guaranteeing migrants' human rights and the legitimacy of drawing distinctions between different categories of migrant – may tilt in favour of maintaining the status quo by virtue of their vague meaning and political rhetorical power and consequently justify the discriminatory treatment which is extant in EU migration and asylum law. This book does not come down on a concrete position in this respect but does aim to clearly articulate the basis for any potential arguments for reform.

2.3.3 Forced Migrants

2.3.3.1 *Persons Seeking Temporary Protection*

As noted earlier, there is no clear articulation in the text of the Temporary Protection Directive of the reasons justifying the difference in treatment between persons seeking temporary protection, other categories of forced migrant or other categories of migrant in general. This uncertainty is a potential source of domination for persons seeking temporary protection and may also be a basis for making a claim of unjustifiable discrimination on the basis of immigration status. If there are ostensibly no reasons justifying such discrimination, then how can same be justified at all, particularly given the vulnerability of all categories of forced migrants? It could be objected that no such measures should be provided for forced migrants at all because they are not owed any obligations of justice. Rather, they are merely owed humanitarian obligations of rescue.[69] While it is conceded that forced migrants are indeed not owed any duties of justice and are instead owed humanitarian duties,

69 *The Ethics of Immigration* (n 64) ch 10; *Strangers in Our Midst* (n 64) ch 5; and Michael Gibney, 'The ethics of refugees' (2018) 13 Philosophy Compass 1. Various theorists alternate between describing such obligations as being 'humanitarian' or 'human rights' obligations. For example, David Miller, *National Responsibility and Global Justice* (OUP 2007) ch 7 and David Miller, *Justice for Earthlings: Essays in Political Philosophy* (CUP 2013) ch 7 suggests that states have obligations of global justice which consist of their human rights obligations.

that does not mean that the content of these duties is different. In the case of forced migrants, while the ground of the duty to act is different, the content of the duty is the same, if not even greater. In other words, a political community's humanitarian duties to forced migrants are the same or even greater than its general obligations of justice to its own citizens. The question of whether persons seeking temporary protection should benefit from such preferential treatment is a vexed one.

While persons seeking temporary protection are not the paradigm case of forced migrant, nonetheless there is likely a strong policy case in favour of granting them the sorts of rights available to refugees and persons eligible for subsidiary protection status outlined above. This is particularly evident in the aftermath of the Russian invasion of Ukraine in 2022 and the consequent mass influx of persons from Ukraine to the EU. This was the first occasion on which the Temporary Protection Directive was activated and ultimately resulted in the European Commission adopting a recommendation on the recognition of professional qualifications of such persons.[70] While that measure will be explored in detail in Chapter 5 of this book, it merits noting at this stage that, obviously, it is not binding. Such persons currently benefitting from temporary protection in the EU cannot therefore rely on the Commission's recommendation as a source of rights. However, the very fact that such a policy measure was introduced in the first place suggests that there were problems with the operation of the Temporary Protection Directive. If that inference is accurate, then it follows that the policy case in favour of the provision of targeted qualification recognition procedures, integration measures and even education and training facilities to persons seeking temporary protection may be sufficiently strong and relevant to merit reconsidering or revising at least certain parts of the Temporary Protection Directive itself. Such a policy case for affording such rights and entitlements to this category of forced migrants could feed into and justify the argument that the specific discriminatory treatment of persons seeking temporary protection relative to other categories of forced migrants, migrants and EU member state nationals in respect of these measures on the basis of immigration status and nationality respectively is unjustifiable. By contrast, the other more abstract arguments noted above – based on migrants' human rights and the legitimacy of drawing distinctions between different categories of migrant – may tilt in favour of maintaining the status quo and

70 Commission Recommendation (EU) 2022/554 on the recognition of qualifications for people fleeing Russia's invasion of Ukraine [2022] OJ L107I/1.

consequently justifying the discriminatory treatment which is extant in EU migration and asylum law.

2.3.3.2 *Asylum Seekers*

This book does not question the legitimacy of states' entitlement to restrict migrants' access to the labour market tout court. However, if it could be established empirically that asylum seekers were less likely to face discrimination and inadequate skills recognition if they were immediately afforded access to the labour market, certain skills' utilisation measures and opportunities on the same basis as member state nationals or other categories of forced migrant, then there would be a strong policy case in favour of affording them immediate access thereto. By contrast, the other more abstract arguments noted earlier – based on migrants' human rights and the legitimacy of drawing distinctions between different categories of migrant – may tilt in favour of maintaining the status quo and consequently justifying the discriminatory treatment which is extant in EU migration and asylum law.

2.3.3.3 *Refugees and Persons Eligible for Subsidiary Protection Status*

Refugees and beneficiaries of subsidiary protection are offered what might be considered the 'gold standard' in terms of measures designed to facilitate the use, development and recognition of their skills. They are guaranteed equality of treatment in respect of access to and participation in the labour market, procedures for the recognition of their skills – even in the context of loss of documentary evidence of qualifications – and are to be given access to integration programmes designed to facilitate their needs. Importantly, they are also given opportunities to train and upskill on equal terms with member state nationals. These measures are provided to refugees and beneficiaries of subsidiary protection on the basis that they are the paradigm case of forced migrant. Indeed, some of these measures may not even be provided to EU member state nationals, such as facilitating the recognition of professional qualifications where no documentary evidence is provided. The reason justifying these measures is therefore somewhat distinct and exceptional.

2.3.4 Irregular Migrants

This book does not challenge political communities' rights to restrict or regulate migration in general and the consequent restriction of rights afforded to such persons. However, there would seem to be at least some reasons to afford victims of human trafficking the same or equivalent sorts of measures provided to forced migrants, such as providing targeted integration measures or special exemptions from the requirement to provide documentary evidence of their qualifications. By contrast, the other more abstract arguments noted earlier – based on migrants' human rights and the legitimacy of drawing distinctions between different categories of migrant – may tilt in favour of maintaining the status quo and consequently justifying the discriminatory treatment which is extant in EU migration and asylum law.

3 EU External Relations Law

3.1 *Overview*

Part Five, Title V TFEU governs the EU's external relations. According to art 205 TFEU, Part Five, Title V TFEU is guided by the principles established in Title V, Chapter 1 TEU, the fundamentals of which are

> democracy, the rule of law, the universality and indivisibility of human rights and fundamental freedoms, respect for human dignity, the principles of equality and solidarity, and respect for the principles of the United Nations Charter and international law.[71]

Accordingly, the EU should respect, protect and promote those principles in its external relations. As was demonstrated in Chapter 2, however, the EU's member states are in breach of their international and European human rights and labour law obligations insofar as nationality discrimination is not generally prohibited under EU law. To improve coherence in the EU's external relations, therefore, this breach should be remedied as there suggested. According to art 3(2) TFEU, the EU is competent to complete international agreements when it is necessary to do so for the purposes of the functioning of the EU's internal competences, e.g., the effective operation of the Single Market and the implementation of a common commercial policy, or on the basis of a legislative act. This competence is essentially repeated in art 216 TFEU. In this vein, the Union shall develop close relations with its neighbours in an effort to foster its values.[72] This section accordingly considers the extent to which qualification recognition and equal treatment with member state nationals is provided

71 TEU, art 21(1). See generally Piet Eeckhout, *EU External Relations Law* (2nd edn, OUP 2011); Bart van Vooren and Ramses Wessel (eds), *EU External Relations Law: Text, Cases and Materials* (CUP 2014); and Pieter Jan Kuijper, Jan Wouters, Frank Hoffmeister, Geert de Baere and Thomas Ramopoulos (eds), *The Law of EU External Relations: Cases, Materials and Commentary on the EU as an International Legal Actor* (2nd edn, OUP 2015).

72 TEU, art 8.

for in EU external relations law through an analysis of the EU's partnership, association and trade agreements with third-countries. It also considers the link between education and training and the effective recognition of migrants' professional qualifications.

3.2 *Partnership, Association and Trade Agreements*[73]

3.2.1 Overview

In its Communication, *Trade for All: Towards a more responsible trade and investment policy*, the Commission noted the need to improve synergies between EU trade and migration policies, referring in particular to the *European Agenda on Migration* previously discussed in the introductory chapter to this text. Specifically, the Commission concluded that it would promote the recognition of qualifications in trade agreements negotiated with third-countries so as to reduce market access costs for service providers and improve external migration flows.[74] In this sub-section, the EU's current association and trade agreements are considered to assess what the current role of qualification recognition and equal treatment is in the EU's external relations. It is significant that, in these agreements, discrimination on the basis of nationality is often prohibited and equal treatment with EU nationals is therefore guaranteed. However, it is important to bear in mind that if third-country nationals do not have a right of entry to or residence in the EU, then a right to equal treatment or the recognition of qualifications will be of little, if any, value.[75]

3.2.2 (Almost) Full Mutual Recognition: EEA States and Switzerland

Part III of the EEA Agreement guarantees the free movement of persons, services and capital between the EU and EEA states.[76] Article 30 of the Agreement

---

73 See Elspeth Guild, *The Legal Elements of European Identity: EU Citizenship and Migration Law* (Kluwer Law International 2004); Christopher Hillion and Panos Koutrakos (eds), *Mixed Agreements Revisited: The EU and its Member States in the World* (Hart 2010); Katharina Eisele, *The External Dimensions of the EU's Migration Policy: Different Legal Positions of Third-Country Nationals in the EU: A Comparative Perspective* (Brill Nijhoff 2014); Daniel Thym and Margarite Zoeteweij-Turhan (eds), *Rights of Third-Country Nationals under EU Association Agreements: Degrees of Free Movement and Citizenship* (Brill Nijhoff 2015); and Steve Peers, *EU Justice and Home Affairs Law Volume I: EU Immigration and Asylum Law* (4th edn, OUP 2016).

74 Commission, 'Trade for All: Towards a more responsible trade and investment policy' (Communication) COM(2015) 497 final, 7–8, 11.

75 *The Legal Elements of European Identity* (n 73) 153–159; and *The External Dimensions of the EU's Migration Policy* (n 73) 338.

76 Agreement on the European Economic Area between the European Communities, their Member states and the Republic of Austria, the Republic of Finland, the Republic

provides that the contracting parties thereto shall ensure, in accordance with measures contained in an annex to the Agreement, the mutual recognition of qualifications of workers and self-employed persons moving between jurisdictions. The relevant annex has been updated to incorporate the Recognition Directive[77] (the major subject of Chapter 4 of this book) but no measure incorporating the Administrative Cooperation Directive[78] has yet been adopted. Thus, the terms of the un-amended Recognition Directive apply to EEA nationals. Their qualifications are recognised in roughly the same way as those of EU nationals.

The EC-Swiss Confederation Free Movement of Persons Agreement similarly guarantees the free movement of persons, services and capital between the EU and Switzerland.[79] Specifically, Part 1 guarantees the right to equal treatment with nationals in respect of access to, and the pursuit of, an economic activity, and living, employment and working conditions[80] and imposes an obligation on the contracting parties to take all necessary measures to ensure the mutual recognition of qualifications.[81] Annex III to the Agreement, which has been amended on numerous occasions,[82] applies the Recognition Directive to Switzerland but the Administrative Cooperation Directive has not yet been applied. Swiss nationals are therefore in the same position as EEA nationals in respect of their skills and qualifications.

The fact that these agreements facilitate the free movement of persons and the mutual recognition of qualifications suggests a relatively high level of (economic) integration between the EU and these states. It suggests that there are

---

of Iceland, the Principality of Liechtenstein, the Kingdom of Norway, the Kingdom of Sweden and the Swiss Confederation [1994] OJ L1/3.

77 Parliament and Council Directive 2005/36/EC on the recognition of professional qualifications [2005] OJ L 255/22; EEA Joint Committee, 'Annual Report of the Joint Committee 2007: Functioning of the EEA Agreement' (22 February 2008) para 47.

78 Parliament and Council Directive 2013/55/EU amending Directive 2005/36/EC on the recognition of professional qualifications and Regulation (EU) No 1024/2012 on administrative cooperation through the Internal Market Information System [2013] OJ L 354/132.

79 Agreement between the European Community and its Member states, of the one part, and the Swiss Confederation, of the other, on the free movement of persons [2002] OJ L114/6.

80 EC-Swiss Confederation Free Movement of Persons Agreement, arts 7(a) and 9.

81 ibid art 9.

82 Decision No 2/2011 of the EU-Swiss Joint Committee established by Article 14 of the Agreement between the European Community and its Member states, of the one part, and the Swiss Confederation, of the other, on the free movement of persons of 30 September 2011 replacing Annex III (Mutual recognition of professional qualifications) thereto [2011] OJ L277/20.

increasing ties of cooperation, coordination and possibly even shared identity. And while the relationship between the EU and these states may not give rise to obligations of justice, it is plausible to think that one mutual obligation of the parties would be to facilitate the effective guarantee of the right to work for members of all states parties. In other words, one might expect that some additional measures would be made available to migrants coming from these states to the EU to appropriately instantiate their right to work. Of some relevance in this respect is the prohibition of discrimination on the ground of nationality and the obligation to coordinate their respective social security systems found in both the EEA Agreement[83] and the EC-Swiss Confederation Free Movement of Persons Agreement.[84] A general guarantee of equal treatment implies that EEA and Swiss nationals should be equally entitled to access education and training opportunities with member state nationals. EEA and Swiss nationals are therefore accorded treatment identical to member state nationals moving within the EU. While both the EEA Agreement and the EC-Swiss Confederation Free Movement of Persons Agreement abolish any discrimination on the grounds of nationality and provide for qualification recognition, no targeted integration measures are evident from the text of the documents. The agreements might be considered deficient in this respect.

There are two potential remedial responses to this situation. The first response is interpretive: if the guarantee of equal treatment contained in the respective agreements could be interpreted broadly enough to enable EEA and Swiss nationals to benefit from additional measures necessary to instantiate their right to work, such as integration measures and education and training opportunities, then these agreements may be sufficient as they stand. The second is to consider these measures as a matter of policy. If it could be established as a matter of policy that, as a result of additional measures, migrants from the EEA and Switzerland did not suffer discrimination or inadequate skills recognition, then there would be a strong policy case in favour of them. However, such a policy argument may not be compelling in the case of EEA and Swiss nationals because they are already so highly integrated into the EU. It would be necessary to determine the extent to which EEA and Swiss nationals suffer inadequate skills' recognition and discrimination in the EU. This point remains to be verified.

83 EEA Agreement, art 4 and Annex VI.

84 EC-Swiss Confederation Free Movement of Persons Agreement, arts 2 and 8.

3.2.3 CETA and Mutual Recognition Agreements

The Comprehensive Economic and Trade Agreement (CETA) between Canada and the EU provides for the free movement of professionals between the EU and Canada for the purposes of temporary service provision.[85] Service providers are to be afforded national treatment or equal treatment with nationals of the states parties to CETA.[86] Chapter 11 thereof provides for the mutual recognition of qualifications which is designed to facilitate a 'fair, transparent and consistent regime for the mutual recognition of professional qualifications' by the parties and sets out the conditions for the negotiation of mutual recognition agreements (MRAs) between the competent authorities of the parties. Article 11.2.3 provides that the parties will not adopt mutual recognition practises which are either discriminatory or disguised restrictions on trade in services. Furthermore, art 11.4.3 provides that an MRA cannot require recognition to be conditional upon the ability of a service supplier to meet any citizenship or residency requirement, nor the necessity to have completed or obtained education, training or professional qualifications in the party's jurisdiction.

Annex 11-A provides non-binding guidance on the negotiation of MRAs. Of particular interest is the four-step recognition process contained therein. According to this process, the following four steps should be adopted in every MRA to simplify the recognition process: (a) verification of equivalency; (b) evaluation of substantial differences; (c) compensatory measures; and (d) identification of the conditions for recognition. MRAs should also include, inter alia, certain requirements beyond professional qualifications, such as: having an office address, maintaining an establishment or being a resident; language skills; proof of good character; professional indemnity insurance; compliance with the host jurisdiction's requirements for use of trade or firm names; and compliance with the host jurisdiction ethics, for example, independence and good conduct.[87] At present, at least one MRA has been negotiated between the Architects' Council of Europe and its equivalent Canadian body.[88]

CETA is more limited than the EEA Agreement and the EC-Swiss Confederation Free Movement of Persons Agreement. It reflects a more

85 Comprehensive Economic and Trade Agreement (CETA) between Canada, of the one part, and the European Union and its Member states, of the other part [2017] OJ L11/23, ch 9–10.

86 CETA, art 9.3.

87 CETA, Annex 11A(6).

88 ACE, 'ACE signed an agreement with the Canadian Architectural Licensing Authority to facilitate the mobility of Architects between the EU and Canada' (23 April 2018) <https://www.ace-cae.eu/services/news/?tx_ttnews%5BbackPid%5D=1&tx_ttnews%5Btt_news%5D=1684&cHash=c8f538fe489e5af7ed6fd9b40b18ff8b> (accessed 5 December 2019).

fragmented degree of integration between the EU and Canada. For example, the free movement of persons is limited to temporary service providers alone and the guarantee of equal treatment under art 9.3 is afforded to service providers, giving them equal treatment with nationals of the host state. Given this limited degree of economic integration, the sorts of measures one would generally envisage as being necessary to secure the well-being of migrants may not be considered necessary. However, recall from Chapter 1 that there are different types of service providers, some of which may be employed workers. Specifically, intra-corporate transferees are generally employees. These people may benefit from the additional measures envisaged earlier, namely, integration measures, as well as education and training opportunities. Unlike the EEA Agreement and EC-Swiss Confederation Free Movement of Persons Agreement, however, it is probably not possible to interpret such measures into CETA in the absence of an equal treatment guarantee, but the argument from policy remains sound, subject to the caveat that it is necessary to determine the extent to which persons moving to the EU on foot of CETA actually suffer inadequate qualification recognition and wrongful discrimination. If they do not, then no such additional measures may be necessary.

3.2.4 'CETA-Minus' Arrangements

A number of other association and trade agreements provide potential avenues for the recognition of qualifications of certain third-country nationals. Specifically, the following agreements make provision for the (eventual) establishment of mutual recognition agreements: EU-Andean Trade Agreement;[89] EU-Armenia CEPA;[90] Bosnia and Herzegovina Stabilisation and Association Agreement;[91] Economic Partnership Agreement with CARIFORUM states;[92] Central America-EU Association Agreement;[93] EU-Chile Association

89 Trade Agreement between the European Union and its member states, of the one part, and Columbia and Peru, of the other part [2012] OJ L353/3, art 129.

90 Comprehensive and Enhanced Partnership Agreement between the European Union and the European Atomic Energy Community and their Member States, of the one part, and the Republic of Armenia, of the other part [2018] OJ L23/4, art 161.

91 Stabilisation and Association Agreement between the European Communities and their Member states, of the one part, and Bosnia and Herzegovina, of the other part [2015] OJ L164/2, art 55.

92 Economic Partnership Agreement between the CARIFORUM States, of the one part, and the European Community and its Member states, of the other part [2008] OJ L289/1/3, arts 85 and 114.

93 Agreement establishing an Association between Central America, on the one hand, and the European Union and its Member states, on the other [2012] OJ L363/3, art 177.

Agreement;[94] EC-Georgia Association Agreement;[95] EU-Japan Economic Partnership Agreement;[96] Euro-Mediterranean Agreement with Jordan;[97] EU-Korea Free Trade Agreement;[98] EC-Kosovo Stabilisation and Association Agreement;[99] EC-Macedonia Stabilisation and Association Agreement;[100] EC-Moldova Association Agreement;[101] EC-Montenegro Stabilisation and Association Agreement;[102] EU-Singapore Free Trade Agreement;[103] EU-Ukraine Association Agreement;[104] and the EU-Vietnam Free Trade Agreement.[105]

Many of the above-mentioned agreements require national authorities to encourage professional regulatory authorities to enter into discussion with their counterparts in the other contracting party and consider the possibility of mutual recognition. This is, however, a weak obligation. Like CETA, these agreements lack an equal treatment guarantee. However, as previously suggested, if it could be established empirically that workers (of any kind) from

94 Agreement establishing an association between the European Community and its Member states, of the one part, and the Republic of Chile, of the other part [2002] OJ L352/3, art 103.

95 Association Agreement between the European Union and the European Atomic Energy Community and their Member states, of the one part, and Georgia, of the other part [2014] OJ L261/4, art 96.

96 Agreement between the European Union and Japan for an Economic Partnership [2018] OJ L330/3, art 8.35(2).

97 Euro-Mediterranean Agreement establishing an Association between the European Communities and their Member states, of the one part, and the Hashemite Kingdom of Jordan, of the other part [2002] OJ L129/3, art 35.

98 Free Trade Agreement between the European Union and its Member states, of the one part, and the Republic of Korea, of the other part [2011] OJ L127/6, art 7.21.

99 Stabilisation and Association Agreement between the European Union and the European Atomic Energy Community, of the one part, and Kosovo, of the other part [2006] OJ L71/3, art 56.

100 Stabilisation and Association Agreement between the European Communities and their Member States, of the one part, and the former Yugoslav Republic of Macedonia, of the other part [2004] OJ L84/13, art 52.

101 Association Agreement between the European Union and the European Atomic Energy Community and their Member states, of the one part, and the Republic of Moldova, of the other part [2014] OJ L260/4, art 222.

102 Stabilisation and Association Agreement between the European Communities and their Member states, of the one part, and the Republic of Montenegro, of the other part [2010] OJ L108/3, art 57.

103 Free Trade Agreement between the European Union and the Republic of Singapore [2019] OJ L294/3, art 8.16.

104 Association Agreement between the European Union and its Member States, of the one part, and Ukraine, of the other part [2014] OJ L161/3, art 106.

105 Free Trade Agreement between the European Union and the Socialist Republic of Viet Nam [2020] OJ L186/3, art 8.21.

these countries are less likely to be affected by discrimination and inadequate skills recognition by affording them additional opportunities to have their qualifications recognised, integrate into the labour market and upskill or reskill, then there would be a compelling policy argument in favour of affording them equal treatment with member state nationals immediately.

3.2.5 The EU-UK Trade and Cooperation Agreement[106]

Perhaps unsurprisingly, the EU-UK Trade and Cooperation Agreement merits separate attention in this context. The mutual recognition of professional qualifications is not guaranteed at all in the EU-UK TCA; and professional bodies in the respective Parties to the Agreement are not even 'encouraged' to develop mutual recognition agreements. Rather, such bodies are merely permitted to make recommendations to the Partnership Council established by the Agreement. Once they do so, the Partnership Council must ('shall') then review its consistency with the Agreement within a reasonable period of time. After such review, the Council 'may' then, by way of annex to the Agreement, set out the conditions for the mutual recognition of qualifications in a given sector.

However, there is one aspect of the EU-UK TCA which bears some similarity to CETA: that is the provision of an annex to the Agreement (Annex 24) which provides, like the equivalent annex in CETA (Annex 11-A), guidelines on the development of arrangements concerning the mutual recognition of professional qualifications. The guidelines contained in this Annex must be taken into account by the Partnership Council when developing arrangements governing mutual qualification recognition, but they are, nonetheless, non-binding. The guidelines are accordingly characterised by a high degree of flexibility. While they set out the 'typical' contents of a mutual recognition arrangement, it is noted that any such arrangement need not slavishly follow the structure envisaged in the guidelines. Any arrangement may also be limited in nature, merely addressing administrative issues, for example. In terms of the structure of the guidelines contained in the Annex, the scope of any mutual recognition arrangement, conditions for recognition, procedural arrangements, the effect of recognition and administration of any arrangement are all identified as issues which could form the content of a mutual recognition arrangement. Thus, mutual recognition arrangements between the Parties could, amongst other things, specify the professional qualifications necessary for recognition,

106 Trade and Cooperation Agreement between the European Union and the European Atomic Energy Community, of the one part, and the United Kingdom of Great Britain and Northern Ireland, of the other part [2021] OJ L149/10.

the degree of discretion allowed to professional recognition authorities in determining whether to recognise a given qualification as well as the potential use of compensatory measures to permit partial recognition. The Annex goes on to address, in further detail, the two conditions set out in Article 24.C above, namely, the economic value of any mutual recognition arrangement and the compatibility of the Parties' respective qualification regimes. In respect of the economic value of mutual recognition arrangements, the Annex envisages joint recommendations submitted to the Partnership Council analysing relevant aspects of the Parties' economies such as the existing level of market openness, industry needs, and business opportunities. Any such economic analysis need not, however, be comprehensive: a mere identification of business and consumer need will suffice. In respect of the compatibility of the Parties' qualification regimes, the Annex outlines, in relative detail, a three-step process: first, an assessment of the scope of practice and qualifications needed to practise a profession should be conducted; second, an evaluation of the divergence, if any, between these two aspects of the Parties' respective qualification regimes will be necessary; and third, an analysis of the recognition mechanisms of the respective Parties should be carried out. If, on analysis, it turns out that there is a substantial divergence between the scope of practice and qualifications needed to practise a profession in the respective Parties, then compensatory measures, such as a period of supervised access to the profession in question, a test, a temporary limitation of the scope of practice or any combination of these measures, may be provided for in a mutual recognition arrangement.

Annex 24 is accordingly rich in the guidance it provides to professional authorities in preparing joint recommendations for submission to the Partnership Council. While strictly non-binding, it does expand upon the relatively sparse text of art 158 in a number of areas. Annex 24 does go very far in expanding upon the limited text of art 158, even more so than the equivalent annex of CETA. What effect the Agreement will have on mutual recognition is difficult to determine at this point in time.

The EU-UK TCA is more limited than the EEA Agreement and the EC-Swiss Confederation Free Movement of Persons Agreement. It reflects a more fragmented degree of integration between the EU and the UK. For example, the guarantee of equal treatment under art 137 is afforded to service providers, giving them equal treatment with nationals of the host state. Given this limited degree of economic integration, the sorts of measures one would generally envisage as being necessary to secure the well-being of migrants may not be considered necessary. However, recall from Chapter 1 that there are different types of service providers, some of which may be employed workers. Specifically, intra-corporate transferees are generally employees. These people may benefit from the additional measures envisaged earlier, namely, integration measures, as well as education and training opportunities. Unlike the EEA Agreement and EC-Swiss Confederation Free Movement of Persons Agreement, however, it is probably not possible to interpret such measures into the EU-UK TCA in the absence of an equal treatment guarantee, but the argument from policy remains sound, subject to the caveat that it is necessary to determine the extent to which persons moving to the EU on foot of EU-UK TCA actually suffer inadequate qualification recognition and wrongful discrimination. If they do not, then no such additional measures may be necessary.

3.2.6 Equal Treatment and National Treatment

Another potential avenue facilitating access to qualification recognition, integration measures and education and training opportunities may be the guarantee of equality and non-discrimination made in many such agreements. This possibility was first raised in *Razanatsimba*, in which the applicant, a Madagascan national, sought admission to the Lille Bar having met all other qualification requirements except that of nationality.[107] The applicant relied on art 62 of the EEC-African Caribbean and Pacific (ACP) States Convention (now art 13, annex II of the Cotonou Agreement),[108] which provided that the respective parties to the Convention must treat nationals and firms on a non-discriminatory basis in matters of establishment and the provision of services. According to the European Court of Justice, art 62 did not require of member states or ACP states to treat nationals of the other group equally. Rather, 'the wording of the article does not purport to provide equality of treatment between nationals of an ACP state and those of a Member State of the EEC'.[109] In particular, 'that articles does not oblige either the ACP States or the Member States of the EEC to give to the nationals of a State belonging to the other group treatment identical to that reserved to their own nationals'.[110] Instead, 'that wording refers to the two groups of States bound by the Lomé Convention, the ACP States and the Member States of the EEC, and provides that any State belonging to one of the two groups shall treat nationals of any State belonging to the other group on a non-discriminatory basis'.[111] The Court went on to

107 Case 65/77 *Razanatsimba* [1977] ECR 2229.

108 Partnership Agreement between the Members of the African, Caribbean and Pacific Group of States of the one part, and the European Community and its Member States of the other part [2013] OJ L173/1.

109 [1977] ECR 2229 [13].

110 [1977] ECR 2229 [14].

111 [1977] ECR 2229 [12].

consider whether ACP nationals may be entitled to equality of treatment in respect of particular advantages accorded by member states to nationals of ACP states and concluded that it was acceptable for member states to provide preferential treatment to nationals of certain ACP states which did not benefit nationals of all ACP states equally.

Compare the result in *Razantsimba*, however, with the more recent decision in *Simutenkov*, in which the applicant, a Russian national and football player resident and working in Spain, was required to hold a 'non-Community' football licence.[112] The applicant applied for a Community licence but was refused. Relying on the equal treatment guarantee in the EC-Russia Partnership and Cooperation Agreement,[113] the applicant challenged this decision. According to the European Court of Justice, the equal treatment guarantee contained therein was directly effective. The rule concerning the non-Community licence was consequently found to be invalid. However, in *Pavlov*, the Court held that equal treatment in working conditions does not include access to a profession itself.[114] In that case, the applicant, a Bulgarian national, completed his legal studies in Vienna and then worked as an employee in a lawyer's office in Vienna. The applicant held a residence permit and establishment permit in Austria authorising him to work therein. The applicant applied to be included on the list of trainee lawyers and to be issued with a certificate of entitlement to appear in court as required under Austrian law. However, it was a requirement of Austrian law that person concerned meet a nationality requirement; that is, that they be Austrian, an EU citizen or a citizen of an EEA State or the Swiss Confederation. The applicant, accordingly, failed to meet that criterion. Challenging the decision, the applicant relied on an equal treatment clause in the EC-Bulgaria Association Agreement[115] which provided that workers of Bulgarian nationality resident in the EU must not be discriminated against on the ground of nationality, in particular as regards working conditions. However, that agreement further provided that, inter alia, the parties to the EC-Bulgaria Association Agreement will examine what steps are necessary to provide for the mutual recognition of qualifications.[116] In the light of this provision, the

112 Case C-265/03 *Simutenkov* [2005] ECR I-2579.

113 Agreement on partnership and cooperation establishing a partnership between the European Communities and their Member States, of one part, and the Russian Federation, of the other part [1997] OJ L327/3, art 23.

114 Case C-101/10 *Pavlov* [2011] ECR I-05951.

115 Europe Agreement between the European Communities and their Member States, of the one part, and the Republic of Bulgaria, of the other part [1994] OJ L358/1, art 38.

116 EC-Bulgaria Association Agreement, art 47.

CJEU held that the EC-Bulgaria Association Agreement did not provide for the total abolition of discrimination on the ground of nationality, in particular as it relates to access to regulated professions rather than working conditions. In other words, the conditions for access to a profession did not constitute working conditions but rather fell to be considered separately under the provisions of the Agreement on establishment.

Non-discrimination clauses concerning the treatment of workers are also contained in the: Ankara Agreement;[117] Euro Mediterranean Agreement with Algeria;[118] EC-Azerbaijan Agreement;[119] Bosnia and Herzegovina Stabilisation and Association Agreement;[120] EC-Macedonia Stabilisation and Association Agreement;[121] EC-Montenegro Stabilisation and Association Agreement;[122] Euro-Mediterranean Agreement with Morocco;[123] EC-Serbia Stabilisation and Association Agreement;[124] Euro-Mediterranean Agreement with Tunisia;[125] and EU-Ukraine Association Agreement.[126] These clauses do not, however, apply to the temporary provision of services, although similar provisions affording 'national treatment' to temporary service provision appear in many of these agreements. It is plausible that the equal treatment guarantees in these agreements could be used to apply the same procedure for the recognition of qualifications as applies to nationals of the member states but, in the light of *Pavlov*, equal treatment in working conditions may not include within its scope access to a profession. However, it is possible to partially distinguish

117 Agreement establishing an Association between the European Economic Community and Turkey [1977] OJ L361/1, art 9.

118 Euro-Mediterranean Agreement establishing an Association between the European Community and its Member states, of the one part, and the People's Democratic Republic of Algeria, of the other part [2005] OJ L265/2, art 67.

119 Partnership and Cooperation Agreement between the European Communities and their Member States, of the one part, and the Republic of Azerbaijan, of the other part [1999] OJ L246/3, art 20.

120 Bosnia and Herzegovina Stabilisation and Association Agreement, art 47.

121 EC-Macedonia Stabilisation and Association Agreement, art 44.

122 EC-Montenegro Stabilisation and Association Agreement, art 49.

123 Euro-Mediterranean Agreement establishing an association between the European Communities and their Member states, of the one part, and the Kingdom of Morocco, of the other part [2000] OJ L70/2, art 64.

124 Stabilisation and Association Agreement between the European Communities and their Member states of the one part, and the Republic of Serbia, on the other part [2013] OJ L278/16, art 49.

125 Euro-Mediterranean Agreement establishing an association between the European Communities and their Member states, of the one part, and the Republic of Tunisia, of the other part [1998] OJ L97/2, art 64.

126 EU-Ukraine Association Agreement, art 17.

the judgment in *Pavlov* insofar as it was based on a particular interpretation of the EC-Bulgaria Association Agreement[127] which is unlikely to apply with full rigour to all of the agreements noted above. According to the Court of Justice in that case, '[n]othing in the Association Agreement (...) allows it to be deduced (...) that the contracting parties intended to eliminate all discrimination based on nationality as regards access to regulated professions by Bulgarian nationals'.[128] The Court also noted that the non-discrimination clause in that agreement was contained in the title on workers and no equivalent guarantee was provided in the title concerning establishment and service provision. It will thus only be in the light of a holistic interpretation of an equal treatment guarantee and its place within an association and trade agreement that we can judge with certainty whether or not it will extend to the recognition of qualifications on equal terms with member state nationals. The fact that the equal treatment guarantees found in these agreements are so open to varied interpretations may provide a source of domination for third-country nationals seeking to have their qualifications recognised.

Like the EEA Agreement and the EC-Swiss Confederation Free Movement of Persons Agreement, these agreements contain equal treatment clauses prohibiting discrimination on the grounds of nationality in respect of working conditions. It is therefore plausible that a broad interpretation of the equal treatment guarantees contained therein could be used to afford migrants entering the EU on the basis of these agreements some of the measures identified in the previous section, viz, qualification recognition procedures, integration measures and education and training facilities. However, the uncertainty inherent in such vague guarantees of equal treatment may be a source of domination for such migrants. An argument from policy along the lines of that previously mentioned and subject to the same caveats is also possible.

3.2.7 Education and Training

A close study of the EU's partnership, trade and association agreements reveals another (albeit, more remote) basis for recognising or giving effect to migrants' professional qualifications. It lies in the provisions thereof concerning education and training. My early academic research suggested that effective and efficient labour mobility and access to the labour market is premised on people's qualifications actually being substantively equivalent. In other words, people's qualifications must be the same or similar to some extent. And for

127 Europe Agreement between the European Communities and their Member States, of the one part, and the Republic of Bulgaria, of the other part [1994] OJ L358/1.

128 [2011] ECR I-05951 [27].

qualifications to be the same or similar, education curricula must also be the same or similar. Notice that this transcends the role of qualification recognition in simply facilitating access to the labour market. Rather, it presupposes quite a high degree of cooperation and integration in respect of education as a necessary precursor not merely to access to the labour market but to effective participation therein. Education and training, in other words, prepares people for work.[129]

Extrapolating and generalising this point, institutionalising educational links with third-countries might eventually provide the EU and its member states with fertile sources of human capital sufficient to satisfy the needs of employers and consumers in the Single Market. Indeed, the EU and many of its international partners are obligated to cooperate in relation to education, human resource development and up-skilling. For example, many of the EU's partnership, association and trade agreements include clauses concerning cooperation to improve the living and working conditions of nationals of the EU's trading partners through improvements to their education system and investing in 'human resource development', thereby enabling the development of the skills of those nationals. Specifically, the following agreements contain clauses concerning cooperation, to varying degrees, in respect of education: the EEA Agreement;[130] Euro-Mediterranean Agreement with Algeria;[131] EU-Armenia CEPA;[132] EC-Azerbaijan Agreement;[133] EC-Bangladesh Agreement;[134] Bosnia and Herzegovina Stabilisation and Association Agreement;[135] Economic Partnership Agreement with CARIFORUM states;[136] the Cotonou Agreement;[137] Euro-Mediterranean Agreement with Egypt;[138] EU-Central America Agreement;[139] EC-Georgia Association Agreement;[140]

---

129 See my 'Trade in Services, Migration and Recognition of Professional Qualifications post-Brexit' in Simon Tans and Marc Veenbrink (eds), *Upgrading Trade in Services in EU and International Trade Law* (Wolf 2019).

130 EEA Agreement, arts 1(2)(f) and 78.

131 Euro-Mediterranean Agreement with Algeria, arts 74–78.

132 EU-Armenia CEPA, art 93.

133 EU-Azerbaijan Agreement, arts 44, 53 and 62.

134 EC-Bangladesh Agreement, art 10.

135 Bosnia and Herzegovina Stabilisation and Association Agreement, art 100.

136 Economic Partnership Agreement with CARIFORUM states, art 196(2)(c).

137 Cotonou Agreement, art 25.

138 Euro-Mediterranean Agreement with Egypt, art 42.

139 EU-Central America Agreement, art 42.

140 EC-Georgia Association Agreement, arts 358–359.

EC-Indonesia Agreement;[141] EU-Iraq Partnership and Cooperation Agreement;[142] Euro-Mediterranean Agreement with Israel;[143] EU-Japan Agreement;[144] Euro-Mediterranean Agreement with Jordan;[145] EU-Kazakhstan Partnership and Cooperation Agreement;[146] EC-Kosovo Stabilisation and Association Agreement;[147] Euro-Mediterranean Agreement with Lebanon;[148] EC-Macedonia Stabilisation and Association Agreement;[149] EC-Mexico Economic Partnership, Political Coordination and Cooperation Agreement;[150] EC-Moldova Association Agreement;[151] EC-Montenegro Stabilisation and Association Agreement;[152] Euro-Mediterranean Agreement with Morocco;[153] EU-New Zealand Partnership Agreement;[154] EC-Pakistan Cooperation Agreement;[155] Euro-Mediterranean Interim Association Agreement with the Palestine Liberation Organisation;[156] EC-Russia Partnership and Cooperation

141 Framework Agreement on comprehensive partnership and cooperation between the European Community and its Member States, of the one part, and the Republic of Indonesia, of the other part [2014] OJ L125/17, art 25.

142 Partnership and Cooperation Agreement between the European Union and its Member States, of the one part, and the Republic of Iraq, of the other part [2012] OJ L204/20, arts 82–84.

143 Euro-Mediterranean Agreement establishing an association between the European Communities and their Member States, of the one part, and the State of Israel, of the other part [2000] OJ L147/3, art 59.

144 Agreement between the European Union and Japan for an Economic Partnership [2018] OJ L330/3, art 16(1).

145 Euro-Mediterranean Agreement with Jordan, art 63.

146 EU-Kazakhstan Partnership and Cooperation Agreement, art 244.

147 EC-Kosovo Stabilisation and Association Agreement, art 107.

148 Euro-Mediterranean Agreement establishing an Association between the European Community and its Member States, of the one part, and the Republic of Lebanon, of the other part [2006] OJ L143/2, art 43.

149 EC-Macedonia Stabilisation and Association Agreement, art 91.

150 Economic Partnership, Political Coordination and Cooperation Agreement between the European Community and its Member States, of the one part, and the United Mexican States, of the other part [2006] OJ L276/45, art 30.

151 EC-Moldova Association Agreement, arts 122–123.

152 Stabilisation and Association Agreement between the European Communities and their Member states, of the one part, and the Republic of Montenegro, of the other part [2010] OJ L108/3, art 102.

153 Euro-Mediterranean Agreement with Morocco, art 46.

154 Partnership Agreement on Relations and Cooperation between the European Union and its Member States, of the one part, and New Zealand, of the other part [2016] OJ L321/3, art 40.

155 Cooperation Agreement between the European Community and the Islamic Republic of Pakistan on partnership and development [2004] OJ L378/23, art 4.

156 Euro-Mediterranean Interim Association Agreement on trade and cooperation between the European Community, of the one part, and the Palestine Liberation Organisation

Agreement;[157] Serbia Stabilisation and Association Agreement;[158] EC-South Africa Trade, Development and Cooperation Agreement;[159] Euro-Mediterranean Agreement with Tunisia;[160] and EU-Ukraine Association Agreement.[161]

Of these agreements, several provisions stand out as meriting specific notation. First is that contained in the EU-Armenia CEPA which provides that the parties shall cooperate with a view to approximating the education systems of Armenia to those of the EU. This reflects a very high degree of cooperation and integration between the EU and Armenia in respect of education. Such approximation should, as a matter of principle, facilitate more effective recognition of professional qualifications. Also of interest are the clauses contained in the EC-Indonesia Agreement and the Euro-Mediterranean Agreement with Israel which both contain clauses which identify the role which education and training play in facilitating 'mutual understanding'. Specifically, these agreements oblige the parties to them to 'promote cooperation' in respect of education and training with particular regard to the manner in which education and training can facilitate mutual understanding. While certainly a weak obligation, it would be beneficial if these provisions and those noted in the EU-Armenia CEPA were generalised and institutionalised throughout the EU's external relations so that more effective recognition of professional qualifications was ensured for migrants coming to the EU.

Conclusion

Part 1 of this book laid the legal foundations for migrants' integration in Europe. These constitute the basis for at least one derivative right of the core right to work which Part 2 of this book addresses, namely, the right of migrants to have their professional qualifications recognised for the purposes of accessing work

(PLO) for the benefit of the Palestinian Authority of the West Bank and the Gaza Strip, of the other part [1997] OJ L187/3, art 38.

157 Agreement on partnership and cooperation establishing a partnership between the European Communities and their Member States, of one part, and the Russian Federation, of the other part [1997] OJ L327/3, art 56(3).

158 Serbia Stabilisation and Association Agreement, art 102.

159 Agreement on Trade, Development and Cooperation between the European Community and its Member states, of the one part, and the Republic of South Africa, of the other part [1999] OJ L311/3, art 89.

160 Euro-Mediterranean Agreement with Tunisia, art 46.

161 EU-Ukraine Association Agreement, arts 430–436.

in the EU. Part 2 of this book attempts to provide a remedial response to the inadequate skills' recognition third-country nationals habitually experience in the EU by analysing the extent to which that right is guaranteed in EU law and policy. Reflecting on the extent to which that right has been guaranteed in one dimension – namely, in the context external migration – this chapter has reached the following four sets of conclusions.

First, international and European law provides a very limited lens through which to understand and critique EU law and policy in respect of qualification recognition. The right to have one's qualifications recognised, formal or informal, can be understood as a derivative right of the fundamental human right to work. International labour law envisages the need for 'special measures' to accommodate the recognition of qualifications of non-nationals, while international economic law provides the foundations for the mutual recognition of qualifications between states. In addition, the Council of Europe has acknowledged the needs of refugees to have their qualifications recognised. At present, however, these sources of international and European law are quite vague and indeterminate in terms of the practical requirements states must comply with to implement their terms. This fact renders these provisions much less useful than other areas thereof already considered in Part 1 of this book in relation to the rights to work and to equality and non-discrimination. Moreover, many of the provisions of international and European law considered in Section 1 of this chapter are not currently binding on the EU and its member states.

Second, EU migration and asylum law provides a number of different measures to facilitate the integration of migrants coming to the EU. However, there is no harmonised pre-departure procedure for the recognition of the qualifications of any migrants coming to the EU. On arrival and residence in the EU, migrants are afforded a complex patchwork of rights which vary greatly – according to their status in EU law – from being afforded no right to have their qualifications recognised to having their qualifications recognised in circumstances even where they lack any verifying documentation. It is not always clear why this is the case nor are the actual rights and entitlements of migrants always clear on the face of the relevant legislation. This variation and uncertainty may be a source of domination for some migrants but could be alleviated by a comprehensive clarification and restatement of EU migration and asylum law. Furthermore, the majority of categories of migrants arriving in the EU are not afforded the 'gold standard' of measures designed to facilitate their integration into the labour market, namely, equal treatment in respect of qualification recognition procedures, targeted and mandatory integration measures (such as language training relevant to their profession) and education and training opportunities. It is possible that these measures could be provided on foot of an expansive interpretation of EU migration and asylum law. Alternatively, building on the argument made in Part 1 of this book, it could be argued that this differential treatment constitutes unlawful discrimination, on the basis of either nationality or immigration status, which is without any rational or reasonable basis in data-driven policies and is consequently unjustifiable. On the other hand, it could be argued that the discriminatory treatment is justified on the basis of (vague) international and European obligations set out previously or by virtue of the (vague) political legitimacy of drawing distinctions between different categories of migrant. This chapter has not finally reached a conclusion on this matter but has pointed to certain problems with and attempted to clearly articulate some of the reasons for and against the status quo.

Third, much of the EU's external relations are characterised by partial cooperation and integration with third-countries. This is fine; the EU is not obliged to establish the free movement of persons in its external affairs or to integrate fully with third-countries. But, if it does cooperate – in whole or in part – with such states, then it should at least consider affording migrants some of the rights discussed in Section 2. This is not currently the case for any of the agreements considered. Moreover, some are quite vague in the extent to which they provide for qualification recognition, integration measures and opportunities for education and training. This ambiguity may be a source of domination for third-country nationals seeking to rely on the terms thereof. The same sorts of arguments made in respect of EU migration and asylum law concerning interpretation and policy could be made in respect of the EU's partnership, trade and association agreements, although such policy arguments may be weaker, given that the EU already has close relationships with the states party to these agreements and there may consequently be less discrimination and inadequate qualification recognition. This needs to be verified.

Fourth and finally, my research suggests that institutionalising coordinated education systems between the EU's member states and third-countries could improve the matching of supply and demand, thereby contributing to people's well-being through making it easier for people to exercise their autonomy in and through their work. At present, there are very limited binding legal obligations in place between the EU, its member states and third-countries concerning cooperation in respect of education and training. Overtime, the implementation of these obligations may facilitate more effective recognition of migrants' professional qualifications, insofar as they require the coordination or even approximation of education and training systems. If education and training systems are substantially equivalent, then it stands to reason that the professional qualifications produced thereby will be more easily recognised, so that migration works.

CHAPTER 4

Internal Migration

Introduction

The previous chapter described and critically analysed the circumstances in which migrants coming to the EU might have their professional qualifications recognised. This chapter now aims to describe and analyse the circumstances in which migrants moving within the EU can have their professional qualifications recognised. It transcends the spatial limitations of external migration, being concerned not with recognition procedures within individual EU member states but rather with an aspect of the substantive law of the EU; in other words, EU free movement law. Accordingly, this chapter considers the primary tool for the recognition of qualifications within the Single Market, namely, Parliament and Council Directive 2005/36/EC on the recognition of professional qualifications, as amended (Recognition Directive).[1] The vast majority of regulated professions in the EU are dealt with by the Recognition Directive. A select number of professions are specifically addressed under separate legislation.[2] For present purposes, these are set aside. The analysis below

1 [2005] OJ L255/22. And see the amendments made thereto in Parliament and Council Directive 2013/55/EU on the recognition of professional qualifications and Regulation (EU) No 1024/2012 on administrative cooperation through the Internal Market Information System [2013] OJ L354/132 (Administrative Cooperation Directive).

2 These are statutory auditors, governed by Parliament and Council Directive 2006/43/EC on statutory audits of annual accounts and consolidated accounts [2006] OJ L157/87; seafarers, governed by Parliament and Council Directive 2008/106/EC on the minimum level of training of seafarers (recast) [2008] OJ L323/33; insurance intermediaries, governed by Parliament and Council Directive 2002/92/EC on insurance mediation [2003] OJ L9/3; certain transport operators, under Council Directive 96/26/EC on admission to the occupation of road haulage operator and road passenger transport operator and mutual recognition of diplomas, certificates and other evidence of formal qualifications intended to facilitate for these operators the right to freedom of establishment in national and international transport operations [1996] OJ L124/1; professionals handling toxic products, under Council Directive 74/557/EEC on the attainment of freedom of establishment and freedom to provide services in respect of activities of self-employed persons and of intermediaries engaging in the trade and distribution of toxic products [1974] OJ L307/5 and Council Directive 74/556/EEC laying down detailed provisions concerning transitional measures relating to activities, trade in and distribution of toxic products and activities entailing the professional use of such products including activities of intermediaries [1974] OJ L307/1; lawyers, governed by Council Directive 77/249/EEC to facilitate the effective exercise by lawyers of freedom to provide services [1977] OJ L78/17 (First Lawyers' Directive) and Parliament and Council Directive 98/5/EC to facilitate

 | DOI:10.1163/9789004724068_008

may well have implications for those professions, but they are not directly addressed here.

This is the only chapter of this book devoted entirely to a very specific dimension of EU free movement law. It is concerned with the somewhat obscure and under-explored right to the recognition of professional qualifications, a derivative concern of the fundamental freedoms of movement of workers, services and establishment, as provided for in Part Three, Title IV TFEU. The specific governing provision of EU law in this context is art 53 TFEU, which is the only express textual basis for the regulation of the recognition of professional qualifications in the entirety of EU constitutional law. That provision empowers the EU to issue directives, but not regulations, for the mutual recognition of diplomas, certificates and other formal qualifications so as to make it easier to pursue professions across the EU. A sparse provision, it and its predecessors have nonetheless formed the basis for constructing a detailed, somewhat controversial and exceptionally complex regulatory scheme, now subsumed and consolidated into a single legislative instrument: the Recognition Directive. The mutual recognition of professional qualifications in the Single Market has spawned a great deal of case law before the CJEU, some of which will be discussed here insofar as it is relevant.

This chapter is structured as follows. The first section provides an introduction to the fundamental principle of EU law governing the recognition of professional qualifications within the Single Market: the principle of mutual recognition. This is necessary so that the reader can understand the distinctive approach adopted to the recognition of professional qualifications within the Single Market. While the concept of mutual recognition was mentioned in in passing the previous chapter, it was not explained. Accordingly, the explanation of that principle as it is understood in EU law will serve to clarify the previous chapter and discussion that follows in the present one. Section 2 of this chapter then outlines the conditions for the application of the Recognition Directive, while Section 3 describes how the principle of mutual recognition works, as applied by the Recognition Directive, and reflects upon its implications for the regulation of professions in the EU. Section 4 considers who may benefit from the Recognition Directive. Section 4 focuses specifically on the potential for migrants to benefit from the Recognition Directive. A short conclusion follows summarising the key findings of this chapter.

---

practice of the profession of lawyer on a permanent basis in a Member State other than that in which the qualification was obtained [1998] OJ L77/36 (Second Lawyers' Directive); and commercial agents, governed by Council Directive 86/653/EEC on the coordination of the laws of the Member States relating to self-employed commercial agents [1986] OJ L382/17.

1 The Principle of Mutual Recognition

1.1 *Origins*

Mutual recognition is an important tool in the project of European integration.[3] But what is it? The starting point in understanding mutual recognition is *Cassis de Dijon* in which the European Court of Justice first stated the now infamous principle that if a good is lawfully produced and marketed in one member state, then it should in principle be permitted to circulate in any other member state.[4] The only limitations to this principle evinced at the time were restrictions based on certain 'mandatory requirements' such as 'the effectiveness of fiscal supervision, the protection of public health, the fairness of commercial transactions and the defence of the consumer'.[5] Unfortunately, this bare statement does not greatly enlighten this fundamental principle.

1.2 *The Principle*

The best way to strengthen our view on what mutual recognition is and requires is to clarify our principles. A thought experiment may help to do so. Thus, consider the following scenario. Suppose that two nation states are generally characterised – socially, economically, culturally – by the following starting position relative to each other, and desire to transition to the following end state relative to each other:

Starting State:	(Partial or Total) Diversity
End State:	(Partial or Total) Uniformity[6]

When transitioning from the starting state to the end state, there are at least two approaches we could take. Put briefly, they are (partial or total) competitive

3 Paul Craig, 'The Evolution of the Single Market' in Catherine Barnard and Joanne Scott (eds), *The Law of the Single European Market* (Hart 2002) 7; Susanne Schmidt, 'Mutual Recognition as a New Mode of Governance' (2007) 14 JEPP 667; Kalypso Nicolaïds, 'Trusting the Poles? Constructing Europe through Mutual Recognition' (2007) 14 JEPP 682; Christine Janssens, *The Principle of Mutual Recognition in EU Law* (OUP 2013); and Kalypso Nicolaïdis, 'Mutual Recognition: Promise and Denial, from Sapiens to Brexit' (2017) 70 CLP 227.

4 Case 120/78 *Cassis de Dijon* [1979] ECR 650 [14]; and see Commission, Communication concerning the consequences of the judgment given by the Court of Justice on 20 February 1979 in case 120/78 ('Cassis de Dijon') [1980] OJ C256/2.

5 Kenneth Armstrong, 'Mutual Recognition' in *The Law of the Single European Market* (n 4) and Markus Möstl, 'Preconditions and Limits of Mutual Recognition' (2010) 47 CML Rev 405 agree.

6 Cf 'Mutual Recognition as a New Mode of Governance' (n 3).

federalism and (partial or total) harmonisation. Harmonisation is the more challenging of these two methods because it requires the parties to agree, quite specifically and forthrightly, on the formation of one or several uniform standards. When transitioning from a state of (partial or total) diversity to one of (partial or total) uniformity, harmonisation is an obvious choice, but it is practically difficult to implement. Competitive federalism, by contrast, puts diverse systems of value – social, economic, regulatory – into competition.[7] To say that two or more systems of value are in competition is not to guarantee that uniformity will emerge, but competitive pluralism is at least consistent with the eventual emergence of one or several uniform standards by any given community. The benefits of this approach lie in its subtlety. There need not be an agreement to create uniform standards, but the competition engendered may result in a desire amongst the parties to create uniform standards due to converging standards and values. Competitive federalism is well-captured by mutual recognition as outlined in *Cassis de Dijon*. There is a general agreement or rule that goods must freely circulate, subject to relatively minimal exceptions. Over time, consumer tastes and demands then adjust, and patterns of uniformity emerge in markets for goods, services and labour. It is often suggested, however, that mutual recognition may engender a 'race to the bottom' in regulatory standards, but it is by no means clear that this would occur.[8] Indeed, some research suggests that the very opposite might happen, namely, a 'race to the top'.[9] Ultimately, it will depend on a large variety of factors in the market in question.[10]

---

7 'Mutual Recognition' (n 5) 243–244; Catherine Barnard and Simon Deakin, 'Market Access and Regulatory Competition' in *The Law of the Single European Market* (n 3); Catherine Barnard, *EU Employment Law* (4th edn, OUP 2012) 38; Charles Tiebout, 'A Pure Theory of Local Expenditure' (1956) 64 Journal of Political Economy 416; Akiko Suwa Eisenmann and Thierry Verdier, 'Reciprocity and the Political Economy of Harmonisation and Mutual Recognition of Regulatory Measures' Centre for Economic Policy Research Discussion Paper Series No 3147 (January 2002).

8 See, inter alia, Catherine Barnard, 'Social Dumping and the Race to the Bottom: Some Lessons for the European Union from Delaware?' (2000) 25 EL Rev 57; Hanne Søndergård Birkmose, 'A 'Race to the Bottom' in the EU?' (2006) 13 MJ 35; and Gareth Davies, 'Trust and Mutual Recognition in the Services Directive' in Ioannis Lianos and Okeoghene Odudu (eds), *Regulating Trade in Services in the EU and the WTO: Trust, Distrust and Economic Integration* (CUP 2012).

9 See Susanne Schmidt, 'The Impact of Mutual Recognition: Inbuilt Limits and Domestic Responses to the Single Market' (2002) 9 JEPP 935 and Jacques Pelkmans, 'Mutual Recognition in Goods and Services' in Fiorella Kostoris Padoa Schioppa (ed), *The Principle of Mutual Recognition in the European Integration Process* (Palgrave Macmillan 2005).

10 See Kalypso Nicolaïdis, 'Globalisation with Human Faces: Managed Mutual Recognition and the Free Movement of Professionals' in *The Principle of Mutual Recognition in the*

What, then, does the principle of mutual recognition demand? Competing accounts are available, but Kalypso Nicolaïdis offers perhaps the most intuitive and relevant.[11] According to Nicolaïdis, in a regulatory context mutual recognition is a process which involves mutual comparative assessments of rules, standards and norms, in selected areas, by respective national public institutions and regulatory authorities, according to prior agreement. This comparative analysis involves the acquisition of knowledge and information of foreign regulatory regimes by the respective national institutions and authorities. As a result of this mutual learning, national regulators may adapt their own administrative, regulatory and legislative techniques to make their regulatory systems more attractive. It may also result in the production of harmonised standards between the parties in areas of mutual interest and comparability.[12] Ultimately, the successful operation of this process results in an embedded relationship of mutual trust, confidence and respect between administrators and national authorities across borders for their respective laws, policies and administrative decisions.[13] But this does not entail an absolute acceptance of such laws, policies or decisions. Indeed, as the exceptions to *Cassis de Dijon* suggest, there are limits to mutual recognition. Rather than engage in conflict or ignore the other side, it suggests that if a conflict between regulation arises or differences in regulatory approach emerge, then national administrators and law-makers should instead engage in dialogue over the coherence and sensibility of maintaining potentially self-interested regulations which are likely to negatively affect such a relationship of trust. However, it is not clear

---

European Integration Process (n 9) 169 et seq; and Daniel Esty and Damien Geradin (eds), *Regulatory Competition and Economic Integration: Comparative Perspectives* (OUP 2001).

11 See Kalypso Nicolaïdis and Michelle Egan, 'Transnational Market Governance and Regional Policy Externality: Why Recognise Foreign Standards?' (2001) 8 JEPP 454; Kalypso Nicolaïdis and Gregory Shaffer, 'Transnational Mutual Recognition Regimes: Governance without Global Government' (2004) 68 Law and Contemporary Problems 263; 'Globalisation with Human Faces: Managed Mutual Recognition and the Free Movement of Professionals' (n 10); 'Trusting the Poles? Constructing Europe through Mutual Recognition' (n 3); Kalypso Nicolaïdis and Susanne Schmidt, 'Mutual Recognition 'on Trial': the Long Road to Services Liberalisation' (2007) 14 JEPP 717; and 'Mutual Recognition: Promise and Denial, from Sapiens to Brexit' (n 3).

12 See Wolfgang Kerber and Roger Van den Bergh, 'Mutual Recognition in the Global Trade Regime: Lessons from the EU Experience' in *Regulating Trade in Services in the EU and the WTO: Trust, Distrust and Economic Integration* (n 8).

13 See Case C-330/03 *Colegio de Ingenieros de Caminos, Canales y Puertos* [2006] ECR I-801 [21].

that regulations which are blatantly self-interested and not 'other-regarding' in the Single Market are always withdrawn or reviewed peaceably over dialogue between member state authorities.[14] Nonetheless, Nicolaïdis' account provides a useful lens through which we can understand mutual recognition.

2 The Recognition Directive

2.1 *Operation of the Recognition Directive*

There are three cumulative threshold questions for applying the mutual recognition schemes under the Recognition Directive, each of which shall be addressed in turn.

2.1.1 Does the National of a Member State Concerned Have a Professional Qualification?[15]

According to art 3(1)(b), 'professional qualifications' are qualifications attested by evidence of formal qualifications; an attestation of competence referred to in art 11(a)(i); or professional experience. Evidence of formal qualifications includes 'diplomas, certificates and other evidence' issued by the competent authority of a member state which certifies the successful completion of training, completed primarily in the EU.[16] This automatically excludes the possibility of qualification recognition for many third-country nationals. However, art 3(3) states that evidence of formal qualifications obtained in a third-country shall be regarded as a formal qualification for the purposes of the Recognition Directive if the person in question has three years professional experience in the member state in question. The Recognition Directive therefore charges the national competent authorities with primary responsibility for the recognition of qualifications of third-country nationals.

But what if a qualification obtained outside the EU is recognised in at least one member state; is another member state obliged to recognise it? In *Tawil-Albertini*[17] and *Haim*[18] the Court of Justice held that the national competent

---

14 See the cases discussed in Stephen Weatherill, 'Why there is no Principle of Mutual Recognition in EU Law (and why that matters to consumer lawyers)' in Kai Purnhagen and Peter Rott (eds), *Varieties of European Economic Law and Regulation: Liber Amicorum for Hans Micklitz* (Springer 2014) and Stephen Weatherill, 'The Principle of Mutual Recognition: it Doesn't Work, because it Doesn't Exist' (2018) 43 EL Rev 224.

15 Recognition Directive, arts 2(1), 2(2), 3(1)(b), 3(1)(c), 3(1)(f), 3(3), 11(a)(i).

16 Recognition Directive, art 3(1)(c).

17 Case C-154/93 *Tawil-Albertini* [1994] ECR I-451.

18 Case C-319/92 *Haim* [1994] ECR I-425.

authorities of the host member state are not bound by the prior recognition of other member states. However, in *Hocsman* the Court of Justice narrowed the scope of its previous holding, stating that national competent authorities must nonetheless 'take into consideration all the diplomas, certificates and other evidence of formal qualifications of the person concerned and his relevant experience, by comparing the specialised knowledge and abilities so certified and that experience with the knowledge and qualifications required by the national rules'.[19] This may require the national competent authority of the host member state to verify whether prior recognition of a professional qualification by another member state as equivalent 'was given on the basis of criteria comparable to those whose purpose (...) is to ensure that Member States may rely on the quality of the diplomas (...) awarded by the other Member States'.[20] By analogy, the same reasoning must hold for third-country nationals who obtained a qualification outside the EU, are lawfully working in the territory of a member state in that profession, exercise free movement rights to work in another member state and seek to have that qualification recognised there.

According to art 11(a)(i) of the Recognition Directive, an attestation of competence is proof of qualification, issued by a competent authority of a member state, on the basis of the completion of certain training courses, exams, pursuit of the profession in question for three consecutive years or an equivalent duration on a part-time basis in the past ten years or attesting that the holder has acquired certain general knowledge. Finally, professional experience is full-time, or equivalent part-time, lawful practice of the profession in question. The education, training and experience constituting the professional qualification must have been obtained mainly, but not wholly, in the EU.[21] The same reasoning applied to formal qualifications above should, in principle, apply to professional experience. The potential range of qualifications which might be recognised is therefore quite broad.

Persons seeking to have their qualifications recognised must be fully qualified.[22] In *Morgenbesser*, the applicant had obtained a master's degree in law in Paris and worked in a Parisian law firm for some time, before seeking recognition of her degree for the purposes of working as a *praticante* in Italy.[23]

19 Case C-238/98 *Hocsman* [2000] ECR I-6623 [35].
20 [2000] ECR I-6623 [39].
21 Case C-286/06 *Commission v Spain* [2008] ECR I-8025.
22 Tinne Heremans, *Professional Services in the EU Internal Market* (Hart 2012) 216–217.
23 Case C-313/01 *Morgenbesser* [2003] ECR I-13493.

However, her application for recognition at the Bar of Genoa was rejected as she did not hold a law degree issued or recognised by an Italian university. The applicant then sought to have her master's degree in law recognised as equivalent to an Italian law degree by an Italian university. The university required the applicant to sit thirteen examinations and prepare a thesis during an accelerated course of study. According to the Court, the profession of *praticanti* in Italy did not constitute a regulated profession but rather formed part of the course of training to become an *avocat* in Italy. The fact that many Italian *praticanti* failed to qualify as *avvocati* but nonetheless continued to work as *praticanti* did not mean that it constituted a profession independent of the profession of *avvocati* but rather constituted, by necessary implication, poor regulation. Moreover, as the applicant had failed to obtain the *certificat d'aptitude à la profession d'avocat* necessary to become a *stagiaire* at the French Bar, she did not have the relevant equivalent qualification. However, the authorities of the host state were nonetheless required to undertake a comparative analysis of the qualifications of the applicant for the purposes of admission to the training process in Italy.[24] Thus, while those professionals who are not fully qualified are not guaranteed recognition of equivalence, the competent authorities are nonetheless required to undertake an assessment of their qualifications.

2.1.2 Has That National Moved from One Member State to Another for the Purpose of Pursuing Their Profession?[25]

This question concerns the distinction between the free movement of services, on the one hand, and the freedom of establishment and the free movement of workers, on the other hand. If a national of a member state moves to another member state to provide services on a temporary or occasional basis, then no question of the recognition of professional qualifications arises.[26] In general, member state nationals exercising their right to provide services on a temporary or occasional basis do not need to have their qualifications recognised by the host member state. However, in certain circumstances, the host member state may require the submission of evidence of professional qualifications, such as on the first occasion on which services are to be provided.[27] In addition, if the regulated profession in question in the host member state involves

24 [2003] ECR I-13493 [50]-[59].

25 Recognition Directive, art 2(1); Case C-152/94 *van Buydner* [1995] ECR I-3985; Cases C-225/95, C-226/95 and C-227/95 *Kapasakalis, Skiathitis and Kougiankas* [1998] ECR I-4243; Case C-342/14 *X-Steuerberatungsgesellschaft* [2016] 2 CMLR 39.

26 Recognition Directive, Title II; Case C-39/07 *Commission v Spain* [2008] ECR I-3435 [37].

27 Recognition Directive, art 7(2)(c).

certain public health or safety implications, then the competent authority of the host member state may check the professional qualifications of the service provider insofar as doing so pursues the purpose of avoiding serious damage to the health or safety of service recipients. On the basis of this check, if the host member state concludes that there are substantial differences between the qualifications required of its nationals and the service provider, then the service provider may be required to pass an aptitude test.[28] The administrative cooperation of home and host state authorities is also guaranteed in the case of justified doubts on behalf of the host state authority, where the host state authority requires certain information or documents, concerning the qualifications and integrity of the professional in question.[29]

Professionals exercising their free movement rights for the purposes of providing services must comply with the rules governing the profession of the host member state insofar as they are directly related to professional qualifications. In *Konstantinides*, the CJEU confirmed that rules concerning the calculation of fees and advertising were not directly related to the actual professional practice of medicine and thus the applicant, a Greek medical doctor who provided services in Germany on a temporary and occasional basis, was not required to adhere to those rules.[30] The Court noted that the types of rules which are directly related to a profession include the definition of the profession, the use of titles – a point referred to earlier – and 'serious professional malpractice which is directly and specifically linked to consumer protection and safety'.[31] Rules such as those in *Konstantinides*, which were only indirectly related to a profession, are instead considered as restrictions on the free movement of services under art 56 TFEU.

2.1.3 Is That Profession a Regulated Profession in the Host Member State?[32]

According to art 3(1)(a) of the Recognition Directive, a 'regulated profession' is

> a professional activity or group of professional activities, access to which, the pursuit of which, or one of the modes of pursuit of which is subject, directly or indirectly, by virtue of legislative, regulatory or administrative provisions to the possession of specific professional qualifications; in

28 Recognition Directive, art 7(4).
29 Recognition Directive, art 8.
30 Case C-475/11 *Konstantinides* [2014] 1 CMLR 33.
31 [2014] 1 CMLR 33 [38].
32 Recognition Directive, art 3(1)(a).

> particular, the use of a professional title limited by legislative, regulatory or administrative provisions to holders of a given professional qualification shall constitute a mode of pursuit. Where the first sentence of this definition does not apply, a profession [practised by the members of an association or organisation listed in Annex I to the Directive] shall be treated as a regulated profession.

This concept is an EU law concept and its parameters are to be determined by the CJEU.[33] In *Aranitis*, the question for the Court of Justice was whether the profession of geologist was a regulated profession in Germany where, although there were no administrative provisions, laws or regulations governing the profession, in practice, only persons holding the title 'Diplom-Geologe' – which could only be obtained in Germany – sought employment as a geologist.[34] The Court confirmed that, notwithstanding that German employers would, in practice, only employ persons holding the above title, that profession could not be considered to be directly or indirectly regulated, as there were no laws, regulations or administrative provisions concerning the profession nor was de facto market regulation sufficient to constitute the indirect regulation of a profession. *Aranitis* nonetheless leaves open the possibility of indirectly regulating a profession in some other way.

What does a person do if their profession is not considered a 'regulated profession', as in *Aranitis*? In *Vlassopoulou*, the Court of Justice confirmed that an independent duty to apply the principle of mutual recognition arises directly from art 53 TFEU.[35] Accordingly, on application by a professional, the competent authority must take into account and assess, comparatively, the diplomas, certificates and any other evidence of qualifications of that professional. The purpose of such an assessment is to consider whether, and to what extent, the qualifications of that person are identical, or at least equivalent, to the qualifications so certified by the host state's requirements. The competent national authority is permitted to take into account objective differences between the respective legal frameworks and fields of activity in the professional's home

33 Case C-234/97 *Fernández de Bobadilla* [1999] ECR I-4773; Case C-285/07 *Burbaud* [2003] ECR I-8219; Case C-586/08 *Rubino* [2009] ECR I-12013; Cases C-372 and 373/09 *Peñarroja Fa* [2011] ECR I-1785; Case C-298/14 *Brouillard* [2016] 2 CMLR 7.

34 Case C-164/94 *Aranitis* [1996] ECR I-135. See also Cases C-372 and 373/09 *Peñarroja Fa* [2011] ECR I-1785 concerning court translators.

35 Case C-340/89 *Vlassopoulou* [1991] ECR I-2357; Case C-104/91 *Borrell* [1992] ECR I-3003; Case C-19/92 *Kraus* [1993] ECR I-1663; Case C-319/92 *Haim* [1994] ECR I-425; Case C-164/94 *Aranitis* [1996] ECR I-135; Case C-238/98 *Hocsman* [2000] ECR I-6623; Case C-313/01 *Morgenbesser* [2003] ECR I-13493; Case C-298/14 *Brouillard* [2016] 2 CMLR 7.

member state and the host member state. If the national competent authority concludes that the professional's qualifications are either identical or equivalent to those required by the profession in the host member state, then the authority must recognise them for the purposes of access to and exercise of that profession. However, if the authority concludes that there is only partial correspondence between the qualifications held by the professional and those required by the authorities of the host member state, then the host Member State may require that professional to demonstrate proof of the qualifications which are necessary.[36] According to the Court, an applicant may do so by demonstrating proof of the acquisition of knowledge or practical experience in the host member state, or the acquisition of professional experience in the home member state. National authorities must provide reasoned decisions for the outcome of this process.[37]

2.2 *Mutual Recognition in the Recognition Directive*

2.2.1 The Methods of Recognition

2.2.1.1 *Overview*

The Recognition Directive consolidates and expands upon the methods of recognition previously adopted in the so-called transitional, sectoral and horizontal directives.[38] The Recognition Directive consists of a general recognition scheme[39] and the automatic recognition of professional qualifications on the basis of professional experience, education and so-called 'common training principles'.[40]

2.2.1.2 *General Recognition Scheme*

In respect of the first method, art 10 provides that it is to apply to all those regulated professions which are not covered by the other schemes and to certain exceptional cases which do not fall under those other schemes.[41] This fall-back scheme ensures such persons access to and exercise of their profession in another member state, provided that, if access to and exercise of same is contingent upon possession of a specific professional qualification, then they

36 [1991] ECR I-2357 [15]-[19].

37 [1991] ECR I-2357 [20]-[22].

38 For a historical overview of these many complex legislative instruments, see my 'Recognition of Professional Qualifications in the Single Market: A Recap' (2019) 30(5) EBLR 785, 790–795.

39 Recognition Directive, Title III, Chapter I.

40 Recognition Directive, Title III, Chapters II-IIIA.

41 Case C-238/98 *Hocsman* [2000] ECR I-6623; Case C-31/00 *Dreessen* [2002] ECR I-663; Case C-477/13 *Angerer* ECLI:EU:C:2015:239.

possess an 'attestation of competence' or other 'evidence of formal qualifications' from the competent authority in the member state in which they previously practised their profession. If the profession is not regulated in the member state of origin, then access to and pursuit of that profession in the host member state will be ensured if the person concerned has practised their profession for at least one year full-time or an equivalent period part-time in the past ten years and can provide either an attestation of competence or evidence of formal qualifications.[42] In *Toki*, the Court of Justice explained the purpose of the need for professional experience: professional experience is required so as to provide the host member state with safeguards equivalent to state regulation through market regulation in states with limited market intervention.[43]

Under this scheme, the host member state is permitted to restrict or delay access on a number of grounds. First, according to art 13(4), the host member state is entitled to refuse access to and pursuit of a profession if the profession in question requires nationals to hold a diploma certifying that the holder has completed post-secondary education of at least four years duration, whereas the national pursuing that profession in their home state only holds an attestation of competence.[44] Second, the host member state may require the professional to complete an adaptation period or an aptitude test, subject to the principle of proportionality and the provision of a reasoned decision, if there are substantial differences between the training of the professional and the training pursued in the host member state;[45] the pursuit of the profession requires precise knowledge of national law or rules;[46] or the training period is one year shorter in that in the host member state.[47]

In *Colegio de Ingenieros de Caminos, Canales y Puertos*, the Court of Justice emphasised the need to adhere to the principle of proportionality in the application of such restrictions and noted the seriousness of such restrictions. As the Court noted, '[a] non-application of those measures might be significant, *and even decisive*, for a national of one Member State wishing to take up a regulated profession in another Member State'.[48] The competent authority of the host member state may also permit partial access to the profession only

42 Recognition Directive, art 13.
43 Case C-424/09 *Toki* [2011] ECR I-2587 [30]-[32].
44 Similar derogations and equivalence assessments are provided for in Recognition Directive, art 14(3).
45 Recognition Directive, art 14(1), (4). See also Case C-313/01 *Morgenbesser* [2003] ECR I-13493.
46 Recognition Directive, art 14(3), first and third paragraphs.
47 Recognition Directive, art 14(3), fourth paragraph.
48 [2006] ECR I-801 [24] (emphasis added).

in the most extreme circumstances. According to art 4f(1) of the Recognition Directive, the professional must be fully qualified in their home member state, the difference between the profession in the home and host member states must be so large that the application of other compensation measures would be tantamount to requiring the applicant to undergo the full course of training ordinarily required of nationals of the host member state to be admitted to the profession, and the activity in question can be objectively distinguished from other activities in the regulated profession in the host member state.

2.2.1.3 *Automatic Recognition Schemes*

The second scheme provides for the automatic recognition of professional experience. According to art 16, if access to and pursuit of a profession listed in Annex IV to the Recognition Directive – generally, manufacturing, assembly, transport, maintenance, communications, personal service, certain itinerant and intermediary services – requires the possession of general, commercial or professional knowledge and abilities, then the host member state shall recognise previous experience as sufficient proof, subject to specific periods of past experience in some cases.[49] The third type of recognition scheme concerns the automatic recognition of qualifications on the basis of coordination of certain minimum training conditions listed in Annex V to the Recognition Directive for medical doctors, specialised doctors, nurses, dental practitioners, specialist dental practitioners, midwives, veterinary surgeons, pharmacists and architects in a manner substantially similar to the sectoral directives.[50] The Commission is empowered to update the knowledge and skills embodied in the coordinated minimum training requirements, subject to the right of member states to organise their education systems.[51]

The final automatic recognition scheme concerns the recognition of qualifications obtained on the basis of 'common training principles'.[52] According to art 49a(1) of the Recognition Directive, a 'common training framework' is 'a common set of minimum knowledge, skills and competences necessary for the pursuit of a specific profession'. The Administrative Cooperation Directive, which introduced this provision by way of amendment to the Recognition Directive, provides some insight on the purpose of common training frameworks. Recital 25 of the Administrative Cooperation Directive states that their introduction should 'promote a more automatic character of recognition of

49 Recognition Directive, arts 17–19.
50 Recognition Directive, Title III, Chapter III.
51 Recognition Directive, art 21(6).
52 Recognition Directive, Title III, Chapter IIIA.

professional qualifications for those professions which do not currently benefit from it'. Furthermore, common training frameworks could be helpful in providing automatic recognition to certain specialisations not harmonised in the liberal professions. Professional organisations represented at EU level and national professional organisations should be able to submit suggestions for common training principles to the Commission. According to art 49a(2) of the Recognition Directive, common training frameworks must satisfy a number of conditions:

(i) They must facilitate more professionals to move across member states;
(ii) The profession must be regulated in at least one-third of the member states;
(iii) The common set of knowledge and skills collated combines the knowledge and skills required in at least one-third of the member states;
(iv) The common training framework must be based on the European Qualification Framework;
(v) It must have been prepared during a transparent consultation process; and
(vi) It must permit nationals of any member state to be eligible to pursue their profession in another member state without being required to join or register with a professional organisation.

To date, no common training frameworks have been adopted.

2.2.2 The Effects of Mutual Recognition

While the principal effect of these mutual recognition schemes is to require access to a given profession on the basis of the recognition of qualifications,[53] clearly reflecting the access dimension of the previously-discussed right to work, the case law of the CJEU provides a number of insights into the incidental or indirect effects of these mutual recognition schemes on the organisation, structure and regulation of professions which merit consideration. A first concerns the extent to which the recognition of qualifications requires or permits admission to the host member state's labour market conditions. In *Beuttenmüller*, the Court of Justice confirmed and clarified that the right of access to and pursuit of a profession guaranteed by the then Diplomas'

53 Recognition Directive, art 4(1).

Directive did not extend to remuneration and other employment conditions in the host Member State.[54] Any such claims must be dealt with under the relevant EU equality legislation.

A second issue concerns the organisation and structure of certain professions across the member states. A case well illustrating the potential effect of the Recognition Directive in this respect is *Burbaud*, in which the Court of Justice considered the organisation of the profession of hospital manager in France.[55] The applicant, a Portuguese national, obtained a law degree and a hospital administrator qualification from Portuguese institutions. She worked as a hospital administrator for several years in Portugal, before moving to France, obtaining a doctorate in French law in France and acquiring French nationality. The applicant then applied for admission to the hospital managers' corps of the French public service but was denied admission. The operative reason for denying the applicant admission was that she had not taken an entrance exam required in France to undergo training to become a hospital manager.

The Court first found that the profession of hospital manager in the French public service was a 'regulated profession' within the meaning of the Diplomas' Directive. Next, the Court held that the qualification obtained after completion of the training course required constituted a 'professional qualification' within the meaning of the Diplomas' Directive. Initially, the Court upheld the entrance examination, insofar as it served a 'dual purpose': first, successful performance in the examination facilitated entry to the French state's training college for hospital managers; and, second, successful performance also led to recruitment as trainees in the public service. If the applicant's Portuguese qualification was found to be equivalent to that awarded at the end of the training course in France, then she would still be required to take the entrance exam but would be exempted from the course itself and the final examination.

The Court then recognised that requiring nationals of other member states to pass an entrance exam to a training course for which they already hold the final qualification constituted an obstacle to the free movement of workers. As such, it required justification. According to the Court, the effect of the entrance exam in such circumstances was to downgrade nationals of other member states and was not necessary to the legitimate objective of seeking the best candidates for the job. The applicant could not therefore be required to undertake the entrance exam.

54 Case C-102/02 *Beuttenmüller* [2004] ECR I-5405 [45].

55 Case C-285/01 *Burbaud* [2003] ECR I-8219.

Burbaud thus illustrates the significant effects that the competition engendered by the principle of mutual recognition can have on professions in the EU and the consequent effect on the governance of those same professions. For, first, the operation of the principle of mutual recognition provides excellent evidence of one way in which our competitive pluralistic culture works. Insofar as working in the EU constitutes a form of participation in the ongoing construction and entrenchment of the Single Market, migrant workers who seek to practise their profession in another member state directly contribute to this process where their right to work requires the liberalisation of professional regulation. To recall some of my analysis in Chapter 2, workers, as autonomous actors, are competing to advance their own conception of the good in and through their work. But, as there noted, there are limits to permissible competition in the form of prohibited harm or domination. Where people's pursuit of the good seems to be hindered through unnecessary, dominating regulation, such as that in *Burbaud* itself, it is right that they be able to challenge it; and, by contrast, where their flourishing is hindered by a *lack* of regulation, it is right that they be able to challenge such a failure to positively regulate. An example of this may be where professions are forced to merge or split, thus creating newly regulated professions.

At present, at least some economic data suggests that further *deregulation* of regulated professions across the EU, such as making it easier for people to access and participate in the labour market, would facilitate greater participation in the labour market, lower prices for consumers and improve allocative efficiency across the Union.[56] And these changes should lead to the satisfaction of people's well-being in the EU because (i) people will have a wider and/or better range of options to choose from and (ii) it will be easier to pursue at least some of those options given, amongst other things, lower prices and easier access conditions. Second, *Burbaud* illustrates how our competitive pluralistic culture *itself* generates norms governing behaviour, a point first made in Chapter 2.III.A. By facilitating people's access to the labour market through the right to work, equal treatment and the right to have one's qualifications recognised for the purpose of accessing one's profession, such rights provide routes for people to challenge contemporary norms, either by having them reduced through deregulation or replaced by reregulation.

56 Commission, 'Reform recommendations for regulation in professional services' (Communication) COM(2016) 820 final, 7–8. See also Parliament and Council Directive 2018/958/EU on a proportionality test before adoption of new regulation of professions [2018] OJ L173/25.

Nasiopoulos also illustrates these points.[57] In that case, the Court confirmed that where the exercise of one regulated profession in the host member state could be separated distinctly from that of another, the dissuasive effect caused by the impossibility of partial recognition of the professional qualification in question was too serious to be offset by the fear of potential harm to the rights of recipients of services. For example, suppose

$$\text{Profession I} = \text{Activities } (X + Y + Z)$$

and

$$\text{Profession II} = \text{Activities } (A + X + Y)$$

According to *Nasiopoulos*, a person practising Profession I must be granted partial recognition to practice Profession II, even though they are clearly somewhat different. In that case, the plaintiff obtained a qualification as a medical masseur-hydrotherapist after two and a half years of training in Germany. He then moved to Greece and sought access to the profession of physiotherapist, which there required a higher degree of at least three years duration. His application was rejected. The Court adopted a broad sectoral approach noting that as both professions were in the paramedical sector, they could not avoid the mutual recognition system. Once again, the effects of the principle of mutual recognition embodied in the Recognition Directive can be seen very clearly. As the overwhelming emphasis is on facilitating access to and participation in the labour market through the recognition of qualifications, that same mandate may require the reregulation of professions due to increased competition in the labour market. Indeed, in *Colegio de Ingenieros de Caminos, Canales y Puertos*, the Court acknowledged that 'partial recognition of professional qualifications could, theoretically, have the effect of fragmenting the professions regulated in a Member State into various activities'.[58] In such cases, the Court noted,

> the legitimate objective of protection of consumers and other recipients of services may be achieved through less restrictive means, particularly the obligation to use the professional title of origin or the academic title both in the language in which it was awarded and in its original form, and in the official language of the host Member State.[59]

57 Case C-575/11 *Nasiopoulos* [2014] 1 CMLR 7 [34].
58 [2006] ECR I-801 [32].
59 [2006] ECR I-801 [38].

This suggests that, where possible, partial recognition must be facilitated in all but the most extreme circumstances, implying that the possibility of increased fragmentation of professions and the consequent institutionalisation of individualised legal regulation is heightened. This should not be viewed as problematic; rather, it reflects the demands of our contemporary culture and the centrality of work to people's lives. Given that productivity is the hallmark of work, which is itself such a fluid concept, it should come as no wonder that old professions are constantly being challenged and fragmented by emerging forms of business and new ways of using skill sets. Once again, therefore, the recognition of professional qualifications can be understood as contributing to the further entrenchment of the Single Market by liberalising seemingly restrictive regulations and practices which dampen competition.

Notwithstanding the significant consequences this may have on the profession in question, the possibility of professions merging as a result of the mutual recognition process has also been recognised. In *Council national de l'ordre des médecins*, the French state introduced regulations governing a specialisation in oral surgery which would provide elements of specialist dental and medical surgery.[60] This specialisation already existed in certain other member states and was listed in Annex v of the Recognition Directive. The question for the Court was whether the Recognition Directive precluded such a development. According to the Court, the Recognition Directive did not preclude such a development. Such a training course could be open to persons who have completed basic medical training or basic dental training. However, *Peśla* forces us to resist drawing stronger conclusions about the far-reaching implications of mutual recognition for the regulation, organisation and structure of professions.[61] In that case, the Court observed

> Article [45 TFEU] does not, in order to be given practical effect, require that access to a professional activity in a Member State be subject to lower requirements than those normally required of nationals of that State (…) However, although Article [45 TFEU] does not, of itself, require a lowering of the level of knowledge required of the law of the host Member State (…), that article cannot be interpreted as depriving the Member States of the possibility of relaxing the relevant qualification requirements.[62]

60 Case C-492/12 *Council national de l'ordre des médecins* ECLI:EU:C:2013:576.

61 Case C-345/08 *Peśla* [2009] ECR I-11677.

62 [2009] ECR I-11677 [50], [56]. See also Case C-125/16 *Malta Dental Technologists Association and Reynaud* ECLI:EU:C:2017:707 [47]-[49].

Thus, there are some limits to the need to reorganise or reconfigure professions due to the recognition of qualifications. While professions may need to reorganise their access, training and practice structures, or even merge partially or wholly, they cannot be obliged to lower their educational, training or technical standards independently of the need to facilitate partial recognition or reorganise. In other words, a race to the bottom in terms of quality standards is not required, although it is possible.

In relation to educational standards, the principle of mutual recognition facilitates the proliferation of standards which originated in third-countries, albeit in limited circumstances. In *Commission v Spain*, the Court confirmed that it is sufficient if education and training constituting a professional qualification is received mainly, but not wholly, in the EU.[63] Moreover, as noted in section III.A above, qualifications wholly obtained in third-countries may be recognised in certain limited circumstances under the Recognition Directive. This means that professions in the Single Market may be affected not only by standards of the member states but also global standards from outside the EU. However, this is less likely to have such a substantial impact, because the number of third-country nationals exercising their limited free movement rights in the EU is much smaller than the number of member state nationals exercising free movement rights. Nonetheless, the possibility remains that third-country nationals can play a distinctive role in the process of EU integration generally by using the skills which they have obtained outside the EU when working in the EU. In so doing, they provide new sources of value which enables the EU to remain competitive, thereby contributing to the well-being of its peoples through the provision of a wide range of options which satisfies the contemporary demands of our culture.[64]

A final implication of the principle of mutual recognition in this context is the fine line between the abuse of rights in EU law, on the one hand, and taking advantage of the benefits of a more attractive regulatory system in another member state, on the other hand. In *Torresi*, this question arose directly under the Second Lawyers' Directive.[65] The applicants, having obtained a law degree in Italy, then obtained a law degree in Spain and were registered as lawyers in Spain. Shortly thereafter, they sought registration in Italy. The Italian courts referred a question to the Court of Justice, expressing concern that the

63 Case C-286/06 *Commission v Spain* [2008] ECR I-8025.

64 See my 'Recognition of Professional Qualifications Post-Brexit' (*Regulating for Globalisation*, 6 February 2019) <http://regulatingforglobalization.com/2019/02/06/recognition-of-professional-qualifications-post-brexit/> (accessed 7 June 2019).

65 Case C-58/13 *Torresi* EU:C:2014:2088.

applicants, if they were registered in Italy, would then immediately return to Spain, thus resulting in an apparent abuse of their rights of free movement and freedom of establishment. While the Court of Justice confirmed that abuse of EU law rights cannot be tolerated, the circumstances of the case did not give rise to such an abuse. Specifically, the fact that a national obtains a law degree in one member state, moves to another member state to obtain the professional qualification of lawyer, and then returns to their own member state to practise under that title does not constitute an abuse of EU law rights. Moving to another member state to benefit from a more favourable legislative or administrative regime cannot be considered abusive. This is a clear example of the competition fostered by the principle of mutual recognition.

This case of course needs to be distinguished from cases of actual abuse or poor regulation. In *Consiglio Nazionale degli Ingegneri*, the holder of an Italian mechanical engineering degree sought recognition of his degree as a professional qualification in Spain.[66] The competent authority in Spain recognised his degree for the purposes of the Recognition Directive, and the applicant enrolled in the register of industrial technical engineers in Spain. However, the applicant had not obtained any professional qualification as an engineer in Italy prior to seeking recognition in Spain. The question of recognition should not, therefore, have arisen in the first place before the Spanish authorities. Without ever practising in Spain, the applicant then immediately sought recognition of his Spanish qualification in Italy so that he could enrol on the Italian Register of Engineers. His Spanish qualification was recognised in Italy and this was challenged by the applicant professional body before the CJEU. The Court of Justice accepted that the recognition of the mechanical engineering degree by the competent Spanish authority had not been based on any examination of the professional qualifications or professional experience held by the degree holder. Moreover, the degree holder had not been subject to any examination or assessment by the Spanish authority. Consequently, the Spanish enrolment certificate based on the Spanish authority's recognition of equivalence was not a 'diploma' requiring recognition by the Italian competent authority. Ultimately, the case stands out as illustrating a failure to appropriately adhere to the regulatory procedures in question.

66 Case C-311/06 *Consiglio Nazionale degli Ingegneri* [2009] ECR I-415. Cf Case C-118/09 *Koller* [2010] ECR I-13627.

2.2.3 Restrictions on Mutual Recognition[67]

Permissible restrictions on the operation of the principle of mutual recognition in the context of the Recognition Directive or the general rules under art 53 TFEU are those which adhere to the general rules on restricting rights of free movement.[68] Thus, restrictions must be based on considerations of public policy, public security or public health. Derogations based on such considerations must be read in the light of the general principles of EU law, such as fundamental human rights and proportionality.[69] Alternatively, it is possible to justify restrictions on the basis of the public interest, provided that restrictions so justified in the public interest are non-discriminatory and proportionate.[70] Such restrictions may have the effect of maintaining or constituting high standards in certain professions. In addition to certain restrictions noted in the case law discussed above, several other restrictions have been found by the CJEU to be excessive. Requiring further qualifications than those stated in the annexes to the Recognition Directive is contrary to EU law.[71] Similarly, the need to prove special qualifications in certain fields has been held to infringe EU law.[72] Additional examinations for foreign qualified architects were also held to be contrary to the Recognition Directive,[73] as was an authorisation test for estate agents working in Belgium involving an aptitude test in law.[74]

In *Commission v Greece* numerous restrictions imposed by the Greek competent authorities were found to be excessive.[75] Specifically, the Greek competent authorities systematically refused to recognise qualifications obtained from a private body in Greece which was accredited by the competent authority

---

67 See generally Catherine Barnard, *The Substantive Law of the EU: The Four Freedoms* (7th edn, OUP 2022) 277 et seq and Panos Koutrakos, Niamh Nic Suibhne and Phil Syrpis (eds), *Exceptions to EU Free Movement Law: Derogation, Justification and Proportionality* (Hart 2016).

68 Articles 45(3), 52(1) and 62 TFEU.

69 Case C-100/01 *Ministre de l'Intérieur v Olazabal* [2002] ECR I-10981; Case C-108/96 *MacQuen* [2001] ECR I-837; Case C-17/92 *Federación de Distribuidores Cinematográficos v Estado Español et Unión de Productores de Cine y Televisión* [1993] ECR I-2239.

70 Case C-76/90 *Säger* [1991] ECR I-4221; Case C-19/92 *Kraus* [1993] ECR I-1663; Case C-319/92 *Haim* [1994] ECR I-425; Case C-55/94 *Gebhard* [1995] ECR I-4165; Case C-108/96 *MacQuen* [2001] ECR I-837; Case C-279/00 *Commission v Italy* [2002] ECR I-1425; Case C-294/00 *Gräbner* [2002] ECR I-6515; Case C-330/03 *Colegio de Ingenieros de Caminos, Canales y Puertos* [2006] ECR I-801.

71 Case C-365/13 *Ordre des architectes* ECLI:EU:C:2014:280.

72 Case C-111/12 *Ordine degli Ingegneri di Verona e Provincia and Others* [2013] 2 CMLR 39.

73 Case C-43/06 *Commission v Portugal* [2007] ECR I-73.

74 Case C-197/06 *Van Leuken* [2008] ECR I-2627.

75 Case C-274/05 *Commission v Greece* [2008] ECR I-7969.

of another member state; the transposing legislation incorrectly qualified the right to choose between an adaptation period and an aptitude test; the Greek competent authority was wrongly empowered to assess the certificates which were supposed to be automatically recognised; persons who held professional qualifications could not have them recognised in the public service for the purpose of promotion; and a professional organisation for engineers refused to recognise foreign qualified engineers in accordance with the terms of the Recognition Directive. This case in particular serves as an important lesson to protectionist member state practices.

2.3 *Beneficiaries of the Recognition Directive*

2.3.1 The Law

As should be clear from the discussion so far, the beneficiaries of the Recognition Directive are first and foremost EU citizens exercising their free movement rights under EU law. Given that third-country nationals do not generally enjoy such rights, the Recognition Directive does not generally apply to them. Rather, the Recognition Directive applies to third-country nationals in very specific circumstances only. To be clear, only some categories of regular migrants do have limited mobility rights within the EU. Specifically, migrants who do have mobility rights to differing degrees within the EU under EU law are long-term residents,[76] highly-qualified workers,[77] researchers, students, trainees, volunteers and au pairs,[78] intra-corporate transferees,[79] family members of an EU citizen,[80] citizens of states party to the EEA Agreement[81] and citizens

76 Council Directive 2003/109/EC concerning the status of third-country nationals who are long-term residents [2004] OJ L16/44 (Long-Term Residents' Directive), ch III.

77 Parliament and Council Directive (EU) 2021/1883 on the conditions of entry and residence of third-country nationals for the purposes of highly qualified employment [2021] OJ L382/1 (Blue Card Directive), ch V.

78 Parliament and Council Directive 2016/801/EU on the conditions of entry and residence of third-country nationals for the purposes of research, studies, training, voluntary service, pupil exchange schemes or educational projects and au pairing (recast) [2016] OJ L132/21 (Researchers', Students', Volunteers' and Au Pairs' Directive), ch VI.

79 Parliament and Council Directive 2014/66/EU on the conditions of entry and residence of third-country nationals in the framework of an intra-corporate transfer [2014] OJ L157/1 (ICT Directive), ch V.

80 The primary scheme is embodied in Council Directive 2003/86/EC on the right to family reunification [2003] OJ L251/12 (Family Reunification Directive). See the discussion in Steve Peers, *EU Justice and Home Affairs Law Volume 1: Immigration and Asylum Law* (4th edn, OUP 2016) ch 6.

81 Agreement on the European Economic Area between the European Communities, their Member states and the Republic of Austria, the Republic of Finland, the Republic

of states party to the EC-Swiss Confederation Agreement.[82] Forced and irregular migrants do not have free movement rights under EU law. They therefore completely fall outside the scope of the Recognition Directive. Those migrants who do have free movement rights in varying degrees may only benefit from the terms of the Recognition Directive where they rely on their free movement rights to move from one member state to another member state. A number of variations of this scenario merit critical attention and disambiguation.

The first is where a migrant has a professional qualification from outside the EU, resides in a member state and moves to another member state on the basis of the host member state's immigration law. Can that person benefit from the terms of the Recognition Directive in those circumstances? The answer seems to be no. Although their qualification may have been recognised in the member state they resided in and therefore require consideration by their host member state, that person has not exercised free movement rights, and therefore the threshold noted earlier has not been met. Any assessment of their qualifications in these circumstances is outside the scope of EU law. The second is where a migrant resides in and obtains a professional qualification from one member state and then moves to another member state on the basis of the host member state's immigration law. Can that person benefit from the terms of the Recognition Directive in those circumstances? The answer seems to be no: while they have a professional qualification and therefore meet one element of the test applicable, they have not exercised any free movement rights and therefore falls outside the scope of the Recognition Directive and EU law. The third scenario is where a migrant holds a professional qualification obtained outside the EU, resides in a member state and then moves to another member state on the basis of EU free movement law. If that professional qualification was previously recognised as at least equivalent to professional qualifications obtained in the member state of residence, then it may need to be taken into account. If it was not, then the threshold criteria set out above are not met and the Recognition Directive does not apply. Fourth and finally is the paradigm scenario falling within the terms of the Recognition Directive: where a migrant obtains a professional qualification from the member state in which they reside and then moves to another member state on the basis of EU free movement law, then they will be able to take advantage of the terms of the

of Iceland, the Principality of Liechtenstein, the Kingdom of Norway, the Kingdom of Sweden and the Swiss Confederation [1994] OJ L1/3.

82 Agreement between the European Community and its Member states, of the one part, and the Swiss Confederation, of the other, on the free movement of persons [2002] OJ L114/6.

Recognition Directive. In other words, migrants holding professional qualifications obtained in a member state exercising free movement rights for the purposes of practising their profession fall within the scope of the Recognition Directive.

2.3.2 Analysis

If and to the extent that migrants have and exercise their free movement rights, they will then be entitled to the same qualification recognition, targeted integration measures and access to education and training as EU citizens moving across borders. This stands in stark contrast to the position of migrants first arriving in the EU whose rights are quite uncertain. In general terms, migrants have a high degree of certainty as to what their free movement rights are within the EU and consequently the extent to which they can have their professional qualifications recognised.

Nonetheless, there is an obvious difference in treatment between migrants and EU citizens in respect of their free movement rights. While the EU has acknowledged, through arts 45(2) CFREU and 79(2) TFEU, that third-country nationals should have the right to free movement in at least some circumstances, relatively few categories of migrants have any free movement rights within the Single Market whereas EU citizens have a wide range of free movement rights. Specifically, while many labour migrants and voluntary migrants have some free movement rights, forced and irregular migrants have no free movement rights within the EU. Clearly, then, migrants are treated differently relative to EU member state nationals and other categories of migrants in respect of free movement within the EU. In other words, in granting different levels and degrees of free movement rights to migrants, EU migration and asylum law is discriminatory on the ground of nationality and immigration status. The question which naturally arises is how to address such discrimination. The same sorts of arguments noted and made in the previous chapter – expansively interpreting EU migration and asylum law, making policy-based arguments, respecting migrants' human rights and the legitimacy of drawing distinctions between different categories of migrants – apply here mutatis mutandis. A brief consideration of the relevance and application of these arguments to the mutual recognition of professional qualifications within the Single Market will be provided here. However, it is important not to conflate the arguments in favour of migrants' free movement rights, on the one hand, and their right to have their professional qualifications recognised, on the other hand. This book is concerned with describing and analysing the latter, not the former. While the two are linked in the specific context of internal migration, nonetheless, there does not appear to be any intrinsic or inherent link between them, only a contingent and contextual one.

The argument suggesting that EU migration and asylum law could be interpreted more broadly so as to include within the express guarantee of equal treatment an implicit right to free movement is essentially a weak one. The text of the relevant legislation is clear on the issue of free movement. The stronger argument for reform is one based on the policy justifying the legal position. As a matter of principle, reforming EU migration and asylum law to permit the free movement of third-country nationals within the EU could have several practical benefits.[83] For one, it may bring economic benefits. Empirically-speaking, third-country nationals are more likely to move across borders than member state nationals and are often understood as contributors to the project of EU integration even more so than member state nationals.[84] In addition, permitting the free movement of third-country nationals would also

83 Thomas Hoogenboom, 'Integration into Society and Free Movement of Non-EC Nationals' (1992) 3 EJIL 36; Willy Alexander, 'Free Movement of Non-EC Nationals: A Review of the Case Law of the Court of Justice' (1992) 3 EJIL 53; Andrew Evans, 'Third-Country Nationals and the European Union' (1994) 5 EJIL 205; Anna Kocharov, 'What intra-Community mobility for third-country workers?' (2008) 33 EL Rev 913; Sara Iglesias Sánchez, 'Free Movement of Third-Country Nationals in the European Union? Main Features, Deficiencies and Challenges of the new Mobility Rights in the Area of Freedom, Security and Justice' (2009) 15 ELJ 791; Sara Iglesias Sánchez, 'Free movement as a precondition for integration of third-country nationals in the EU' in Elspeth Guild, Kees Groenendijk and Sergio Carrera (eds), *Illiberal Liberal States: Immigration, Citizenship and Integration in the EU* (Ashgate 2009); Anja Wiesbrock, 'Free movement of third-country nationals in the European Union: the illusion of inclusion' (2010) 35 EL Rev 455; Anja Wiesbrock, 'Granting Citizenship-related Rights to Third-Country Nationals: An Alternative to the Full Extension of European Union Citizenship?' (2012) 14 EJML 63; Paula García Andrade, 'Privileged Third-Country Nationals and Their Right of Free Movement and Residence to and in the EU: Questions of Status and Competence' in Elspeth Guild, Cristina Gortázar Rotaeche and Dora Kostakopoulou (eds), *The Reconceptualisation of European Union Citizenship* (Brill 2014); Sara Iglesias Sánchez, 'Free Movement Law within the European Union: Workers, Citizens and Third-Country Nationals' in Marion Panizzon, Gottfried Zürcher and Elisa Fornalé (eds), *The Palgrave Handbook of International Labour Migration: Law and Policy Perspectives* (Palgrave Macmillan 2015); Lucia Della Torre and Tesseltje de Lange, 'The 'importance of staying put': third-country nationals' limited intra-EU mobility rights' (2018) 44 Journal of Ethnic and Migration Studies 1409; and Petra Weingerl and Matjaž Tratnik, 'Climbing the Wall around EU Citizenship: Has the Time Come to Align Third-Country Nationals with Intra-EU Migrants?' (2022) 33(1) EJIL 15.

84 A Turmann, 'A New European Agenda for Mobility' in *CEPS-ECHR Taskforce* (2004) cited in 'Free movement of third-country nationals in the European Union: the illusion of inclusion' (n 85); and European Migration Network Synthesis Report, *Intra-EU Mobility of Third-Country Nationals* (European Commission 2013) 5.

make the Single Market a more attractive place to live in the global 'market for migrants', making the EU better able to compete with the USA in particular.[85] Indeed, it is clear from the introductory chapter to this book that this is an imperative of the European Commission and recent proposals for reform have been advocated in this context, which will be noted in the next chapter. In outline, therefore, there appear to be at least some good policy reasons in favour of expanding the range of circumstances in which at least some migrants may move freely within the EU.

However, the policy rationale for the general exclusion of qualifications obtained from third-countries from the Recognition Directive and consequent indirect exclusion of migrants therefrom is clear: unlike the member states, third-countries are not bound by the principle of mutual recognition which underlies the Recognition Directive and are therefore not required to coordinate their qualification recognition systems with those of the EU's member states. Unlike the recognition of qualifications of migrants when first coming to the EU, the mutual recognition of professional qualifications within the Single Market is a question of the integrity and quality of professional services regulation and provision in the EU. As should be evident from the outline of the principle of mutual recognition in Section 1, it is a distinctive governance tool which is one of the primary implements of European economic integration.

Indeed, permitting the mutual recognition of professional qualifications obtained outside the EU with the Single Market may effectively allow third-countries to control, albeit very much indirectly, the quality of professional qualifications in the EU. This possibility is particularly poignant post-Brexit. Allow me to explain. The UK's higher education system attracts many students from the EU and will likely continue to do so for the foreseeable future. If professional qualifications obtained therein continue to be mutually recognised and thereby facilitate access to and participate in professions in the EU, then the UK will still have an influence on the regulation of professions in the EU. Furthermore, even if professional qualifications obtained in the UK are not formally mutually recognised in the EU, it is still plausible that at least some professions in the EU may track the professional qualification standards set in the UK. On the other hand, the general exclusion of third-country qualifications from the terms of the Recognition Directive appears to leave member states with a degree of discretion in relation to the procedures governing the recognition of qualifications obtained in third-countries. On its own, such

85 FH Buckley, 'The market for migrants' in Jagdeep Bhandari and Alan Sykes (eds), *Economic Dimensions of International Law: Comparative and Empirical Perspectives* (CUP 1998).

discretion may be a source of domination for third-country nationals and persons holding professional qualifications obtained in a third-country insofar as they may not be entitled to procedural equality with member state nationals or persons holding professional qualifications obtained in the EU, although this is unlikely by virtue of the guarantee of equality before the law.

The policy arguments in favour of expanding the rights of free movement of migrants within the EU are therefore somewhat more mixed than in the previous chapter. While there is obviously discrimination and potentially inadequate qualification recognition in existence, the justification for this is clear on the face of the Recognition Directive. This relative clarity stands in contrast with the provisions of EU migration and asylum law considered in the previous chapter which were unclear on their face, resulting in an obvious potential source of domination for migrants coming to the EU.

Turning thence to the other argumentative strategies deployed in the previous chapter – concerning the obligation to respect migrants' human rights under international and European law and the legitimacy of distinctions between different categories of migrant – first, there is no binding source of international and European law entailing or implying a commitment to ensuring the freedom of movement of migrants within the EU. Specifically, there is no express or implied obligation under international and European law to permit migrants to move freely within the EU, as opposed to within the EU's member states.

Second, the argument suggesting that drawing distinctions between different categories of migrants is legitimate – such that migrants' rights approximate with those of citizens overtime – is quite compelling in the context of free movement rights generally. This is because EU free movement law is the essence of the EU's zeitgeist. For example, not all EU citizens have equal free movement rights: those who are most active and contribute the most or can sustain themselves independently have the strongest or weightiest free movement rights, whereas those who do not have more limited free movement rights. It should therefore come as no surprise that only some regular migrants, such as highly-skilled workers and long-term residents, are among the few who are entitled to exercise free movement rights within the EU by virtue of their contribution to their host member state. It stands to reason that only those migrants who are most likely to contribute to the EU's economic agenda in the medium- to long-term should have extensive free movement rights, as is the case with EU citizens themselves.

Irregular migrants and forced migrants do not have rights of free movement within the EU. This would appear to be for reasons of immigration and border control which are determined by other parts of EU migration and asylum law and by virtue of the rights and responsibilities of the EU's member states under international and European law concerning forced and irregular migrants. To even begin to reflect on the right to free movement of irregular and forced migrants requires a broader investigation of the rights and responsibilities of the EU's member states under national, EU and international law towards such migrants, which is far beyond the scope of this text.

Conclusion

This chapter has concluded the description and critical analysis of the 'hard law' governing the recognition of professional qualifications in EU law. It has addressed the mutual recognition of professional qualifications within the Single Market. The following conclusions have been reached.

First, it is clear that there are several competing conceptions of mutual recognition at operation in the context of the recognition of qualifications, reflecting differing stages in the transition from very diverse to relatively uniform standards across different professional sectors. Second, the recognition procedures are generally quite flexible, and can very seriously impact on the regulation, organisation and structure of certain national professions. This is a good example of the role and effect of the regulatory competition fostered by mutual recognition in the single market. Third, the combined application of art 53 TFEU and the Recognition Directive in general and to third-country nationals specifically can be restated as follows.

1. A person must hold a professional qualification either obtained in the EU or obtained outside the EU but previously recognised by a member state. This excludes many third-country nationals who hold professional qualifications obtained outside the EU and not previously recognised therein. However, the argument made in Chapter 3 suggests that persons holding qualifications from third-countries should be entitled to strict procedural equality with persons holding qualifications obtained in the EU.
2. A person must then move to another member state by exercising their free movement rights. Again, this excludes many third-country nationals who do not have free movement rights within the Single Market.
3. The profession in question must be a regulated one. If it is not regulated, the Recognition Directive does not apply and, instead, an

independent duty to recognise qualifications arises by virtue of the direct effect of art 53 TFEU.

Chapter 2 argued that discrimination on the ground of nationality should be abolished in general, subject to specific, reasoned exceptions. Generally speaking, migrants do not have free movement rights within the EU. They are therefore treated differently relative to EU nationals in respect of their free movement rights and consequently their right to have their professional qualifications recognised when moving within the EU. While there may be good reasons in favour of granting migrants free movement rights in a broader range of circumstances than is presently the case, there are also good reasons to limit their right to have their qualifications recognised when moving within the Single Market. These reasons derive from the special role which the principle of mutual recognition plays in the construction of the EU and its consequent use in the Recognition Directive. While it is a highly-complex legislative instrument, the Recognition Directive is generally clear and migrants can know and understand their rights on the basis of its text. Their general and indirect exclusion from its terms arises not by virtue of any flaw in the regulation of the recognition of professional qualifications but by virtue of its constituting part of EU free movement law, which is primarily aimed at and designed for the benefit of EU citizens.

CHAPTER 5

Soft Law and Policy

Introduction

This chapter concludes Part 2 of this book and the specific focus on the recognition of professional qualifications of migrants in Europe provided thereby. Having previously attempted to comprehensively describe and analyse the 'hard' law governing this issue in Chapters 3 and 4, this chapter explores some of the EU's historic and existing soft law and policy measures, as well as emerging developments, in the context of both internal and external migration. It does so by describing and analysing certain measures which have been adopted on the basis of the EU's various policy competences in respect of migration and asylum, external relations and education and training which touch on or have implications for the recognition of professional qualifications.

This chapter is structured as follows. Section 1 addresses measures which the EU has adopted on the basis of its migration and asylum competences. These include integration measures specifically targeted at third-country nationals as well as relevant EU funds supporting the integration of migrants in Europe. Consideration is also given to recent developments and proposals for reform, such as the European Commission's recent recommendations on the recognition of professional qualifications of third-country nationals generally and migrants fleeing the Russo-Ukrainian War in particular, as well as the proposal for a Regulation establishing an EU Talent Pool. These measures are described and critically reflected upon. Section 2 addresses measures which have been adopted on the basis of the EU's external relations competences. These include the EU's Neighbourhood and Enlargement policies, mobility partnerships, international development and cooperation policy and more. Finally, Section 3 describes the regulation of the recognition of non-formal and informal learning which the EU has adopted. A short conclusion follows summarising the key findings of this chapter.

1 EU Migration and Asylum Policy

1.1 *Overview*

Article 79(4) TFEU provides that the Parliament and Council may adopt measures, excluding the harmonisation of laws, which provide 'incentives and

 | DOI:10.1163/9789004724068_009

support' to the member states in facilitating the integration of third-country nationals legally resident in the EU. There are a number of contemporary integration policy measures and funds which are relevant to the recognition of third-country nationals' qualifications here outlined and analysed.

1.2 *Integration Policies and Initiatives*

1.2.1 Background

A full background to all EU policies concerning the integration of third-country nationals is essentially extraneous to the purpose of this chapter; useful and detailed analyses are available elsewhere.[1] It is, however, necessary to note that the importance of qualification recognition was not recognised in the EU's earliest integration policies, namely the Tampere European Council Conclusions[2] and the Hague Programme.[3] Although the recognition of the skills of third-country nationals was taken into account on numerous occasions,[4] it was not until the adoption of the Stockholm Programme in 2009 that the European Council fully recognised the need to adopt 'coherent immigration policies as well as better integration assessments of the skills in demand on the European labour markets'.[5] In the Stockholm Programme, the European Council also

1 Jan Niessen and Thomas Huddleston (eds), *Legal Frameworks for the Integration of Third-Country Nationals* (Nijhoff 2009); Micaela Malena and Sonia Morano-Foadi, 'Integration Policy at European Union Level' in Sonia Morano-Foadi and Micaela Malena (eds), *Integration for Third-Country Nationals in the European Union: The Equality Challenge* (Edward Elgar 2012); Clíodhna Murphy, *Immigration, Integration and the Law: The Intersection of Domestic, EU and International Law Regimes* (Ashgate 2013) ch 6; Blanca Garcés-Mascareñas and Rinus Penninx (eds), *Integration Processes and Policies in Europe: Contexts, Levels and Actors* (SpringerOpen 2016); and Pierre Georges Van Wolleghem, *The EU's Policy on the Integration of Migrants: A Case of Soft-Europeanisation?* (Palgrave Macmillan 2019). In respect of asylum seekers and refugees specifically, see the special edition of (2019) 25 Transfer 13–129.

2 Tampere Presidency Conclusions, 15–16 October 1999.

3 Brussels Presidency Conclusions, 5–4 November 2004; Council, 'The Hague Programme: Strengthening Freedom, Security and Justice in the European Union' [2005] OJ C53/1.

4 Justice and Home Affairs Council Conclusions, *Common Basic Principles on Immigrant Integration*, Council Document 14615/04, Brussels, 19 November 2004, Common Basic Principle 3; Commission, 'A Common Agenda for Integration: Framework for the Integration of Third Country Nationals in the European Union' (Communication) COM(2005) 389 final, 16; Commission, 'A Common Immigration Policy for Europe – Principles, Actions and Tools' (Communication) COM(2008) 359 final, 6; and Commission, 'Strengthening the Global Approach to Migration – Increasing Coordination, Coherence and Synergies' (Communication) COM(2008) 611 final, 4.

5 European Council, *The Stockholm Programme – An Open and Secure Europe serving and protecting citizens* (Brussels, 2 December 2009) 63.

invited the Commission and Council to evaluate existing policies that should 'improve skills recognition and labour matching between the European Union and third countries and the capacity to analyse labour market needs (…) and skills matching in the country of origin'.[6]

Subsequently, in the *Conclusions of the Council and the Representatives of the Governments of the Member states on Integration as a Driver for Development and Social Cohesion*, the Council and Representatives recognised the need to 'find new ways to recognise qualifications, training or professional skills and work experience of immigrants'.[7] The immediate follow-up to the Council's analysis was the formulation of the *European Agenda for the Integration of Third-Country Nationals* by the Commission, which emphasised, inter alia, the need to recognise foreign qualifications and support pre-departure qualification recognition measures in the migrant's country of origin.[8] This theme was repeatedly echoed thereafter in the Commission's Communications on *Migration*,[9] *The Global Approach to Migration and Mobility* (the '*GAMM*', previously discussed in the introductory chapter)[10] and *An Open and Secure Europe*.[11] A recent report for the International Organisation for Migration provides extensive reflections on the practical implementation of these policies.[12] It first notes that while there is, strictly speaking, no clear legal basis for pre-departure qualification recognition measures at EU level, at least one broad interpretation[13] of the provisions of the Family Reunification Directive and the Long-Term Residents' Directive concerning 'integration measures', previously discussed in Chapter 3 above, may permit the adoption of pre-departure qualification recognition measures by the member states. However, as previously

6 ibid.

7 Council of the European Union, *Conclusions of the Council and the Representatives of the Governments of the Member states on Integration as a Driver for Development and Social Cohesion* (Brussels, 4 May 2010) 4.

8 Commission, 'European Agenda for the Integration of Third-Country Nationals' (Communication) COM(2011) 455 final, 7, 10–11.

9 Commission, 'Migration' (Communication) COM(2011) 248 final, 16.

10 Commission, 'The Global Approach to Migration and Mobility' (Communication) COM(2011) 743 final.

11 Commission, 'An Open and Secure Europe: Making it Happen' (Communication) COM(2014) 154 final, 4.

12 Alin Chindea, *Headstart to Integration: A Global Review of Pre-departure Support Measures for Migrants* (IOM 2015).

13 That of Sergio Carrera and Anja Wiesbrock, *Civic Integration of Third-Country Nationals: Nationalism versus Europeanisation in the Common EU Immigration Policy* (Centre for European Policy Studies 2009).

suggested, it would be preferable if this were clarified so that there was a clear legal basis upon which pre-departure measures could be developed.[14]

1.2.2 The European Migration Forum

Subsequently, in January 2015 the European Economic and Social Committee (EESC) organised the first meeting of the European Migration Forum (EMF), 'a platform for dialogue between civil society and the European institutions, on issues relating to migration, asylum and the integration of third-country nationals'.[15] The EMF replaced the European Integration Forum (EIF), established in 2009 by the EESC, which met biannually. The EIF had briefly considered the issue of qualification recognition at its fourth,[16] eighth[17] and ninth[18] meetings – notwithstanding that it had been envisaged to constitute a significant aspect of its work from the outset[19] – but quite full consideration was given to the issue at the EMF's meeting in 2018. Specifically, workshops at that meeting addressed, inter alia, (i) best practice in skills recognition and (ii) matching refugees' skills with labour market needs.

In respect of the first issue, participants recognised the significance of supplying migrants with information concerning skills' recognition processes. The availability of a range of validation tools was supported, including visual and multi-lingual tools. Mentoring was also seen as an important skills recognition and enhancement strategy; a third-country national may better understand and develop their own skills through dialogue with a colleague. In respect of the second workshop, participants emphasised the importance, actual and potential, of civil society organisations and digital tools in matching skills. Best

14 See generally Kees Gronendijk, 'Pre-Departure Integration Strategies in the European Union: Integration or Immigration Policy?' (2011) 13 EJML 1.

15 EESC, 'European Migration Forum' <https://www.eesc.europa.eu/en/sections-other-bodies/other/european-migration-forum> accessed 17 April 2018.

16 EESC, 'Summary Report: Fourth Meeting of the European Integration Forum, Brussels, 6–7 December 2010' 2 available at <https://ec.europa.eu/migrant-integration/eiforum/4th-european-integration-forum> accessed 18 April 2018.

17 EESC, 'Summary Report: Eighth Meeting of the European Integration Forum, Brussels, 16–17 October 2012' 6 available at <https://ec.europa.eu/migrant-integration/eiforum/8th-european-integration-forum-the-contribution-of-migrants-to-economic-growth-in-the-eu> accessed 18 April 2018.

18 EESC, 'Summary Report: Ninth Meeting of the European Integration Forum, Brussels, 4–5 June 2013' 6 available at <https://ec.europa.eu/migrant-integration/eiforum/8th-european-integration-forum-the-contribution-of-migrants-to-economic-growth-in-the-eu> accessed 18 April 2018.

19 Commission, 'An Area of Freedom, Security and Justice serving the Citizen' (Communication) COM (2009) 262 final, 25.

practices identified by participants included the need to move to different areas within a single member state to obtain work; fast-track training schemes; mentoring; and the possibility of changing status or altering the residence rights of asylum seekers.[20] While the Forum is quite obviously discursive in nature, it may nonetheless play an important role in facilitating an exchange of ideas and best practices between member state authorities and national civil society organisations. And while it is understandable that the EMF's discussions focussed on asylum seekers and refugees given the occurrence of the European Migrant Crisis at the time, it is unfortunate that it did not take the opportunity to address the skills' recognition needs of third-country nationals more generally.

At the EMF's meeting in April 2019, ten recommendations were adopted, some of which are of particular relevance. Specifically, at a workshop entitled, 'What is the Future of EU Legal Migration Policy?', the EMF concluded that a single directive should be adopted harmonising the admission conditions and rights for all third-country nationals, including equal treatment and intra-EU mobility rights. Establishing a structured process for consulting with NGOs, local authorities and the social partners was also recommended at this workshop. At another workshop, entitled, 'From global to local governance of migration: the role of local authorities in managing migration', the possibility of collaboration and cooperation amongst local groups, such as NGOs and local authorities was also envisaged. Harmonising integration processes across the Union and providing targeted funding to facilitate same was also recommended.[21] Reference was further made in passing to the possibility of adopting a directive facilitating the recognition of qualifications of third-country nationals.[22] While it is clear that these recommendations are of value, these measures were not discussed at the EMF's subsequent meetings in 2021, 2022 or 2023 and have not subsequently been adopted by the EU's institutions.

The second measure of practical significance to be adopted was the *European Dialogue on Skills and Migration*, a platform for employers, public sector bodies and other stakeholders to discuss labour migration and labour

20 EESC, 'European Migration Forum – 4th Meeting' <https://www.eesc.europa.eu/en/agenda/our-events/events/european-migration-forum-4th-meeting> accessed 17 April 2018; and see the downloads available on the same page which provide a summary of the event.

21 EESC, 'The 10 recommendations adopted by the Forum' <https://www.eesc.europa.eu/sites/default/files/files/recommendations_adopted_by_the_european_migration_forum_5th_meeting.pdf> accessed 11 December 2019.

22 EESC, 'European Migration Forum' (10 April 2019) available at <https://dmsearch.eesc.europa.eu/search/public> accessed 11 December 2019.

market integration of third-country nationals. Thus far, two meetings have been held under the auspices of the *Dialogue*, at which two conclusions of relevance were reached. The first acknowledged that there is a need for improved qualification recognition across the EU. In particular, it was acknowledged that recognition of qualifications in one member state should be more easily recognised in another member state, without necessarily harmonising legislation on qualification recognition. The Dialogue emphasised the role that employers, public service providers and other stakeholders play in assessing qualifications, and the need for these stakeholders to create partnerships with equivalent third-country organisations. The possibility of compensation measures to make up for skills disparities between third-country nationals and member state standards was also recognised. The second key conclusion was the need to match employers' needs and migrants' skills and competences. While this conclusion was primarily targeted at refugees, company visits, orientation days, and 'speed-dating' arrangements between all third-country migrants and potential employers is envisaged as a positive strategy. In general, these suggestions should be welcomed, generalised, systematised and institutionalised across the Union. One important development emerging from the Dialogue which does seem very practical is *Employers Together for Integration*, an initiative which places employers at the centre of integration processes. Several large north European companies are participating in the programme, and are offering internship, apprenticeship and corporate degree programmes and scholarship opportunities to refugees. This sort of active engagement with migrants should be welcomed and expanded to other categories of third-country nationals, not merely refugees. Given that it also not a systematic programme, it would however be better if a comprehensive approach were adopted. Unfortunately, however, to this author's knowledge, the *European Dialogue on Skills and Migration* is now defunct.

A final and similar measure is the *European Partnership for Integration*, a partnership between the Commission and the social and economic partners which aims to foster refugee integration as soon as possible, particularly through labour market access and participation. The Commission and social and economic partners agree to gather and share information concerning best practices in, inter alia, skills and qualification recognition and enhancement, providing feedback to public authorities on the success or failure of public policies in this area. The core activities of the partnership involve information exchanges, the establishment of networks and ensuring 'synergies' with other initiatives.

1.2.3 Action Plan on the Integration of Third-Country Nationals

Of course, the major project undertaken by the Commission in this field of late is the *Action Plan on the integration of third country nationals*, issued after the beginning of the European Migrant Crisis in 2015.[23] The *Action Plan* sets out several tasks to be undertaken by the Commission and the member states in relation to third-country nationals generally. These measures addressed all the main stages in the migration and employment process, namely, pre-departure education recognition, labour market participation, access to basic services, active participation and social inclusion, and tools for coordination, funding and monitoring. Under these headings, the most important and relevant actions and measures were the following:

- Launching projects to support effective pre-departure and pre-arrival measures under the Asylum, Migration and Integration Fund;
- Providing Erasmus+ online language assessment and learning for around 100,000 newly arrived third country nationals, in particular refugees;
- Promoting the upskilling of low-skilled and low-qualified persons in the context of the *New Skills Agenda for Europe* (previously discussed in the introductory chapter);
- Developing a 'Skills Toolkit for Third Country Nationals' under the *New Skills Agenda for Europe* to support timely identification of skills and qualifications for asylum seekers, refugees and other third country nationals;
- Improving transparency and understanding of qualifications acquired in third-countries, through the revision of the European Qualifications Framework (EQF), that will enhance its implementation and extend its scope to include the possibility to establish links with qualifications frameworks of other regions of the world; and
- Funding projects promoting 'fast track' insertion into labour market and vocational training.[24]

Setting aside funding for now, perhaps the most significant of these developments is the *New Skills Agenda for Europe*.[25] According to the Commission in its communication thereon, it shall take, inter alia, the following measures, namely,

23 Commission, 'Action Plan on the Integration of Third Country Nationals' (Communication) COM(2016) 377 final.

24 ibid 18–21.

25 Commission, 'A New Skills Agenda for Europe: Working together to strengthen human capital, employability and competitiveness' (Communication) COM(2016) 381 final.

- a revision of the EQF which promotes the comparability of qualifications between countries covered by the EQF and other countries, such as countries in the European Neighbourhood Policy;
- the development of a 'Skills Profile Tool for Third Country Nationals';
- cooperating with national authorities to support the recognition of third-country nationals' qualifications; and
- making online language learning modules available for newly arriving migrants.

As of May 2020, the EQF has been revised, and the Commission is now preparing to implement the changes.[26] The revised EQF recommendation makes little reference to professional qualifications, except to note that common training frameworks adopted under the Recognition Directive, the subject of Chapter 4, are to be based on EQF levels.[27] However, it is possible that the EQF may touch on the recognition of professional qualifications in one other way. It recommends that the Commission, in cooperation with the Member states, and stakeholders, considers the 'development and application of criteria and procedures to enable, in accordance with international agreements, the comparison of third countries' national and regional qualifications frameworks with the EQF'.[28] While there is thus no duty undertaken by the Commission as such, nor any action on the part of the Commission on this issue as of yet, it does support the possibility of increased recognition of skills in the future. This possibility may, eventually, provide a basis for third-country qualifications to be more easily compared and recognised with those obtained in the EU. Moreover, a number of comparative studies between the EQF and other frameworks have recently been undertaken, including between Hong Kong, Australia and New Zealand.[29]

The second step proposed by the Commission, namely the development of a 'Skills Profile Tool for Third Country Nationals', has been implemented.[30]

---

26 Council Recommendation on the European Qualifications Framework for lifelong learning and repealing the recommendation of the European Parliament and of the Council of 23 April 2008 on the establishment of the European Qualifications Framework for lifelong learning [2017] OJ C189/15.

27 [2017] OJ C189/15, recital 20.

28 [2017] OJ C189/15, art 13.

29 See, for example, GHK, *Study on the (potential) role of qualifications frameworks in supporting mobility of workers and learners: European Commission and Australian Department of Education, Employment and Workplace Relations Joint EU-Australia Study* (DEEWR and DG EAC 2011).

30 Commission, 'EU Skills Profile Tool for Third Country Nationals' <https://ec.europa.eu/migrantskills/#/> accessed 24 January 2018.

The fourth step – the provision of online language learning – has now been made available by the Commission through the Erasmus+ programme. This measure is actually targeted at EU migrants, but the Commission has ensured that special modules are available for refugees. The same provision should be made for third-country nationals shortly arriving and currently in the EU. The fact that these language modules have been made available to EU nationals highlights how the problem of integration is not confined to third-country nationals but also affects member state nationals. Indeed, many of my concerns for third-country nationals' integration in general can be mapped on to member state nationals when moving within the EU.

The third step – cooperating with national authorities – has also occurred. A repository of promising practices in aid of the social and labour market integration of refugees has been established by DG Employment, Social Affairs and Inclusion, and several of these are quite insightful and relevant to the recognition of qualifications.[31] Examples include the pilot project of the Austrian Public Employment Service "Skills check for the vocational integration of refugees" (*AMS-Pilotprojekt "Kompetenzcheck zur beruflichen Integration von Asylberechtigten"*) which involves a skills assessment, assisting applicants for recognition in undertaking the recognition procedure, a verification of skills on the basis of field trials and the writing up of a detailed CV for the purposes of labour market access. Similar processes have been adopted in Germany under the "Every person has potential – labour market integration of asylum seekers (Early Intervention)" (*"Jeder Mensch hat Potenzial – Arbeitsmarktintegration von Asylbewerberinnen und Asylbewerbern (Early Intervention)"*) and Prototyping Transfer – recognition of professional and vocational qualifications via qualification analyses (*"Prototyping Transfer-Berufsanerkennung mit Qualifikationsanalysen"*) projects. A similar Dutch project is also quite advanced. "Recognition of Refugee Qualifications" (*"Diplomawaardering voor vluchtelingen"*) provides a number of useful services such as producing descriptions of the educational systems and qualifications of refugees' countries of origin and organising workshops on the issue of qualification recognition for refugees. As these are pilot projects, however, we await a final, definitive systematic and institutionalised response by the EU and the member states. Indeed, while all of the above measures are laudable, they lack systematisation and institutionalisation, features which, as noted in the introductory chapter, the law as an institutional normative system can distinctively provide.

---

31 DG Employment, Social Affairs and Inclusion, 'Repository of Promising Practices' <http://ec.europa.eu/social/main.jsp?langId=en&catId=1208> accessed 25 January 2018.

1.2.4 Action Plan on Integration and Inclusion 2021–2027

The *Action Plan on the integration of third country nationals*, issued after the beginning of the European Migrant Crisis in 2015, was succeeded by the *Action Plan on Integration and Inclusion 2021–2027*.[32] Adopted in 2020, the Commission envisaged a series of key action points for the EU and its member states in the context of education and training, employment and skills and a series of ancillary actions supporting effective integration and inclusion in those sectors. In these sectors, the following were the most important and relevant action points for the Commission:

- Fostering cooperation between national authorities in charge of integration and national centres for the recognition of qualifications (ENIC-NARIC networks);
- Supporting transparent recognition practices of qualifications of refugees through the Erasmus Programme;
- Promoting exchanges between member states on providing complementary/bridging courses for migrants;
- Providing information on recognition practices and on skills and qualifications for migrants using the full potential of the Europass portal;
- Promoting the transparency of qualifications systems, including through the EQF;
- Work with members states to further develop comprehensive and accessible language learning programmes, including intermediate and advanced courses, through funding and exchanges of experiences;
- Sharing and scaling up practices on skills assessment through the European Integration Network, the European Network of Public Employment Service and the updated Europass platform;
- Further developing the EU Skills Profile Tool for Third Country Nationals and promoting its use among public authorities and other organisations, including before arrival, particularly in the case of resettlement and complementary pathways; and
- Launching a new Eurobarometer on integration.

Not all of these action points have been implemented as of the time of writing. Indeed, the Commission's one-year review of the *Action Plan on Integration and Inclusion 2021–2027* in 2021 did not indicate any progress on the above measures. However, some have been actioned while others are underway. For

32 Commission, 'Action Plan on Integration and Inclusion 2021–2027' (Communication) COM(2020) 758 final.

example, the Eurobarometer on integration was published in 2022. Polling some 26,510 respondents, the strongest conclusion of the survey was that 'immigrants should have educational qualifications and skills that are sufficient to find a job in order for their integration to be successful'.[33] In January 2024, Eurostat launched the migrant integration and inclusion dashboard, an interactive visualisation tool which offers a comprehensive overview of data related to the migrant population in the EU.[34] In May 2024, the Commission published an analysis of bridging courses for migrants to complement qualifications acquired in third-countries provided across the EU.[35] The analysis was published on the European Website on Integration, the only official EU-wide source of up-to-date information and good practices on migrant integration.[36] The analysis suggested that member states do 'not have a comprehensive approach to provision of bridging courses at the national level' but the feedback received from member states clearly demonstrated 'not only the importance of these courses … but also the importance of facilitating access to them'. The types of bridging courses typically available across the member states include free industrial-specific language learning support, programmes that specifically target refugees, initiatives designed to facilitate labour market access for third-country nationals, such as work experience and civic integration courses, and many more. The Commission is expected to publish a mid-term review of the *Action Plan on Integration and Inclusion 2021–2027* by the end of 2024.

33 Commission, 'Special Eurobarometer: integration of immigrants in the European Union' (20 June 2022) <https://migrant-integration.ec.europa.eu/library-document/special-eurobarometer-integration-immigrants-european-union_en> (accessed 26 August 2024).

34 Eurostat, 'Migrant integration and inclusion dashboard' <https://ec.europa.eu/eurostat/cache/dashboard/migrant-integration-inclusion/> (accessed 26 August 2024).

35 Commission, 'Bridging courses for migrants to complement qualifications acquired in third countries: approaches and practices in EU Member States' (30 May 2024) < https://migrant-integration.ec.europa.eu/special-feature/bridging-courses-migrants-complement-qualifications-acquired-third-countries_en> (accessed 26 August 2024).

36 Commission, 'European Website on Integration' <https://migrant-integration.ec.europa.eu/home_en> (accessed 26 August 2024).

1.3 *Recent Developments and Proposals for Reform*

1.3.1 Recommendation on the Recognition of Qualifications for People Fleeing Russia's Invasion of Ukraine

The European Commission issued a recommendation on the recognition of qualifications for people fleeing Russia's invasion of Ukraine in April 2022.[37] This recommendation followed the activation of the Temporary Protection Directive by the Council of the European Union in 2022,[38] which designated certain persons fleeing Russia's invasion of Ukraine as benefitting from temporary protection. The Temporary Protection Directive provides such persons with a clear legal status under EU law and grants them access to 'employed or self-employed activities, subject to rules applicable to the profession' as well as in activities such as educational opportunities for adults, vocational training and practical workplace experience. While, as noted earlier, it is unclear on the basis of the wording of the Temporary Protection Directive whether its subjects are entitled to equal treatment with member state nationals in respect of the procedures governing the recognition of their professional qualifications, as suggested below, the tenor of the Commission's recommendation indicates that persons benefitting from temporary protection should be treated the same as refugees and persons eligible for subsidiary protection status.

The recitals to the recommendation are insightful. First, they note that, empirically-speaking, third-country nationals and refugees in particular often have to take jobs below their qualification level. Facilitating the effective recognition of their qualifications may better enable them to use and develop their skills in a manner commensurate with the qualifications they already have. Second, it notes that the Commission's *Action Plan on Integration and Inclusion for 2021–2027* recognises that facilitating the recognition of qualifications acquired in third-countries and increasing their comparability with EU qualifications is essential to faster and fairer inclusion of refugees in the labour market. However, third, the Commission acknowledges the member states have exclusive competence to regulate the recognition of professional qualifications of third-country nationals, unless an international agreement applies. This means that the recognition procedures may differ greatly across the member states. In this vein, the Commission expressly recognises that Directive 2005/36/EC does not generally apply to third-country nationals.

37 Commission Recommendation (EU) 2022/554 on the recognition of qualifications for people fleeing Russia's invasion of Ukraine [2022] OJ L107I/1.

38 Council Implementing Decision (EU) 2022/382 establishing the existence of a mass influx of displaced persons from Ukraine [2022] OJ L 71/1.

Nonetheless, the Commission endeavoured to provide some concrete, practical guidelines to the member states when assessing the professional qualifications of people fleeing Russia's invasion of Ukraine. These guidelines concern the organisation of the recognition of professional qualifications for people enjoying temporary protection, facilitating academic recognition for such persons, the provision of information to the member states on the use of electronic tools for enabling qualification recognition, practical tips on dealing with incomplete evidence of qualifications, specific requirements for certain professions, as well as facilitating the exercise of regulated professions. While the recommendation is strictly non-binding and hortative in nature, its undertones are imperative. The Commission recommended that member states issue their recognition decisions 'swiftly', ensuring that 'only essential documents are required', to 'accept other forms of proof than original documents', dispense with certified translations and to reduce or eliminate the fees associated with the recognition process. Overall, the Commission recommended that member states adopt 'a flexible approach' to recognition and to 'consider checking qualifications of professionals only if it is essential'. Ukrainian higher education qualifications should be automatically recognised and such recognition in one member state should be accepted in other member states. Member state authorities should liaise with the Ukrainian authorities to obtain confirmation of the qualification achieved where possible.

The specific guidelines for certain professions and for the exercise of regulated professions are perhaps the most significant part of this recommendation. The Commission encouraged member states to consider how persons enjoying temporary protection could be employed in healthcare services, such as by developing short-term up-skilling programmes to meet the minimum training standards for certain healthcare professions, or to allow such persons to perform certain activities with a different status than that of a full member of a profession. In addition, the Commission recommended that Ukrainian-qualified teachers and other educational professionals should be employed in schools where Ukrainian-educated children now attend and that language training be provided to such education professionals. In terms of facilitating the exercise of regulated professions, the Commission recommended that the member states 'do not introduce or maintain any requirement for companies to prove that they could not hire an EU citizen before recruiting a person enjoying temporary protection'.

It is important to remember that Commission recommendations are strictly non-binding on member states. However, they are persuasive. The recommendations in respect of people fleeing the Russian invasion of Ukraine are powerful and wide-ranging. In large part, they are very practical, pointed and impactful in effect; designed to facilitate the better integration of such persons into Europe's economy and society; and focussed on tangible impacts on such persons' welfare. Indeed, the Commission's own assessment of the recommendation indicated that the recognition of professional qualifications of such persons was as successful as that of EU nationals.[39] However, they also amount, in substance, to an elision of the distinction in EU law between persons benefitting from temporary protection and refugees and persons eligible for subsidiary protection status, at least in respect of the right to the recognition of professional qualifications. While some forced migration activists may welcome this development, from the perspective of EU law it is difficult to justify. Moreover, the entire recommendation stands in stark contrast to the manner in which Syrian and other refugees were treated in the aftermath of the European migration crisis of 2015. There was, in fact, no such Commission recommendation in respect of such forced migrants nor such generous preferential treatment. Persons fleeing Ukraine are being treated far better than those migrants ever were. In addition, from the perspective of the Single Market, at least some of these recommendations are difficult to swallow. The suggestion, for example, that professional qualifications should only be assessed 'if it is essential' rides roughshod over the entire EU qualification recognition acquis and consequently diminishes the quality and integrity of the Single Market.

1.3.2 Recommendation on the Recognition of Professional Qualifications of Third-Country Nationals

The background to the Commission's recommendation in 2023 on the recognition of professional qualifications of third-country nationals[40] is somewhat different. In her 2022 State of the Union Address, Commission President Ursula von der Leyen specifically noted that, given the record-high job vacancies and skills shortages in the EU, 'we need to speed up and facilitate the recognition of qualifications … of third country nationals'.[41] Accordingly, in the Commission's workplan for 2023 which was published shortly thereafter, a new 'initiative' to facilitate the recognition of qualifications of third-country nationals was

39 European Commission, *Assessment of Commission Recommendation (EU) 2022/554 of 5 April 2022 on the Recognition of Qualifications for People Fleeing Russia's Invasion of Ukraine* (June 2023) 3.

40 Commission Recommendation (EU) 2023/2611 on the recognition of qualifications of third-country nationals [2023] OJ L 2023/2611.

41 European Commission, '2022 State of the Union Address by President von der Leyen' (14 September 2022) <https://ec.europa.eu/commission/presscorner/detail/en/speech_22_5493> (accessed 14 January 2024).

envisaged to 'attract the right skills' to the EU.[42] In its communication on *Skills and Talent Mobility*, the Commission announced, over a year after the publication of its workplan for 2023, its adoption of its recommendation on the recognition of professional qualifications of third-country nationals. As the Commission put it,

> Simpler, better procedures in this area will help employers to know what a qualification gained outside the EU means in practice, ensuring third-country nationals are able to perform the jobs they are recruited for and have comparable qualifications to their EU counterparts.[43]

The recommendation is expressly designed to apply to third-country nationals who are in the process of obtaining a visa or work and residence permit in a member state or are already legally resident in the EU. Specifically, it applies to skills and qualification recognition requirements in the context of access to a regulated profession, access to a learning programme or where required as part of a labour migration process. The reference to 'skills' in this context is important: the recommendation seeks to target not only formal qualifications, but any skill which a third-country national may be able to evidence. The Commission elucidates five general 'principles' which should guide the recognition of skills and qualifications of third-country nationals. These concern the reduction of barriers to skills and qualification recognition, the need for member states to adopt a 'skills first' approach, the reduction of use of labour market tests, the mitigation of the 'brain drain' from third-countries and not extending the requirement for the recognition of skills and qualifications of third-country nationals to circumstances other than those to which the recommendation applies, such as in respect of professions that are not regulated. They should guide member states' overall approach to skills' and qualification recognition.

The recommendation then goes on to identify a series of recommendations in respect of the organisation of the recognition of the skills and qualifications of third-country nationals concerning capacity building of member state qualification recognition authorities, cooperation with third-countries to facilitate easier qualification recognition, even pre-arrival to the EU, the provision of easily accessible and digestible information and support to third-country

---

42 European Commission, 'Commission work programme 2023: A Union standing firm and united' (Communication) COM(2022) 548 final, 11.

43 European Commission, 'Skills and Talent Mobility' (Communication) COM(2023) 715 final, 7.

nationals on national qualification procedures and processes improved national procedures, such as by providing third-country nationals with instant acknowledgement-receipts after submitting online applications for recognition. These recommendations are quite granular and amount, in substance, to a work programme for member state qualification recognition authorities. For example, the Commission goes so far as to recommend that staff of such authorities develop their foreign language skills to enable them to better provide services to third-country nationals. On the issue of costs of recognition applications, however, the Commission's position is somewhat less ambitious; it simply recommends that national authorities should publish transparent information about the costs associated with recognition procedures and that the costs should not exceed the actual cost of the procedure and are comparable with those costs applied to EU citizens in similar circumstances.

In the final parts of this recommendation, the Commission makes a series of detailed recommendations in respect of the recognition professional qualifications specifically and the recognition of skills and qualifications for labour migration. The former consist of three overarching recommendations in respect of documents and formalities, recognition decisions and priority regulated professions. Perhaps the most controversial of these is that member states should issue recognition decisions within 2 months at most and within 4 weeks in general. This is likely to place great resource pressures on national authorities. The Commission also recommends that in respect of priority regulated professions, third-country nationals should be able to practise their profession after submitting their application for recognition but while the examination of their application is pending. This suggestion implies that the demands of economic efficiency in member state labour and service markets should override the clear procedures which have been set down in member state law and trample over the clear procedural limits set by Directive 2005/36/EC. This may be a hard pill for many national authorities to swallow. The recommendations in respect of the recognition of skills and qualifications for labour migration are more limited, emphasising cooperation between member state authorities, clarity of communication of information to third-country nationals about qualification recognition procedures and enabling third-country nationals to have their qualifications recognised before arriving in the EU.

1.3.3 Proposal for a Regulation Establishing an EU Talent Pool

The Commission's 2023 recommendation above is but one facet of its *Skills and Talent Mobility* package. The other major initiative which is of relevance in the present context is its proposal for a regulation establishing an EU Talent

Pool.[44] That proposal envisages, *inter alia*, the establishment of a pool of jobseekers from third-countries who will be able to look for jobs online via an automated matching tool. This tool will facilitate the matching of third-country jobseekers with jobs in the EU by matching their qualifications and experience with those job profiles. Unlike the relevant parts of the EU's migration and asylum acquis considered earlier, this proposal and the Commission recommendation will apply to third-country nationals before they arrive in the EU, thereby facilitating the anticipatory recognition of their professional qualifications. Specifically, the recitals to the proposal for a regulation establishing an EU Talent Pool suggest that

> the recognition of qualifications and validation of skills of registered jobseekers from third countries should be conducted in the participating Member States upon request of the jobseeker or the employer in accordance with the national law and practices.

While this does not go so far as to require member states to set up a qualification recognition procedure for third-country nationals outside the EU (as it expressly defers to national law and practices in this respect), nonetheless it is a welcome development. It remains to be seen how this bold statement will be received by the other EU institutions. The Commission Recommendation on the recognition of qualifications of third-country nationals is, however, expressly designed to apply to third-country nationals who are in the process of obtaining a visa or work and residence permit in a member state or are already legally resident in the EU. Other, practical initiatives are also envisaged as part of the Commission's *Skills and Talent Mobility* package, such as improving the transparency of and access to recognition processes across the EU, using EU tools to help understand the value of qualifications and skills gained in third-countries relevant for meeting EU labour market shortages, exploring the possibility of a broader reform of the EU system on the recognition of qualifications and validation of skills and cooperating with third-countries to establish 'Talent Partnerships' – partnerships with certain third-countries to facilitate managed labour migration with mutually beneficial, tailor-made priorities[45] and the establishment of a Labour Migration Platform to enhance discussions and cooperation on legal migration and employment and support

44 Commission, 'Proposal for a Regulation of the European Parliament and of the Council establishing an EU Talent Pool' COM(2023) 716 final.

45 These have yet to be established. See Lucas Rasche, 'EU Talent Partnerships: Fit for Purpose?' (Hertie School Policy Brief, 16 June 2021).

the effective operationalisation of EU-level initiatives. At a high-level it can be observed that these proposals are welcome in principle, although they are likely to be highly controversial if ever implemented.

1.4 *Funds Supporting Integration*

1.4.1 European Social Fund[46] and European Social Fund Plus[47]

According to art 2(1) of the instrument establishing the ESF, the fund was designed to, inter alia, 'promote high levels of employment and job quality, improve access to the labour market [and] support the geographical and occupational mobility of workers'. The ESF is based on a regulation, not a directive, as envisaged by art 164 TFEU. This is but another example of the diversity of regulatory approaches adopted by the EU in this area. Article 2(3) thereof states that the ESF should 'benefit people, including disadvantaged people such as the long-term unemployed, people with disabilities, *migrants, ethnic minorities* [and] *marginalised communities*' (my emphasis). Article 10 provides for transnational cooperation, 'with the aim of promoting mutual learning, thereby increasing the effectiveness of policies supported by the ESF'. In relation to migrants, this is currently achieved through the Thematic Network on Migrants, which facilitates discussion between the member states of their own integration projects, the coordination of projects between member states through the provision of online databases, networking and publications, as well as annual conferences.[48] The ESF funded member state projects which further certain thematic objectives established in the Common Provisions Regulation I, the most relevant of which are 'promoting sustainable and quality employment and supporting labour mobility', 'promoting social inclusion, combating poverty and any discrimination', and 'investing in education, training and vocational training for skills and life-long learning'.[49] Some such projects appear to

---

46 Parliament and Council Regulation (EU) 1304/2013 on the European Social Fund [2013] OJ L347/470.

47 Parliament and Council Regulation (EU) 2021/1057 establishing the European Social Fund Plus (ESF+) and repealing Regulation (EU) 1296/2013 [2021] OJ L231/21.

48 Commission, 'ESF Transnational Cooperation: Migrants' <https://ec.europa.eu/esf/transnationality/forums/migrants> accessed 16 April 2018.

49 Regulation 1303/2013/EU of the European Parliament and of the Council laying down common provisions on the European Regional Development Fund, the European Social Fund, the Cohesion Fund, the European Agricultural Fund for Rural Development and the European Maritime and Fisheries Fund and laying down general provisions on the European Regional Development Fund, the European Social Fund, the Cohesion Fund and the European Maritime and Fisheries Fund and repealing Council Regulation (EC) No 1083/2006 [2013] OJ L347/320 (Common Provisions Regulation I), art 9.

contribute to the recognition of qualifications. For example, *EPIC*, an Irish programme targeted at migrants based in Dublin, provides cultural and practical information on living and working in Ireland. EPIC works with Irish employers to deliver additional skills training, including social media training and participating in mock interviews, for migrants.[50] There are also a number of projects which are targeted directly at refugees. The Metal Engineering Qualifications programme in Germany, for example, provided an education programme for refugees, who, on successful completion of the programme, received a professional qualification, between May 2015 and October 2016.[51]

The ESF operated during the period 2014–2020. The ESF+ is the successor to the ESF and operates for the period 2021–2027. Like the ESF, it is designed to support the member states to 'achieve high employment levels, fair social protection and a skilled and resilient workforce ready for the future world of work, as well as inclusive and cohesive societies'. In this vein, ESF+ funding should 'provide support to promote the socio-economic integration of third-country nationals, including migrants'. And like the ESF, the ESF+ funds member state projects which further certain thematic enabling conditions established in the Common Provisions Regulation II, the most relevant of which are 'improving access to employment … for long-term unemployed and disadvantaged groups on the labour market', 'modernising labour market institutions and services to assess and anticipate skills needs and ensure timely and tailor-made assistance and support to labour market matching, transitions and mobility', 'improving the quality, inclusiveness, effectiveness and labour market relevance of education and training systems including through validation of non-formal and informal learning', 'promoting lifelong learning, in particular flexible upskilling and reskilling opportunities for all' and 'fostering active inclusion with a view to promoting equal opportunities, non-discrimination and active participation, and improving employability, in particular for disadvantaged groups'.[52] For example, in Ireland, funding is provided through the ESF+ to support migrant

50 Business in the Community, 'Are you a Jobseeker?' <https://www.bitc.ie/business-action-programmes/business-action-on-employment/are-you-a-jobseeker/> accessed 26 January 2018; Commission, 'Projects: 'EPIC' Outcomes for Migrant Jobseekers in Ireland' <http://ec.europa.eu/esf/main.jsp?catId=46&langId=en&projectId=1997> accessed 26 January 2018.

51 Commission, 'Projects: Metalwork qualifications for young refugees' <http://ec.europa.eu/esf/main.jsp?catId=46&langId=en&projectId=2197> accessed 26 January 2018.

52 Parliament and Council Regulation (EU) 2021/1060 laying down common provisions on the European Regional Development Fund, the European Social Fund Plus, the Cohesion Fund, the Just Transition Fund and the European Maritime, Fisheries and Aquaculture Fund and financial rules for those and for the Asylum, Migration and Integration Fund, the Internal Security Fund and the Instrument for Financial Support for Border

employability include employment training, workplace language training, training in CV preparation, interview skills, work placements, referral to other services (where appropriate), and mentoring, all with the objective of placement of the participants in either employment, improved employment or further training. Similar projects in Austria, Bulgaria, Serbia and Turkey also received funding from the Employment and Social Innovation strand of the ESF+, a part of the fund which is directly managed by the European Commission.

1.4.2 Asylum, Migration and Integration Fund[53]

The AMIF Regulation I supported integration and other programmes for the period 2014–2020, taking over from the Refugee Fund,[54] the Integration Fund[55] and the Return Fund.[56] The AMIF provides funding for actions supporting different categories of migrants, primarily on the basis of national funding programmes drawn up by the member states. Thus, for regular migrants, the AMIF supported pre-departure measures in third-countries as well as integration measures in the member states. Specifically, the AMIF supported, inter alia,

- information packages and campaigns to raise awareness and promote intercultural dialogue, including via user-friendly communication and information technology and websites;
- the assessment of skills and qualifications, as well as enhancement of transparency and compatibility of skills and qualifications in a third country with those of a Member State;
- training enhancing employability in a Member State;
- comprehensive civic orientation courses and language tuition; and
- measures focusing on education, including language training and preparatory actions to facilitate access to the labour market.[57]

In relation to forced migrants, by contrast, the only relevant actions which the AMIF supported were the provision of material aid, including assistance at the

Management and Visa Policy [2021] OJ L231/159 (Common Provisions II Regulation), art 15 and Annex III.

53 Parliament and Council Regulation (EU) 516/2014 establishing the Asylum, Migration and Integration Fund [2014] OJ L150/168 (AMIF Regulation I) and Parliament and Council Regulation (EU) 2021/1147 establishing the Asylum, Migration and Integration Fund [2021] OJ L251/1 (AMIF Regulation II).

54 Decision 573/2007/EC establishing the European Refugee Fund [2007] OJ L144/1.

55 Decision 435/2007/EC establishing the European Integration Fund [2007] OJ L168/18.

56 Decision 527/2007/EC establishing the European Return Fund [2007] OJ L144/45.

57 AMIF Regulation I, arts 8–9.

border, education, health and psychological care; and the provision of support services such as translation and interpretation, education, training, including language training, and other initiatives which are consistent with the status of the person concerned.[58] An example of a project targeted at forced migrants which was funded by the AMIF is the Skills2Work project, which promoted the labour market integration of the beneficiaries of international protection in nine member states. The project supported the asylum reception framework by providing information and services concerning skills recognition and validation.[59] Finally, in respect of irregular migrants, the AMIF envisages funding 'measures to launch the progress of reintegration for the returnee's personal development, such as cash-incentives, training, placement and employment assistance and start-up support for economic activities'.[60] The AMIF also part-funds the European Migration Network, a network which aims to provide the information demands of the EU's institutions and the member states.[61]

Interestingly, it has been suggested that the European Integration Fund, a predecessor to the AMIF, 'induced the creation of a systematic integration policy at national level'.[62] This is a good example of the theme of governance at work. While the EU's competence in this area remains exceptionally limited, it is nonetheless possible that a 'Europeanisation' of national policies has occurred to some degree, even in the absence of hard legal measures. However, whether this conclusion can claim to be comprehensively accurate is doubtful. In its interim evaluation of the operation of the AMIF, for example, the Commission concluded that member states have prioritised short-term integration measures, such as civic integration policies – the kind of measures discussed under the terms of the Family Reunification and Long-Term Residents' Directives above – and, to a slightly lesser extent, medium-term integration measures, such as access to the labour market.[63] But, as the argument of this book thus far has suggested, effective access for third-country nationals requires more than a bare right to work. More is often necessary.

In respect of the period 2021–2027, €9.88 billion is available under the AMIF Regulation II to support, inter alia, the strengthening and development of the

---

58 AMIF Regulation I, art 5.

59 IOM Global Office Brussels, 'Valuing Skills of Beneficiaries of International Protection' <https://globalofficebrussels.iom.int/skills2work> accessed 12 May 2025.

60 AMIF Regulation I, art 12(e).

61 Council Decision 2008/381/EC establishing a European Migration Network [2008] OJ L131/7, art 1.

62 *The EU's Policy on the Integration of Migrants* (n 1) 4.

63 Commission, *Interim Evaluation of the Asylum, Migration and Integration Fund: Final Report* (Publications Office of the European Union 2018) 41–42.

EU's migration and asylum system, promoting and contributing to the effective integration and inclusion of third-country nationals. Funding for specific measures in this context include the assessment and recognition of skills and qualifications, including professional experience, acquired in a third country, as well as their transparency, and their equivalence with those of a member state as well as counselling, education, language and other training, such as civic orientation courses and professional guidance.[64] In addition, part of the AMIF consists of a Thematic Facility which comprises funding that can be allocated on an emergency basis to projects addressing the needs of forced migrants. The Thematic Facility funds the promotion of transnational projects and partnerships fostering the integration of migrants in the labour market, such as by contributing to facilitating and speeding up the assessment, recognition and validation of skills and qualifications of third-country nationals.

2 EU External Relations Policy

2.1 *Overview*

The EU's external competences in this context are several. First is the competence under art 216 TFEU to reach international agreements with third-countries. The exercise of this competence was largely discussed in Chapter 3. The element of that competence which is of relevance here is the possibility of cooperating to facilitate skills' development and qualification recognition. The second is the Union's competence to develop relationships with its neighbours under art 8 TEU, countries which are likely to be particularly close with the Union. Relations with neighbouring countries must be founded on the values of the Union. Third is the Union's competence to cooperate with third-countries specifically in relation to education and training under arts 165(3) and 166(3) TFEU. Finally, there is the Union's competence under Part Five, Title III TFEU concerning cooperation with third-countries and humanitarian aid. According to art 208(2) TFEU, the EU's concern in this area is poverty alleviation and eradication. According to art 209(1) TFEU, the Parliament and Council shall adopt the necessary measures to implement the Union's development cooperation policy, which may relate to multiannual cooperation programmes with developing countries or programmes with a thematic approach. However, the Union's competence in this area is a shared competence; as art 4(4) TFEU states, the exercise of the Union's competence in this area is without prejudice

64 AMIF Regulation II, Annex III.

to the exercise of the member states' competence. Each of these competences are addressed in turn.

2.2 *Mobility Partnerships*

Mobility Partnerships between the EU, some of its member states and third-countries are non-binding arrangements, primarily targeted at countries in the EU Neighbourhood, which facilitate mobility, visa facilitation and readmission agreements and pre-departure measures.[65] Such arrangements are currently in place between the EU and Moldova (2008), Cape Verde (2008), Georgia (2009), Armenia (2011), Morocco (2013), Azerbaijan (2013), Tunisia (2014), Jordan (2014) and Belarus (2016). These arrangements facilitate the creation of dedicated 'Migration and Mobility Resource Centres' which serve as a one-stop shop for individuals seeking information and support on validation of their qualifications, skills upgrading and skills needs at national or regional levels or in the EU and provide pre-departure, return and reintegration measures.[66]

65 See, inter alia, Roderick Parkes, 'EU Mobility Partnerships: A Model of Policy Coordination?' (2009) 11 EJML 327; Nastasja Reslow, 'Deciding on EU External Migration Policy: The Member States and the Mobility Partnerships' (2012) 34 European Integration 223; Natasja Reslow, 'The Role of Third-Countries in EU Migration Policy: The Mobility Partnerships' (2012) 14 EJML 393; Stefan Angenbendt, 'Mobility Partnerships – The Future of European Migration Policy?' (2012) 1 Migration and Development 216; Paula García Andrade, 'The Legal Feasibility of the EU's External Action on Legal Migration: The Internal and the External Intertwined' (2013) 15 EJML 263; Julia Maisenbacher, 'The Political Economy of Mobility Partnerships – Structural Power in the EU's External Migration Policy' (2015) 20 New Political Economy 871; Nastasja Reslow, 'EU 'Mobility' Partnerships: An Initial Assessment of Implementation Dynamics' (2015) 3 Politics and Governance 117; Stefan Brocza and Katharina Paulhart, 'EU Mobility Partnerships: A Smart Instrument for the Externalisation of Migration Control' (2015) 3 European Journal of Futures Research 15; Leonhard den Hertog, 'Funding the EU-Morocco 'Mobility Partnership': Of Implementation and Competences' (2016) 18 EJML 275; Natasja Reslow, '"Not everything that counts can be counted": Assessing 'success' of EU external migration policy' (2017) 55 IM 156; Fanny Tittel-Mosser, 'The Unintended Legal and Policy Relevance of EU Mobility Partnerships: A Comparative Implementation Analysis of Morocco and Cape Verde' (2018) 20 EJML 314; Natasja Reslow, 'Making and Implementing Multi-Actor EU External Migration Policy: The Mobility Partnerships' in Sergio Carrera, Arie Pieter Leonhard den Hertog, Marion Panizzon and Dora Kostakopoulou (eds), *EU External Migration Policies in an Era of Global Mobilities: Intersecting Policy Universes* (Brill/Nijhoff 2018); and Fanny Tittel-Mosser, 'Mobility Partnerships: A Tool for the Externalisation of EU Migration Policy? A Comparative Study of Morocco and Cape Verde' in Sergio Carrera, Juan Santos Vara and Tineke Strik (eds), *Constitutionalising the External Dimensions of EU Migration Policy in Times of Crisis* (Edward Elgar 2019).

66 Commission, 'The Global Approach to Migration and Mobility' (Communication) COM(2011) 743 final 14.

For example, the Belarussian Mobility Partnership envisages that cooperation will entail 'pre-departure training' as well as the facilitation of 'mutual recognition of vocational and academic qualifications' with specific reference to the Lisbon Convention, including the development 'of curricula in such a manner as to enhance recognition of respective qualifications'. Similarly, the Georgian Mobility Partnership envisages measures designed to tackle the 'brain drain and brain waste' by, inter alia, facilitating the recognition of qualifications, labour-matching tools and educational programmes.

In principle, these centres are beneficial and provide precisely the sort of measures here envisaged. It would, accordingly, be helpful if these centres were institutionalised throughout the EU's external relations. However, they are not without their drawbacks. First, these arrangements are simply that; arrangements, not legally binding agreements. They do not provide third-country nationals with rights which they can rely upon. This is not necessarily problematic but the point nonetheless merits noting. Second, most of these agreements are of relatively recent vintage and much research remains to be done in respect of their actual implementation in practice. The vast majority of the materials cited at note 65 are concerned with the extent to which the Mobility Partnerships have been negotiated and funded, while less of those materials are concerned with how successfully they have been implemented in practice. Of the literature which does address the implementation of the Mobility Partnerships, Nastaja Reslow and Fanny Tittel-Mosser's contributions stand out as meriting attention.

Across two papers, Reslow considers the implementation and success of the Mobility Partnerships agreed to date in a general way.[67] In other words, Reslow abstracts from specific Mobility Partnerships and identifies ways in which they can be implemented and adjudged successful. In terms of implementation, one point which emerges is that the fact that they are voluntary and non-binding may be of benefit; member states must choose to participate in the Mobility Partnerships. In terms of success, while the Commission noted in its exceptionally early review (2009) that the Mobility Partnerships are 'promising, innovative and comprehensive tools',[68] Reslow, rather than reaching a conclusion as to their success, develops an analytical framework which, going forward, may be used to assess their success. This framework emphasises 'goal

67 'EU 'Mobility' Partnerships: An Initial Assessment of Implementation Dynamics' (n 65); and '"Not everything that counts can be counted": Assessing 'success' of EU external migration policy' (n 65).

68 Commission, 'Mobility Partnerships as a Tool of the Global Approach to Migration' SEC(2009) 1240, 8.

achievement, political success, normative justification, costs, time and external factors' as relevant to determining the success of the Mobility Partnerships in practice.[69] Such a framework, however, faces a number of obstacles. First, there is a significant lack of data available by which to judge the success of Mobility Partnerships in practice. Second, the analytical framework will itself require some amendment to function effectively. Third and relatedly, given the generality of such a framework, case studies may be necessary to apply it in practice.

Accordingly, and by contrast, Tittel-Mosser's analysis involves a more fine-grained case study approach. She focuses on the implementation of the Mobility Partnerships with Morocco and Cape Verde. Of particular relevance is her focus on the changes made in Moroccan and Cape Verdean law since the development of the Mobility Partnerships, such as the liberalisation of certain restrictions on access to and practise of some professions, as well as the development of national immigration and integration policies. As Tittel-Mosser notes, while there is, strictly speaking, not a causal relationship between the development of the Mobility Partnerships and these changes, there is at least a correlation.

2.3 *European Neighbourhood Policy and Enlargement*

2.3.1 European Neighbourhood Policy

The ENP is the EU's policy governing its relations with its southern and eastern neighbours, namely: Algeria, Egypt, Israel, Jordan, Lebanon, Libya, Morocco, Palestine, Syria, Tunisia, Armenia, Azerbaijan, Belarus, Georgia, Moldova and Ukraine.[70] Among other things, the ENP requires the development and implementation of country-specific action plans on an annual basis. These action

69 '"Not everything that counts can be counted": Assessing 'success' of EU external migration policy' (n 66) 165.

70 See, inter alia, Roland Dannreuther, 'Developing the Alternative to Enlargement: The European Neighbourhood Policy' (2006) 11 EFA Rev 183; Paul James Cardwell, *EU External Relations and Systems of Governance: The CFSP, Euro-Mediterranean Partnership and Migration* (Routledge 2009); Bart van Vooren, 'A case-study of "soft law" in EU external relations: the European Neighbourhood Policy' (2009) 34 EL Rev 696; Bart van Vooren, *EU External Relations Law and the European Neighbourhood Policy: A Paradigm for Coherence* (Routledge 2012); Sieglinde Gstöhl (ed), *The European Neighbourhood Policy in Comparative Perspective: Models, Challenges, Lessons* (Routledge 2016); Sieglinde Gstöhl and Simon Schunz (eds), *Theorising the European Neighbourhood Policy* (Routledge 2016); Dimitris Bouris and Tobias Schumacher (eds), *The Revised European Neighbourhood Policy: Continuity and Change in EU Foreign Policy* (Palgrave Macmillan 2017); and Tobias Schumacher, Andreas Marchetti and Thomas Demmelhuber (eds), *The Routledge Handbook on the European Neighbourhood Policy* (Routledge 2018).

plans are developed by the particular council established under the relevant association and trade agreement between the EU and third-countries in the EU Neighbourhood. They are then formally adopted by the Commission on the basis of an implementing decision, the details of which are contained in annexes thereto, and are binding on the EU.[71] Some of these action plans require that countries in the ENP develop, inter alia, national qualification frameworks (NQFs) in line with the EQF, outlined earlier; labour market skills matching tools, ie, qualification recognition systems; and educational exchanges between participating third-country students and EU students.[72] Finally, in terms of financing, in addition to the annual action plans which draw directly on the EU's budget, the EU has adopted a European Neighbourhood Instrument specifically designed to provide funding for certain measures in respect of countries in the neighbourhood, such as promoting capacity building in education and training through the improved use and development of skills.[73]

All of these steps seem welcome. Aligning third-country NQFs with the EQF will make education in those countries more comparable to that in the EU. As suggested earlier, this facilitates what can be described as the 'externalisation' of the Single Market; namely, the creation of a robust external dimension which ensures that the EU is better able to secure its internal goals. Creating similar education and training systems outside the EU may prepare third-country nationals to participate in the Single Market before they even arrive. It may even better facilitate the recognition of their qualifications and, consequently, their ability to work in the EU. The possibility of educational exchanges is to be welcome insofar as it facilitates the circulation of knowledge and the possibility for third-country nationals to bring greater knowledge and skills back to their country of origin. If such exchanges were institutionalised across the EU's partnership, trade and association agreements, they may

71 Parliament and Council Regulation (EU) 232/2014 establishing a European Neighbourhood Instrument [2014] OJ L77/27; Parliament and Council Regulation (EU) 2021/947 establishing the Neighbourhood, Development and International Cooperation Instrument – Global Europe [2021] OJ L209/1; and 'A case-study of "soft law" in EU external relations: the European Neighbourhood Policy' (n 70) 709–710.

72 See, eg, Commission Implementing Decision on the Annual Action Plan 2018 in favour of the Republic of Azerbaijan for 2018 C(2018) 8177 final, Annex; Commission Implementing Decision on the Annual Action Plan 2017 in favour of the Republic of Armenia to be financed from the general budget of the European Union C(2017) 8195 final, Annex 1.

73 Parliament and Council Regulation 232/2014/EU establishing a European Neighbourhood Instrument [2014] OJ L77/27, Annex II.

serve to improve mutual understanding, reduce discrimination and alleviate the risks of any 'brain drain'.

2.3.2 Enlargement Policy

The EU's enlargement policy concerns the potential accession of certain neighbouring countries in Europe, such as those in the Western Balkans (Bosnia and Herzegovina, Montenegro, Albania, Serbia, Kosovo, North Macedonia (formerly FYROM)) and Turkey, to the EU.[74] In its enlargement policy, the EU monitors the progress of such countries in meeting certain basic, minimum standards in relation to, amongst other things, their national institutions, education and training, fiscal stability and market rules. The Commission draws up reports on each country's progress towards compliance with such EU norms and standards on an annual basis. Thus far, the development and recognition of qualifications have featured in these reports. Turkey, Kosovo, North Macedonia and Montenegro have adopted and implemented an NQF which references the EQF, an approach recommended in the updated Council Recommendation on the EQF in 2017. In respect of the recognition of skills and qualifications, the Commission reports that while some potential and actual candidate accession states have implemented a recognition scheme, obstacles to recognition, such as nationality and language requirements, remain.[75] Moreover, such recognition schemes have generally been quite partial, applying to a handful professions only.[76] Several states, such as Montenegro and Serbia, have yet to adopt any legislation on the recognition of professional qualifications. Nonetheless, all states are encouraged to continue aligning their recognition frameworks with EU norms. The Commission's reports also disclose an extensive concern for the quality of education available in these states and the relevance of such education for participation in the labour market. In most cases, the Commission has recommended more extensive investment in respect of the education systems of accession states, as well as increasing participation rates

74 See, inter aila, Helene Sjursen (ed), *Questioning EU Enlargement: Europe in Search of Identity* (Routledge 2006).

75 See, eg, Commission, 'Turkey 2018 Report accompanying the 2018 Communication on EU Enlargement Policy' (Staff Working Document) SWD(2018) 153 final, 65.

76 See, eg, Commission, 'Bosnia and Herzegovina 2016 Report accompanying the 2016 Communication on EU Enlargement Policy' (Staff Working Document) SWD(2016) 365 final, 42; Commission, 'The former Yugoslav Republic of Macedonia 2018 Report accompanying the 2018 Communication on EU Enlargement Policy' (Staff Working Document) SWD(2018) 154 final, para 5.3; Commission, 'Albania 2018 Report accompanying the 2018 Communication on EU Enlargement Policy' (Staff Working Document) SWD(2018) 151 final, 56.

in education.[77] In terms of funding, the Parliament and Council have adopted two funding instruments specifically in respect of pre-accession states, one of which has since expired.[78] The funding instrument from 2014–2020 envisaged funding being provided for, inter alia, education, skills and lifelong learning, specifically through adapting vocational education and training to labour market demands and improving the quality and relevance of higher education and training.[79] The total budget for the period 2014–2020 under the instrument for all pre-accession states was €11.7bn. Under the current funding instrument, the total budget for the period 2021–2027 is €14.162billion.[80]

2.4 *International Cooperation and Policy Dialogue*

Commission DG Education and Training cooperates in education and training with third-countries to prioritise, inter alia, the advancement of the EU as a centre of excellence in education and training; to support partner countries in the modernisation of their legal system; and to promote common values and closer understanding between different peoples and cultures. The EU has thus established a policy dialogue with several partner states and groups, namely with the countries in the EU Neighbourhood through the Eastern Partnership (Armenia, Azerbaijan, Belarus, Georgia, Moldova and Ukraine), Southern Mediterranean Partnership and Western Balkans Platform on Education and Training (Albania, Bosnia and Herzegovina, North Macedonia, Kosovo, Montenegro and Serbia), with Africa through the EU-Africa Partnership, and with several countries in the Americas and Asia. These dialogues provide opportunities for EU and non-EU officials and member state representatives to meet, discuss competing goals, form joint agendas and goals and produce reports or evaluations on respective recognition methods, policies and cooperation.

---

77 See, eg, Commission, 'Albania 2018 Report accompanying the 2018 Communication on EU Enlargement' (Staff Working Document) SWD(2018) 151 final, ch 26; Commission, 'Montenegro 2019 Report accompanying the 2019 Communication on EU Enlargement Policy' (Staff Working Document) SWD(2019) 217 final, ch 26.

78 Council Regulation 1085/2006/EC establishing an Instrument for Pre-Accession Assistance [2006] OJ L210/82.

79 Parliament and Council Regulation (EU) 231/2014 establishing an Instrument for Pre-accession Assistance (IPA II) [2014] OJ L77/11, Annex II(d); and see Wolfgang Koeth, 'The New Instrument for Pre-Accession Assistance (IPA II): Less Accession, More Assistance?' (EIPA Working Paper 2014/W/01).

80 Parliament and Council Regulation (EU) 2021/1529 establishing the Instrument for Pre-accession assistance (IPA III) [2021] OJ L330/1.

An example of this is the joint study commissioned by the EU-Australia Partnership on the role of qualifications frameworks in facilitating the mobility of workers and learners in 2011. The study noted the significance of professional organisations in recognising qualifications, and several problems surrounding the lack of professional qualification recognition. These problems included the lack of professional networks, the great diversity of professional bodies and organisations, and the different qualification assessment and recognition methodologies adopted in respect of vocational, academic and professional qualifications.[81] The study was completed against the background of the European Commission – Government of Australia Joint Declaration on Cooperation in Education and Training in 2007, which required cooperation by both parties on, inter alia, 'facilitating the quality of student/learner and professional mobility by promoting transparent, mutual recognition of qualifications and periods of study, training, and where appropriate, portability of credits'. Since the report in 2011, the EU-Australia Partnership has agreed to foster linkages between the EQF and the Australian Qualifications Framework for the purposes of better facilitating the recognition of qualifications.[82] Similarly, in its third Policy Dialogue with Southern Mediterranean Countries on Higher Education as part of the Southern Mediterranean Partnership, the Commission encouraged participating partner countries to adopt the EQF in the development of their national qualification frameworks,[83] and the Astana Declaration of the Second Meeting of Ministers for Education of the member states of the European Union and of the Central Asian Countries encouraged members of the EU's Education Initiative for Central Asia to consider the recent Council Recommendation on the EQF and take it into account in forming and updating their respective national qualification frameworks.[84] In addition, the EQF has

81 GHK, *Study on the (potential) role of qualifications frameworks in supporting mobility of workers and learners: European Commission and Australian Department of Education, Employment and Workplace Relations Joint EU-Australia Study* (DEEWR and DG EAC 2011).

82 EU-Australia Education and Training Policy Dialogue, 'Fourth European Union-Australia Education and Training Policy Dialogue: Joint Statement' (Brussels, 12 March 2012); EU-Australia Education and Training Policy Dialogue, 'Fifth European Union-Australia Education and Training Policy Dialogue: Joint Statement' (Melbourne, 4 March 2013).

83 Commission, *Report on the Third Policy Dialogue with Southern Mediterranean Countries on Higher Education* (Brussels, 12–13 July 2016) 12.

84 Astana Declaration of the Second Meeting of Ministers for Education of the Member states of the European Union and of the Central Asian Countries (Astana, 23 June 2017).

been, or soon will be, adopted by a number of countries participating in the Western Partnership[85] and the Eastern Partnership.[86]

2.5 *International Cooperation and Development*

Commission DG International Cooperation and Development reaches out to many countries across the world in a wide variety of ways through the EU's trade relationships and the provision of technical and financial assistance and grants to developing countries for the development of their national and regional political, economic, social and cultural institutions. The EU's work in this area is vast and significant.[87] Any comments I make here should therefore be considered introductory and relevant solely to the recognition of the skills of third-country nationals. More specifically, it is worth considering briefly some of the measures which have been adopted in this area that are of relevance to recognition of skills.

Perhaps the key measure in this area is the Development Cooperation Instrument (DCI)[88] which provided funding during the period 2014–2020, the DCI took over from an earlier measure which ran for the period 2006–2013.[89] The DCI funded thematic programmes, such as the development of education and training, through, inter alia, the development and implementation of annual action plans (AAPs). AAPs were financing decisions adopted by the Commission in respect of the EU's external relations under the auspices of the DCI; and several of these have addressed skills development and recognition. The first was the 2016 AAP for Africa, which provided funding for the recognition of educational qualifications obtained in different African educational

85 DG Education and Culture, *From University to Employment: Higher Education Provision and Labour Market Needs in the Western Balkans Synthesis Report* (European Commission 2016).

86 'Mutual Learning for Better Qualifications Regional Conference October 2015: Conference Conclusions and Follow-up Actions' (6–8 October 2015).

87 See, eg, Wil Hout (ed), *EU Development Policy and Poverty Reduction: Enhancing Effectiveness* (Ashgate 2007); Martin Holland and Matthew Doidge, *Developing Policy of the European Union* (Red Globe Press 2012); Stefan Gänzle, Sven Grimm and Davina Makhan (eds), *The European Union and Global Development: An 'Enlightened Superpower' in the Making?* (Palgrave Macmillan 2012); Robert Schütze, 'EU Development Policy: Constitutional and Legislative Foundation(s)' (2013) 15 CYELS 699; and Sarah Beringer, Sylvia Maier and Markus Thiel (eds), *EU Development Policies: Between Norms and Geopolitics* (Palgrave Macmillan 2019).

88 Parliament and Council Regulation 233/2014/EU establishing a financial instrument for development cooperation for the period 2014–2020 [2014] OJ L77/44.

89 Parliament and Council Regulation 1905/2006/EC establishing a financial instrument for development cooperation [2006] OJ L378/41.

institutions. Specifically, the funding aimed to promote the recognition of qualifications and skills obtained during periods of study abroad. By facilitating recognition between educational institutions in Africa, it is hoped that this will lead to greater internationalisation and harmonisation of educational curricula across Africa.[90] This may even eventually lead to the mutual recognition of qualifications between African professional bodies. This issue was also recognised in a recent Joint Communication, in which the Commission noted the need to 'better organise intra- and inter-regional labour mobility, facilitating institutional dialogue and cooperation along the migratory routes, and facilitating 'brain circulation' through recognition of skills and qualification, dialogue on visas, and promotion of students, researchers and academic mobility'.[91] Several other AAPs have noted the need to implement national qualifications frameworks in the context of higher education, but in general no link has yet been made between educational qualifications and professional qualifications.[92] Given that coordinated education and training is an important precursor to effective qualification recognition, only after education reforms have been institutionalised and entrenched is the issue of qualification recognition likely to arise.

The European Development Fund (EDF) was the primary financing instrument for the EU's development policy with ACP countries under the Cotonou

90 Commission, 'Implementing Decision on the Annual Action Programme 2016 of the DCI Pan-Africa Programme' (Implementing Decision) C(2016) 4513 final, Annex I.

91 Commission, 'A renewed partnership with the countries of Africa, the Caribbean and the Pacific' (Joint Communication) JOIN(2016) 52 final, 17.

92 See, for example, Commission, 'Implementing Decision on the Annual Action Programme 2014 in favour of Belarus to be financed from the general budget of the European Union' (Implementing Decision) C(2014) 6937 final, Annex III; Commission, 'Implementing Decision on the Annual Action Plan 2015 in favour of Pakistan to be financed from the general budget of the European Union' (Implementing Decision) C(2015) 9335 final, Annex I; Commission, 'Implementing Decision on the Annual Action Plan 2016 Part III in favour of the Asia region to be financed from the general budget of the European Union' (Implementing Decision) C(2016) 5218 final, Annex I; Commission, 'Implementing Decision on the Annual Action Plan 2016 in favour of the Caribbean Region to be financed from the 11th European Development Fund' (Implementing Decision) C(2016) 6434 final, Annex III; Commission, 'Implementing Decision on the Annual Action Programme 2014 in favour of Belarus to be financed from the general budget of the European Union' (Implementing Decision) C(2014) 6937 final, Annex III; Commission, 'Decision on the Annual Action Programme 2017 in favour of Angola to be financed from the 11th European Development Fund' (Implementing Decision) C(2016) 7077 final, Annex; Commission, 'Decision on the Annual Action Programme 2017 part 2 in favour of the Pacific Region to be financed from the 11th European Development Fund' (Implementing Decision) C(2017) 4903 final, Annex I.

Agreement. The 11th EDF, which operated from 2014–2020, provides approximately €32 billion for development activities in ACP states.[93] Historically, the EDF has mainly provided targeted development aid in the areas of agriculture and infrastructure, which have been key to decreasing poverty in ACP states. However, increasingly, funding has shifted towards developing human capital through enhancing skills and education of persons in ACP states.[94] However, both the DCI and EDF and other funding instruments have now been subsumed and consolidated into the Neighbourhood, Development and International Cooperation Instrument – Global Europe.[95] The NDICI – Global Europe provides funding from 2021–2027 with an overall allocation of €79.5 billion during that period. The NDICI – Global Europe allocates funding to geographic programmes, thematic programmes and rapid response actions to countries around the world. Of relevance to the present book are those projects which support 'decent employment and employability through the development of skills and competences, education and vocational training'. As with the DCI, the NDICI – Global Europe entails the adoption of AAPs by the Commission. However, as of the time of writing, no further AAPs have noted or focussed on the recognition of professional qualifications, although many continue to address the issue of upskilling, reskilling and continuously developing human capital.

3 EU Education and Training Policy

The point of recognising skills obtained in non-formal and informal contexts is to institutionalise knowledge, competencies and skills which would otherwise remain informal.[96] Recall that Part Three, Title XII TFEU provides

---

93 Cotonou Agreement, Annex IC; Council Regulation 2015/323/EU on the financial regulation applicable to the 11th European Development Fund [2015] OJ L58/17; and Council Regulation 2018/1877/EU on the financial regulation applicable to the 11th European Development Fund [2018] OJ L307/1.

94 See Roman Grynberg and Alice Clarke (eds), *The European Development Fund and Economic Partnership Agreements* (Commonwealth Secretariat 2006); Alisa Herrero, Anna Knoll, Cecilia Gregersen and Willy Kokolo, 'Implementing the Agenda for Change: An Independent Analysis of the 11th EDF Programming' European Centre for Development Policy Management Discussion Paper No 180 (September 2015).

95 Parliament and Council Regulation (EU) 2021/947 establishing the Neighbourhood, Development and International Cooperation Instrument – Global Europe [2021] OJ L209/1.

96 See generally Patrick Werquin, *Recognising Non-Formal and Informal Learning: Outcomes, Policies and Practices* (OECD 2010) and Madhu Singh, *Global Perspectives on Recognising Non-Formal and Informal Learning: Why Recognition Matters* (Springer Open 2015).

for education and training in the Union. Education and training in the EU is a shared competence; the Union's competence is accordingly limited to 'encouraging cooperation between member states'.[97] Any measures adopted by the Union in this area are therefore likely to be limited; indeed, harmonisation of laws is expressly excluded. Instead, the Council may adopt non-binding recommendations in respect of education policy. The key measure in respect of the recognition and validation of non-formal and informal learning is the Council Recommendation on the validation of non-formal and informal learning (the Recommendation).[98] In the recitals to the Recommendation, the Council notes that validating non-formal and informal learning can 'play an important role in enhancing employability and mobility, as well as increasing motivation for lifelong learning, particularly in the case of socio-economically disadvantaged or the low-qualified'.[99] The Recommendation therefore acknowledges the need to recognise the skills of those who are likely to be most vulnerable and at risk of social exclusion and isolation. It gives such groups the opportunity to live their way of life through the recognition of the skills they have acquired, even though they may not be traditionally recognised as being of significant economic value in the community. And the breadth or scope of application of the Recommendation is significant. For example, the Recommendation defines 'informal learning' as 'learning resulting from daily activities related to work, family or leisure and is not organised or structured in terms of objectives, time or learning support; it may be unintentional from the learner's perspective'.[100] Expressly included in the definition of 'informal learning' is 'activities at home (eg taking care of a child)'.[101]

According to the Recommendation, the member states should have in place, no later than 2018, arrangements for the validation of non-formal and informal learning, providing candidates with the possibility of obtaining some sort of qualification, in whole or in part, in respect of their non-formal and informal learning. According to the Council, validating such learning through the provision of qualifications 'can increase (...) participation in lifelong learning and (...) access to the labour market'.[102] While much of the above is welcome,

97 TFEU, art 165(1).

98 [2012] OJ C398/1. See also CEDEFOP, *European guidelines for validating non-formal and informal learning* (Publications Office of the European Union 2015).

99 The Recommendation, recital 1.

100 The Recommendation, Annex (c).

101 ibid.

102 ibid, art 1(3)(c).

there are several drawbacks to the Recommendation. For one, it is only a recommendation. There is no obligation on the member states to implement its terms. Whether or not this measure is nonetheless successful depends on the extent to which it establishes norms guiding member states conduct. This is an empirical question beyond the scope of this book. In respect of this recommendation specifically, in 2016 Lilli Casano demonstrated that the member states have been slow to implement its terms and many member states have simply made no effort at all. In general, her research remains accurate to date. Moreover, where efforts have been made, key stakeholders such as employers' associations and trade unions have not been sufficiently involved. Furthermore, there has been a strong tendency towards 'formalisation', ie, validation of skills obtained in an informal context but without a correlate focus on ensuring that people can subsequently benefit from such validation, ie, obtaining paid employment.[103] Finally, no account is taken of the role which validation of non-formal or informal learning might play in respect of third-country nationals specifically, although they may be considered to be a 'disadvantaged' group as noted in the recitals. Indeed, as the Commission noted in its recent *Fitness Check on EU Legislation on legal migration*,

> there is no (…) automatic coverage by third-country nationals (already residing in the EU) by existing validation arrangements. Moreover, equal treatment under the legal migration directives refers to the 'recognition of diplomas, certificates and other professional qualifications' and not more specifically to equal access to 'schemes for the assessment, validation and accreditation of prior learning and experience'.[104]

Conclusion

This chapter concluded Part 2 of this book. It did so by describing and reflecting upon the 'soft' – as opposed to the 'hard' – regulation of migrants' integration in Europe, with a particular focus on those measures concerning the recognition of professional qualifications, as well as certain ancillary supporting measures, such as education and training and targeted integration measures. The conclusions reached in this chapter are as follows.

---

103 Lilli Casano, 'The Future of European Labour Law and the Right to Employability: Which Role for the Validation of Non-Formal and Informal Learning?' (2016) 7 ELLJ 498.

104 Commission, 'Fitness Check on EU Legislation on legal migration' (Staff Working Document) SWD(2019) 1055 final, 133.

First, while many of the specific measures adopted to facilitate the integration of migrants in the EU are precisely of the kind which this book is most concerned with, they lack the institutionalisation, systematisation and formalisation which legal regulation can bring. For example, the Commission's recent recommendations on the recognition of professional qualifications of migrants are not binding. However, they are nonetheless evidence of a minor revolution occurring in respect of the treatment of migrants in EU and member state law. It will be interesting to see how the other EU institutions and the member states respond to these recommendations, whether they will be incorporated into member state law or practice and whether they will positively impact the experience of third-country nationals working in the EU. Given their granularity and controversial nature, the fact that they were not incorporated into a directive, as the European Parliament had apparently expected,[105] is perhaps not surprising. Indeed, given the current political climate at EU and member state level, openly treating third-country nationals the same as EU citizens in some circumstances – and even preferentially in other circumstances – is unlikely to fly.

Second, in its external relations policies, the EU cooperates with numerous third-countries in respect of education and training to various degrees. Much of the EU's work in this context involves an exercise of its soft power. That is, the EU either encourages or indirectly requires (through funding conditionality) that third-countries align their education and training systems with the EU's so as to better facilitate the recognition of professional qualifications specifically and consequently labour mobility generally. Having said that, in global terms, a lot of the EU's activity in the context of its external relations merely involves the provision of funding to improve education and training systems, which is akin to humanitarian-style work. Unlike the measures adopted in the context of EU migration and asylum policy, however, many of the 'action plans' adopted by the EU in the context of its external relations policy are actually binding on the EU.

Third, so much for the EU's policies concerning the recognition of formal qualifications; what about the recognition of informal and non-formal learning? This understudied issue surely merits some attention in a text concerned with the recognition of qualifications. Through its education and training policies, the EU has developed measures which are currently at an embryonic

105 Policy Department for Citizens' Rights and Constitutional Affairs, *The EU Legal Migration Package: Towards a Rights-based Approach to Attracting Skills and Talent to the EU* (European Parliament 2022) 25, 62, 63, 68.

stage. These require further reflection and entrenchment, possibly through the law. Moreover, migrants have not even been taken into account in this context. This is notwithstanding the fact that they frequently have skills, learned in non-formal or informal settings, which could benefit from recognition, thereby enabling them to more effectively participate in the Single Market.

Conclusion

Introduction

Migrants working in the EU regularly face discrimination and inadequate skills' recognition, experiences which affect their well-being. Accordingly, this book has investigated the extent to which the EU guarantees the well-being of migrants in accessing work through its laws and policies, with a particular focus on skills' recognition and freedom from discrimination as aspects of their well-being, as a means to facilitate and enable their integration into European societies and economies. The answer this book has provided to this question is that the Single Market has not been entirely adequately designed to secure those aspects of third-country nationals' well-being in accessing work. This final chapter consolidates the argument of the book and reflects upon it with a critical lens. It is structured as follows. Section 1 summarises the argument of the book and the critical conclusions reached in each chapter. Section 2 reflects on the overarching success or failure of EU law and policy in this area. Section 3 reflects on the recognition of professional qualifications generally, the major subject of Part 2 of this book. Section 4 addresses the theme of governance. In the light of all of these critical reflections, Section 5 provides a collection of practical proposals for reform. Finally, Section 6 addresses some of the empirical data necessary to confirm some of the conclusions here reached and the practical steps that can be taken to implement them. A short conclusion follows.

1 The Argument of This Book

The core argument of this book can be summarised as follows.

1. Migration to and within the EU is one of the foundations of shared prosperity, unity and diversity in Europe. However, migrants coming to and moving within Europe habitually experience wrongful discrimination and inadequate recognition of the skills or professional qualifications. They are frequently overqualified and underemployed. This problem calls for resolution. This book therefore attempts to describe and critically reflect on the legal foundations of migrant integration in Europe, with a view to making practical proposals on how this problem might be resolved.

 | DOI:10.1163/9789004724068_010

2. The right to work is one of the legal foundations of migrants' integration in Europe. It is a fundamental right in international, European, EU and member state law. For the purposes of this text, the most important and relevant dimension of that right is its facilitation of access to and participation in the workforce, whether as an employee or self-employed person. It can be used to challenge laws and policies which are designed to constitute and correct the market. However, as a matter of law, migrants are only afforded the right to work when they are guaranteed equal treatment with member state nationals on the ground of nationality.
3. In the EU, the right to equal treatment and non-discrimination functions as migrants' right to have rights. In other words, migrants' rights in the EU are determined on the basis of the extent of their entitlement to equal treatment and non-discrimination with member state nationals on the ground of nationality. There are reasons which suggest that the general abolition of discrimination on the ground of nationality could have some good consequences, such as improving migrants' integration and reducing the wrongful discrimination which they habitually experience. International and European law requires that discrimination on the ground of nationality is generally prohibited. However, this is not the case in EU law. Rather, discrimination on the ground of nationality is only prohibited in specific circumstances. EU law doctrine does not appear to be entirely coherent in this respect nor does it comply with binding international and European law. While it initially appeared that the prohibition of discrimination on other grounds, such as race and ethnic origin, might lead to or entail the prohibition of discrimination on the ground of nationality, the Court of Justice has since confirmed that these grounds are not generally related or converging. This is regrettable.
4. The right to have one's professional qualifications recognised has a limited but nonetheless clear and express basis in international and European law. Migrants are to be afforded 'special measures' to have their qualifications recognised. However, under EU migration and asylum law, there is no harmonised pre-departure procedure for the recognition of the qualifications of any migrants coming to the EU. On arrival and residence in the EU, migrants are afforded a complex patchwork of rights which vary greatly – according to their status in EU law – from being afforded no right to have their qualifications recognised to having their qualifications recognised in circumstances even where they lack any verifying documentation. It is not always clear why this is the case nor are the actual rights and entitlements of migrants always clear on the face of the relevant legislation. Furthermore, the majority of categories

of migrants arriving in the EU are not afforded the 'gold standard' of measures designed to facilitate their integration into the labour market, namely, equal treatment in respect of qualification recognition procedures, targeted and mandatory integration measures (such as language training relevant to their profession) and education and training opportunities. Under EU external relations law, migrants from third-countries with which the EU has partnership, trade or association agreements are afforded a patchwork of rights, varying from almost full mutual recognition of their professional qualifications to being afforded equal treatment with member state nationals. Many of these partnership, trade or association agreements are somewhat uncertain in terms of their implications for the recognition of professional qualifications. This ambiguity may be a source of domination for third-country nationals seeking to rely on the terms thereof. However, interestingly, the EU has negotiated some legally-binding terms in some of these agreements concerning the coordination of education and training systems. Over time, this could improve the recognition of professional qualifications between the EU and those countries.

5. The right to the recognition of professional qualifications is expressly provided for in EU free movement law. The relevant Treaty provisions and the Recognition Directive have generated a huge volume of complex case law on this issue. However, migrants cannot generally benefit from these provisions because and insofar as they do not have free movement rights. There are reasons for this general exclusion which apply with particular force in the context of the recognition of professional qualifications: these reasons derive from the need to guarantee the quality and integrity of regulated services in the Single Market. The law is relatively clear on this issue and migrants. Consistent with the rationale of EU free movement law, only those most highly-skilled migrants have free movement rights and the consequent entitlement to have their professional qualifications recognised.

6. In terms of soft law and policies, there are three branches of EU policy which are relevant. EU migration and asylum policies provide the member states with supports in respect of the recognition of professional qualifications and ancillary rights and protections. The Commission has recently adopted two recommendations to the member states on the specific issue of the recognition of professional qualifications of migrants, suggesting just how significant the problem has become. Parts of these recommendations contradict express provisions of EU law, ride roughshod over national law and are incoherent. Others are helpful and timely.

EU external relations policies in respect of the recognition of professional qualifications are more limited. The most relevant of these policies are in the context of the EU's Neighbourhood, where funding conditionality to countries in the Neighbourhood requires that they align their national qualification frameworks with the EQF and adopt legislation facilitating the recognition of professional qualifications. This involves the EU exercising its 'soft power'. Finally, EU education and training policy in this area has involved the adoption of a recommendation on the recognition of non-formal and informal learning. However, this recommendation was adopted during the height of austerity and is not specifically targeted at migrants, although they may indirectly benefit from it.

2 Judging EU Law and Policy

The critical analysis conducted in Parts 1 and 2 of this book suggest that changes in culture may be necessary in the EU. The first is a change in legal culture. By 'legal culture', I essentially mean a change in the practice of the law. And the primary site of legal practice is that of legislators, legal officials and courts. Thus, for example, in Chapter 2 I argued that nationality should be made a prohibited ground of discrimination as a matter of EU equality and anti-discrimination law on the basis of some theoretical and legal doctrinal arguments. I also there stated that it is possible that the CJEU will take part in this cultural change, although that does seem increasingly unlikely. There are some good reasons of legal doctrine to depart from the status quo and courts can play a role in amending legal doctrine in the light of these reasons. I have not, however, identified all of the reasons which factor in the balance of reasons; the argument has been largely one sided and tilted in favour of the preferences and interests of third-country nationals. A full analysis of all of the reasons in favour of and against such a significant change in the EU's legal culture remains to be completed.

Making nationality discrimination a prohibited ground of discrimination is not the only area where judicial reform is possible and perhaps even necessary. It is also possible that, insofar as the rights contained in EU migration and asylum, external relations and free movement law are justiciable before the CJEU, the Court could exercise its jurisdiction to develop an expansive interpretation of those rights. Interpretation, it was suggested in Chapter 3, is but one way in which EU law as it currently stands could be understood to grant third-country nationals rights to greater resources than they currently have. However, while international and European law provide a fairly solid basis for developing a reformist integrated interpretation of EU anti-discrimination and equality law, as argued in Chapter 2, in the light of the review of the fairly sparse and even vague corresponding provisions of international and European law in Chapter 3, the same cannot be said for a possible reformist integrated interpretation of EU migration and asylum, external relations and free movement law.[1]

The second and concurrent change, largely implicitly suggested by the analysis provided in Part 2 of this book, is a broader change in political culture. This point was made most clearly in Chapter 3 where it was suggested that to afford third-country nationals greater rights and resources was largely a matter of policy. Political theory and legal doctrine tended to run out of argumentative steam at this point, leaving room instead for policy makers to make arguments based on economic and social analyses of the consequences of granting third-country nationals greater rights and resources, as well as the consequences of third-country nationals actually making use of such rights and resources. One example of such an argument was provided in Chapter 4 where it was suggested that, from at least one economic perspective, further deregulation of regulated professions would make it easier for people to participate in the EU's labour market. Such arguments fall within the 'interpretive space' provided by political theory to make arguments which are consistent with its requirements. There are, however, some minor exceptions to this view. Failing to provide for the recognition of the non-formally and informally obtained skills of third-country nationals seems like an obvious gap in EU law and policy. The lack of a strong legal basis to develop integration measures, discussed in Chapter 5, may also be viewed as problematic.

Nonetheless, whether or not such change in political culture is practically or politically possible or plausible is, of course, very controversial and uncertain. The EU has faced and continues to encounter significant challenges, some of which are so great that they have questioned the very existence and nature of the EU itself. On at least one view of history, the greatest changes brought about in political culture are triggered by significant economic, social and cultural crises. The EU will no doubt continue to face further crises in the future; whether or not they lead to a widening and deepening of the project of EU integration can only involve quite a significant degree of speculation. While some of the reasons applicable in assessing how such a change in political culture might be brought about have been outlined in this book, a complete all-things-considered analysis of the balance of reasons remains to be completed.

1 On the integrated approach to interpretation, see Virginia Mantouvalou, 'Labour Rights in the European Convention on Human Rights: An Intellectual Justification for an Integrated Approach to Interpretation' (2013) 13 HRLR 529.

3 The Recognition of Professional Qualifications

Part 2 of this book investigated, in relative detail, a legal right which has yet to be discussed extensively by many EU lawyers, namely, the right to have one's qualifications recognised. This right only came to light because of this book's emphasis on the role of people's skills in accessing and participating in the Single Market. That is, skills form part of people's capacity for freedom of choice or well-being and consequently their formation, exercise and development may be taken into account as part of a more general exploration of how to guarantee people's well-being in society. It is perhaps most surprising that this right has not attracted much if any juridical attention in respect of persons seeking to access the labour market generally. That is to say, this right has not been deployed by people attempting to have their qualifications recognised by employers within their own member state for the purposes of participating in the labour market. Employers regularly and often rightly discriminate between people on the ground of their skills. It is possible that, in doing so, they violate the right to have one's qualifications recognised. This right, like many other rights, at its core is a guarantee of procedural equality of treatment consisting of the obligation to fairly and objectively assess, in a non-discriminatory manner, people's qualifications standards in the light of criteria known in advance. If employers fail to adhere to such a guarantee of procedural equality, then they may violate the right to have one's qualifications recognised.

This book is primarily concerned not with employers as authorities governing access to the labour market but with public and/or private professional regulatory bodies. Moreover, it focussed on the application of that right in the context of movement across borders by third-country nationals moving to and within the EU. As to the first such context, that right has been guaranteed in a fairly haphazard fashion. While it is generally guaranteed to some extent in international and European law, albeit occasionally quite vaguely, as a matter of EU migration and asylum law not all third-country nationals coming to the EU are entitled to have their qualifications recognised on an equal basis with member state nationals. Moreover, as a matter of EU external relations law some third-country nationals, particularly those from third-countries with which the EU has close relations, are entitled to have their qualifications recognised on an equal basis with member state nationals while many others are not. In other words, some third-country nationals are privileged in EU law. This is not inherently problematic as it is legitimate to discriminate between people and peoples on the basis of their skills, but some third-country nationals should not be benefited at the expense of others. Migrants should be entitled to have their qualifications recognised in a procedurally fair manner. In terms of making it easier for third-country nationals to have their qualifications recognised when moving to the EU, it was suggested that the EU and its member states should coordinate their education and training systems, at least to some extent, with those of third-countries, particularly those from which there is a high degree of inward migration to the EU. A review of the EU's external relations to date suggests that this process appears to be underway. This is a welcome development insofar as it may reduce the inadequate skills' recognition third-country nationals habitually experience when coming to the EU.

Consideration was also given to the extent to which third-country nationals may have their professional qualifications recognised when moving within the Single Market. Perhaps surprisingly, the EU has developed a highly sophisticated mutual recognition system to facilitate the recognition of professional qualifications of persons moving within the EU. This contrasts sharply with, say, the USA where the recognition of professional qualifications is completely decentralised and regulated at state level. This system enables its beneficiaries to challenge over-regulation and under-regulation of regulated professions, thereby facilitating greater access to and participation in work. The structural links between the right to work and the right to have one's qualifications recognised are clear here: like the right to work generally, the right to have one's qualifications recognised derives from a concern to both prohibit hindrances to and positively promote people's liberty to work which is crucial to people's well-being. However, this system almost exclusively applies to persons who have obtained a professional qualification within a member state and have the right, as a matter of EU free movement law, to move freely within the Single Market. The vast majority of third-country nationals cannot, therefore, benefit from this system, and there appear to be good reasons for this.

In terms of non-binding measures, the EU has again adopted a plethora of programmes such as Mobility Partnerships, measures facilitating the recognition of non-formal and informal learning and targeted integration measures designed to facilitate, inter alia, the recognition of qualifications of third-country nationals coming to the EU. Given the increasing significance of the right to have one's qualifications recognised in facilitating effective access to the labour market, however, it is surprising that these measures, all of which are very welcome, are non-binding in nature. Indeed, given that complex patchwork of legal and non-legal measures adopted by the EU and its member states to date, it should come as no surprise that the European Migration Forum considered, at its meeting in April 2019, the possibility of adopting a directive harmonising the conditions for the recognition of professional qualifications of third-country nationals coming to the EU. This possibility would be welcome if it could be demonstrated to reduce the arbitrary power to which third-country nationals are subject to in being treated differently from member state nationals and to make it easier for third-country nationals to have their qualifications recognised in practice. While this book does not conclusively endorse such a measure given its uncertain scope at present, if it met the aforementioned criteria, then it would indeed be a welcome development. Unfortunately, however, no further reflection on this issue was made at subsequent meetings of the EMF in 2021 and 2023.

4 The Theme of Governance

In the introduction to this book, governance was identified as a central theme. It was there noted that this book is primarily concerned with traditional or 'hard law' modes of governance. However, it should by now be clear that the EU adopts a wide variety of modes and means of governance to achieve a diverse range of goals. At this stage, there are essentially three issues which arise for discussion. A first is whether and to what extent the measures adopted by the EU actually achieve their purported goals. This is a question of the efficacy of the modes of governance adopted, which largely depends on empirical research for verification. There is or ought to be a strong pro tanto case that hard law is better able to institutionalise and systematise norms and standards because that is a necessary conceptual property of traditional legal regulation. In other words, because law is an institutionalised normative order, it is more likely to be able to achieve comprehensive goals with widespread implications. Unless it can be empirically established that soft legal regulation is better able to instantiate these properties than hard legal regulation, then my general preference for same remains sound. This is particularly relevant for those measures discussed in Chapter 6.v, where it was suggested that integration measures specifically targeted at third-country nationals should be based on legal regulation. Some of the measures there discussed were essentially pilot schemes. This is, of course, permissible. Some experimentation at the outset of developing a policy is valuable. But over time, these measures should be promoted through legal regulation. This would not only institutionalise and systematise these measures; it would also enable third-country nationals to rely on legally enforceable rights which secure crucial aspects of their well-being.

The second issue is the nature and value of the goals of legal regulation. How extensive and far reaching are the aims of the EU's governance in the areas discussed in this book? Are they adequate; are they sufficiently ambitious? As noted in the introductory chapter to this book, the law will occasionally become 'reflexive', adapting and even ameliorating its goals to govern other social systems. While the law may indeed by reflexive, in many cases its reflexivity must be limited in the light of the ambitious goals it must achieve. It is presumed that some goals can only be achieved through hard law, possibly in a top-down fashion, such as through courts, an approach I suggested in Chapter 2 in respect of expanding the guarantee of equal treatment and non-discrimination currently afforded to third-country nationals in the EU. In respect of areas of the law in which courts cannot or should not play a role, legislation is likely to be the most appropriate form of governance. Whether legislation will actually be adopted to implement some of the changes suggested above largely depends on political will.

A final but important point of reflection is on the role of international modes of governance. EU law is of course a form of transnational governance, but its special characteristics largely distinguish it from other forms of international regulation. International and European law has nonetheless offered an extensive doctrinal armoury from which to draw upon in critiquing EU law and policy. And while not always strictly binding nor even readily enforceable, the EU and its member states can use it to legitimise their laws and practices. In other words, in adhering to agreed standards in international and European law, the EU and its member states can better secure the external dimension of the well-being of their peoples insofar as, by doing so, they cohere to agreed standards designed to secure the well-being of the peoples of free states.

5 Practical Proposals for Reform

In terms of potential practical reforms which may resolve some of the problems which I have identified throughout the argument of this book, this author suggests the following modest possibilities as a start, which may lead to fruitful resolution of these problems in the future.

1. The personal and material scope of application of the right to equality and non-discrimination on the ground of nationality should be reconsidered. The current position as a matter of EU law is inconsistent with binding international and European law. Several Advocates General of the CJEU have noted this inconsistency, yet the Court of Justice has expressly resiled from resolving this issue judicially. It may be that Treaty reform is necessary to resolve the issue. In any event, further debate of the issue is at the very least required. This could occur formally, by way of a judicial conference of the judges of the CJEU, a meeting of the Constitutional Affairs or Civil Liberties, Justice and Home Affairs Committees of the European Parliament or a special Eurobarometer

on nationality discrimination or other public polling mechanism. More informally, it could occur through an academic conference dedicated to the issue of equal treatment and non-discrimination on the ground of nationality.

2. The rights afforded to migrants before and on arrival in the EU as regards the recognition of their professional qualifications and ancillary measures, such as integration measures and education and training, should be clarified in the first instance. Clarification could occur through an imprimatur of sorts by way of a Commission communication.[2] Alternatively, a group of academic experts could draft and publish a brief restatement of this part of EU migration and asylum law. The European Commission could commission such a publication. A similar clarification or restatement of the rights afforded to migrants from third-countries with which the EU has established partnership, association or trade agreements may also be helpful.
3. The patchwork of rights afforded to migrants before and on arrival in the EU should be reconsidered. For example, should a pre-arrival/departure measure, such as that envisaged by the proposal for a regulation establishing an EU Talent Pool, be adopted? Should language training be made compulsory for all migrants? Should more categories of migrants have access to education and training? Why aren't all regular migrants afforded the 'gold standard' of measures to facilitate their integration in the EU? Again, in the first instance, debate or discussion as to whether any potential or possible reform might occur, if at all. Again, officially, a meeting of the Civil Liberties, Justice and Home Affairs Committee of the European Parliament, a special Eurobarometer on the rights and entitlements of migrants or other public polling mechanism may be appropriate. Less officially, an academic conference could be organised on the law governing the recognition of professional qualifications in the EU generally. Such an academic conference could help to generate new knowledge about the law governing the recognition of professional qualifications generally, not merely as it concerns migrants, but also EU citizens.
4. The overarching communication and content of EU migration and asylum policy needs to be made more coherent and lawful. Parts of EU migration and asylum policy are clearly consistent with EU law; others

2 A good example is the Communication from the Commission concerning the consequences of the judgment given by the Court of Justice on 20 February 1979 in case 120/78 ('Cassis de Dijon') [1980] OJ C256/2.

are expressively and potentially inconsistent with EU law. This undermines the rule of law and the principle of legality. Specifically, the Commission's two recent recommendations on the recognition of professional qualifications are potentially inconsistent with the principle of subsidiarity and the rule of law, resulting in the potential to create uncertainty amongst member state authorities as to whether or not they should follow the recommendations. The tone and content of these recommendations could therefore be reconsidered.

5. Having said that, EU migration and asylum policy also needs an injection of ambition. The EU competence in this area is confined to providing the member states with 'incentives and supports' in facilitating the integration of migrants. While many 'supports' have been made available, as were extensively noted in Chapter 5, relatively few 'incentives' are provided to the member states. Making full use of the entirety of the EU's competence in this context may therefore benefit from fresh consideration and some renewed vitality to generate not merely new fora, discussions or meetings, but practical propositions and tools to facilitate migrant integration.
6. EU external relations policy in the context of the recognition of professional qualifications and related measures consists of a patchwork of complex measures dealt with by various different directorates-general of the Commission. There is a risk that this could lead to a lack of 'joined-up' thinking across the board. For example, the EU's external relations policies are not systematic; they are generally targeted at certain third-countries with which the EU and its member states have historic ties or for strategic reasons. This indicates bittiness and may be suggestive of incoherence. If not already in existence, it is possible that a working group or forum within the Commission across the various directorates-general responsible may assist in improving the coherence of these areas.

6 Explanatory Gaps

While I have endeavoured to identify some concrete reforms, in some cases it has not been possible to do so in the absence of specific and detailed empirically verified arguments and claims. Moreover, in some parts, the argument made in this book contained some explanatory gaps which need to be filled by further research in order to be complete. Accordingly, it is helpful to here consider some explanatory gaps which this book has identified as necessary to fill in order to justify more substantial conclusions.

The first area in which further data is required is in respect of the prevalence of nationality discrimination across the EU. In Chapter 2, I identified some sources of empirical data suggesting that discrimination on grounds closely associated with nationality, such as ethnicity, remain prevalent in the EU. It would, however, be preferable if there was also specific evidence concerning the prevalence of discrimination on the ground of nationality. Such empirical evidence would have to distinguish between host state nationals, EU migrant nationals and third-country nationals. Only with that level of evidence could it be convincingly established whether or not nationality discrimination is decreasing. Further evidence demonstrating the link, if any, between equality and anti-discrimination norms and the reduction of discrimination would also be helpful to strengthen the case in favour of making nationality a prohibited ground of discrimination. These are largely sociological questions.

A second and related area in which further research is required is the political plausibility of the arguments made in this book. That is, the question is whether the claims I have made here are politically palatable. This could perhaps be established through surveys or identifying how and to what extent similar policies have been developed elsewhere, or in specific member states of the European Union, and assessing their success. And given that my claims are based on the EU as a whole, such research would generally have to be conducted on an EU-wide scale. Similarly, research would need to be conducted on the role of courts, particularly the CJEU, in the process of EU integration both in general and with a particular focus on third-country nationals. Should courts be involved in the process of EU integration? If so, how and to what extent? Research should also be conducted considering how to cultivate political palatability where none currently exists. These and other questions are for political scientists to investigate.

A third source of empirical evidence required was noted in Chapter 2 concerning third-country nationals' entitlement to additional measures related to the recognition of professional qualifications, such as mandatory integration measures and access to education and training. It was there noted that if it could be proven, as a matter of policy, that third-country nationals were less likely to suffer discrimination and inadequate skills' recognition if they were immediately afforded access to such measures on the same or similar grounds as member state nationals, then there would be a compelling policy case in favour of so affording third-country nationals such access. Accordingly, to test that hypothesis, what would be required at the very least would be pilot schemes affording third-country nationals immediate access to such measures. A control group, which did not have access to such measures, would also need to be established to verify the hypothesis. This is essentially a question of social policy.

Conclusion

This book has concluded that the EU does not entirely adequately secure certain aspects of the well-being at work of third-country nationals coming to or currently in the EU. It has identified some potential reforms and action points which could be undertaken to improve the law in this area and ultimately better cohere with the legal foundations of migrant integration as outlined in Part 1. Some of these reforms are purely matters of legal doctrine, such as the argument for equal treatment on the ground of nationality in Chapter 2; others involve more complex and multifaceted analyses of legal and political theory; and others still involve engagement with broader debates in the social sciences more generally. Moreover, whether or not those reforms will eventually, if ever, be made is, unfortunately, very uncertain. But this book has attempted to nudge the debate in the right direction by identifying some of the reasons which can and should motivate a deepening of the project of EU integration by and through the work of third-country nationals. Migrants clearly play a vital role in that project and could better do so if their well-being was adequately secured.

Bibliography

Books

Ales E, Bell M, Deinert O and Robin-Olivier S (eds), *International and European Labour Law: A Commentary* (Nomos/Hart 2018).

Alston P (ed), *Labour Rights as Human Rights* (OUP 2005).

Alston P and Goodman R, *International Human Rights: Text and Materials* (OUP 2013).

Amalfitano C, *General Principles of EU Law and the Protection of Fundamental Rights* (Edward Elgar 2018).

Arnull A, *The European Union and its Court of Justice* (2nd edn, OUP 2006).

Arnull A and Chalmers D (eds), *The Oxford Handbook of European Union Law* (OUP 2015).

Atrey S, *Intersectional Discrimination* (OUP 2019).

Baderin M and Ssenyonjo M (eds), *International Human Rights Law: Six Decades after the UDHR and Beyond* (Ashgate 2010).

Bansak C, Simpson N and Zavodny M, *The Economics of Immigration* (2nd ed, Routledge 2021).

Bantekas I, Stein MA and Anastasiou D (eds), *The UN Convention on the Rights of Persons with Disabilities: A Commentary* (OUP 2018).

Barnard C and Scott J (eds), *The Law of the Single European Market* (Hart 2002).

Barnard C, *EU Employment Law* (4th edn, OUP 2012).

Barnard C, *The Substantive Law of the EU: The Four Freedoms* (6th edn, OUP 2019).

Bastia T and Skeldon R (eds), *Routledge Handbook of Migration and Development* (Routledge 2020).

Bauder H, *Labour Movement: How Migration Regulates Labour Markets* (OUP 2006).

Bell M, *Anti-Discrimination Law and the European Union* (OUP 2002).

Bell M, *Racism and Equality in the European Union* (OUP 2008).

Beringer S, Maier S and Thiel M (eds), *EU Development Policies: Between Norms and Geopolitics* (Palgrave Macmillan 2019).

Bernitz U, Groussot X and Schulyok F (eds), *General Principles of EU Law and European Private Law* (Wolters Kluwer 2013).

Boeri T, Brücker H, Docquier F and Rapport H, *Brain Drain and Brain Gain: The Global Competition to Attract High-Skilled Migrants* (OUP 2012).

von Bogdandy A and Bast J (eds), *Principles of European Constitutional Law* (2nd edn, Hart/Beck 2010).

Bogg A, *The Democratic Aspects of Trade Union Recognition* (Hart 2009).

Bogg A, Costello C and Davies ACL (eds), *Research Handbook in EU Labour Law* (Edward Elgar 2016).

Bogg A, Costello C, Davies ACL and Prassl J (eds), *The Autonomy of Labour Law* (Hart 2015).

Bogg A, Costello C, Davies ACL, Prassl J, Rowbottom J and Young AL (eds), *The Constitution of Social Democracy: Essays in Honour of Keith Ewing* (Hart 2020).

Bouris D and Schumacher T (eds), *The Revised European Neighbourhood Policy: Continuity and Change in EU Foreign Policy* (Palgrave Macmillan 2017).

Brennan G, Eriksson L, Goodin R and Southwood N, *Explaining Norms* (OUP 2013).

Brock G and Blake M, *Debating Brain Drain: May Governments Restrict Emigration?* (OUP 2015).

Bruun N, Lörcher K, Schömann I and Clauwert S (eds), *The European Social Charter and the Employment Relation* (Hart 2017).

Buckinx B, Trejo-Mathys J and Waligore T (eds), *Domination and Global Political Justice: Conceptual, Historical and Institutional Perspectives* (Routledge 2015).

de Búrca G and Weiler JHH (eds), *The European Court of Justice* (OUP 2001).

de Búrca G and Weiler JHH, de Witte B (eds), *Social Rights in Europe* (OUP 2005).

de Búrca G and Weiler JHH, de Witte B, Scott J (eds), *Law and New Governance in the EU and the US* (Hart 2006).

Busby N, *A Right to Care? Unpaid Work in European Employment Law* (OUP 2011).

Cardwell PJ, *EU External Relations and Systems of Governance: The CFSP, Euro-Mediterranean Partnership and Migration* (Routledge 2009).

Carens J, *The Ethics of Immigration* (OUP 2013).

Cerna L, *Immigration Policies and the Global Competition for Talent* (Palgrave Macmillan 2016).

Craig P and de Búrca G, *EU Law: Texts, Cases and Materials* (6th edn, OUP 2015).

Craven M, *The International Covenant on Economic, Social and Cultural Rights: A Perspective on its Development* (OUP 1995).

Davies G and Avbelj M (eds), *Research Handbook on Legal Pluralism in EU Law* (Edward Elgar 2018).

Dawson M, *New Governance and the Transformation of European Law: Coordinating EU Social Law and Policy* (CUP 2011).

Dorssemont F, Lörcher K and Schömann I (eds), *The European Convention on Human Rights and the Employment Relation* (Hart 2013).

Dorssemont F, Lörcher K and Schömann I, Clauwaert S and Schmitt M (eds), *The Charter of Fundamental Rights of the European Union and the Employment Relation* (Hart 2019).

Dworkin R, *Taking Rights Seriously* (HUP 1977).

Dworkin R, *A Matter of Principle* (HUP 1985).

Dworkin R, *Sovereign Virtue: The Theory and Practice of Equality* (HUP 2002).

Edgell S, Gottfried H and Granter E (eds), *The SAGE Handbook of the Sociology of Work and Employment* (SAGE Publications 2016).

Eidelson B, *Discrimination and Disrespect* (OUP 2015).

Eeckhout P, *EU External Relations Law* (2nd edn, OUP 2011).

Eisele K, *The External Dimension of the EU's Migration Policy: Different Legal Positions of Third-Country Nationals in the EU: A Comparative Perspective* (Brill/Nijhoff 2014).

Elgeström O and Jönsson C (eds), *European Union Negotiations: Processes, Networks and Institutions* (Routledge 2005).

Esty D and Geradin D (eds), *Regulatory Competition and Economic Integration: Comparative Perspectives* (OUP 2001).

Fabbrini F, *Economic Governance in Europe: Comparative Perspectives and Constitutional Challenges* (OUP 2016).

Ferri D and Cortese F (eds), *The EU Social Market Economy and the Law: Theoretical Perspectives and Practical Challenges for the EU* (Routledge 2018).

Fick B, *International Labour Law* (Edward Elgar 2015).

Fletcher M, Herlin-Karnell E and Matera C (eds), *The European Union as an Area of Freedom, Security and Justice* (Routledge 2017).

Fredman S, *Human Rights Transformed: Positive Rights and Positive Duties* (OUP 2008).

Fredman S, *Discrimination Law* (2dn edn, OUP 2011).

Freedland M and Costello C (eds), *Migrants at Work: Immigration and Vulnerability in Labour Law* (OUP 2014).

Freedland M, Costello C and Prassl J (eds), *Viking, Laval and Beyond* (Hart 2014).

Freeman M, Chinkin C and Rudolf B (eds), *The UN Convention on the Elimination of All Forms of Discrimination Against Women: A Commentary* (OUP 2012).

Friðriksdóttir B, *What Happened to Equality? The Construction of the Right to Equal Treatment of Third-Country Nationals in European Union Law on Labour Migration* (Brill/Nijhoff 2017).

Gänzle S, Grimm S and Makhan D (eds), *The European Union and Global Development: An 'Enlightened Superpower' in the Making?* (Palgrave Macmillan 2012).

Garcés-Mascareñas B and Penninx R (eds), *Integration Processes and Policies in Europe: Contexts, Levels and Actors* (SpringerOpen 2016).

Geiger R, Khan D-E and Kotzur M (eds), *European Union Treaties: A Commentary* (Beck/Hart 2015).

Gstöhl S (ed), *The European Neighbourhood Policy in Comparative Perspective: Models, Challenges, Lessons* (Routledge 2016).

Gstöhl S and Simon Schunz (eds), *Theorising the European Neighbourhood Policy* (Routledge 2016).

de Guchetneire P, Pécoud A and Cholewinksi R (eds), *Migration and Human Rights: The United Nations Convention on Migrant Workers' Rights* (CUP 2009).

Guild E, *The Legal Elements of European Identity: EU Citizenship and Migration Law* (Kluwer Law International 2004).

Guild E, Groenendijk K and Carerra S (eds), *Illiberal Liberal States: Immigration, Citizenship and Integration in the EU* (Ashgate 2009).

de Haas H, *How Migration Really Works: 22 Things You Need to Know about the Most Divisive Issue in Politics* (Penguin 2024).

Hellman D, *When is Discrimination Wrong?* (HUP 2011).

Heremans T, *Professional Services in the EU Internal Market* (Hart 2012).

Hillion C and Koutrakos P (eds), *Mixed Agreements Revisited: The EU and its Member States in the World* (Hart 2010).

Holland M and Doidge M, *Developing Policy of the European Union* (Red Globe Press 2012).

Honohan I and Hovdal-Moan M (eds), *Domination, Migration and Non-Citizens* (Routledge 2015).

Horsley T, *The Court of Justice of the European Union as an Institutional Actor: Judicial Lawmaking and its Limits* (CUP 2018).

Hout W (ed), *EU Development Policy and Poverty Reduction: Enhancing Effectiveness* (Ashgate 2007).

Ineli-Ciger M, *Temporary Protection in Law and Practice* (Brill Nijhoff 2018).

Jaklic K, *Constitutional Pluralism in the EU* (OUP 2014).

Jan Kuijper P, Wouters J, Hoffmeister F, de Baere G and Ramopoulos T (eds), *The Law of EU External Relations: Cases, Materials and Commentary on the EU as an International Legal Actor* (2nd edn, OUP 2015).

Janssens C, *The Principle of Mutual Recognition in EU Law* (OUP 2013).

Jaspers T, Pennings F and Peters S (eds), *European Labour Law* (Intersentia 2019).

Jones E, Menon A and Weatherill S (eds), *The Oxford Handbook of the European Union* (OUP 2012).

Jørgensen K E and Laatikainen K V (eds), *Routledge Handbook on the European Union and International Institutions: Performance, Policy, Power* (Routledge 2013).

Joseph S and Castan M, *The International Covenant on Civil and Political Rights: Cases, Materials and Commentary* (3rd edn, OUP 2013).

Kellerbauer M, Klamert M and Tomkin J (eds), *The EU Treaties and the Charter of Fundamental Rights: A Commentary* (OUP 2019).

Khaitan T, *A Theory of Discrimination Law* (OUP 2015).

Koutrakos P, Nic Suibhne N and Syrpis P (eds), *Exceptions to EU Free Movement Law: Derogation, Justification and Proportionality* (Hart 2016).

Kuijper PJ, Wouters J, Hoffmeister F, de Baere G and Ramopoulos T (eds), *The Law of EU External Relations: Cases, Materials and Commentary on the EU as an International Legal Actor* (2nd edn, OUP 2015).

Lester S, Mercurio B and Davies A, *World Trade Law: Text, Materials and Commentary* (3rd edn, Hart 2018).

Lianos I and Odudu O (eds), *Regulating Trade in Services in the EU and the WTO: Trust, Distrust and Economic Integration* (CUP 2012).

Lim, *Immigration and Social Equality: The Ethics of Skill-Selective Immigration Policy* (OUP 2023).

Lippert-Rasmussen K, *Born Free and Equal? A Philosophical Inquiry into the Nature of Discrimination* (OUP 2014).

Lippert-Rasmussen K (ed), *The Routledge Handbook of the Ethics of Discrimination* (Routledge 2018).

Mantouvalou V (ed), *The Right to Work: Legal and Philosophical Perspectives* (Hart 2015).

Maupain F, *The Future of the International Labour Organisation in the Global Economy* (Hart 2013).

Meardi Guglielmo (ed), *Research Handbook on Migration and Employment* (Edward Elgar 2024).

Mendes J and Venzke J (eds), *Allocating Authority: Who Should Do What in European and International Law?* (Hart 2018).

Micklitz H-W (eds), *Constitutionalisation of European Private Law* (OUP 2014).

Miller D, *Strangers in Our Midst: The Political Philosophy of Immigration* (HUP 2016).

Moeckli D, Shah S and Sivakumaran S (eds), *International Human Rights Law* (3rd edn, OUP 2018).

Morano-Foadi S and Malena M (eds), *Integration for Third-Country Nationals in the European Union: The Equality Challenge* (Edward Elgar 2012).

Muir E, *EU Equality Law: The First Fundamental Rights Policy of the EU* (OUP 2018).

Murphy C, *Immigration, Integration and the Law: The Intersection of Domestic, EU and International Law Regimes* (Ashgate 2013).

Murray J, *Transnational Labour Regulation: The ILO and EC Compared* (Kluwer Law International 2001).

Nicolaïdis K and Howse R (eds), *The Federal Vision: Legitimacy and Levels of Governance in the United States and the European Union* (OUP 2001).

Niessen J and Huddleston T (eds), *Legal Frameworks for the Integration of Third-Country Nationals* (Nijhoff 2009).

Panizzon M, Zürcher G and Fornalé E (eds), *The Palgrave Handbook of International Labour Migration: Law and Policy Perspectives* (Palgrave Macmillan 2015).

Peers S, Hervey T, Kenner J and Ward A (eds), *The EU Charter of Fundamental Rights: A Commentary* (Hart/Beck 2014).

Peers S, Hervey T, Kenner J and Ward A (eds), *The EU Charter of Fundamental Rights: A Commentary* (2nd ed, Hart 2021).

Peers S, *EU Justice and Home Affairs Law Volume 1: EU Immigration and Asylum Law* (4th edn, OUP 2016).

Peers S, *EU Justice and Home Affairs Law Volume 1: EU Immigration and Asylum Law* (5th ed, OUP 2023).

Prassl J, *The Concept of the Employer* (OUP 2016).

Pribán J, *Sovereignty in Post-Sovereign Society: A Systems Theory of European Constitutionalism* (Routledge 2015).

Quershi A and Ziegler A, *International Economic Law* (3rd edn, Sweet and Maxwell 2011).

Raz J, *The Morality of Freedom* (OUP 1986).

Ripoll Servent A and Trauner F (eds), *The Routledge Handbook of Justice and Home Affairs Research* (Routledge 2017).

Ross M and Borgmann-Prebil Y (eds), *Promoting Solidarity in the European Union* (OUP 2010).

Ruhs M, *The Price of Rights: Regulating International Labour Migration* (Princeton University Press 2013).

Saul B, Kinley D and Mowbray J, *The International Covenant on Economic, Social and Cultural Rights: Commentary, Cases and Materials* (OUP 2014).

Schumacher T, Marchetti A and Demmelhuber T (eds), *The Routledge Handbook on the European Neighbourhood Policy* (Routledge 2018).

Schütze R, *European Constitutional Law* (2nd edn, CUP 2016).

Schioppa F K P (ed), *The Principle of Mutual Recognition in the European Integration Process* (Palgrave Macmillan 2005).

Schmidt SK, *The European Court of Justice and the Policy Process: The Shadow of Case Law* (OUP 2018).

de Schutter O, *International Human Rights Law: Cases, Materials and Commentary* (2nd edn, CUP 2014).

Shakespeare T, *Disability Rights and Wrongs Revisited* (2nd edn, Routledge 2014).

Singh M, *Global Perspectives on Recognising Non-Formal and Informal Learning: Why Recognition Matters* (Springer Open 2015).

Sjursen H (ed), *Questioning EU Enlargement: Europe in Search of Identity* (Routledge 2006).

Song S, *Immigration and Democracy* (OUP 2019).

Tans S, *Service Provision and Migration: EU and WTO Service Trade Liberalisation and Their Impact on Dutch and UK Immigration Rules* (Brill/Nijhoff 2017).

Thelen K, *How Institutions Evolve: The Political Economy of Skills in Germany, Britain, the United States and Japan* (CUP 2004).

Thornberry P, *The International Convention on the Elimination of All Forms of Racial Discrimination: A Commentary* (OUP 2016).

Thym D and Zoeteweij-Turhan M (eds), *Rights of Third-Country Nationals under EU Association Agreements: Degrees of Free Movement and Citizenship* (Brill Nijhoff 2015).

Thym D and Zoeteweij-Turhan M (eds), *EU Migration Law* (OUP 2023).

Tobin J (ed), *The UN Convention on the Rights of the Child: A Commentary* (OUP 2019).

Tridimas T, *The General Principles of EU Law* (3rd edn, OUP 2019).

van Vooren B, *EU External Relations Law and the European Neighbourhood Policy: A Paradigm for Coherence* (Routledge 2012).

van Vooren B and Wessel R (eds), *EU External Relations Law: Text, Cases and Materials* (CUP 2014).

Weatherill S, *Law and Values in the EU* (OUP 2016).

Weiler JHH, *The Constitution of Europe: "Do the New Clothes Have an Emperor?" and Other Essays on European Integration* (CUP 1999).

Whitman R (ed), *Normative Power Europe: Empirical and Theoretical Perspectives* (Palgrave Macmillan 2011).

Williams A, *The Ethos of Europe: Values, Law and Justice in the EU* (CUP 2012).

de Witte D, *Justice in the EU: The Emergence of Transnational Solidarity* (OUP 2015).

Van Wolleghem PG, *The EU's Policy on the Integration of Migrants: A Case of Soft-Europeanisation?* (Palgrave Macmillan 2019).

Chapters in Edited Books

Adamo S and Binder T, 'Union Citizens and the Recognition of Professional Qualifications: Where Do We Go from Here?' in Sybe de Vries, Elena Ioriatti, Paulo Guarda and Elisabetta Pulice (eds), *EU Citizens Economic Rights in Action: Re-Thinking Legal and Factual Barriers in the Internal Market* (Edward Elgar 2018).

Barnard C, 'Free movement of natural persons and citizenship of the Union' in Barnard C and Peers S (eds), *European Union Law* (2nd edn, OUP 2017).

Betts A and Cerna L, 'High-Skilled Labour Migration' in Betts A (ed), *Global Migration Governance* (OUP 2011).

Blair M, 'An Economic Perspective on the Notion of 'Human Capital' in Burton-Jones A and Spender J-C (eds), *The Oxford Handbook of Human Capital* (OUP 2011).

Bonavita V, 'The EU Charter of Fundamental Rights and the Social Dimension of International Trade' in Di Federico G (ed), *The EU Charter of Fundamental Rights: From Declaration to Binding Instrument* (Springer 2011).

Van den Brink T and de Vries S, 'A Silk Road for Professional Qualifications? EU Models of Integration and their Potential in Sino-EU Relations' in Van Der Wende M, Kirby WC, Liu NC and Marginson S (eds), *China and Europe on the New Silk Road: Connecting Universities across Eurasia* (OUP 2020).

Brouwer E and de Vries K, 'Third-country nationals and discrimination on the ground of nationality: article 18 TFEU in the context of article 14 ECHR and EU migration law: time for a new approach' in van de Brink M, Burri S and Goldschmidt J (eds), *Equality and Human Rights: Nothing but Trouble? Liber amicorum Titia Loenen* (SIM 2015).

Buckley FH, 'The market for migrants' in Bhandari J and Sykes A (eds), *Economic Dimensions of International Law: Comparative and Empirical Perspectives* (CUP 1998).

Cerna L, 'European High-Skilled Migration Policy: Trends and Challenges' in Czaika M (ed), *High-Skilled Migration: Drivers and Policies* (OUP 2018).

Cerna L and Czaika M, 'European Policies to Attract Talent: The Crisis and Highly Skilled Migration Policies' in Anna Triandafyllidou and Irina Isaakyan (eds), *High Skill Migration and Recession: Gendered Perspectives* (Palgrave Macmillan 2015).

Connell J, 'International Trade in Health Workers' in Culyer A (ed), *Encyclopaedia of Health Economics, Volume 2* (Elsevier 2014).

Ferreira-Pereira L, 'Human Rights, Peace and Democracy: Is 'Model Power Europe' a Contradiction in Terms?' in Bindi F (ed), *The Foreign Policy of the European Union: Assessing Europe's Role in the World* (Brookings Institute 2010).

Fine S, 'Immigration and Discrimination' in Fine S and Ypi L (eds), *Migration in Political Theory: The Ethics of Movement and Membership* (OUP 2016).

Fredman S, 'Combating Racism with Human Rights: The Right to Equality' in Fredman S (ed), *Discrimination and Human Rights: The Case of Racism* (OUP 2001).

García Andrade P, 'Privileged Third-Country Nationals and Their Right of Free Movement and Residence to and in the EU: Questions of Status and Competence' in Guild E, Gortázar Rotaeche C and Kostakopoulou D (eds), *The Reconceptualisation of European Union Citizenship* (Brill 2014).

Groenendijk K, 'Citizens and third-country nationals: differential treatment or discrimination' in Carlier J-Y and Guild E (eds), *The Future of Free Movement of Persons in the EU* (Bruylant 2006).

Groenendijk K, 'Are third-country nationals protected by the Union law prohibition of discrimination on grounds of nationality?' in Barwig K and Dobbelstein R (eds), *Den Fremden akzeptieren – Festschrift fuer Gisbert Brinkmann* (Nomos 2012).

Guild E and Peers S, 'Out of the Ghetto? The Personal Scope of EU Law' in Peers S and Rogers N (eds), *EU Immigration and Asylum Law: Text and Commentary* (Brill 2006).

Konstadinides T and O'Meara N, 'Fundamental Rights and Judicial Protection' in Acosta Arcarazo D and Murphy C (eds), *EU Security and Justice Law: After Lisbon and Stockholm* (Hart 2014).

McCormack-George D, 'Trade in Services, Migration and Recognition of Professional Qualifications post-Brexit' in Simon Tans and Marc Veenbrink (eds), *Upgrading Trade in Services in EU and International Trade Law* (Wolf 2019).

McCrudden C, 'Theorising European Equality Law', in Costello C and Barry (eds), *Equality in Diversity: The New Equality Directives* (Irish Centre for European Law 2003).

McCrudden C and Kountouris H, 'Human Rights and European Equality Law' in Meenan H (ed), *Equality Law in an Enlarged European Union* (CUP 2007).

Michaels R, 'The Functional Method of Comparative Law' in Reimann M and Zimmermann R (eds), *The Oxford Handbook of Comparative Law* (OUP 2007).

Miller D, 'Immigration: The Case for Limits' in Cohen A and Heath Wellmann C (eds), *Contemporary Debates in Applied Ethics* (Blackwell 2005).

Morano-Foadi S and de Vries K, 'The Equality Clauses in the EU Directives on Non-discrimination and Migration/Asylum' in Morano-Foadi S and Malena M (eds), *Integration for Third-Country Nationals in the European Union: The Equality Challenge* (Edward Elgar 2012).

Moreau S, 'In Defence of a Liberty-based Account of Discrimination' in Hellman D and Moreau S (eds), *Philosophical Foundations of Discrimination Law* (OUP 2013).

Neyer J, 'Europe's Justice Deficit: Justification and Legitimacy in the European Union' in Neyer J and Wiener A (eds), *Political Theory of the European Union* (OUP 2011).

Novitz T, 'Legal Power and Normative Sources in the Field of Social Policy: Normative Power Europe at Work?' in Orbie J (ed), *Europe's Global Role: External Policies of the European Union* (Ashgate 2008).

Ramcharan B, 'Equality and Non-discrimination' in Henkin L (ed), *The International Bill of Rights: The Covenant on Civil and Political Rights* (Columbia University Press 1981).

Reslow N, 'Making and Implementing Multi-Actor EU External Migration Policy: The Mobility Partnerships' in Carrera S, den Hertog A P L, Panizzon M and Kostakopoulou D (eds), *EU External Migration Policies in an Era of Global Mobilities: Intersecting Policy Universes* (Brill/Nijhoff 2018).

van Riemsdijk M, 'Politics of Free Movement in the European Union: Recognition and Transfer of Professional Qualifications' in Maas W (ed), *Democratic Citizenship and the Free Movement of People* (Brill 2013).

Roberts P, 'Interdisciplinarity in Legal Research' in McConville M and Hong Chui W (eds), *Research Methods for Law* (Edinburgh University Press 2007).

Ryan B, 'In Defence of the Migrant Workers Convention: Standard Setting for Contemporary Migration' in Juss S (ed), *The Ashgate Research Companion to Migration Theory and Policy* (Ashgate 2013).

Ryan B, and Mantouvalou V, 'The Labour and Social Rights of Migrants in International Law' in Rubio Martin R (ed), *Human Rights and Immigration* (OUP 2014).

de Schutter O and Deakin S, 'Reflexive Governance and the Dilemmas of Social Regulation' in de Schutter O and Deakin S (eds), *Social Rights and Market Forces: Is the Open Coordination of Employment and Social Policies the Future of Europe?* (Bruylant 2005).

Streeck W, 'From Market Making to State Building? Reflections on the Political Economy of European Social Policy' in Liebfried S and Pierson P (eds), *European Social Policy: Between Fragmentation and Integration* (Brookings Institute 1995).

Tittel-Mosser D, 'Mobility Partnerships: A Tool for the Externalisation of EU Migration Policy? A Comparative Study of Morocco and Cape Verde' in Carrera S, Santos Vara J and Strik T (eds), *Constitutionalising the External Dimensions of EU Migration Policy in Times of Crisis* (Edward Elgar 2019).

Tryfonidou A, 'The Outer Limits of Article 28 EC: Purely Internal Situations and the Development of the Court's Approach through the Years' in Barnard C and Odudu O (eds), *The Outer Limits of European Union Law* (Hart 2009).

de Vries K, 'The Non-National as 'The Other': What Role for Non-Discrimination Law?' in Jesse M (ed), *European Societies, Migration and the Law: The 'Others' amongst 'Us'* (CUP 2021).

Wahl N, 'The Freedom to Conduct a Business' in Amtenbrink F, Davies G, Kochenov D and Lindeboom J (eds), *The Internal Market and the Future of European Integration: Essays in Honour of Lawrence Gormley* (CUP 2019).

Weatherill S, 'Why there is no Principle of Mutual Recognition in EU Law (and why that matters to consumer lawyers)' in Purnhagen K and Rott P (eds), *Varieties of European Economic Law and Regulation: Liber Amicorum for Hans Micklitz* (Springer 2014).

Journal Articles

Adepoju A, van Noorloos F and Zoomers A, 'Europe's Migration Agreements with Migrant-Sending Countries in the Global South: A Critical Review' (2010) 48 IM 42.

Aggestam L, 'Ethical Power Europe' (2008) 84 International Affairs 1.

Aissi J, Peels R and Samaan D, 'Evaluating the effectiveness of labour provisions in trade agreements: An analytical and methodological framework' (2018) 157 Int'l Lab Rev 671.

Alexander W, 'Free Movement of Non-EC Nationals: A Review of the Case Law of the Court of Justice' (1992) 3 EJIL 53.

Anderson B, 'Migration, immigration controls and the fashioning of precarious workers' (2010) 24 WES 300.

Angenbendt S, 'Mobility Partnerships – The Future of European Migration Policy?' (2012) 1 Migration and Development 216.

Arendt H, 'The Rights of Man: What are They?' (1949) 3(1) Modern Review 467.

Armstrong K, 'Rediscovering Civil Society: The European Union and the White Paper on Governance' (2008) 8 ELJ 102.

Atrey S, 'Redefining Frontiers in EU Discrimination Law' [2017] PL 185.

Atrey S, 'Race discrimination in EU Law after *Jyska Finans*' (2018) 55 CML Rev 625.

Atrey S, 'The Intersectional Case of Poverty in Discrimination Law' (2018) 18 HRL Rev 411.

Barnard C, 'Social Dumping and the Race to the Bottom: Some Lessons for the European Union from Delaware?' (2000) 25 EL Rev 57.

Barnard C, 'The Social Partners and the Governance Agenda' (2008) 8 ELJ 80.

Barnard C and Fraser Butlin S, 'Free Movement v Fair Movement: Brexit and Managed Migration' (2018) 25 CML Rev 203.

Barnard C, Fraser Butlin S and de Vries S, 'The 'Social Market Economy' in a (Heterogenous) Social Europe: Does it Make a Difference?' (2019) 15 Utrecht LR 47.

Bell M and Waddington L, 'Reflecting on Inequalities in European Equality Law' (2003) 28 EL Rev 349.

Benedi Lahuerta S, 'Race Equality and TCNs, or How to Fight Discrimination with a Discriminatory Law' (2009) 15 ELJ 738.

Benedi Lahuerta S, 'Taking EU Equality Law to the Next Level: In Search of Coherence' (2017) 7 ELLJ 348.

Bidwell P, Humphries N, Dicker P, Thomas S, Normand C and Brugha R, 'The National and International Implications of a Decade of Doctor Migration in the Irish Context' (2013) 110 Health Policy 29.

Birkmose HS, 'A 'Race to the Bottom' in the EU?' (2006) 13 MJ 35.

Black J, 'Constitutionalising Self-Regulation' (1996) 59 MLR 24.

Black J, 'Proceduralising Regulation, Part II' (2001) 21 OJLS 33.

Blake M, 'Positive and negative rights of migration: a reply to my critics' (2016) 9 Ethics and Global Politics 1.

Blake M, 'In defence of departure: Justice and the right to leave' (2017) 36 South African Journal of Philosophy 168.

Blažytė G and Žibas K, 'Integration of beneficiaries of international protection in the Lithuanian labour market: policies and practices' (2019) 25 Transfer 113.

Boland T, 'Seeking a Role: Disciplining Jobseekers as Actors in the Labour Market' (2017) 30 WES 334.

Bradford A, 'Exporting standards: The externalisation of the EU's regulatory power via markets' (2015) 42 International Review of Law and Economics 158.

Britt Djuve A and Cecilie Kavli H, 'Refugee integration policy the Norwegian way – why good ideas fail and bad ideas prevail' (2019) 25 Transfer 25.

Brock G, 'Just responses to problems associated with the brain drain: Identity, community and obligation in an unjust world' (2017) 36 South African Journal of Philosophy 156.

Brock G and Blake M, 'Global justice and the brain drain' (2016) 9 Ethics and Global Politics 1.

Brock G and Blake M, 'Guest editors' introduction: Justice, the brain drain and Africa: Introduction to a symposium on *Debating Brain Drain*' (2017) 36 South African Journal of Philosophy 1.

Brocza S and Paulhart K, 'EU Mobility Partnerships: A Smart Instrument for the Externalisation of Migration Control' (2015) 3 European Journal of Futures Research 15.

Brown R, 'Promoting labour rights in the global economy: Could the United States' new model trade and investment frameworks advance international labour standards in Bangladesh?' (2016) 155 Int'l Lab Rev 383.

Butler G, 'The Coming of Age of the Court's Jurisdiction in the Common Foreign and Security Policy' (2017) 13 EUConst 673.

Campbell S, '"What's a Sundial in the Shade?": Brain Waste Among Refugee Professionals Who Are Denied Meaningful Opportunity for Credential Recognition' (2016) 68 Emory LJ 139.

Campling L, Harrison J, Richardson B and Smith A, 'Can labour provisions work beyond the border? Evaluating the effects of EU free trade agreements' (2106) 155 Int'l Lab Rev 357.

Capuano S and Migali S, 'The Migration of Professionals within the EU: Any Barriers Left?' (2017) 25 Review of International Economics 760.

Castles S, 'Guestworkers in Europe: A Resurrection?' (2007) 40 IMR 741.

Casano L, 'The Future of European Labour Law and the Right to Employability: Which Role for the Validation of Non-Formal and Informal Learning?' (2016) 7 ELLJ 498.

Ceccorulli M, 'Back to Schengen: the collective securitisation of the EU free-border area' (2019) 42 West European Politics 302.

Cerna L, 'Understanding the diversity of EU migration policy in practice: the implementation of the Blue Card Directive' (2013) 34 Policy Studies 180.

Cerna L, 'The EU Blue Card: Preferences, Policies and Negotiations between Member States' (2014) 2 Migration Studies 73.

Cerna L, 'Attracting High-Skilled Immigrants: Policies in Comparative Perspective' (2014) 52 IM 69.

Cerna L, 'The crisis as an opportunity for change? High-skilled immigration policies across Europe' (2016) 42 Journal of Ethnic and Migration Studies 1610.

Cerna L and Chou MH, 'The regional dimension in the global competition for talent: Lessons from framing the European Scientific Visa and Blue Card' (2013) 21 JEPP 76.

Cerna L and Chou MH, 'Defining 'Talent': Insights from Management and Migration Literatures for Policy Design' (2019) 47 PSJ 819.

Claassen R, 'Making Capability Lists: Philosophy versus Democracy' (2011) 59 Political Studies 491.

Collins H, 'Regulating the Employment Relation for Competitiveness' (2001) 30 ILJ 17.

Collins H, 'Discrimination, Equality and Social Inclusion' (2003) 66 MLR 16.

Collins H, 'An Emerging Human Right to Protection against Unjustified Dismissal' (2020) 50(1) ILJ 36.

Countouris N, 'The Concept of 'Worker' in European Labour Law: Fragmentation, Autonomy and Scope' (2018) 47 ILJ 192.

Damjanovic D, 'The EU Market Rules as Social Market Rules: Why the EU Can be a Social Market Economy' (2013) 50 CML Rev 1685.

Dannreuther R, 'Developing the Alternative to Enlargement: The European Neighbourhood Policy' (2006) 11 EFA Rev 183.

Dawson M, 'New governance and the displacement of Social Europe: the case of the European Semester' (2018) 14 EUConst 191.

Della Torre L and de Lange T, 'The 'importance of staying put': third-country nationals' limited intra-EU mobility rights' (2018) 44 Journal of Ethnic and Migration Studies 1409.

Demeyere G, 'Discrimination, Freedom and the Limits of Contract' (2009) 10 IJDL 219.

Dennison J and Geddes A, 'Brexit and the perils of 'Europeanised' migration' (2018) 25 JEPP 1137.

Donoso A and Mancilla A, 'Doctors *with* borders? An authority-based approach to the brain drain' (2017) 36 South African Journal of Philosophy 69.

Ebert FC, 'Labour provisions in EU trade agreements: What potential for channelling labour standards-related capacity building?' (2016) 155 Int'l Lab Rev 407.

Eckes C, 'Common Foreign and Security Policy: The Consequences of the Court's Extended Jurisdiction' (2016) 22 ELJ 492.

Elgström O, 'Outsiders' Perceptions of the European Union in International Trade Negotiations' (2007) 45 JCMS 949.

Elsig M, 'The EU's Choice of Regulatory Venues for Trade Negotiations: A Tale of Agency Power?' (2007) 45 JCMS 927.

Evans A, 'Third-Country Nationals and the European Union' (1994) 5 EJIL 205.

Ferracioli L, 'Immigration, self-determination and the brain drain' (2015) 41 Review of International Studies 99.

Ferracioli L, 'Vulnerable populations and the duty to exclude' (2016) 9 Ethics and Global Politics 1.

Ferrera M and Burelli C, 'Cross-National Solidarity and Political Stability in the EU after the Crisis' (2019) 57 JCMS 94.

Fredman S, 'Emerging from the Shadows: Substantive Equality and Article 14 of the European Convention on Human Rights' (2016) 16 HRLR 273.

Fudge J and Herzfeld Olsson P, 'The EU Seasonal Workers Directive: When Immigration Control Meets Labour Rights' (2014) 16 EJML 439.

Fudge J and Herzfeld Olsson P, 'Labour Rights as Human Rights: Turning Slogans into Legal Claims' (2015) 37 Dalhousie LJ 601.

Fudge J and Herzfeld Olsson P, 'Migration and Sustainable Development in the EU: A Case Study of the Seasonal Workers' Directive' (2015) 31 IJCLLIR 331.

Gansemans A, Martens D, D'Haese M and Orbie J, 'Do Labour Rights Matter for Export? A Qualitative Comparative Analysis of Pineapple Trade in the EU' (2017) 5 Politics and Governance 93.

Garben S, 'On Recognition of Qualifications for Academic and Professional Purposes' (2011) 16 TLR 127.

Garben S, 'The European Pillar of Social Rights: An Assessment of its Meaning and Significance' (2019) 21 CYELS 101.

García Andrade P, 'The Legal Feasibility of the EU's External Action on Legal Migration: The Internal and the External Intertwined' (2013) 15 EJML 263.

Gardner J, 'Liberals and Unlawful Discrimination' (1989) 9 OJLS 1.

Gardner J, 'Discrimination as Injustice' (1996) 16 OJLS 353.

Gardner J, 'On the Ground of Her Sex(uality)' (1998) 18 OJLS 167.

Gardner J, 'Discrimination: the Good, the Bad and the Wrongful' (2018) 118 Proceedings of the Aristotelian Society 55.

Gibney M, 'The ethics of refugees' (2018) 13 Philosophy Compass 1.

Giubboni S, 'Freedom to Conduct a Business and EU Labour Law' (2018) 14 EUConst 172.

Gronendijk K, 'Pre-Departure Integration Strategies in the European Union: Integration or Immigration Policy?' (2011) 13 EJML 1.

Hafiz H, 'Structural Labour Rights' (2021) 119(4) Mich L Rev 651.

Harrison J, Barbu M, Campling L, Richardson B and Smith A, 'Governing Labour Standards through Free Trade Agreements: Limits of the European Union's Trade and Sustainable Development Chapters' (2019) 57 JCMS 260.

Hendrickx F, Marx A, Rayp G and Wouters J, 'The architecture of global labour governace' (2016) 155 Int'l Lab Rev 339.

den Hertog L, 'Funding the EU-Morocco 'Mobility Partnership': Of Implementation and Competences' (2016) 18 EJML 275.

Hogan H, 'The Origins and Development of Article 16 of the Charter of Fundamental Rights' (2023) 2 European Law Open 753.

Hoogenboom T, 'Integration into Society and Free Movement of Non-EC Nationals' (1992) 3 EJIL 36.

Howard E, 'The Case for a Considered Hierarchy of Discrimination Grounds in EU Law' (2006) 13 MJ 445.

Hublet C, 'The Scope of Article 12 of the Treaty of the European Communities *vis-à-vis* Third-Country Nationals: Evolution at Last?' (2009) 15 ELJ 757.

Iglesias Sánchez S, 'Free Movement of Third-Country Nationals in the European Union? Main Features, Deficiencies and Challenges of the new Mobility Rights in the Area of Freedom, Security and Justice' (2009) 15 ELJ 791.

Iglesias Sánchez S, 'Fundamental Rights Protection for Third-Country Nationals and Citizens of the Union: Principles for Enhancing Coherence' (2013) 15 EJML 137.

Iglesias Sánchez S, 'Purely Internal Situations and the Limits of EU Law: A Consolidated Case Law or a Notion to be Abandoned?' (2018) 14 EUConst 7.

Jacqueson C and Pennings F, 'Equal Treatment of Mobile Persons in the Context of a Social Market Economy' (2019) 15 Utrecht LR 64.

Jesse M, 'Integration measures, integration exams and immigration control: *P and S* and *K and A*' (2016) 53 CML Rev 1065.

Kissack R, 'The Performance of the European Union in the International Labour Organization' (2011) 33 Journal of European Integration 651.

Kocharov A, 'What intra-Community mobility for third-country workers?' (2008) 33 EL Rev 913.

Kolben K 'A Supply Chain Approach to Trade and Labour Provisions' (2017) 5 Politics and Governance 60.

Kortese L, 'Exploring Professional Recognition in the EU: A Legal Perspective' (2016) 4(1) Journal of International Mobility 43.

Koutrakos P, 'Judicial Review in the EU's Common Foreign and Security Policy' (2018) 67 ICLQ 1.

Krastev I, 'Eastern Europe's Illiberal Revolution' (2018) 97 Foreign Affairs 49.

Kumur Potnuru B and Sam V, 'India-EU Engagement and International Migration: Historical Perspectives, Future Challenges and Policy Imperatives' (2015) 27 IIMB Management Review 35.

Kyvik Nordås H, 'Does Mutual Recognition of Professional Qualifications Stimulate Service Trade? The Case of the European Union' (2016) 48 Applied Economics 1852.

Laslett J, 'The Mutual Recognition of Diplomas, Certificates and other Evidence of Formal Qualifications in the European Community' (1990) 17 LIEI 1.

van Leeuwen B, 'The Doctor in Free Movement Law: Expertise, Duty and Accountability' (2023) CYELS 1.

Lonbay J, 'Free Movement of Persons, Recognition of Qualifications and Working Conditions' (1989) 38 ICLQ 211.

Lonbay J, 'Free Movement of Persons, Recognition of Qualifications and Working Conditions' (1994) 43 ICLQ 217.

Ma R and Allen D, 'Recruiting across cultures: A value-based model of recruitment' (2009) 19 Human Resource Management Review 334.

MacKay D, 'Are Skill-Selective Immigration Policies Just?' (2016) 42 Social Theory and Practice 123.

Maisenbacher J, 'The Political Economy of Mobility Partnerships – Structural Power in the EU's External Migration Policy' (2015) 20 New Political Economy 871.

Mantouvalou V, 'Are Labour Rights Human Rights?' (2012) 3 ELLJ 151.

Mantouvalou V, 'Labour Rights in the European Convention on Human Rights: An Intellectual Justification for an Integrated Approach to Interpretation' (2013) 13 HRL Rev 529.

Mantouvalou V, 'The Protection of the Right to Work through the European Convention on Human Rights' (2014) 16 CYELS 313.

Martin-Ortega O and Methven O'Brien C, 'Advancing Respect for Labour Rights Globally through Public Procurement' (2017) 5 Politics and Governance 69.

Marx A, Lein B and Brando N, 'The Protection of Labour Rights in Trade Agreements: The Case of the EU-Columbia Agreement' (2016) 50 JWT 587.

Marx A, Lein B, Brando N and Wouters J, 'Redesigning enforcement in private labour regulation: will it work?' (2016) 155 Int'l Lab Rev 435.

Marx A, Lein B, Brando N, Wouters J, Ebert F and Hachez N, 'Dispute Settlement for Labour Provisions in EU Free Trade Agreements: Rethinking Current Approaches' (2017) 5 Politics and Governance 49.

McCormack-George D, 'The Right to Work in Irish Law' (2020) 42 DULJ 119.

McCormack-George D, 'Asylum Seekers and the Right to Work in Irish Law' (2019) 61 IJ (ns) 174.

McCormack-George D, 'Equal Treatment of Third-Country Nationals in the European Union: *Why Not?*' (2019) 21 EJML 53.

McCormack-George D, 'Recognition of Professional Qualifications in the Single Market: A Recap' (2019) 30 EBLR 785.

McCormack-George D, 'Recognition of Professional Qualifications of Third-Country Nationals in the European Union: A Comment' (2024) 15 ELLJ (forthcoming).

Melo Araujo B, 'Labour Provisions in EU and US Mega-Regional Trade Agreements: Rhetoric and Reality' (2018) 67 ICLQ 233.

Migali S, 'Migration and Institutions: Evidence from Internal EU Mobility' (2018) 41 World Economy 29.

Mjöll Arnardóttir O, 'The Differences that Make a Difference: Recent Developments on the Discrimination Grounds and the Margin of Appreciation under Article 14 of the European Convention on Human Rights' (2014) 14 HRLR 647.

Morano-Foadi S, 'Third Country Nationals Versus EU Citizens: Discrimination Based on Nationality and the Equality Directives' (21 December 2010) available at <https://papers.ssrn.com/sol3/papers.cfm?abstract_id=1729141> (accessed 9 July 2019).

Morano-Foadi S, and Stelios Andreadakis, 'The Convergence of the European Legal System in the Treatment of Third-Country Nationals: The ECJ and ECtHR Jurisprudence' (2011) 22 EJIL 1071.

Moreau S, 'What is Discrimination?' (2010) 38 Phil and Pub Aff 143.

Möstl M, 'Preconditions and Limits of Mutual Recognition' (2010) 47 CML Rev 405.

Muir E, 'Enhancing the Protection of Third-Country Nationals against Discrimination: Putting EU Anti-Discrimination Law to the Test' (2011) 18 MJ 136.

Nic Shuibhne N, 'Free Movement of Persons and the Wholly Internal Rule: Time to Move On?' (2002) 39 CML Rev 731.

Nicolaïds K, 'Trusting the Poles? Constructing Europe through Mutual Recognition' (2007) 14 JEPP 682.

Nicolaïds K and Egan M, 'Transnational Market Governance and Regional Policy Externality: Why Recognise Foreign Standards?' (2001) 8 JEPP 454.

Nicolaïds K and Egan M and Schmidt S, 'Mutual Recognition 'on Trial': the Long Road to Services Liberalisation' (2007) 14 JEPP 717.

Nicolaïds K and Egan M, Schmidt S and Shaffer G, 'Transnational Mutual Recognition Regimes: Governance without Global Government' (2004) 68 Law and Contemporary Problems 263.

Nicolaïds K and Egan M, Schmidt S and Shaffer G, 'Mutual Recognition: Promise and Denial, from Sapiens to Brexit' (2017) 70 CLP 227.

Novitz T, 'The Paradigm of Sustainability in a European Social Context: Collective Participation in Protection of Future Interests?' (2015) 31 IJCLLIR 243.

Ó Cinnéide C, 'The Constitutionalisation of Equality within the EU Legal Order: Sexual Orientation as a Testing Ground' (2015) 22 MJ 370.

O'Connell R, 'Cinderella comes to the ball: Article 14 and the right to non-discrimination in the ECHR' (2009) 29 LS 211.

O'Connell R, 'The Right to work in the ECHR' (2012) EHRLR 176.

O'Connor N, 'Whose Autonomy is it Anyway? Freedom of Contract, the Right to Work and the General Principles of EU Law' (2020) 49(3) ILJ 285.

Oberman K, 'Can Brain Drain Justify Immigration Restrictions?' (2013) 123 Ethics 427.

Odin Ekman Å and Engblom S, 'Expanding the Movement of Natural Persons Through Free Trade Agreements? A Review of CETA, TPP and ChAFTA' (2019) 35 IJCLLIR 163.

Oehri M, 'Civil Society Activism under US Free Trade Agreements: The Effects of Actorness on Decent Work' (2017) 5 Politics and Governance 40.

Orbie J and Van Roozendaal G, 'Labour Standards and Trade: In Search of Impact and Alternative Instruments' (2017) 5 Politics and Governance 1.

Orbie J, Van den Putte L and Martens D, 'The Impact of Labour Rights Commitments in EU Trade Agreements: The Case of Peru' (2017) 5 Politics and Governance 6.

Parkes R, 'EU Mobility Partnerships: A Model of Policy Coordination?' (2009) 11 EJML 327.

Peers S, 'The Court of Justice lays the Foundations for the Long-Term Residents Directive: *Kamberaj, Commission v Netherlands, Mangat Singh*' (2013) 50 CML Rev 529.

Peeters M, 'Free Movement of Medical Doctors: The New Directive 2005/36/EC on Recognition of Professional Qualifications' (2005) 11 EJHL 373.

Poot J and Strutt A, 'International Trade Agreements and International Migration' (2010) 33 The World Economy 1923.

de la Porte C, 'Is the Open Method of Coordination Appropriate for Organising Activities at European Level in Sensitive Policy Areas?' (2008) 8 ELJ 38.

Portes J and Forte G, 'The economic impact of Brexit-induced reductions in migration' (2017) 33 Oxford Review of Economic Policy S31.

Prassl J, 'Freedom of Contract as a General Principle of EU Law? Transfers of Undertakings and the Protection of Employer Rights in EU Labour Law' (2013) 42 ILJ 434.

Rasche L, 'EU Talent Partnerships: Fit for Purpose?' (Hertie School Policy Brief, 16 June 2021).

Reslow N, 'Deciding on EU External Migration Policy: The Member States and the Mobility Partnerships' (2012) 34 European Integration 223.

Reslow N, 'The Role of Third-Countries in EU Migration Policy: The Mobility Partnerships' (2012) 14 EJML 393.

Reslow N, 'EU 'Mobility' Partnerships: An Initial Assessment of Implementation Dynamics' (2015) 3 Politics and Governance 117.

Reslow N, '"Not everything that counts can be counted": Assessing 'success' of EU external migration policy' (2017) 55 IM 156.

van Riemsdijk M, 'Obstacles to the Free Movement of Professionals: Mutual Recognition of Professional Qualifications in the European Union' (2013) 15 EJML 47.

Riethof M, 'The International Labour Standards Debate in the Brazilian Labour Movement: Engagement with Mercosur and Opposition to the Free Trade Area of the Americas' (2017) 5 Politics and Governance 30.

Roos C and Zaun N, 'Norms Matter! The Role of International Norms in EU Policies on Asylum and Immigration' (2014) 16 EJML 45.

Ross M, 'Freedom of Establishment and Freedom to Provide Services' (1989) 14 EL Rev 162.

Ruhs M and Martin P, 'Numbers vs Rights: Trade-Offs and Guest Worker Programs' (2008) 41 IMR 249.

Ruhs M, 'Migrant Rights, Immigration Policy and Human Development' (2010) 11 Journal of Human Development and Capabilities 259.

Schenner J and Neergaard A, 'Asylum-seekers and refugees within Europe and labour market integration' (2019) 25 Transfer 13.

Schenner J, Neergaard A, Cavanna P and Ollus N, 'Asylum-seekers and the 'hyper-precarity trap' in Austria, Finland and Italy' (2019) 25 Transfer 81.

Schütze R, 'EU Development Policy: Constitutional and Legislative Foundation(s)' (2013) 15 CYELS 699.

Segers M, 'Eclipsing Atlantis: Trans-Atlantic Multilaterialism in Trade and Monetary Affairs as a Pre-History to the Genesis of Social Market Europe (1942–1950)' (2019) 57 JCMS 60.

Selby Smith C and Ridoutt L, 'The importance employers attach to employee qualifications' (2007) 45 Asia Pacific Journal of Human Resources 180.

Scott J and Trubek D, 'Mind the Gap: Law and New Approaches to Governance in the European Union' (2002) 8 ELJ 1.

Schmidt S, 'The Impact of Mutual Recognition: Inbuilt Limits and Domestic Responses to the Single Market' (2002) 9 JEPP 935.

Schmidt S, 'Mutual Recognition as a New Mode of Governance' (2007) 14 JEPP 667.

Scott C, 'The Governance of the European Union: The Potential for Multi-Level Control' (2008) 8 ELJ 59.

Söhn J, 'Initial employment pathways of immigrants in Germany. Why legal contexts of reception matter – an analysis of life-course data' (2019) 25 Transfer 43.

Spaventa E, 'Seeing the Wood for the Trees? On the Scope of Union Citizenship and its Constitutional Effects' (2008) 45 CML Rev 13.

Stanczyk L, 'Managing skilled migration' (2016) 9 Ethics and Global Politics 1.

Šuta Ž and Pišek Šuta K, 'Professional Qualifications Recognition of Doctors in the EU: A Perspective on EU Citizens and Third-Country Nationals' (2023) 16(1) Medicine, Law and Society 149.

Teklè T, 'Labour Rights and the Case Law of the European Court of Justice: What Role for International Labour Standards?' (2018) 9 ELLJ 236.

Tesón F, 'Brain Drain' (2008) 45 San Diego L Rev 899.

Teubner G, 'Substantive and Reflexive Elements in Modern Law' (1983) 17 Law and Society Review 239.

Thym D, 'EU Migration Law and its Constitutional Rationale: A Cosmopolitan Outlook' (2013) 50 CML Rev 709.

Thym D, "Citizens' and 'Foreigners' in EU Law. Migration Law and its Cosmopolitan Outlook' (2016) 22 ELJ 296.

Thym D, 'Towards a contextual conception of social integration in EU immigration law. Comments on *P and S* and *K and A*' (2016) 18 EJML 89.

Tittel-Mosser F, 'The Unintended Legal and Policy Relevance of EU Mobility Partnerships: A Comparative Implementation Analysis of Morocco and Cape Verde' (2018) 20 EJML 314.

Trubek D, 'Towards a Social Theory of Law: An Essay on the Study of Law and Development' (1982) 82 Yale LJ 1.

Ulmer K, 'Trade Embedded Development Models' (2015) 31 IJCLLIR 305.

Van den Putte L and Orbie J, 'EU Bilateral Trade Agreements and the Surprising Rise of Labour Provisions' (2015) 31 IJCLLIR 263.

Van den Roozendaal G, 'Where Symbolism Prospers: An Analysis of the Impact on Enabling Rights of Labour Standards Provisions in Trade Agreements with South Korea' (2017) 5 Politics and Governance 19.

Verschueren H, 'Employment and Social Security Rights of Third-Country Nationals under the EU Labour Migration Directives' (2018) 20 EJSS 100.

Velyvyte V, 'The Right to Strike in the European Union after Accession to the European Convention on Human Rights' (2015) 15 HRLR 73.

Vogt J, 'A Little Less Conversation: The EU and the (Non) Application of Labour Conditionality in the Generalised System of Preferences (GSP)' (2015) 31 IJCLLIR 285.

Vogt J, 'The Bangladesh Sustainability Compact: An Effective Tool for Promoting Workers' Rights?' (2017) 5 Politics and Governance 80.

Vončina B and Marin N, 'What issues do refugees face in integrating into labour markets? Evidence from Slovenia' (2019) 25 Transfer 101.

van Vooren B, 'A case-study of "soft law" in EU external relations: the European Neighbourhood Policy' (2009) 34 EL Rev 696.

Waegenbaur R, 'Free Movement in the Professions: The New EEC Proposal on Professional Qualifications' (1986) 23 CML Rev 91.

Weatherill S, 'Use and Abuse of the EU's Charter of Fundamental Rights: On the Improper Veneration of 'Freedom of Contract'' (2014) 10 ERCL 167.

Weatherill S, 'The Principle of Mutual Recognition: it Doesn't Work, because it Doesn't Exist' (2018) 43 EL Rev 224.

Weber F, 'Labour Market Access for Asylum Seekers and Refugees under the Common European Asylum System' (2016) 18 EJML 34.

Weingerl P and Tratnik M, 'Climbing the Wall around EU Citizenship: Has the Time Come to Align Third-Country Nationals with Intra-EU Migrants?' (2022) 33(1) EJIL 15.

Wiesbrock A, 'Free movement of third-country nationals in the European Union: the illusion of inclusion' (2010) 35 EL Rev 455.

Wiesbrock A, 'Granting Citizenship-related Rights to Third-Country Nationals: An Alternative to the Full Extension of European Union Citizenship?' (2012) 14 EJML 63.

Wikström E and Sténs A, 'Problematising refugee migrants in the Swedish forestry sector' (2019) 25 Transfer 63.

Woolfson C, Fudge J and Thörnqvist C, 'Migrant precarity and future challenges to labour standards in Sweden' (2014) 35 Economic and Industrial Democracy 695.

Zahn R and Mangan D, 'Labour Standards and Sustainable Development: Unpicking the EU's Approach' (2015) 31 IJCLLIR 233.

Reports

European Migration Network, *Labour Market Integration of Third-Country Nationals in EU Member States: Synthesis Report for the EMN Study* (2019).

OECD/European Union, *Indicators of Immigrant Integration 2015: Settling In* (OECD Publishing 2015).

ILO, *Migrant Workers* (Geneva 1980).

ILO, *Migrant Workers* (Geneva 1999).

ILO, *Promoting fair migration* (Geneva 2016).

Special Eurobarometer 437, *Discrimination in the EU in 2015: Report* (European Commission 2015).

Fundamental Rights Agency, *Second European Union Minorities and Discrimination Survey: Main Results* (Publications Office of the European Union 2017).

Donlevy V, Curtarelli M, McCoshan A and Meierkord A, *Study on Obstacles to Recognition of Skills and Qualifications: Final Report* (ECORYS/European Commission 2016).

Eisele K, 'Falling Through the Cracks: Third-Country Nationals and the Recognition of Qualifications in the EU' in Carrera S, Guild E and Eisele K (eds), *Rethinking the Attractiveness of EU Labour Immigration Policies: Comparative Perspectives on the EU, the US, Canada and Beyond* (CEPS 2014).

Eisenmann A Sand Verdier T, 'Reciprocity and the Political Economy of Harmonisation and Mutual Recognition of Regulatory Measures' Centre for Economic Policy Research Discussion Paper Series No 3147 (January 2002).

Böhning WR and Werquin J, *Some Economic, Social and Human Rights Considerations concerning the Future Status of Third-Country Nationals in the Single European Market* (ILO 1990).

Turmann A, 'A New European Agenda for Mobility' in *CEPS-ECHR Taskforce* (2004).

European Migration Network Synthesis Report, *Intra-EU Mobility of Third-Country Nationals* (European Commission 2013).

Global Education Monitoring Report, *What a waste: Ensure migrants and refugees' qualifications and prior learning are recognised* (UNESCO 2018).

ILO, *General Survey of Reports on the Paid Educational Leave Convention (No 140) and Recommendation (No 148) 1974, and the Human Resources Development Convention (No 142) and Recommendation (No 150) 1975* (ILO 1991).

Quality and Recognition in Higher Education (OECD 2004).

European Commission, *Obstacles to Recognition of Qualifications* (2017).

European Commission, *Assessment of Commission Recommendation (EU) 2022/554 of 5 April 2022 on the Recognition of Qualifications for People Fleeing Russia's Invasion of Ukraine* (June 2023).

OECD and EU, *Recruiting Immigrant Workers: Europe 2016* (2016).

Werquin P, *Recognising Non-Formal and Informal Learning: Outcomes, Policies and Practices* (OECD 2010).

CEDEFOP, *European guidelines for validating non-formal and informal learning* (Publications Office of the European Union 2015).

Chindea A, *Headstart to Integration: A Global Review of Pre-departure Support Measures for Migrants* (IOM 2015).

Carrera S and Wiesbrock A, *Civic Integration of Third-Country Nationals: Nationalism versus Europeanisation in the Common EU Immigration Policy* (Centre for European Policy Studies 2009).

GHK, *Study on the (potential) role of qualifications frameworks in supporting mobility of workers and learners: European Commission and Australian Department of Education, Employment and Workplace Relations Joint EU-Australia Study* (DEEWR and DG EAC 2011).

Koeth W, 'The New Instrument for Pre-Accession Assistance (IPA II): Less Accession, More Assistance?' (EIPA Working Paper 2014/W/01).

Grynberg R and Clarke A (eds), *The European Development Fund and Economic Partnership Agreements* (Commonwealth Secretariat 2006).

Commission, *Interim Evaluation of the Asylum, Migration and Integration Fund: Final Report* (Publications Office of the European Union 2018).

Commission, *Report on the Third Policy Dialogue with Southern Mediterranean Countries on Higher Education* (Brussels, 12–13 July 2016).

Pijpers R, Beckers P, Grootjans N, van Naerssen T, Paardekooper L and Smith L, *Skills Recognition, Diversity Management and Voluntary Work with regard to Third Country Nationals in the Netherlands: A Case Study on the Healthcare Sector in the Arnhem-Nijmegen Region* (Radboud University 2015).

Theses

Hogan H, *The Freedom to Conduct a Business: The Origins and Development of Article 16 of the Charter of Fundamental Rights of the European Union* (European University Institute PhD Thesis 2024).

Wiesner NC, *Recognition of Third-Country Professional Qualifications: An Evaluation of the Current Framework in the European Union. The Case of Healthcare Workers* (Utrect University LLM Thesis 2023).

Official Documents

United Nations

CESCR, 'The Right to Work: General Comment No 18' (24 November 2005)

CCPR, 'General Comment No 18: Non-discrimination' (10 November 1989)

CESCR, 'General Comment No 20: Non-discrimination in economic, social and cultural rights' (2 July 2009)

International Labour Organisation

Application of International Labour Standards 2018: Report of the Committee of Experts on the Application of Conventions and Recommendations (Report III Part A)

General Survey of Reports on the Paid Educational Leave Convention (No 140) and Recommendation (No 148) 1974, and the Human Resources Development Convention (No 142) and Recommendation (No 150) 1975 (ILO 1991)

Council of Europe

ECSR, 'Conclusions II, Statement of Interpretation on Article 1(2)'
Explanatory Report to the European Social Charter (Revised)
Committee of the Convention on the Recognition of Qualifications concerning Higher Education in the European Region, 'Revised Recommendation on Criteria for the Assessment of Foreign Qualifications' (Strasbourg, 23 June 2010)
Steering Committee for Higher Education and Research, 'Policies and Instruments for Recognition of Qualifications and Mobility: Reference Document' (Strasbourg, 21–22 September 2004)
Committee of the Convention on the Recognition of Qualifications concerning Higher Education in the European Region, 'Recommendation on the Recognition of Refugees' Qualifications under the Lisbon Recognition Convention and Explanatory Memorandum' (Strasbourg, 14 November 2017)

European Union

European Council

Lisbon Conclusions (23 and 24 March 2000)
European Council Conclusions (19 December 2005)
The Stockholm Programme – An Open and Secure Europe serving and protecting citizens (Brussels, 2 December 2009)

Council of the European Union

Tampere Presidency Conclusions, 15–16 October 1999
Brussels Presidency Conclusions, 5–4 November 2004
'The Hague Programme: Strengthening Freedom, Security and Justice in the European Union' [2005] OJ C53/1.
Justice and Home Affairs Council Conclusions, *Common Basic Principles on Immigrant Integration*, Council Document 14615/04, Brussels, 19 November 2004
Conclusions of the Council and the Representatives of the Governments of the Member states on Integration as a Driver for Development and Social Cohesion (Brussels, 4 May 2010)

European Commission

'Working together for jobs and growth: A new start for the Lisbon Strategy' (Communication) COM(2005) 24 final

'Europe 2020: A strategy for smart, sustainable and inclusive growth' (Communication) COM(2010) 2020

'Migration' (Communication) COM(2011) 248 final

'Global Europe: Competing in the World – A Contribution to the EU's Growth and Jobs Strategy' (Communication) COM(2006) 567 final

'European Competitiveness Report 2008' (Communication) COM(2008) 774 final

'On the External Dimension of the Lisbon Strategy for Growth and Jobs: Reporting on market access and setting the regulatory framework for more effective international regulatory cooperation' (Communication) COM(2008) 874 final

'Trade for All: Towards a more responsible trade and investment policy' (Communication) COM(2015) 497 final

'The Global Approach to Migration and Mobility' (Communication) COM(2011) 743 final

'Strengthening the Global Approach to Migration: Increasing Coordination, Coherence and Synergies' (Communication) COM(2008) 611 final

'An Area of Freedom, Security and Justice serving the Citizen' (Communication) COM (2009) 262 final

'Report on the implementation of the Global Approach to Migration and Mobility' COM(2014) 96 final

'A European Agenda on Migration' (Communication) COM(2015) 240 final

'New Skills for New Jobs' (Communication) COM(2008) 868 final

'An Agenda for new skills and jobs: A European contribution towards full employment' (Communication) COM(2010) 682 final

'Rethinking Education: Investing in skills for better socio-economic outcomes' (Communication) COM(2012) 669 final

'A New Skills Agenda for Europe: Working together to strengthen human capital, employability and competitiveness' (Communication) COM(2016) 381 final

'Fitness Check on EU Legislation on legal migration' (Staff Working Document) SWD(2019) 1055 final

'Mobility Partnerships as a Tool of the Global Approach to Migration' SEC(2009) 1240

'European Agenda for the Integration of Third-Country Nationals' (Communication) COM(2011) 455 final

'Migration' (Communication) COM(2011) 248 final

'An Open and Secure Europe: Making it Happen' (Communication) COM(2014) 154 final

'Action Plan on the Integration of Third Country Nationals' (Communication) COM(2016) 377 final

'Turkey 2018 Report accompanying the 2018 Communication on EU Enlargement Policy' (Staff Working Document) SWD(2018) 153 final

'Bosnia and Herzegovina 2016 Report accompanying the 2016 Communication on EU Enlargement Policy' (Staff Working Document) SWD(2016) 365 final

'The former Yugoslav Republic of Macedonia 2018 Report accompanying the 2018 Communication on EU Enlargement Policy' (Staff Working Document) SWD(2018) 154 final

'Albania 2018 Report accompanying the 2018 Communication on EU Enlargement Policy' (Staff Working Document) SWD(2018) 151 final

'Albania 2018 Report accompanying the 2018 Communication on EU Enlargement' (Staff Working Document) SWD(2018) 151 final

'Montenegro 2019 Report accompanying the 2019 Communication on EU Enlargement Policy' (Staff Working Document) SWD(2019) 217 final

'A renewed partnership with the countries of Africa, the Caribbean and the Pacific' (Joint Communication) JOIN(2016) 52 final

'Implementing Decision on the Annual Action Programme 2014 in favour of Belarus to be financed from the general budget of the European Union' (Implementing Decision) C(2014) 6937 final

'Implementing Decision on the Annual Action Plan 2015 in favour of Pakistan to be financed from the general budget of the European Union' (Implementing Decision) C(2015) 9335 final

'Implementing Decision on the Annual Action Plan 2016 Part III in favour of the Asia region to be financed from the general budget of the European Union' (Implementing Decision) C(2016) 5218 final

'Implementing Decision on the Annual Action Plan 2016 in favour of the Caribbean Region to be financed from the 11th European Development Fund' (Implementing Decision) C(2016) 6434 final

'Implementing Decision on the Annual Action Programme 2014 in favour of Belarus to be financed from the general budget of the European Union' (Implementing Decision) C(2014) 6937 final

'Decision on the Annual Action Programme 2017 in favour of Angola to be financed from the 11th European Development Fund' (Implementing Decision) C(2016) 7077 final

'Decision on the Annual Action Programme 2017 part 2 in favour of the Pacific Region to be financed from the 11th European Development Fund' (Implementing Decision) C(2017) 4903 final

'Reform recommendations for regulation in professional services' (Communication) COM(2016) 820 final

'A Common Agenda for Integration: Framework for the Integration of Third Country Nationals in the European Union' (Communication) COM(2005) 389 final

'A Common Immigration Policy for Europe – Principles, Actions and Tools' (Communication) COM(2008) 359 final

'Strengthening the Global Approach to Migration – Increasing Coordination, Coherence and Synergies' (Communication) COM(2008) 611 final

'Skills and Talent Mobility' (Communication) COM(2023) 715 final

'Commission work programme 2023: A Union standing firm and united' (Communication) COM(2022) 548 final

'Action Plan on Integration and Inclusion 2021–2027' (Communication) COM(2020) 758 final

'The European Green Deal' (Communication) COM(2018) 640 final

'Establishing a European Pillar of Social Rights' (Staff Working Document) SWD/2017/0201 final

'A New Pact on Migration and Asylum' (Communication) COM(2020) 609 final

Index

Printed in the United States
by Baker & Taylor Publisher Services